What They Say about Us

*"One organization with a long record of success
in helping people find jobs is The Five O'Clock Club."*

FORTUNE

*"Many managers left to fend for themselves are turning to the camaraderie offered by [The Five
O'Clock Club]. Members share tips and advice, and hear experts."*
The Wall Street Journal

"If you have been out of work for some time . . . consider The Five O'Clock Club."
The New York Times

*"Wendleton has reinvented the historic gentlemen's fraternal oasis and built it into a chain of
strategy clubs for job seekers."*
The Philadelphia Inquirer

"Organizations such as The Five O'Clock Club are building . . . an extended professional family."
Jessica Lipnack, author, *Professional Teams*

*"[The Five O'Clock Club] will ask not what you do, but 'What do you want to do?' . . . [And] don't
expect to get any great happy hour drink specials at this joint. The seminars are all business."*
The Washington Times

*"The Five O'Clock Club's proven philosophy is that job hunting is a learned skill like any other. The
Five O'Clock Club becomes the engine that drives [your] search."*
Black Enterprise

*"Job hunting is a science at The Five O'Clock Club. [Members] find the discipline, direction and
much-needed support that keeps a job search on track."*
Modern Maturity

*"Wendleton tells you how to beat the odds—even in an economy where pink slips are more common
than perks. Her savvy and practical guide[s] are chockablock with sample résumés, cover letters,
worksheets, negotiating tips, networking suggestions and inspirational quotes from such far-flung
achievers as Abraham Lincoln, Malcolm Forbes and Lily Tomlin."*
Working Woman

*"On behalf of eight million New Yorkers, I commend and thank The Five O'Clock Club. Keep the faith
and keep America working!"*
David N. Dinkins, former mayor, City of New York

What Job Hunters Say

"During the time I was looking for a job I kept Kate's books by my bed. I read a little every night, a little every morning. Her common-sense advice, methodical approach, and hints for keeping the spirits up were extremely useful."
> Harold Levine, coordinator, Yale Alumni Career Resource Network

"I've just been going over the books with my daughter, who is 23 and finally starting to think she ought to have a career. She won't listen to anything I say, but you she believes."
> Newspaper columnist

"Thank you, Kate, for all your help. I ended up with four offers and at least 15 compliments in two months. Thanks!"
> President and CEO, large banking organization

"I have doubled my salary during the past five years by using The Five O'Clock Club techniques. Now I earn what I deserve. I think everyone needs The Five O'Clock Club."
> M. S., attorney, entertainment industry

"I dragged myself to my first meeting, totally demoralized. Ten weeks later, I chose from among job offers and started a new life. Bless You!"
> Senior editor, not-for-profit

"I'm an artistic person, and I don't think about business. Kate provided the disciplined business approach so I could practice my art. After adopting her system, I landed a role on Broadway in Hamlet."
> Bruce Faulk, actor

"I've referred at least a dozen people to The Five O'Clock Club since I was there. The Club was a major factor in getting my dream job, which I am now in."
> B. R., research head

"My Five O'Clock Club coach was a God-Send!!! She is truly one of the most dynamic and qualified people I've ever met. Without her understanding and guidance, I wouldn't have made the steps I've made toward my goals."
> Operating room nurse

"The Five O'Clock Club has been a fantastic experience for my job search. I couldn't have done it without you. Keep up the good work."
> Former restaurant owner, who found his dream job with an organization that advises small businesses

What Human Resources Executives Say about
The Five O'Clock Club Outplacement

*"**This thing works.** I saw a structured, yet nurturing, environment where individuals searching for jobs positioned themselves for success. I saw 'accountability' in a nonintimidating environment. I was struck by the support and willingness to encourage those who had just started the process by the group members who had been there for a while."*
> Employee relations officer, financial services organization

*"**Wow! I was immediately struck by the electric atmosphere** and people's commitment to following the program. Job hunters reported on where they were in their searches and what they had accomplished the previous week. The overall environment fosters sharing and mutual learning."*
> Head of human resources, major law firm

*"The Five O'Clock Club program is **far more effective** than conventional outplacement. Excellent materials, effective coaching and nanosecond responsiveness combine to get people focused on the central tasks of the job search. Selecting The Five O'Clock Outplacement Program was one of my best decisions this year."*
> Sr. vice president, human resources, manufacturing company

*"**You have made me look like a real genius** in recommending The Five O'Clock Club [to our divisions around the country]!"*
> Sr. vice president, human resources, major publishing firm

The Five O'Clock Club®

Advising Professionals, Managers, and Executives for Over 25 Years

SHORTCUT YOUR
JOB SEARCH
THE BEST WAYS TO
GET MEETINGS

KATE WENDLETON

THOMSON

DELMAR LEARNING

Australia Canada Mexico Singapore Spain United Kingdom United States

THOMSON

DELMAR LEARNING

Shortcut Your Job Search: The Best Ways to Get Meetings
Kate Wendleton

Vice President, Career Education SBU:
Dawn Gerrain

Director of Editorial:
Sherry Gomoll

Acquisitions Editor:
Martine Edwards

Developmental Editor:
Kristen Shenfield

Editorial Assistant:
Jennifer Anderson

Director of Production:
Wendy A. Troeger

Production Manager:
J.P. Henkel

Production Editor:
Rebecca Goldthwaite

Technology Project Manager:
Sandy Charette

Director of Marketing:
Wendy E. Mapstone

Channel Manager:
Gerard McAvey

Marketing Coordinator:
Erica Conley

Cover Design:
TDB Publishing Services

Library of Congress Cataloging-in-Publication Data
Wendleton, Kate.
    Shortcut your job search : the best way to get meetings / Kate Wendleton.
        p. cm.
    At head of title: The Five O'Clock Club.
    Includes bibliographical references and index.
    ISBN 1-4180-1502-4
    1. Job hunting. 2. Employment interviewing. 3. Career development. I. Title: Short cut your job search. II. Five O'Clock Club (New York, N.Y.) III. Title.

HF5382.7.W459 2006
650.14—dc22
                                                            2005050669

NOTICE TO THE READER

For the thousands of members of The Five O'Clock Club—
These stories are theirs.

Without effort we cannot attain any of
our goals in life, no matter what the
advertisements may claim to the contrary.
Anyone who fears effort, anyone who backs off
from frustration . . . will never get anywhere.

Erich Fromm, *For the Love of Life*

Preface

Dear Member or Prospective Member of The Five O'Clock Club:

You probably think there is only one best way to get interviews in your target market. You may personally believe ads are best for you, or search firms or networking. You are probably incorrect. Chances are, the technique that helped you get your last job will not be the best technique for you this time around. The situation has changed. You are older now and have more to offer, the kind of job you want next may have changed, and the job market has certainly changed.

Luckily, we have spent the last 25-plus years researching and keeping up-to-date on job-search techniques that work. You can benefit from our efforts on your behalf. It is very difficult for job searchers themselves to know which techniques will work best this time around. Therefore, we suggest you take an organized, methodical *research* approach to your own search. Observe what is working for you and what is not—and do more of whatever is working. We'll show you how.

There are four basic techniques for getting meetings in your target market: search firms, ads (in print and online), networking, and contacting companies directly. We urge you to consider all four techniques—and their variations—for your search. The best searches rely on two or more techniques for getting meetings.

Chances are, you are going after published job *openings* rather than unpublished job *possibilities*. If you chase advertised openings, you will automatically have competition for those openings. We suggest that you develop more *possibilities*. This means contacting hiring managers who do not happen to have an opening right now, but would *love* to have someone like you on board. Then we'll want you to keep in touch with those managers (we'll tell you how), and develop 6 to 10 similar contacts.

This may sound like a lot of work, but it's a lot less work than applying for openings and continually being rejected. As a matter of course, Five O'Clock Clubbers regularly develop 6 to 10 leads—and more. We want them to wind up with three concurrent job offers so they will have a choice. You can do this, too.

Chances are, you are not contacting enough organizations. Be sure to read "Measuring Your Targets" and "Current List of Stage-1, Stage-2, and Stage-3 Contacts." In our research, we have found these worksheets to be the most effective ways to make sure you are on the right path in your search.

Believe it or not, a successful search hinges on *having an effective Stage 2*. I know you don't understand what I'm saying right now, but soon you will be glad that there is actually a *methodology* you can follow, a way to measure the effectiveness of your job search—in good economic times and bad.

We found that there is no one job-hunting technique that always works. Job-hunting formulas hold true in the aggregate, but may not for a specific situation. The techniques that work depend, to a large extent, on the industry being pursued, the kind of job you want within that industry, and your own style and personality.

This book series gives you guidelines, but also offers flexibility in deciding which job-hunting approach is right for you. When you understand what is happening and why, you will be in a better position to plan your own job-hunting campaign, and rely less on chance or on what a specific expert tells you.

Job hunting can be thought of as a project—much like any project you might handle in your regular job. Most of the approaches in this book are businesslike rather than intensely psychological. Thinking of job hunting in a business-type way allows you to use the problem-solving skills you might use at work.

I feel duty-bound to address the issue of career planning. Most people are interested in job-hunting techniques but don't want to give much thought to what they should do with their *lives*. So be sure to read our book *Targeting a Great Career* to make sure your career is heading in the right direction. When you uncover what it is you want to do long term, then you can look for a job that will take you in that direction.

These books are the result of years of research into how successful job hunters land the best jobs at the best pay. This series replaces the very successful and popular *Through the Brick Wall* series, and, with the addition of new material, takes job search to an even higher level of sophistication. Together, these books provide the most detailed explanation of the search process:

- *Targeting a Great Career* shows you *what kind* of job you should look for. It is a relatively painless way to think about the career-planning process. In addition, it contains the most comprehensive job-search bibliography available anywhere.
- *Packaging Yourself: The Targeted Résumé* is quite simply the best résumé book on the market. It uses the résumés of real people and tells you their stories. It refers to more than 100 industries and professions.
- *Shortcut Your Job Search: The Best Ways to Get Meetings* (this book) tells you *how to* get job leads—part-time or full-time, freelance or consulting. In addition, it contains worksheets that you may copy for your own use.

- *Mastering the Job Interview and Winning the Money Game* tells you how to interview, get the offer, and negotiate using proven Five O'Clock Club techniques.
- *Navigating Your Career* tells you how to do well in your job and manage your career.

Welcome to the exciting world of managing your own career. And thank you for supporting The Five O'Clock Club through your purchase of this book. Because of people like you, we can keep the program going so we'll be there when you need us. Our goal is, and always has been, to provide the best affordable career advice. And—with you as our partners—we will continue to do this.

Cheers, God bless, and good luck!

Kate Wendleton
New York City, 2005
www.fiveoclockclub.com

Contents

PART THREE Knowing the Right People: How to Get Interviews in Your Target Areas

(IF YOU ALREADY HAVE INTERVIEWS SCHEDULED, GO TO PART FOUR.)

PART FOUR Managing Your Campaign: Are You Conducting a Good Search?

PART FIVE   Career and Job-Search Bibliography

(LOOK AT THIS PART FOR HELP IN RESEARCHING A FIELD OR INDUSTRY.)

PART SIX   What is The Five O'Clock Club? "America's Premier Career Counseling Network"

The
Five
O'Clock
Club

Introduction

People can be divided into three groups: those who make things happen, those who watch things happen—and those who wonder, What happened?

Anonymous

The Five O'Clock Club is a research organization working with job hunters across the country both individually and in small groups.

In the small groups, members report on their searches every week, and counselors report on client cases at Counselor Guild meetings. We transcribe the "graduation speeches" of successful job hunters, and these reports are often published in our newsletter, *The Five O'Clock News*. Because we have done this continuously since 1978, we have monitored job-market changes and have kept up-to-date with what works in today's market.

For example, we know that:

- It takes an average of eight follow-up phone calls to get a meeting. The chapter "How to Handle the Phone: A Life Skill" will help you increase your success rate.

- The average job hunter who comes to The Five O'Clock Club is not targeting enough *positions*. A job hunter must target 200 positions to get a job within a reasonable time frame (*positions*, not openings and not companies). See the section "Measuring Your Targets."

- Job hunters who rely on only one technique for getting meetings (networking, search firms, print or online ads, or contacting companies directly) have weaker searches. Those who consider all four techniques do better.

- The only way to measure the effectiveness of these techniques is not whether they result in job offers, but whether they result in *meetings*.

- Networkers should contact anyone at any level to get information on a field, but they are unlikely to get a job unless they contact those who are one or two levels higher than they are.

- To maintain momentum, job hunters must have 6 to 10 things in the works at all times: five will fall away through no fault of their own!

- The key to the job search process is Stage 2: meet with at least 6 to 10 people who are the right people at the right level in the right organizations. It's okay (or even better) if they do not have a job opening right now. The question to ask is this: "If you had an opening, would you consider bringing someone like me on board?"

    If the answer is yes, just keep in touch with them. Do this with enough companies and you will hear about openings before your competitors do. You are more likely to get offers this way.

- The Internet is great—especially for research. Definitely answer ads on the web, but also use the Internet to develop your target list of companies to contact (your Personal Marketing

Plan), to research companies before you go in for a meeting, and to research the information you need to develop an excellent follow-up piece.

Ah! A Process I Can Follow

When job hunters have been looking for a while and finally find The Five O'Clock Club, they are relieved that:

- There is a methodology they can follow.
- They can tell right away where they are in their searches.
- They can measure the effectiveness of their job search.

Most books tell you simply to network to get interviews. But networking is spotty (i.e., you get meetings only at the places where someone you know knows someone) and networking alone is too slow for most people. Use all four techniques highlighted in this book.

As you will see, these techniques work at all levels—and for all types of people. They have even been used successfully by actors and actresses, and at least one orchestra conductor. Whatever your field, this book will give you the inside track.

When job hunters find jobs, they report to the group. Last week, a man reported that he had been unemployed for three years. His wife had a good job, he spent time with his kids, and he found a few temporary assignments, but he was essentially unemployed, and was trying very hard to get a job. After only four Five O'Clock Club sessions, he found a great one.

The week before, a woman spoke who had been unemployed for a year and a half; she had come to six sessions. Her first session had been a full year earlier, and she had decided to search on her own. After a year, she came back, attended five more sessions, and got a great job.

The week before that, a man who had been unemployed for six months before joining The

Five O'Clock Club found a great job. In his four months with the Club, the group helped him see how he was coming across in interviews (very stiff and preachy) and how to expand his job targets. Some people take longer because they are at the beginning of their search or because they have not searched in many years and need to learn this new skill.

Many job hunters think they have to lower their salary expectations because they are unemployed or have been job searching for a long time. You may have to lower your salary expectations for other reasons but, if you position yourself well, not because of being unemployed—none of these three people did. Their unemployment did not affect their salary negotiations. In our book, *Mastering the Job Interview and Winning the Money Game*, you will learn how to negotiate properly and increase your chances of getting what you deserve—whether you are employed or not.

The Five O'Clock Club techniques work whether a job hunter is employed or unemployed. Most job hunters try to get interviews and then try to do well in them. They are skipping two important parts of the process that come before interviewing, and are therefore probably not doing the two remaining parts very well. At The Five O'Clock Club, we stress that all four parts are important. They are:

- **Assessment:** Deciding what you really want results in better job targets. (See our book *Targeting a Great Career* and Part Two of this book for an introduction to the process.) Assessment also results in better résumés. (See our book *Packaging Yourself: The Targeted Résumé*.)
- **Campaign Preparation and Getting Interviews:** Planning your campaign results in lots of interviews in each job target (this book).
- **Interviewing:** Interviews result in an assessment of the *company's* needs. (See our book *Mastering the Job Interview and Winning the Money Game*.)
- **Interview Follow-Up:** Proactive steps taken after the interview result in job offers. (See our

book *Mastering the Job Interview and Winning the Money Game*.)

As you can see, job hunters who think that interviews lead to offers have skipped a step. Interviews lead to a better understanding of what the company wants. What you do *after* the interview leads to an offer.

Here are a few quick stories to get you started. They were written by David Madison on our staff.

CASE STUDY *Pierre*
Getting a Career Back on Track

Pierre had been away from his chosen field of urban planning for almost a decade, and he knew he was fighting an uphill battle. He found that The Five O'Clock Club approach to correct positioning and research played a major role helping him overcome objections and get back in. He decided to respond to three jobs posted on a website; working with his Five O'Clock Club small group and counselor, he crafted cover letters to show that his experience was a match for the stated requirements, relying heavily on the language of the ad itself to describe his background.

> **Pierre found jobs listed on the Internet,
> but so did thousands of others.
> So he networked to find people
> who knew the hiring manager.**

But once the letter and résumés were on the way, he went into high gear to outclass the competition; since it was an Internet ad, he knew there would be plenty of competition—and he could assume that most of the other candidates would have current experience. He networked heavily to find out as much as he could about the company and the key players. He was able to reach people who knew the hiring manager and

he called the president of an industry association to get suggestions and insights about the company. By the time he went on the interview, it was hard for the hiring manager to see him as unconnected or out of touch—and he landed the job. He attended the Club for two months.

CASE STUDY *Natalie*
Learning the Price of Networking without Positioning

Natalie is one of the leaders in her field, but is the first to admit that her job-search skills left something to be desired. Her position was eliminated in a corporate merger and she found herself in the job market for the first time in 13 years. "I have a stellar résumé," she said. "I had this completely unrealistic expectation that, when I told people I would be available, they would be clamoring to have me." She set out to network on a massive scale, and because of her position and reputation, many doors were opened. A year later, she confesses, "I had an incredible collection of business cards."

But she still didn't have a job, although a few teaching and writing assignments had come her way. Her networking had put her on the trail of The Five O'Clock Club, and she began attending sessions. She credits The Five O'Clock Club, especially the books, with giving her crucial insights about strategy and positioning. She learned that people wouldn't be "clamoring" to have her until she helped them grasp what she could do for them. "The Five O'Clock Club gave me a different way of approaching interviews: trying to identify company needs, positioning myself in terms of their needs." She credits the Club with giving her "heightened awareness" that turned the situation around—and she acknowledges the role of her counselor in inspiring her to listen more carefully. On the interviews, she says, "I could hear his voice in the back of my head!"

Natalie credits the weekly contact with her counselor for "keeping me motivated. The Five

xix

O'Clock Club gave me strategy. I'm just sorry that I didn't find the Club sooner." She attended the Club for almost two months.

People are always blaming their circumstances for what they are. I don't believe in circumstances. The people who get on in this world are the people who get up and look for the circumstances they want, and if they can't find them, make them.

George Bernard Shaw

CASE STUDY *Tanya*
Relying on the Two-Minute Pitch

Tanya also credits The Five O'Clock Club with helping her engineer a major career change. She had been a manager at a not-for-profit organization, and just a year later managed to land where she wanted: as an in-house corporate trainer. As one of the first steps, she followed her counselor's suggestion to join the American Society for Training and Development, and soon after accepted a committee assignment—and began the process of meeting the right people.

**Never make a call unless your
Two-Minute Pitch is ready.**

But she forged ahead on other fronts as well: She spent a lot of time on self-assessment, especially the Seven Stories, and took classes to learn the Internet, Excel, and PowerPoint. Having been in the not-for-profit environment only, she wanted to experience the corporate world before going on interviews in her new chosen field. She signed up for temp jobs to get assignments at major corporations, including American Express and Merrill Lynch. So she got her feet wet in the world of business—and her ego got a nice boost when some of the firms wanted her to come on board full-time.

Tanya accomplished her career change after 11 sessions at The Five O'Clock Club, and is pleased with her new role in a new industry. She is a firm believer in positioning and in always being prepared. The Five O'Clock Club teaches that the follow-up calls are critical in the process, and Tanya warns, "Never make calls unless your Two-Minute Pitch is ready—unless you have your résumé in front of you."

CASE STUDY *Chandler*
Well Positioned . . . to Hire Himself

Chandler came to The Five O'Clock Club intent on finding a new job. After 13 sessions, however, he was able to say, "I hired myself." "I really found that coming here helped me a lot because it helped pull a lot of things together that I couldn't have done on my own." He praised the Seven Stories (see our book *Targeting a Great Career*) especially for confirming his interest in training and teaching, but also for helping him realize that he prizes his independence. Hence he came to see that he didn't want a new job in the sense of being hired by someone. He realized he was giving such signals when an interviewer commented: "I know you can do this job. The question is, Do you want to do it?"

Chandler met a woman at the Club who helped him hook up with an assignment that proved to be a valuable foundation for launching his own consulting practice. He felt that his small group was helpful in keeping him focused, and he credits regular attendance with "keeping me on track." Chandler's experience illustrates the truth that The Five O'Clock Club methodology is valid for consultants as well as traditional employees— it is about life management as well as job-search and career skills. After his 13 sessions at the Club, Chandler said, "I don't see myself being retired. I want to work close to things that are important to me. I feel like I've taken this really giant step forward toward doing that."

A New Definition of Job Hunting

Job hunting in our changing economy is a *continuous* process and requires a new definition. Job hunting now means continually becoming aware of market conditions both inside and outside your present organization, and learning what you have to offer—to both markets. This new definition means you must develop new attitudes about your work life, and new skills for doing well in a changing economy.

Today's economy requires job hunters to be more proactive, more sophisticated, and more willing to go through brick walls to get what they want. Employers don't plan your career for you. You must look after yourself, know what you want, and know how to get it.

Understanding How the Job-Hunting Market Works

Knowing why things work the way they do will give you flexibility and control over your job hunt. Knowing how the hiring system works will help you understand why things go right and why they go wrong—why certain things work and others don't. Then you can modify the system to fit your own needs, temperament, and the workings of the job market you are interested in.

It is simplistic to say that only one job-hunting system works. The job-selection process is more complicated than that. Employers can do what they want. You need to understand the process from their point of view. Then you can plan your own job hunt in your own industry. You will learn how to compete in this market.

Always remember, the best jobs don't necessarily go to the most qualified people, but to the people who are the best job hunters. You'll increase your chances of finding the job you want by using a methodical job-hunting approach.

The Five O'Clock Club Coaching Approach

Our approach is methodical. Our coaches are the best. The Five O'Clock Club coaches are full-time career coaches. Each one has met with hundreds of job hunters. Often within minutes we can pinpoint what is wrong with a person's search and turn it around. In this book, you will get that same information. Like our Five O'Clock Club job hunters, you will learn the techniques and hear the stories of other people so you can job hunt more effectively.

It is other people's experience that makes the older man wiser than the younger man.

Yoruba Proverb

The
Five
O'Clock
Club

PART ONE

Finding Good Jobs
THE CHANGING JOB-HUNTING PROCESS

11 Hints for Job Hunting in a Tight Market

The
Five
O'Clock
Club

If you haven't the strength to impose your own terms upon life, then you must accept the terms it offers you.

T. S. Eliot, *The Confidential Clerk*

1. Expand Your Job-Hunting Targets

If you are searching only in Los Angeles or only in Detroit, for example, think of other geographic areas. If you are looking only in large public corporations, consider small or private companies. If you are looking for a certain kind of position, investigate what other kinds of work you could also do.

2. Expect to Be "In Search" for the Long Haul

The average professional or managerial worker takes six months to get a job. So though you may find something right away, it is sensible to develop financial backup plans. What kind of side work could you do to earn money in the short run? How could you reduce your expenses? Join a job-hunting group to get support, ideas, and contacts.

When you meet someone who doesn't "have" anything for you right now, that's okay. Plan to get in touch with that person again. In fact, you may meet dozens of people who don't have anything right now. Get to know them and their needs better, and tell them about yourself. Build relationships so you can contact them later.

3. Keep Your Spirits Up

An alarming number of job hunters in the United States are becoming discouraged and dropping out of the job market. Don't you be one of them. Read the next section, "When You've Lost the Spirit to Job Hunt."

Be aware that what you are going through is not easy, and that many of the things you are experiencing are being experienced by just about everybody else. Hang in there, get a fresh start, and eventually you will find something.

4. Think about Developing New Skills

If you suspect your old skills are out-of-date, develop new ones. If you can't get a job because you don't have the experience, *get* the experience. The several months that you will probably be searching is long enough for you to develop new skills. Take a course. Do volunteer work to gain expertise that you can then market. Join an association related to your new skill area.

If you need to earn money immediately, try to do something that will enhance your job search. For example, if you decide to do temporary work, and you want a job in the airline industry, consider doing your temporary work with an airline.

Consider doing something for little or no money simply because it would improve your résumé. A Five O'Clock Clubber got a 12-week assignment with a Sears consignee during the Christmas rush. The pay was terrible but the job title was Regional Manager. He needed something to do, and the job looked great on his résumé.

5. Become a Skilled Job Hunter

Being good at your job does not make you good at *getting* jobs. Good job hunters know what they want, what the market wants, and how to present themselves. Stay competitive. Learn how to job hunt like an expert. Your future depends on it.

6. Look for Opportunities

In this economy, opportunities probably will not come knocking on your door. You have to look for them—both inside and outside your present company. Chances are, your present company and even the industry you are in are going to change. So rather than just doing the same old job, think of how you can take on new assignments so you are at the forefront of the changes. Put out feelers to find out whether you are marketable outside your company. Continually test the waters.

When you are on an interview, try to negotiate a job that suits both you and the hiring manager. For example, if the job is for an administrator, and you would like to do some writing, see if they will allow you to do that too.

Don't passively expect to be told where you could fit in. Actively think about your place in their organization. Create a job for yourself.

7. Target What You Want

As Lily Tomlin said, "I always wanted to be somebody, but I should have been more specific." Be sure you select specific geographic areas, specific industries, and specific positions within those industries.

For example, you may want to be a writer in publishing or advertising in Manhattan or Chicago. Find the names of the people to contact in those cities and industries—or people who know people in those targets. If you target, you have a better chance of finding the job you want.

8. Learn How to Get Interviews

There are a lot of techniques for generating interviews. The basic ones are: answering ads, using search firms, contacting companies directly, and networking. Only 10 percent of all jobs are filled through ads and search firms, so it is wise to learn how to contact companies directly and how to network properly.

Identify all of the companies you need to contact, and then contact them as quickly as possible. Make sure you consider *every* technique for getting interviews in your target area. Don't focus on getting a job: Focus on getting interviews.

9. See People Two Levels Higher than You Are

When you are in the initial stages of exploring a target area, you will want to do some library research and contact people at your level to find out about that area and see how well your skills match up.

But after you have decided to conduct a full campaign in a target area, contact people who are at a higher level than you are. They are the ones who are in a position to hire you or recommend that you be hired.

Make sure you talk to lots of people. It will give you practice and actually relax you. You will find out how much in demand you are, and how much you can charge.

10. Work at Your Job Hunt the Same Way You Would Work at a Job

Plan your job-hunting campaign. Work at it 35 hours a week if you are unemployed, and 15 hours a week if you are employed. It's only when you are devoting a certain number of hours a week to your search that you can get some momentum built up. Of course, you also need to be concerned about the *quality* of your campaign. You can have an organized and methodical search by carefully following the process in this book.

11. Follow-Up, Follow-Up, Follow-Up

After you meet with someone who has no job for you, keep in touch with that person by letting him or her know how your search is going or by sending a magazine article that would be of interest, for example. After a job interview, consider what they liked about you and what they didn't, and how you could influence their hiring decision. Follow-up is the main opportunity you have to turn a job interview into a job offer.

You think you understand the situation, but what you don't understand is that the situation just changed.

Putnam Investments advertisement

The
Five
O'Clock
Club

When You've Lost the Spirit to Job Hunt

"I can't explain myself, I'm afraid, Sir," said Alice,
"because I'm not myself, you see."
"I don't see," said the Caterpillar.

Lewis Carroll, *Alice in Wonderland*

They're all doing terrific! You're not. You're barely hanging on. You used to be a winner, but now you're not so sure. How can you pull yourself out of this?

I've felt like that. Everyone in New York had a job except me. I would never work again. I was ruining interviews although I knew better—I had run The Five O'Clock Club for years in Philadelphia. Yet I was unable to job hunt properly. I was relatively new to New York and divorced. Even going to my country house depressed me: A woman wanted me to sell it, join her cult, and have a 71-year-old as my roommate. It seemed to be my fate.

Then I got a call from my father—a hurricane was about to hit New York. When I told him my situation, he directed me to get rid of the cult lady and take the next train out. I got out just as the hurricane blew in, and he and I spent three beautiful days alone at my parents' ocean place. He encouraged me, even playing 10 motivational tapes on "being a winner"! One tape taught me:

The winners in life think constantly in terms of I can,
I will and I am. Losers, on the other hand, concentrate
their waking thoughts on what they should have or
would have done, or what they can't do.

Dr. Dennis Waitley, *The Psychology of Winning*

My father wined and dined and took care of me. We watched a six-hour tape of my family history—the births, and birthdays, Christmases past, marriages, and parties. We talked about life and the big picture. I had no strength. He nurtured me and gave me strength.

What can *you* do if you can't get this kind of nurturing? Perhaps I've learned a few lessons that may help you.

> **There seem to be phases and cycles**
> **in a job hunt—there is the initial**
> **rush, the long haul, the drought,**
> **followed by the first poor job offer**
> **and the later better offers.**

1. Put Things in Perspective

A depressing and difficult passage has prefaced every
new page I have turned in life.

Charlotte Brontë

You've worked 10 or 20 years, and you'll probably work 10 or 20 more. In the grand scheme of things, this moment will be a blip: an aberration in the past.

Focusing on the present will make you depressed and will also make you a poor interviewee. You will find it difficult to brag about your past or see the future. You will provide too much information about what put you in this situation.

Interviewers don't care. They want to hear what you can do for *them.* When they ask why you are looking, give a brief, light, logical explanation, and then drop it.

Focus on what you have done in the past, and what you can do in the future. You *do* have a future, you know, although you may feel locked into your present situation. Even some young people say it is too late for them. But a lot can happen in 10 years—and *most* of what happens is up to you.

My life seems like one long obstacle course, with me as the chief obstacle.

Jack Paar

Woe to him that is alone when he falleth, for he hath not another to help him up.

The Wisdom of Solomon

2. Get Support

The old support systems—extended families and even nuclear families—are disappearing. And we no longer look to our community for support.

Today, we are more alone; we are supposed to be tougher and take care of ourselves. But relying solely on yourself is not the answer. How can you fill yourself up when you are emotionally and spiritually empty?

Job hunters often need some kind of emotional and spiritual support because this is a trying time. Our egos are at stake. We feel vulnerable and uncared for. We need realistic support from people who know what we are going through.

There is no such thing as a self-made man. I've had much help and have found that if you are willing to work, many people are willing to help you.

O. Wayne Rollins

- Join a job-hunting support group to be with others who know what you're going through.

Many places of worship have job-hunting groups open to anyone. During a later job hunt when I was employed, I reported my progress weekly to The Five O'Clock Club I formed in New York. It kept me going.

Statistics show that job hunters with regular career-coaching support get jobs faster and at higher rates of pay. A job-hunting group gives emotional support, concrete advice, and feedback. Often, however, these are not enough for those who are at their lowest.

The more lasting a man's ultimate work, the more sure he is to pass through a time, and perhaps a very long one, in which there seems to be very little hope for him.

Samuel Butler

- If possible, rely on your friends and family. I could count on a call from my former husband most mornings after I returned from breakfast—just so we could both make sure I was really job hunting. I scheduled lunches with friends and gave them an honest report or practiced my job-hunting lines with them.
- Don't abuse your relationships by relying on one or two people. Find lots of sources of support. Consider joining a church, synagogue, or mosque (they're *supposed* to be nice to you).

3. Remember That This Is Part of a Bigger Picture

We, ignorant of ourselves, Beg often our own harms, Which the Wise Power Denies us for our own good; so we find profit by losing of our prayers.

Shakespeare, *Antony and Cleopatra*

. . . so are My ways higher than your ways and My thoughts than your thoughts.

Isaiah 55:9

You are a child of the universe no less than the trees
and the stars; you have a right to be here.
And whether or not it is clear to you, no doubt the
universe is unfolding as it should.

Max Ehrmann

Why me? Why now? Shakespeare thought there might be someone bigger than ourselves watching over everything—a Wise Power. My mother (and probably yours, too) always said "everything happens for the best."

We know that in all things God works for the
good of those who love Him.

Romans 8:28

If you believe things happen for a purpose, *think about the good in your own situation.* What was the *purpose* of my own unemployment? Because of it:

- I experienced a closeness with my father that still affects me;
- I became a better counselor; and
- I stopped working 12-hour days.

Though shattered when they lose their jobs, many say in retrospect it was the best thing that could have happened to them. Some say this time of transition was the most rewarding experience of their lives.

Every adversity has the seed of an
equivalent or greater benefit.

W. Clement Stone

Perhaps you, too, can learn from this experience and also make some sense of it. This is a time when people often:

- decide what they *really* should be doing with their careers—I had resisted full-time career coaching because I liked the prestige of the jobs I had held;

- better their situations, taking off on another upward drive in their careers;
- develop their personalities; learn skills that will last their entire lives, and
- reexamine their values and decide what is now important to them.

For what shall it profit a man, if he shall gain the
whole world, and lose his own soul?

Mark 8:36

The trouble with the rat race is that if you win,
you're still a rat.

Lily Tomlin

4. Continue to Do Your Job

When you were in your old job, there were days you didn't feel like doing it, but you did it anyway because it was your responsibility. *Job hunting is your job right now.* Some days you don't feel like doing it, but you must. Make a phone call. Write a proposal. Research a company. Do your best every day. No matter how you feel. Somehow it will get done, as any job gets done. Some practical suggestions:

- Make your job hunting professional. Organize it. Get a special calendar to use exclusively to record what you are doing. Use The Five O'Clock Club's Interview Record in this book to track more professionally your efforts and results.
- Set goals. Don't think of whether or not you want to make calls and write letters. Of course you don't. Just do them anyway. Spend most of your time interviewing—that's how you get a job.

  Depression ➡ Inactivity ➡ Depression.

- If you're at the three-month mark or beyond, you may be at a low point. It's hard to push on. Get a fresh start. Pretend you're starting all over again.

- Finding a job is your responsibility. Don't depend on anyone else (search firms, friends) to find it for you.

- Watch your drinking, eating, smoking. They can get out of hand. Take care of yourself physically. Get dressed. Look good. Get some exercise. Eat healthful foods. You may need a few days off to recharge.

- Don't postpone having fun until you get a job. If you are unemployed, schedule at least three hours of fun a week. Do something you normally are unable to do when you are working. I went out to breakfast every morning, indulged in reading the *Times,* and then went back to my apartment to job hunt. I also went to the auction houses, and bought a beautiful desk at Sotheby's when I sold my country house.

- Assess your financial situation. What is your backup plan if your unemployment goes on for a certain number of months? If need be, I planned to get a roommate, sell furniture, and take out a loan. It turned out not to be necessary, but by planning ahead, I knew I would not wind up on the street.

- Remember: You are distracted. Job hunters get mugged, walk into walls, lose things. This is not an ordinary situation, and extraordinary things happen. Be on your guard.

- Observe the results of what you do in your job hunt. Results are indicators of the correctness of your actions and can help refine your techniques.

All's well that ends well.

Shakespeare

- Become a good job hunter so you can compete in this market. It takes practice, but the better you are, the less anxious you will be.

In nature there are neither rewards nor punishments—there are consequences.

Robert Green Ingersoll

In the depths of winter I discovered that there was in me an invincible summer.

Albert Camus

Finally, two sayings especially helped me when I was unemployed:

You don't get what you want. You get what you need.
and
When God closes a door, He opens a window.

Good luck.—Kate

An Overview of the Job-Search Process

The
Five
O'Clock
Club

If you only care enough for a result you will almost certainly obtain it. If you wish to be rich, you will be rich; if you wish to be learned, you will be learned; if you wish to be good, you will be good.

William James

The following chart outlines each part of the process. It's best to do every part, however quickly you may do it. Experienced job hunters pay attention to the details and do not skip a step.

The first part of the process is **assessment** (or evaluation). You evaluate yourself by doing the exercises in *Targeting a Great Career,* and you evaluate your prospects by doing some preliminary research in the library or by talking to people.

Assessment consists of the following exercises:

- The Seven Stories Exercise
- Interests
- Values
- Satisfiers and Dissatisfiers
- Your Forty-Year Vision

If you are working privately with a career coach, he or she may ask you to do a few additional exercises, such as a personality test.

Assessment results in:

- a listing of all the targets you think are worth exploring; and
- a résumé that makes you look appropriate to your first target (and may work with other targets as well).

Even if you don't do the entire assessment, the Seven Stories Exercise is especially important because it will help you develop an interesting résumé. Therefore, we have included that exercise in this book.

Research will help you figure out which of your targets:

- are a good fit for you; and
- offer hope in terms of being a good market.

You can't have too many targets as long as you rank them. Then, for *each one,* conduct a campaign to get interviews in that target area.

The circumstances that surround a man's life are not important. How that man responds to those circumstances is important. His response is the ultimate determining factor between success and failure.

Booker T. Washington

Phase I: Campaign Preparation

- Conduct research to develop a list of all the companies in your first target. Find out the names of people you should contact in appropriate departments in those companies.
- Write your cover letter. (Paragraph 1 is the opening; Paragraph 2 is a summary about yourself appropriate for this target; Paragraph 3 contains your bulleted accomplishments ("You may be interested in some of the things I've done"); Paragraph 4 is the close. (Sample letters are included in this book.)

- Develop your plan for getting **lots of interviews in this target**. You have four basic choices:
  - Networking,
  - Direct contact,
  - Search firms, and
  - Ads (print and Internet).

You will read more about these methods for getting interviews later in this book.

Sometimes it's best if a man just spends a moment or two thinking. It is one of the toughest things he will ever do, and that's probably why so few bother to do it.

Alonzo Herndon, born a slave; died a millionaire; Founder, Atlanta Life Insurance Company

Phase II: Interviewing

Most people think interviews result in job offers. But there are usually a few intervening steps before a final offer is made. Interviews should result in getting and giving information.

Did you learn the issues important to each person with whom you met? What did they think were your strongest positives? Where are they in the hiring process? How many other people are they considering? How do you compare with those people? Why might they be reluctant to bring you on board, compared with the other candidates? How can you overcome the decision makers' objections?

One of the most important, yet most overlooked parts of the job-search process, this is covered in extensive detail in this book.

Phase III: Follow-Up

Now that you have analyzed the interview, you can figure out how to follow up with each person with whom you interviewed. Aim to follow up with 6 to 10 companies. Five job possibilities will fall away through no fault of your own.

What's more, with 6 to 10 possibilities, you increase your chances of having three good offers to choose from. You would be surprised: even in a tight market, job hunters are able to develop multiple offers.

When you are in the Interview Phase of Target 1, it's time to start Phase I of Target 2. This will give you more momentum and ensure that you do not let things dry up. Keep both targets going, and then start Target 3.

You ain't goin' nowhere . . . son. You ought to go back to driving a truck.

Jim Denny, Grand Ole Opry manager, firing Elvis Presley after one performance. An interview on October 2, 1954.

Develop Your Unique Résumé

Read all the case studies in *Packaging Yourself: The Targeted Résumé*. You will learn a powerful new way of thinking about how to position yourself for the kinds of jobs you want. Each of the résumés in that book is for a unique person aiming at a specific target. Seeing how other people position themselves will help you think about what you want a prospective employer to know about you.

Now, it is best to go back to the first part of the process, assessment. In *Targeting a Great Career,* you will read actual case studies that will show you how real people benefitted from doing the assessment, including the Forty-Year Vision.

However, if your targets are already defined, just keep reading.

Everyone should learn to do one thing supremely well because he likes it, and one thing supremely well because he detests it.

B. W. M. Young, headmaster, Charterhouse School

Life never leaves you stranded. If life hands you a problem, it also hands you the ability to overcome that problem. Are you ever tempted to blame the world for your failures and shortcomings? If so, I suggest you pause and reconsider. Does the problem lie with the world, or with you? Dare to dream.

Dennis Kimbro, *Think and Grow Rich: A Black Choice*

ASSESSMENT

Consists of:

- The Seven Stories Exercise
- Interests
- Values
- Satisfiers and Dissatisfiers
- Your Forty-Year Vision

Results in:

- As many targets as you can think of
- A ranking of your targets
- A résumé that makes you look appropriate to your first target
- A plan for conducting your search

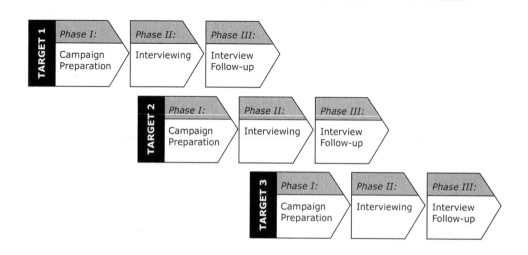

RESULTS

Phase I:
Campaign Preparation.
Results in:

- ❏ Research (list of companies)
- ❏ Résumé
- ❏ Cover letter
- ❏ Plan for getting interviews
  - networking
  - direct contact
  - search firms
  - ads

Phase II:
Interviewing.
Results in:

- ❏ Giving them information to keep them interested in you
- ❏ Getting information so you can "move it along"
- ❏ Plan for follow-up (You may do several in-depth follow-ups with each person)

Phase III:
Follow-Up.
Results in:

- ❏ Aiming to have 6 to 10 things in the works, and

Job Offers!

The
Five
O'Clock
Club

A Systematic Job Hunt

*Man is not born to solve the problems of the universe,
but to find out what he has to do; and to restrain
himself within the limits of his comprehension.*

Goethe

Successful Job Hunting Is a System

Working the system increases your chances of getting the job you want—faster. Working the system also helps relieve your natural anxiety about what you should do next.

The system is the same whether you are employed or unemployed, and even if you are not interested in changing jobs now. The system is the same whether you are looking for full- or part-time employment, consulting, or freelance work.

That's because job hunting in a changing economy means: *continuously becoming aware of market conditions inside as well as outside your present company. And learning what you have to offer—both inside and outside your company.*

The time to become aware of your opportunities is *not* when the pressure is on to find a new job, but *now.*

The Job-Hunting Process

You select or target a job market by selecting a geographic area you'd be willing to work in, an industry or company size (small, medium, or large company), and a job or function within that industry. For example, you may want to be a pressman in the publishing industry in New Hampshire. That's your target market.

Then conduct a campaign for the sole purpose of getting interviews in your target area. A number of those interviews might eventually lead to acceptable job offers.

Job hunting seems to have dozens of equally important steps. There are résumés and cover letters to write, personal contacts to make, search firms to contact, ads to answer, notes to write, and so on. You can lose sight of what is most important.

There are only four main parts in a job-hunting campaign: targeting, getting interviews in each target, interviewing, and following up. Do your best and put your effort into those areas. Everything you do in a job hunt grows out of your targets, which lead to interviews and then to offers. If you have targeted well, can get interviews, are well prepared for them, and know how to turn interviews into offers, you will be focused and less affected by mistakes in other areas of your search.

How Long Will a Job Search Take?

The length of each step in your search can vary considerably. For example, selecting the area in which you want to work (see *Targeting a Great*

Career) can be as simple as saying, "I want to be a controller in a small firm." Or, it can be as complex as saying, "I want a position of leadership in a growing computer services business in any major U.S. city, where I can run my part of the operation, working with fast-paced but ethical people who are imaginative and leaders in their field. The job should lead to the position of partner."

The entire campaign can be very short. Let's say, for example, that:

- You have focused on a specific, realizable target.
- There are openings in the area that interests you.
- You know of someone in a position to hire you.
- You and the hiring manager "strike sparks" during the interview, which progresses naturally.

Start to finish could take several months.

The average job hunt takes longer. Statistics show that it takes an average of six months or more for professionals and middle managers to find the jobs they want. *Career changers take longer.* People who are already employed usually take longer to find a new job because they often don't work as hard at the hunt.

It could take you longer than a month or two because, among other things:

- You may not be clear about what you want.
- What you want may not be realistic.
- Maybe what you want *is* realistic, but there are no immediate openings.
- There may be openings, but you may not know where they are.
- You may hear of openings, but may not know anyone in a position to hire you.
- You may meet someone in a position to hire you, but the two of you don't hit it off.

Devote a large amount of time and energy to your search if you seriously intend to find a suit-

able job. A thorough search is so much work that the job you finally land will seem easy by comparison!

On the other hand, job hunting is like any other skill: You get better at it with practice. You'll learn the techniques and what's right for you. You'll become aware of what's happening in your chosen field, so when you start a formal search it won't take so long.

Make it a rule of life never to regret and never to look back. Regret is an appalling waste of energy; you can't build on it; it's only good for wallowing in.

Katherine Mansfield

The New Approach to Job Hunting

Keep up with changes in your company and your target area. To compete in today's market, you must know:

- yourself,
- the market, both inside and outside your company, and
- how to compete against *trained* job hunters.

Job Hunting—An Everyday Affair

Job hunting is no longer something that happens only when you want to change jobs. Do it informally *all the time* to stay sharp in your present position.

You should always be aware of what may adversely affect your present security. Don't expect your employer to tell you that the company or your department is heading in a different direction. Be ready when the time for change comes. Take advantage of changes so you can move your career in the direction *you* want it to go. Take control and "impose your own terms upon life."

In today's world, many people job hunt virtually all the time. Years ago, when U.S. corporations

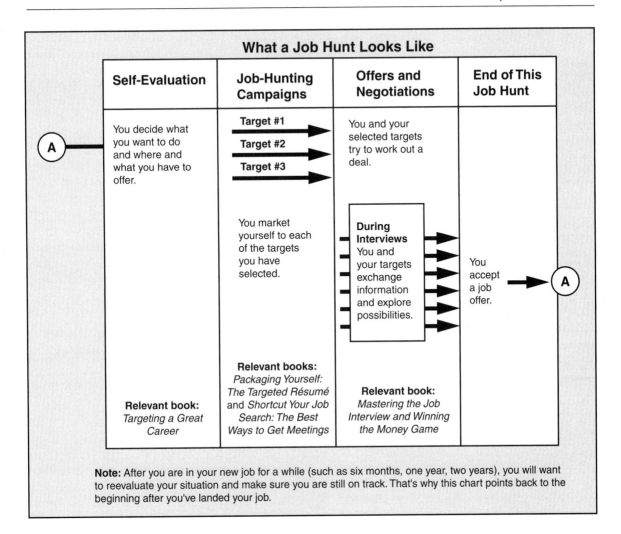

What a Job Hunt Looks Like

Self-Evaluation	Job-Hunting Campaigns	Offers and Negotiations	End of This Job Hunt
You decide what you want to do and where and what you have to offer.	**Target #1** **Target #2** **Target #3**	You and your selected targets try to work out a deal.	
	You market yourself to each of the targets you have selected.	**During Interviews** You and your targets exchange information and explore possibilities.	You accept a job offer.
Relevant book: *Targeting a Great Career*	**Relevant books:** *Packaging Yourself: The Targeted Résumé* and *Shortcut Your Job Search: The Best Ways to Get Meetings*	**Relevant book:** *Mastering the Job Interview and Winning the Money Game*	

Note: After you are in your new job for a while (such as six months, one year, two years), you will want to reevaluate your situation and make sure you are still on track. That's why this chart points back to the beginning after you've landed your job.

were more stable, I met an executive at a major pharmaceuticals company. He had been with that company 30 years, and planned to stay there until retirement.

Yet, while I was talking to him, he reached into his bottom drawer and pulled out an up-to-date résumé. He was not starting a new job hunt; he believed he should always have an up-to-date résumé and keep on looking—even though he had been working at the same company for 30 years! A good number of his job hunts were

"successful" since his outside exploration got him to his high position in the same company.

Job hunting does not necessarily mean you want to change jobs now. Maybe you'll make your next job change a few years down the road. Or maybe someone will change your job for you, without asking. When are you going to start thinking about your next move?

Few things are impossible to diligence and skill.
Samuel Johnson

Plan Your Next Move

Plan your career transitions—your moves from one job to the next—don't have them thrust upon you. First, know which job is right for you: a job in which you will excel and feel satisfied doing. Then see how well your present job fits those desires. Don't leave your job for another one that is equally unsatisfying. On the other hand, don't remain in your current job out of inertia.

Career transitions are prompted by changes in a company—such as when it cuts back or introduces major technological or strategic changes—or by a change in you and your goals for your life. Be alert for a coming transition.

If You're Thinking about Changing Jobs

If you don't like your present job, don't leave yet . . . a good job hunt starts at home. Try to enrich your present job or move elsewhere in the company. Leave only after you are convinced there is nothing there for you.

Whether you want to stay or leave, find out your options and your marketable skills. Figure out what would be a good growth move for you.

One way to find out is to talk informally with people in other companies who are at least two levels higher than you are. They have an overview of the broad spectrum of job possibilities and are also in a position to hire you, or know others who might.

Another way to find out what is marketable is to look at newspaper and Internet ads. This can also give you ideas for growing in your present position.

Let me give you an example. As soon as I accepted the job of vice president of operations for an advertising agency, I started clipping ads for vice president of personnel, controller, vice president of finance, general manager—anything that would apply, even remotely, to my new position. The ads gave me ideas that neither my new employer nor I would have thought of.

I expanded the job and organized the categories of work I should be concentrating on.

These ads also told me the likelihood of being able to get one of those jobs. Even though I clipped lots of ads for vice president of finance, I would never qualify because those positions required skills I did not have and was not interested in acquiring.

Ads also let you see who is hiring and what is in demand. Ads teach you the buzzwords of certain professions, and indicate how to tailor your résumé—just in case.

Your constant job hunt can only be *good* for your present employer. It motivates you to do better, keeping your company more competitive than if you were not aware of what was happening outside.

Practicing Job-Hunting Techniques

Job hunting is a specialized skill just like public speaking or gourmet cooking. You probably wouldn't, for example, get up to speak before an important audience without preparation and practice.

Job hunting takes planning to decide on your message; conduct research; consider your audience and how your message will sound to them; write and rewrite résumés, letters, and interview presentations; and then practice to hear how it all sounds.

Successful job hunting is a formal process. But once you know the basics, you can and should put your own personality into your presentations, just as you would in public speaking.

Follow the "rules" for job hunting the same way you would follow the "rules" for public speaking or cooking. A wise beginner does everything by the book. After you become skilled, you can deviate a bit because you have mastered the basics. You will do what is right for you and the situation you are in. You can exercise sound judgment.

You will then be at the point where it flows. You will find you are operating from an inner strength, and you'll feel what is and is not important. It is *your* job hunt, and you are the one calling the shots. You will feel sure enough to do what is appropriate regardless of what some expert says. You will know when it is to your advantage to break the rules.

Don't develop a siege mentality. Practice job hunting now, even if you happen to enjoy what you're doing, and even if you want to continue in your present job. In fact, you will be more effective in your job if you become sharper about what is happening in the world.

The rules of the game keep changing and that's part of the game. Only those who change along with the rules will be allowed to continue to play.

Our rate of progress is such that an individual human being, of ordinary length of life, will be called on to face novel situations which find no parallel in his past. The fixed person, for the fixed duties, who, in older societies was such a godsend, in the future will be a public danger.
Alfred North Whitehead

The Five O'Clock Club

What to Do If You Are about to Be Fired

I don't deserve this, but I have arthritis and I don't deserve that either.

Jack Benny

When people get fired, many say to themselves, "I'm good at what I do. I won't have trouble finding a job." Unfortunately, job hunting calls for special skills. If you get fired, ask for outplacement help as part of your separation agreement. You cannot purchase the services of an outplacement firm yourself. Your company pays The Five O'Clock Club or other outplacement firm directly. You will get far more and your employer will pay far less if they choose The Five O'Clock Club as their outplacement provider.

On the home page of our website (www.fiveoclockclub.com), go to the bottom left-hand corner and click on "Individuals: get help negotiating severance." You will find extensive information there.

Five O'Clock Club outplacement help can make all the difference in finding new employment quickly and confidently. Most corporate outplacement packages last for one to three months, sometimes just a few days! You are then left to fend for yourself. Many months later, the job hunter may wish he or she had more help.

Five O'Clock Club outplacement packages all last for one full year—even if you land a job quickly—a great benefit. Our one-year package means we will continue working with you even if

you decide to do consulting work for a while, lose your next job, or need help handling the political situation in a new job.

You will receive a guaranteed number of hours of private coaching, one full year in the small group, a set of books, a boxed set of 16 40-minute Five O'Clock Club audio presentations on CD-ROMs, and other benefits. Check our website for the latest offering.

If you are currently employed, or outplacement is not available to you, consider your options. A seminar is fine but will not see you through the job-hunting process. Job-coaching firms often charge from $4,000 to $6,000 up front, and some have been known to lose interest once the fee is paid.

You need advice and support. Job hunting is stressful and lonely. You may feel you are the only one going through what you are going through. You may even feel as though you will never work again.

The Five O'Clock Club was founded to provide "outplacement" help to individuals. More and more organizations are paying for their former employees to receive The Five O'Clock Club's services. However, most of our attendees pay their own way. Those who are already in traditional outplacement often pay to come to the Club on their own. They appreciate the superior coaching at the Club and also enjoy the healthy environment of being in groups with employed, as well as unemployed, people. The room is full of proactive, intelligent people who want to move ahead with their searches—and have fun while doing so.

Join The Five O'Clock Club. We offer job-search training and coaching from professional career coaches. You can also meet with a coach privately (in person or by phone) to help you figure out your job targets, prepare your résumé, or get individualized help on specific parts of your campaign. You will be with others who are trying to accomplish the same things. See the back of this book for more information on the Club.

Unemployed people are sometimes embarrassed by their situation and pretend they are not looking, which is the worst thing they can do. *When you are unemployed and looking for a job, the more people who know what you are looking for, the better.* Spend time regularly with other job hunters, and also with a professional career coach who can give you solid advice.

How to Negotiate Your Severance Package

You may want a career coach to help you during this difficult and sensitive time. Here are some things to consider:

- **Explore your options.**

  During the negotiation, be *pleasantly persistent* as you explore the options available to you. The situation may be more flexible than it originally appears to be.

- **Deal with each compensation issue separately.**

  A severance package is made up of many items. These may include an actual cash settlement, outplacement help, health care and other benefits, and other items, depending on the industry and company. You need to look at each component individually. A large cash settlement, for example, will evaporate quickly if you end up paying for outplacement help and benefits.

- **Push to continue your benefits.**

  It costs a company very little to carry employees on its medical plan. But if you tried to

duplicate coverage on your own, it would cost a small fortune.

- **Develop a mantra.**

  Find one that succinctly describes your feelings. The phrase will keep you focused and give your overall campaign consistency. Use a phrase such as, "I simply want what is fair."

- **Ask for career-coaching help until you find a job.**

  You should never underestimate the amount of time it will take you—or the help you will need—to find another comparable position. Depending on the complexity of your situation and your own psychological makeup, your search may last a long time—some tough searches have taken more than a year. If your company only grants you three months' outplacement assistance, you could find yourself cut off in the middle of your job search. Therefore, ask them to consider using The Five O'Clock Club as their outplacement provider.

- **Don't take money over outplacement.**

  A cash settlement of $3,000—or even $30,000—sounds like a lot, but on your own you will not be able to replicate what you could get with top-of-the-line outplacement services.

> **The fact is that people who get ongoing Five O'Clock Club career coaching throughout their search get better jobs faster, and at higher rates of pay.**

- **Select the outplacement services yourself.**

  Although your firm may have a relationship with an outplacement firm, many companies will allow you to select the outplacement firm with which you want to work. You may call The Five O'Clock Club for referral to one of our coaches for help with your severance negotiation. The coach will charge you on a per-hour basis.

19

- **Use outplacement help to launch your own business.**

  You may dream of going out on your own, and be tempted to take a cash settlement, believing money is the most important ingredient you need to form your new company from scratch. However, a good outplacement firm can help you write a business plan, talk with venture capitalists and merchant bankers, and serve as valued advisors until you are on your feet. This is advice you could never afford on your own. In fact, it costs an outplacement firm more to help someone launch a business than to do a traditional job search. The time involved is longer, and the services required are more complex.

- **You can start outplacement coaching even though you have not completely come to terms with your employer.**

  You can be looking for another job at the same time you are asking your company for a better settlement. But bear in mind: Traditional outplacement firms cannot help you with negotiations with your employer.

- **Find out what other employees have walked away with.**

  Use this information to further your own case.

  Remember: Every situation is unique. Get help while you are negotiating your severance package. The amount you spend on a little bit of coaching, even over the phone, will convince you that you did your very best to get what you deserve and need.

It is work, work that one delights in, that is the surest guarantor of happiness.

Ashley Montagu, *The American Way of Life*

The
Five
O'Clock
Club

How Long Will It Take to Find a Job?

Nothing in the world can take the place of persistence. Talent will not; nothing is more common than unsuccessful men with talent. Genius will not; the world is full of educated derelicts. Persistence and determination alone are omnipotent. The slogan "press on" has solved and always will solve the problems of the human race.

Calvin Coolidge

Most of the factors influencing the length of a job hunt are under your control. Scan the following topics and read the ones of interest to you now. Read the others later.

Factor #1: Career Continuation vs. Career Change

All things being equal, changing careers takes two to three months longer than looking for a job in the field you are in now. If you want to head your career in a new direction, do it—but realize that it will take longer. (See the chapter: "How to Change Careers.")

Factor #2: A Clear Target

You dramatically reduce your chances of finding the job you want if you don't have clearly defined targets.

A job target is a clearly selected geographic area, industry or company size (small, medium, or large company), and function within that industry. For example, a job hunter may target the advertising industry in New York or Chicago, and aim at positions in the account management area. That's one target. That same job hunter may target media sales positions in the publishing industry, also in New York or Chicago. That's a second target. They are related, but require quite different campaigns.

You may feel you are willing to take any job that comes along, but attaining results with such an approach takes longer than with a targeted approach. When you target, your campaign is focused and more convincing to hiring managers. Your pitch is more polished, and you'll find it easier to network. Serendipitous leads can certainly be worthwhile, but the core of your campaign should be targeted.

Factor #3: A Clear Positioning Statement or Pitch within That Target

You are selling an expensive product—yourself—and you cost many thousands of dollars. To sell this product, know what the *customer* (your prospective employer) wants, what you have to offer, and why the customer would want to buy this product. As you position yourself, figure out what to say about yourself in light of what your customer needs. Know how you fit in.

"Take me to the first office building that's hiring."

Factor #4: Favorable Conditions within Your Target Market

If your target area is growing or desperately needs what you are offering, or if there are plenty of jobs for which you would qualify, your job hunt will not take as long.

On the other hand, if you decide to go for a tough target, expect to work hard to overcome the difficulties. Find out how to get in, and then do it.

Factor #5: True Desire to Find a Job

The people most likely to succeed are the ones who sincerely want to find a job, and work hard at getting it.

Job hunting is a job in itself. If you are unemployed, work at it full-time (with time off for a little fun). If you are employed, treat job hunting as a serious part-time job.

Many job hunters do not treat finding a job as their top priority. Some spend time suing their former employer. Others work hard at a job hunt

doing the wrong things: When choosing between doing two things, they seem to choose the one less likely to result in job-hunting progress. Some people spend months in the library getting ready, for example, when they know they should be out meeting people. They may consciously or unconsciously sabotage their own efforts because they were recently fired and are afraid of getting fired again. If you find everything is going wrong all the time, ask yourself if you may be afraid of the future.

Factor #6: Attitude, Attitude, Attitude

You may have the right target, the perfect market, and be the perfect match for a company, but if your attitude is wrong, you'll have a hard time. The worst attitude is expecting someone else to find a job for you. Successful job hunters are those who take responsibility for their own success or failure rather than blaming the career coach or the system when things go wrong.

Attitude includes:

- taking responsibility for your own job hunt,
- the self-confidence you portray,
- being able to think and act like a winner even if you don't feel like it (who wants to hire a loser?), and
- your drive and energy level.

Your attitude is as important as the actual job-hunting techniques you use. Flawless technique is worthless with a bad attitude.

Life shrinks or expands in proportion to one's courage.

Anais Nin

Factor #7: Working The Five O'Clock Club System

In addition to being willing to work hard, you must be willing to work the system. Those most likely to find a job quickly are those who go through every step, even if they go through certain steps quickly or find other steps distasteful.

A job hunt is going to take time. The time you think you're saving by skipping a phase will haunt you later. Do not bypass the system. *There are no shortcuts.*

Factor #8: Good Interviewing and Follow-Up Skills

Some people get lots of interviews but no job offers.

You cannot get a job without an interview, in which you'll have to do well. Interviewing is a skill that requires preparation, practice, and an ability to notice what is important to the interviewer so you can take whatever next steps are required.

Factor #9: Support and Encouragement from Friends and Family/Absence of Personal Disruptions

Recently divorced people, for example, tend to do less well in their jobs and job-hunting efforts. If you have other things on your mind, they may adversely affect your job hunt. Try to be effective despite these problems.

Job hunters usually need emotional support because this can be a trying experience. Our egos are at stake. Job hunting is not an easy thing to do.

Sometimes the support of family and friends is not enough because they are not going through what you are going through. That's why people join job-hunting groups or get outplacement coaching. You need realistic, honest support from people who know what you are going through. Studies have proved that *those who get ongoing coaching during their searches get jobs faster and at higher rates of pay* than those who simply take a course or decide to search on their own.

Factor #10: Previous Job-Hunting Experience

If you haven't job hunted in a while, you're probably rusty. People will ask questions you're not used to answering and you may not sound polished. The process requires skills we don't use in our everyday work lives. Inexperienced job hunters usually take longer than those who are used to marketing themselves. You need to develop the skills that will land the right job for you.

It is only by risking our persons from one hour to another that we live at all. And often enough our faith beforehand in an uncertified result is the only thing that makes the result come true.

William James, *The Will to Believe*

Everyone has a mass of bad work in him which he will have to work off and get rid of before he can do better.

Samuel Butler

The
Five
O'Clock
Club

PART TWO

Deciding What You Want

HOW TO SELECT YOUR JOB TARGETS

Targeting the Job You Want: An Introduction to the Assessment Process

The
Five
O'Clock
Club

There will be many turnings along the way. It will be easy to get lost in attractive bypaths that lead nowhere. Resist deflections.

Mahatma Gandhi

The Five O'Clock Club is a serious program for those who want to work hard at developing a plan and then achieving it. Right now, you probably think of a job search in terms of, "Do I have an offer or don't I?" That is not a helpful way to measure the effectiveness of a job search.

At The Five O'Clock Club, we like it when people have 6 to 10 things in the works. It's our magic range. Five of those will fall away through no fault of your own. We like it when people have three offers to choose from, so they can select the job that positions them best for the long term. That's our mantra. We want you to think two jobs out. Your next job will probably not be your last. So take a job that will position you for the job after that.

We have a shorthand way of talking about our methodology. You will find our lexicon in the back of each of our books. When a counselor asks, "How are you doing in your search?" you'll say something like "I have four things in Stage Two and two in Stage Three." That tells us where you stand. Our lexicon helps us understand each other clearly without having to go into extreme

detail. After all, each person in the group has only a short time in which to talk about his or her search.

> **Study our books as if you were in graduate school. Mark them up, take notes, and constantly reread them. Most people read a little every morning and a little every night.**

Growing vs. Retrenching Industries

The crux of the problem for many people is selecting the fields and industries they want to target. That's what we cover in *Targeting a Great Career*. For now, remember this: If you don't target growing industries, you will have to job hunt more often and will have a more difficult time finding the next position.

At The Five O'Clock Club, we track trends, so we can tell you what is happening in certain industries. For example, the majority of people in banking who lose their jobs leave that industry. The number varies over time, but it is still better if someone in that industry knows the facts at the beginning of his or her search. Otherwise, someone will come into The Five

O'Clock Club, say they've been in banking for 12 years, and everyone they know is in banking, so of course it makes sense for them to target banks. Three months later, they may be still looking for a job.

But if they had known the market situation at the beginning of their search, they might have selected other targets in addition to banking, and would have had a much shorter search.

If your industry is retrenching, and if you decide you want to stay in it, you are more likely to have to relocate with each job move. In addition, you are more likely to have to search more often—it's like the game of musical chairs where they keep taking the chairs away. You become less marketable with each move because the industry is becoming smaller. This happens at every level in the hierarchy—not just the senior levels.

If an industry is retrenching, it is usually not as profitable as high-growth industries. It becomes less fun because it attracts less new blood. Those who remain have to do the mundane, core work, which is not as exciting as new developments. There's no money and no movement.

How many more years do you think you will work? If you want to work only a few more years, it's okay if you land a job in a retrenching industry. But if you want to work more than five years or so, you will probably have to search again. Even if you're over 50, you will probably be working longer than you think. The average American today is living 29 years longer than the average American lived at the turn of the twentieth century. Those years are being tacked on to middle age, not old age. Most of us will be working a lot longer than our predecessors did.

The good news is that you are marketable. If you think your industry is retrenching, brainstorm as many targets as you can at the beginning of your search. When a specific target does not work out, you will have others to fall back on. If you decide to stay in this field, learn some of the new technologies, such as the Internet, that will affect it in the future.

What Successful People Do

When Steven Jobs, the founder of Apple Computers, was fired by John Sculley, the man he brought in to run the company, he felt as though he had lost everything. Apple had been his life. Now he had lost not only his job, but his company. People no longer felt the need to return his phone calls. He did what a lot of us would do. He got depressed. But then:

Confused about what to do next . . . he [Jobs] put himself through an exercise that management psychologists employ with clients unsure about their life goals. It was a little thing, really. It was just a list. A list of all the things that mattered most to Jobs during his ten years at Apple. "Three things jumped off that piece of paper, three things that were really important to me," says Jobs.

Michael Meyer, *The Alexander Complex*

The exercise Steven Jobs went through is essentially what you will do in the Seven Stories Exercise. The threads that ran through his stories formed the impetus for his next great drive: the formation of NeXT computers. If the Seven Stories Exercise is good enough for Steven Jobs, maybe it's good enough for you.

"Successful managers," says Charles Garfield, head of Performance Services, Inc., in Berkeley, California, "go with their preferences." They search for work that is important to them, and when they find it, they pursue it with a passion.

Lester Korn, Chairman of Korn, Ferry, notes in his book *The Success Profile:* "Few executives know, or can know, exactly what they aspire to until they have been in the work force for a couple of years. It takes that long to learn enough about yourself to know what you can do well and what will make you happy. The trick is to merge the two into a goal, then set off in pursuit of it."

I've tried relaxing, but—I don't know—I feel more comfortable tense.

Hamilton cartoon caption

The Results of Assessment: Job Targets—*Then* a Résumé

A job target contains three elements:

- industry or company size (small, medium, or large company)
- position or function
- geographic location

If a change is required, a change in any one of these may be enough.

Looking Ahead—A Career Instead of a Job

Assessment will help you decide what you want to do in your next job as well as in the long run. You will select job targets.

Through your Forty-Year Vision (found in *Targeting a Great Career*), you will have the opportunity to look ahead to see whether a hidden dream may dramatically influence what you will want to do in both the short and long run. I did my own Forty-Year Vision many years ago, and the vision I had of my future still drives me today, even though it was rather vague at the time. Knowing where you would like to wind up in 10, 20, 30, or 40 years can broaden your ideas about the kinds of jobs you would be interested in today.

The Forty-Year Vision is a powerful exercise. It will help you think long-term and put things into perspective.

The Seven Stories Exercise is equally powerful. Without it, many job hunters develop stilted descriptions of what they have accomplished. But the exercise frees you up to brag a little and express things very differently. The results will add life to your résumé and your interviews, and also dramatically increase your self-confidence.

Here's Looking at You

Go through the exercises in *Targeting a Great Career*. Most Five O'Clock Clubbers are glad they did—even if they thought they already knew what kind of job they wanted.

The
Five
O'Clock
Club

Preliminary Target Investigation: Jobs/Industries Worth Exploring

How many things have been looked upon as quite impossible until they have been actually effected?

Pliny the Elder

Although it takes up only a few paragraphs in this book, Preliminary Target Investigation is essential.

Your Preliminary Target Investigation may take only a few weeks if you have high energy and can devote yourself to it full-time. You have to test your ideas for targets in the marketplace to see which ones are worth pursuing. As you research at the library, on the web, and by meeting with people in your fields of choice, you will refine those targets and perhaps develop others. Then you will know where to focus your job search, and the search will be completed much more quickly than if you had skipped this important step.

People who conduct a Preliminary Target Investigation while employed sometimes take a year to explore various fields while they continue in their old jobs. If you are not at all familiar with some of the job targets you have selected, do some Preliminary Target Investigation *now* through the web, library research (be sure to read this section) and networking. You will find that some targets are not right for you. Eliminate them and conduct a full campaign in areas that both seem right for you and offer some reasonable hope of success.

Whether you are employed or between jobs, Preliminary Target Investigation is well worth

your time and a lot of fun. It is the difference between blindly continuing in your old career path because it is the only thing you know, and finding out what is really happening in the world so you can latch on to a field that may carry you forward for many years. This is a wonderful time to explore and find out what the world offers. Most job hunters narrow their targets down too quickly, and wind up later with not much to go after. It is better for you emotionally, as well as practically, to develop now more targets than you need so you will have them when you are actively campaigning. If, on the other hand, you do not have the inclination or time to explore, you can move on. *Just remember, you can come back to this point if your search dries up and you need more targets.*

Most job hunters target only one job type or industry, take a very long time to find out that this target is not working, get depressed, try to think of other things they can do with their lives, pick themselves up, and start on one more target.

The will to persevere is often the difference between failure and success.

David Sarnoff

Instead, **brainstorm as many targets as possible** *before* **you begin your real job search**. Then you can overlap your campaigns, going after a number of targets at once. If some targets do not seem to work as well for you as others, you can drop the targets in which you are no longer interested. And when things don't seem to be going well, you have other targets to fall back on.

1. **List below all of the jobs/industries of interest to you.**

2. If you are not familiar with some targets you have selected, do some Preliminary Target Investigation *now* through library or web research or networking. You will find that some targets are not right for you. Eliminate them and conduct a full campaign in those areas which both seem right for you and offer some reasonable hope of success.

As you find out what is happening in the world, new fields will open up for you. Things are changing so fast that if you conduct a serious search without exploration, you are probably missing the most exciting developments in an area.

Spend some time exploring. Don't narrow your targets down too quickly; you will wind up later with not much to go after. It is better for you emotionally, as well as practically, to develop *now* more targets than you need so you will have them when you are actively campaigning. If you do not have the time or inclination to explore, you can move on to the next step. **Just remember: You can come back to this point if your search dries up and you need more targets.** An easy way to find targets is to complete the worksheet below:

JOBS/INDUSTRIES OF INTEREST TO ME AT THIS POINT:

(Conduct a Preliminary Target Investigation to determine what is really going on in each of them.)

_____

_____

_____

_____

_____

_____

_____

_____

_____

_____

_____

_____

_____

_____

_____

Targeting: The Start of an Organized Search

Dream. Dream big dreams! Others may deprive you of your material wealth and cheat you in a thousand ways, but no man can deprive you of the control and use of your imagination. Men may deal with you unfairly, as men often do; they may deprive you of your liberty; but they cannot take from you the privilege of using your imagination. In your imagination, you always win!

Jesse Jackson

To organize your targeting:

1. Brainstorm as many job targets as possible. You will not conduct a campaign aimed at all of them, but will have backup targets in case certain ones do not work out.

2. Identify a number of targets worthy of preliminary research. (If they are large targets and represent a lot of job possibilities, you will need fewer targets.)

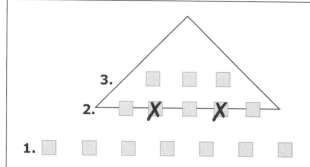

The boxes above represent different job targets. The triangle represents your job search. As you investigate targets, you will eliminate certain ones and spend more time on the remaining targets. You may research your targets by reading or by talking to people. The more you find out, the clearer your direction will become.

During Targeting Phase 1, you brainstormed lots of possible job targets, not caring whether or not they made sense.

During Targeting Phase 2, you conducted preliminary research to determine whether or not you should mount a full campaign aimed at these targets.

During Targeting Phase 3, (a full campaign, covered later in this book, you will focus on the targets warranting a full campaign). This means you will do full research on each target, and consider using all of the techniques for getting interviews: networking, direct contact, search firms, and ads.

3. Research each one enough—through the Internet, the library, and a few networking meetings—to determine whether it is worth a full job-search campaign. This is your Preliminary Target Investigation.

4. If your research shows that a target now seems inappropriate, cross it off your list, and concentrate on the remaining targets. **As you continue to network and research, keep open to other possibilities that may be targets for you. Add those to your list of targets to research.**

     As you add new targets, reprioritize your list so you are concentrating first on the targets that should be explored first. Do *not* haphazardly go after everything that comes your way.

5. If you decide the target is worth pursuing, conduct a full campaign to get interviews:

     - Develop your pitch.
     - Develop your résumé.
     - Develop a list of all the companies in the target area and the name of the person you want to contact in each company.

6. Then contact each organization through networking, direct contact, ads, or search firms.

Serendipitous Leads

Make a methodical approach the basis of your search, but also keep yourself open to serendipitous *lucky leads* outside your target areas. In general, it is a waste of your energy to go after single serendipitous leads. It is better to ask yourself if this lead warrants a new target. If it does, then decide where it should be ranked in your list of targets, and research it as you would any serious target.

Target Selection

After you have done some preliminary research, select the targets you think deserve a full campaign. List first the one you will focus on in your first campaign. If you are currently employed and have time to explore, you may want to select as your first target the most unlikely one, but the one that is the job of your dreams. Then you can concentrate on it and find out for sure whether you are still interested and what your prospects are.

On the other hand, if you must find a job quickly, you will first want to concentrate on the area where you stand the best chance of getting a job—probably the area where you are now working. After you get that job, you can explore your other targets. (To expand your targets quickly, consider broadening your search geographically.)

If you are targeting a geographic area different from where you are now, be sure to conduct a serious, complete campaign aimed at that target. For example, you will want to contact search firms in that area, conduct library and Internet research, perhaps conduct a direct-mail campaign, and network.

Target 1:   Industry or organization size: _____

                  Position/function: _____

                  Geographic area: _____

Target 2:   Industry or organization size: _____

                  Position/function: _____

                  Geographic area: _____

Target 3:   Industry or organization size: _____

                  Position/function: _____

                  Geographic area: _____

Target 4:   Industry or organization size: _____

                  Position/function: _____

                  Geographic area: _____

Target 5:   Industry or organization size: _____

                  Position/function: _____

                  Geographic area: _____

Measuring Your Targets

You've selected three to five (or more) targets on which to focus. Will this be enough to get you an appropriate job?

Let's say, for example, your first target aims at a small industry (10 organizations) having only a few positions that would be appropriate for you.

Chances are, those jobs are filled right now. In fact, chances are there may be no opening for a year or two. The numbers are working against you. Now, if you targeted 20 small industries, each of which has 10 organizations with a few positions appropriate for you, the numbers are more in your favor.

On the other hand, if one of your targets is large and has a lot of positions that may be right for you, the numbers are again on your side.

Let's analyze your search and see whether the numbers are working for or against you.

Fill out the following on your own target markets. You will probably have to make an educated guess about the number. A ballpark figure is all you need to get a feel for where you stand.

Target 1:   Industry or organization size: _____
                         Position/function: _____
                         Geographic area: _____

How big is the market for my *product* in this target?
A. Number of organizations in this target market: _____
B. Number of probable positions suitable for me in the average organization in this target: _____
A x B = Total number of probable positions appropriate for me in this target market: _____

For Target 2:   Industry or organization size: _____
                         Position/function: _____
                         Geographic area: _____

How big is the market for my *product* in this target?
A. Number of organizations in this target market: _____
B. Number of probable positions suitable for me in the average organization in this target: _____
A x B = Total number of probable positions appropriate for me in this target market: _____

For Target 3:   Industry or organization size: _____
                         Position/function: _____
                         Geographic area: _____

How big is the market for my *product* in this target?
A. Number of organizations in this target market: _____
B. Number of probable positions suitable for me in the average organization in this target: _____
A x B = Total number of probable positions appropriate for me in this target market: _____

Rule of thumb:
A target list of 200 positions in a healthy market results in seven interviews, which results in one job offer. Therefore, if there are fewer than 200 potential positions in your targets, develop additional targets or expand the ones you already have. Remember: When aiming at a target of less than 200 potential positions, a more concentrated effort is required.

The Five O'Clock Club

How to Change Careers

I just want to say one word to you. Just one word.
Are you listening? Plastics.

Buck Henry and Calder Willingham, *The Graduate*

T ed had spent 10 years in marketing and finance with a large cosmetics company. His dream was to work in the casino industry. He selected two job targets: one aimed at the cosmetics industry, and one aimed at his dream.

All things being equal, finding a job similar to your old one is quicker. A career change will probably take more time. What's more, the job-hunting techniques are different for both.

Let's take Ted's case. The casino industry was small, focused in Atlantic City and Las Vegas. Everyone knew everyone else. The industry had its special jargon and personality. What chance did Ted have of breaking in?

Ted had another obstacle. His marketing and finance background made him difficult to categorize. His hard-won business skills became a problem.

It's Not Easy to Categorize Career Changers

The easier it is to categorize you, the easier it is for others to see where you fit in their organizations, and for you to find a job. Search firms, for example, generally will not handle career changers. They can more easily market those who want

to stay in the same function in the same industry. Search firms that handled the casino industry would not handle Ted.

You Must Offer Proof of Your Interest and Competence

Many job changers essentially say to a prospective employer, "Give me a chance. You won't be sorry." They expect the employer to hire them on faith, and that's unrealistic. The employer has a lot to lose. First, you may lose interest in the new area after you are hired. Second, you may know so little about the new area that it turns out not to be what you had imagined. Third, you may not bring enough knowledge and skill to the job and fail—even though your desire may be sincere.

The hiring manager should not have to take those risks. It is the job hunter's obligation to prove that he or she is truly interested and capable.

How You as a Career Changer Can Prove Your Interest and Capability

- Read the industry's trade journals.
- Get to know the people in that industry or field.
- Join its organizations; attend the meetings.
- Be persistent.
- Show how your skills can be transferred.

- Write proposals.
- Be persistent.
- Take relevant courses, part-time jobs, or do volunteer work related to the new industry or skill area.
- Be persistent.

. . . civility is not a sign of weakness, and sincerity is always subject to proof.

John F. Kennedy, Inaugural Address, January 20, 1961

Ted, as a career changer, had to offer proof to make up for his lack of experience. One proof was that he had read the industry's trade newspapers for more than 10 years. When he met people in his search, he could truthfully tell them that he had followed their careers. He could also say he had hope for himself because he knew that so many of them had come from outside the industry.

Another proof of his interest was that he had sought out so many casino management people in Atlantic City and Las Vegas. After a while, he ran into people he had met on previous occasions. Employers want people who are sincerely interested in their industry, their company, and the function the new hire will fill. Sincerity and persistence count, but they are usually not enough.

Another proof Ted offered was that he figured out how to apply his experience to the casino industry and its problems. Writing proposals to show how you would handle the job is one way to prove you are knowledgeable and interested in an area new to you. Some people prove their interest by taking courses, finding part-time jobs, or doing volunteer work to learn the new area and build marketable skills.

Ted initially decided to "wing it," and took trips to Atlantic City and Las Vegas hoping someone would hire him on the spot. That didn't work and took two months and some money. Then he began a serious job hunt—following the system explained in the following pages. He felt he was doing fine, but the hunt was taking many months and he was not sure it would result in an offer.

After searching in the casino industry for six months, Ted began a campaign in his old field—the cosmetics industry. Predictably, he landed a job there quickly. Ted took this as a sign that he didn't have a chance in the new field. He lost sight of the fact that a career change is more difficult and takes longer.

Ted accepted the cosmetics position, but his friends encouraged him to continue his pursuit of a career in the casino industry—a small industry with relatively few openings compared with the larger cosmetics industry.

Shortly after he accepted the new position, someone from Las Vegas called him for an interview, and he got the job of his dreams. His efforts paid off because he had done a thorough campaign in the casino industry. It just took time.

Ted was not unusual in giving up on a career change. It can take a long time, and sometimes the pressure to get a paycheck will force people to take inappropriate jobs. That's life. Sometimes we have to do things we don't want to do. There's nothing wrong with that.

What *is* wrong is forgetting that you had a dream. What *is* wrong is expecting people to hire you on faith and hope, when what they deserve is proof that you're sincere and that hiring you has a good chance of working. *What is wrong is underestimating the effort it takes to make a career change.*

In the future, most people will have to change careers. Your future may hold an involuntary career change, as new technologies make old skills obsolete. Those same new technologies open up new career fields for those who are prepared and ready to change. Know what you're up against. Don't take shortcuts. And don't give up too early. Major career changes are normal today and may prove desirable or essential tomorrow.

The strain and discouragement of frankly facing the complex tangle of motives at work in most human situations tempt everyone into the errors of oversimplification.

Henry S. Dennison, *Organization and Management*

For Other Techniques to Help You Change Careers, Take a Look at the Following Chapters in . . .

. . . this book:

- Repositioning Yourself for a Job Change

. . . our book *Mastering the Job Interview and Winning the Money Game:*

- Salary Negotiation: Power and Positioning (see especially "Case Study: Charlie—Negotiating a Career Change")
- Your Two-Minute Pitch: The Keystone of Your Search

. . . our book *Targeting a Great Career*:

- Targeting the Jobs of the Future
- Case Studies: Targeting the Future

. . . our book *Packaging Yourself: The Targeted Résumé*:

- Résumés for Making a Career Change (also see résumés and summaries for the industry or profession you are targeting)

I knew that sweat was a lot of it. I had a cot put in my cutting room. I would recut something maybe five times in a night and run it again and again and again. I just knew it was sweat. I had no special touch or anything like that.

Robert Parrish, Award-winning film editor-director quoted in *The New York Times*

Repositioning Yourself for a Job Change

The
Five
O'Clock
Club

Greatness is not measured by what a man or woman accomplishes, but by the opposition he or she has overcome. . . .

Dr. Dorothy Height, president,
National Council of Negro Women

Feel stuck in your present position? Peel off your old label, slap on a new one, and position yourself for something different.

Whether you're an accountant who wants to go into sales, or an operations person who dreams of being a trainer, the challenge you face is the same: You have to convince people that even though you don't have experience you can handle the new position.

It's a little like show biz: You play the same role for years and then you get typecast. It can be difficult for people to believe that you can play a different role. To move on to new challenges, you have to negotiate into the new job by offering seemingly unrelated skills as an added benefit to the employer. The key to these negotiations is *positioning* yourself.

Positioning

Simply put, positioning yourself means stating your skills and qualities in a way that makes it easy for the prospective employer to see you in the open position or in other positions down the road.

You may want to stay in your present organization, in which case you are positioning yourself to the person in charge of hiring for the particular department you want to enter. Or, you may want to go to a new organization or even a new industry. In this case, you are positioning yourself to a new employer. Either way, the steps are the same:

1. Determine what skills and qualities your prospective employer wants.
2. Search your background to see where you have demonstrated skills and qualities that would apply.
3. Write a summary at the top of your résumé to position yourself.
4. Use the same summary to sell yourself in an interview.

Your summary says it all. It should sell your ability, experience, and personality. It brings together all your accomplishments.

The rest of your résumé should support your summary. For example, if the summary says that you're a top-notch marketer, the résumé should support that. It's completely within your control to tell whatever story you want to tell. You can emphasize certain parts of your background and deemphasize others.

> **You can get typecast. To move on, you have to negotiate into the new job . . . by *positioning* yourself.**

Thinking through your summary is not easy, but it focuses your entire job hunt. It forces you to clarify the sales pitch you will use in interviews.

However, many people *don't* put a summary that positions them on their résumés. They say they want "a challenging job in a progressive and growth-oriented company that uses all my strengths and abilities." That doesn't say anything at all, and it doesn't do you any good.

Résumé: Your Written Pitch

Make sure the first words on your résumé position you for the kind of job you want next, such as *Accounting Manager*. Line *two* of your résumé, also centered, should separate you from all those other accounting managers. For example, it could say, "specializing in the publishing industry." These headlines in your summary could then be followed by bulleted accomplishments that would be of interest to your target market.

Most people write boring résumés. To avoid this, keep in mind to *whom you are pitching*. Tell readers the most important things you want them to know about you. List your most important accomplishments right there in your summary.

It all starts with the Seven Stories Exercise. After you have done this exercise, you will talk about your accomplishments very differently than if you just sit down and try to write a résumé. The Seven Stories Exercise is the foundation for your résumé. Write out your work-related stories in a way that is *expressive* of you as an individual. *Brag* about yourself the way you would brag to the people in your family or your friends. Put *those* words at the top of your résumé to make it much more compelling.

Let's consider a few examples of summaries that *will* work for you:

Pursuing the Dream Job

Jane, a client-relationship manager at a major bank, has handled high-net-worth clients for more than 20 years. She is taking early retirement and thinking about a second career. Two directions are of interest to her: a job similar to what she has done but in a smaller bank; or, the job of her dreams—working as one of the top administrative people for a high-net-worth family (such as the Rockefellers), handling their business office and perhaps doing things that involve her interests: staffing and decorating.

If Jane were to continue on her current career path and go for a position as a relationship manager at a smaller bank, she would highlight the years she has worked at the bank. Her summary, if used in her résumé, would look like this:

> More than 20 years handling all aspects of fiduciary relationships for PremierBank's private banking clients. Successfully increased revenue through new business efforts, client cultivation, and account assessment. Consistently achieved fee increases. Received regular bonus awards.

However, to pursue her dream job, Jane's regular résumé won't do. She has to reposition herself to show that her experience fits what her prospective employer needs. Her summary would read like this:

> **Administrative manager with broad experience in running operations**
>
> - In-depth work with accountants, lawyers, agents, and others.
> - More than 20 years' experience handling all aspects of fiduciary relationships for bank's private banking clients (overall net worth of $800 million).
> - Expert in all financial arrangements (trust and estate accounts, asset management, nonprofits, and tenant shareholder negotiations).

Her résumé would also focus on her work *outside* PremierBank because these activities would interest her prospective employer: first, her work on the board of the luxury apartment building of which she was president for 14 years, and then the post she held for 10 years as treasurer of a nonprofit organization. Finally, Jane would highlight accomplishments at Premier-Bank that would be of interest to a prospective employer, such as saving a client $300,000 in taxes.

Ready to Take Charge

Robert had worked in every area of benefits administration. Now he would like to head up the entire benefits administration area—a move to management. His summary:

14 years in the design and administration of all areas of employee benefit plans

- 5 years with Borgash Benefits Consultants
- Advised some of the largest, most prestigious companies in the country
- Excellent training and communications skills
- MBA in finance

From Supporting to Selling

Jack wants to move into sales after being in marketing support. His prior résumé lacked a summary. Therefore people saw him as a marketing support person rather than as a salesperson—because his most recent job was in marketing support. He has been an executive in the sales promotion area, so his summary stresses his internal sales and marketing, as well as his management, experience:

Sales and marketing professional with strong managerial experience

- Devise superior marketing strategies through qualitative analysis and product repositioning
- Skillful at completing the difficult internal sale, coupled with the ability to attract business and retain clients
- Built strong relationships with the top consulting firms

- A team player with an enthusiastic approach to top-level challenges

Notice how he packages his experience running a marketing department *as sales*. His pitch will be, "It's even more difficult to sell inside because, in order to keep my job, I have to get other people in my company to use my marketing services. I have to do a good job, or they won't use me again."

If you do not have a summary, then, by default, you are positioned by the last job you held. In Jack's case, the employer would receive the new résumé with the new summary and say, "Ah-ha! Just what we need—a salesperson!"

Sophisticated Positioning

Here are how some people repositioned their backgrounds in a sophisticated way. Jeff had been in loan-processing operations in a bank. Outside of financial services, not many organizations do loan processing. To position himself to work in a hospital, Jeff changed his positioning to say *transaction* processing because hospitals process a large numbers of *transactions,* but not loans. Otherwise, they would look at his résumé and say, "We don't need to have loans processed."

In fact, many people who work in banking see themselves as working for information services companies. Money is sent via computer networks and wire transfers. They are passing information, not currency.

Nydia had worked at both banks and pharmaceutical companies. Because of her target, she positioned herself as having worked in *regulated industries.*

David saw himself as an international human resources generalist, but was having difficulty with his search. Since there were no international jobs in his field, he should not have positioned himself as *international.*

Now, think about *your* target market and how you should position your background for your target.

Making a Career Change

Elliott had been in sports marketing years ago, and had enjoyed it tremendously. However, he had spent the past four years in the mortgage industry, and was having a hard time getting back into sports marketing.

The sports people saw him as a career changer and a mortgage man. Even when he explained how marketing mortgages is the same as marketing sports, people did not believe him. He was being positioned by his most recent experience, which was derailing his search.

When job hunters want to change industries—or go back to an old industry—they cannot let their most recent positions act as a handicap. For example, if a person has always been in pharmaceuticals marketing, and now wants to do marketing in another industry, his or her résumé should be rewritten to highlight generic marketing, with most references to pharmaceuticals removed.

In Elliott's case, the summary in his new résumé helps a great deal to bring his old work experience right to the top of the résumé. In addition, Elliott removed the word "mortgage" from the description of his most recent job; his title at the mortgage company now stands out more than the company name. And he removed company and industry jargon, such as the job title *segment director,* which is not easily understood outside his company.

Notice that Elliott's description of what he did for the mortgage business is now written generically—it can apply to the marketing of *any* product. With his new résumé, Elliott had no trouble speaking to people in the sports industry. They no longer saw his most recent experience as a handicap, and he soon had a terrific job as head of marketing for a prestigious sporting-goods company.

If you want to move into a new industry or profession, state what you did generically so people will not see you as tied to the old.

Bring Something to the Party

When it comes down to negotiating yourself into a new position, seemingly unrelated skills from former positions may actually help you get the job.

For example, some of my background had been in accounting and computers when I decided to go into coaching and my CFO (chief financial officer) experience helped me ease into this new career. I agreed to be CFO at a 90-person career-coaching company provided I was also assigned clients to coach. My ability to create a cost-accounting system for them was what I "brought to the party." I was willing to give the company something they wanted (my business expertise) in exchange for doing something I really wanted to do (coaching executives).

Combining the new with the old, rather than jumping feet first into something completely new is often the best way to move your career in a different direction. You gain the experience you need in the new field without having to come in at the entry level. Equally important, it is less stressful because you are using some of your old strengths while you build new ones.

Coming from a background different from the field you are targeting can also give you a bargaining chip. If you are looking at an area where you have no experience, you will almost certainly be competing with people who do have experience. You can separate yourself from the competition by saying, "I'm different. I have the skills to do this job, and I can also do other things these people can't do." It works!

Our résumé book contains dozens of additional positioning (summary) statements. In addition, you will see how the positioning statements are used to set the tone for the rest of the résumé.

Elliott's positioning (summary) statement is on the next page.

ELLIOTT JONES

421 Morton Street   Chase Fortune, KY 23097

SEARS MORTGAGE COMPANY   2002–present
Vice President, Segment Director, Shelter Business

- Director of $4.6 billion residential mortgage business for largest mortgage lender
- Organized and established regional marketing division for largest mortgage lender, including first and second mortgages and mortgage life insurance

SportsLife Magazine   1999–2002

Publisher and Editor
- Published and edited largest health/fitness magazine. Increased circulation by 175%.
  and so on . . .

ELLIOTT JONES

421 Morton Street, Chase Fortune, KY 23097   ejones@yahoo.com

Fifteen years: domestic and international marketing management in the *leisure/sporting goods industry*

- Multibrand expertise specializing in marketing, new business development, strategic planning, and market research.
- Identified customer segments, developed differentiable product platforms, implemented communication strategies, managed sales, oversaw share growth, and generated profit.

SEARS MORTGAGE COMPANY   2003–present
VICE PRESIDENT, BUSINESS DIRECTOR
Residential Real Estate Business

- Business Director of a $4.6 billion business. Managed strategic planning, marketing, product development, and compliance.
- Consolidated four regional business entities into one; doubled product offerings. Grew market share 150 basis points and solidified #1 market position.
- Developed and executed nationally recognized consumer and trade advertising, public relations, and direct-response programs.
- Structured a product-development process, integrating product introductions into the operations and sales segments of the business.
- Organized and established regional marketing division.

SPORTSLIFE MAGAZINE   2000–2003
Publisher and Editor

- Published and edited largest health/fitness magazine. Increased circulation by 175%.

and so on . . .

Summary of What I Have/Want to Offer—Target 1

To Help Me Develop My Written Pitch to That Target

You must know:

- to whom you are pitching; you have to know something about them.
- what they ideally want in a candidate.
- what they are interested in.
- who your likely competitors are.
- what you bring to the party that your competitors do not.

For Target 1:   Geographic area: _____

Industry or company size: _____

Position/function: _____

1. What is the most important thing I want this target to know about me? (This is where you position yourself. If they know nothing else about you, this is what you want them to know.)

_____

2. What is the second most important thing I want this target to know about me? (This could support and/or broaden your introductory statement.)   _____

_____

_____

3. Key selling points: statements/accomplishments that support/**prove** the first two statements:

a. _____

b. _____

c. _____

d. _____

e. _____

Statement of why they should be interested in me/what separates me from my competition:

_____

_____

_____

Other key selling points that may apply even indirectly to this industry or position:

_____

_____

_____

Any objection I'm afraid the interviewer may bring up, and how I will handle it:

_____

Summary of What I Have/Want to Offer—Target 2

To Help Me Develop My Written Pitch to That Target

You must know:
- to whom you are pitching; you have to know something about them.
- what they ideally want in a candidate.
- what they are interested in.
- who your likely competitors are.
- what you bring to the party that your competitors do not.

For Target 2:   Geographic area: _____

Industry or company size: _____

Position/function: _____

1. What is the most important thing I want this target to know about me? (This is where you position yourself. If they know nothing else about you, this is what you want them to know.)
_____

2. What is the second most important thing I want this target to know about me? (This could support and/or broaden your introductory statement.) _____
_____
_____

3. Key selling points: statements/accomplishments that support/**prove** the first two statements:
   a. _____
   b. _____
   c. _____
   d. _____
   e. _____

Statement of why they should be interested in me/what separates me from my competition:
_____
_____
_____

Other key selling points that may apply even indirectly to this industry or position:
_____
_____
_____

Any objection I'm afraid the interviewer may bring up, and how I will handle it:
_____

Summary of What I Have/Want to Offer—Target 3

To Help Me Develop My Written Pitch to That Target

You must know:

- to whom you are pitching; you have to know something about them.
- what they ideally want in a candidate.
- what they are interested in.
- who your likely competitors are.
- what you bring to the party that your competitors do not.

For Target 3:   Geographic area: _____

Industry or company size: _____

Position/function: _____

1. What is the most important thing I want this target to know about me? (This is where you position yourself. If they know nothing else about you, this is what you want them to know.)

_____

2. What is the second most important thing I want this target to know about me? (This could support and/or broaden your introductory statement.) _____

_____

_____

3. Key selling points: statements/accomplishments that support/**prove** the first two statements:

    a. _____

    b. _____

    c. _____

    d. _____

    e. _____

Statement of why they should be interested in me/what separates me from my competition:

_____

_____

_____

Other key selling points that may apply even indirectly to this industry or position:

_____

_____

_____

Any objection I'm afraid the interviewer may bring up, and how I will handle it:

_____

The
Five
O'Clock
Club

PART THREE

Knowing the Right People

HOW TO GET INTERVIEWS IN YOUR TARGET AREAS

The Five O'Clock Club

Precampaign Planning

It is circumstance and proper timing that give an action its character and make it either good or bad.

Agesilaus II

You certainly have done a lot of work so far! You selected three or four targets after conducting a Preliminary Target Investigation, and ranked them so you know which one you want as your first campaign, your second, third, and fourth. You have also developed a preliminary résumé for the first campaign. Now you will plan your *entire* job hunt, just as you would plan any other project. A planned job search will save you time. You will be able to tell what is working and what is not, and change what you are doing accordingly.

Take a look at the chart on page 51. It is a conceptual view of the job-hunting process. There are no time frames for a phase. For some

people, the Evaluation Phase (which is covered in *Targeting a Great Career*) can be as short as 10 minutes. For others, it can take years. The time each step takes depends on you and the situation you face.

Do every step, spending the length of time on them required for your situation. This time is not wasted. It will save time later because your effort will be organized.

Your campaigns aimed at each target (T1, T2) will overlap. You will start one campaign, and when it is in full swing, you will start campaign number two. Each campaign will be condensed, and your total job search will be *shorter* if you follow this approach than if you conducted all of the campaigns together.

As you can see in the chart below, each campaign has three phases. The first phase is Preparation; the second is Interviewing; and the third is Follow-Up. Each phase should be given equal weight.

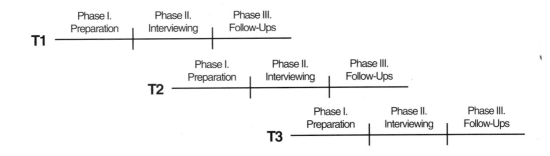

During the Preparation Phase, you:

- Research and make a list of the companies you want to contact.
- Develop your Two-Minute Pitch and your cover letters.
- Make sure your résumé makes you look appropriate to your target.
- Plan your strategy for getting interviews (through networking, direct contact, search firms, and ads).

When you are in the Interview Phase of campaign one, you may start campaign two.

CASE STUDY *Jim*
An Organized Approach

Jim, a marketing manager, had targeted four industries: environmental, noise abatement, shipping, and corporate America, which was a backup target in case the other three did not work. Jim had selected 30 companies in the environmental area, and began to contact them. When he met with an environmental company, he could mention that he had "just met yesterday with another environmental company, and this is what we discussed. What do you think?" *Focusing* on one target at a time can give you credibility and information. Jim can mention other companies with which he is speaking, and let a prospective employer know he is truly interested in the industry. Focus also saves him time. It takes so much time to develop a good pitch, cover letter, and résumé that it only makes sense to sell yourself to a *number* of companies. It's too difficult to try one pitch one day and then a completely different pitch the next. It's better to completely test one pitch and have it down pat. That's why you can start your second campaign when you are in the interview phase of the first campaign.

Furthermore, a condensed campaign allows you to test what is wrong and drop what is not working. Job hunters who go after lots of different targets at the same time usually do not develop a

great pitch for any of them, and cannot tell what is working and what is not.

Jim dropped his first target—the environmental industry—except for following up on two possibilities that seemed promising. He also came up with a number of possibilities from his second and third targets. In the end, he got one job offer from each target, and never started his fourth campaign, corporate America, which he was not interested in anyway. In addition, Jim followed up on serendipitous leads, which also could have yielded something. But a focused search was the core of his campaign, with serendipitous leads on the side.

A focused campaign is shorter, even though you're zeroing in on only one target at a time (until you are in the follow-up stage, in which you are following up on *all* of your targets, and generating more leads in each of them). Many executives who follow a targeted approach can cover four good-sized targets in depth in two months. And many executives have that next position within two-and-a-half to four months!

The distance doesn't matter. Only the first step is difficult.

Mme. DuDeffand

The Timing of Your Campaigns

In the next chapter, you will plan the strategy for getting interviews in your first campaign, which you should implement right away. When you are midway through it, start your second campaign—even if you do not think you will need it.

When you start your first campaign, you will be full of hope. Your résumé will be great, and you will be talking to lots of people. Some will tell you that you should have no problem finding a job. They are being sincere. But job offers dry up. What once seemed like a sure thing does not materialize.

There seem to be phases and cycles in each campaign—there is the initial rush, the long haul,

What a Job Hunt Looks Like over Time

NOTE: You can get a job at any point in a campaign.

Campaign #1

Campaign #2

Campaign #3 →

EVALUATION PHASE
Motivated abilities
Work life requirements
Key accomplishments

TARGETING PHASE
Ranked job targets
Overall job-hunt plan
Preliminary investigation

CAMPAIGN #1 (for target #1)
Campaign strategy
Research of the field
Résumé/pitch preparation
Search firm contact
Research of specific companies
Research through networking
Interview training
Direct-mail campaign
Ads answered
Quality-control checkpoint
Job interviews/negotiations
Assessment of job interviews
Influence notes and follow-up
Reassessment of the situation

CAMPAIGN #2 (for target #2)
Campaign strategy, research,
Résumé preparation, etc.

WEEKLY GROUP MEETINGS (2 hours)

FUN/PERSONAL DEVELOPMENT (3 hours)

CAMPAIGN #3 (optional)

* = Quality-control checkpoints.
  Is your campaign on target?

51

the drought, followed by the first poor job offer and the later better offers. After a letdown, job hunters can lose momentum. They sometimes think they will *never* find a job.

If, however, you have already started that second campaign, you will know that those cover letters are in the mail working for you. You stand a chance of getting some response from the second campaign. You will do better in the interviews from your first campaign because you will not feel so desperate. Your second campaign backs you up.

Your second campaign could include additional people in the same target market as the first. (Do more research and get more names.) It could be a variation of your first target market (a related field or industry) or a new target.

I have had clients start a second campaign even when they were in the final negotiation stages of the first. Those negotiations went better, and helped them land the job because they had the comfort of knowing that the second campaign was in the mail.

If, perchance, your first campaign does *not* work, you will not lose momentum if you are already in the midst of your second—or perhaps even preparing to start your third. It is better not to lose momentum.

Customize Your Campaign

Think of yourself as a corporation. Given equal economic conditions, certain corporations thrive while others fail. Successful companies adjust their approaches to the changes in the economy. And even when the economy is at its worst, certain companies come up winners.

In many respects, job-hunting management resembles the management of a company. The economy has changed dramatically over the past several years; times are more competitive—for companies and for job hunters. Whether you are managing a company or managing your own career, adjust the techniques you use.

Statistics show that certain techniques work better than others in the aggregate. But consider

what might be best for you *and* your situation. The hiring system works differently in different industries and companies. Remain flexible: Do what works in the industry and profession in which you are interested.

In addition, do what works for your personality. For example, certain job hunters phone company executives rather than using the written approach of a direct-mail campaign. What if you find it difficult (as I do) to make calls to people with whom you have had no contact? Or what if you are currently employed and find that heavy use of the phone is out of the question? Or it may be that the industry you are approaching considers this technique an arrogant way to do business.

This same rule applies to the techniques you will find in this book. Use what you want. Do what works for *you*.

Everything comes to him who hustles while he waits.

Thomas A. Edison

A Campaign to Promote Yourself— Just like Promoting a Product

In soloing—as in other activities—it is far easier to start something than it is to finish it.

Amelia Earhart

Airlines run promotional campaigns to get passengers to fly with them. Computer software companies use their promotional efforts to get people to buy their software. You will conduct a promotional campaign to generate interest in your "product."

You and an airline go through the same steps to market your respective products:

- *An airline analyzes the market to determine the kinds of people who are interested in its product, the number of potential customers, and how much need there is for the product.* Analyze your market to determine the kinds of companies that could be interested in you, and the number of companies and positions in your field of interest. Find out how much demand there is for your services in your target market.

- *An airline defines itself by its features,* such as the kind of seating it has, the cities to which it flies to, and so on—and it also defines its personality or style. For example, an airline may say it represents the "friendly skies" or is the "only way to fly." Or it may define itself as a bargain or an exclusive carrier.

  Define yourself not only in terms of your skills and experience but also in terms of your style and personality. There are many qualified people for each position, just as there are a number of airlines offering the same kinds of planes going to the same cities. The differences among airlines is not in their basic product, but in their personality and the way they go about their business.

  You and your competition will often be equally well qualified. The differences will lie in your style and the way you go about your business. For example, a person who ran a department and doubled productivity could have done it in a nasty, threatening way, or could have motivated people to do more, instituted training programs, and encouraged workers to come up with suggestions for improving productivity. Let *your* personality come through.

- *An airline test-markets what it has decided to offer.* If the test results are poor, the airline changes either its basic product (such as its number of seats) or offers the same product in a way that is more attractive to the target market. It could also decide to withdraw from that target market.

  Test what you have decided to offer. If it is not of interest to your target market, change what you are offering, the way you are offering it, or the image you are projecting. For example, you can change what you are offering by getting more experience or training in a certain area. You can change your image by looking

different or by highlighting a certain aspect of your personality that is of interest to your target market. Or you can change your promotional techniques.

On the other hand, you may decide to withdraw from a particular market. Perhaps it is inappropriate for you. An example is when your target market is in the middle of major layoffs. If you can help turn the company around, you have a chance. If you are comparable to the people it is laying off, consider a different target.

Some people pick a target and stick with it no matter what. But you need flexibility and common sense to figure out what may be going wrong in your campaign. You may need more experience or you may need to present yourself differently. Or it may be there is no hope of obtaining an offer in certain markets. No matter how much you may want to work for a foundation, for example, there may not be many positions available. Then even the best job-hunting techniques will not help you. Change your target.

- *An airline assesses its competition, and so will you.* Who is your competition and how well do you stack up in your basic qualifications? What can you offer that is different?

- *An airline asks itself if the timing is right for a campaign it may be planning.* Consider if the timing is right for what *you* want to offer a particular market. Sometimes there is great demand for lawyers or engineers, for example, and at other times there is a glut in the market. When the oil business was booming, there was a demand for people in that field. Aerospace engineers could once name their price. You can easily find out the level of demand by testing what you want.

- *An airline asks itself if it is worth it*—if it can afford to do what it would take to offer its product to a certain market. It decides if its return will be adequate, and it makes sure this venture will satisfy other company needs and support company objectives.

Ask yourself if it is worth it. You may find that a field is not what you thought it was: Perhaps the pay is too low or the hours too long. Or the field may not fit with your long-term goals. Or it may run contrary to your motivated skills or values or what you want in a company or a position. You can lower your expectations or you can look elsewhere.

There is one major difference between what you and the airline have to offer: The airline has a lot of planes and seats, but there is only *one* of you. Be particular about to whom you sell your services. Get a couple of potential offers so you can make a comparison and select what is best for you.

We are here to be excited from youth to old age, to have an insatiable curiosity about the world. . . . We are also here to help others by practicing a friendly attitude. And every person is born for a purpose. Everyone has a God-given potential, in essence, built into them. And if we are to live life to its fullest, we must realize that potential.

Norman Vincent Peale

Weekly Group Meetings

Throughout life our internal lives are enriched by the people we have permitted to touch us.

George E. Vaillant, *Adaptation to Life*

Not everything can be covered in a book. Meeting every week in The Five O'Clock Club with people like yourself can be a tremendous help. They will become familiar with your job search and can give you feedback on your efforts. The experiences of other people can teach you what to do when the same things happen to you. In the group, you can trade stories and techniques, and network with one another.

Believe it or not, weekly group meetings are *fun* and a respite from the discouraging job of job hunting. They can spark you on: Your own situa-

tion seems less hopeless. You feel if they can do it, you can too.

Being in a group with your peers can be more effective than one-on-one coaching with a *pro.* A group can take risks that a coach cannot. For example, even if you have been unemployed for a while, the group may suggest that you not take a position because it is not right for you. You can easily ignore the advice of the group if you want. A coach has to be more careful about giving advice that could adversely affect a person's financial situation. Your peers have more freedom to discuss your needs and to give a variety of *free* advice.

In one of my groups, there was a dynamic public relations man who had been unemployed for two months. The group came to know him well. He received a job offer to do public relations work for a conservative dental firm. When he told us about the offer, the look on his face clearly showed how unhappy he felt about it. Everyone knew that this would not be the right job for him, and the group discouraged him from taking it.

A few weeks later, he received another job offer—this one from a dynamic company in San Francisco. The company had been searching to fill this position for more than six months, and it was thrilled to find him. So was he: For him, the job was the chance of a lifetime.

There is no music in a "rest," Katie, that I know of: but there's the making of music in it. And people are always missing that part of life—melody.

John Ruskin

Time for Personal Development

If you happen to be unemployed, welcome to the club. Some unemployed people think they don't deserve any fun at all. But it is difficult to job hunt for a full 40 hours a week.

If you have only 30 hours of work to do, you may spread it out to fill 40 hours. With too much time on your hands, you may take longer than usual to write a memo or make a phone call or appointment. You may stretch things out so you will always have "something to look forward to." You will wind up stretching out your search.

Wasting time is itself not the bad part. The bad part is losing your flow of adrenaline. Better to spend 35 or 37 hours a week searching for a job and make those hours *intense*—just as you would in a real job—and then reward yourself with three hours of fun that week.

During a period of unemployment, I indulged myself by going to auction houses and spending the time it takes to study furniture. Auctions aren't crowded during the day when everyone else is working. I never regretted the time I spent there. I felt I would never have such a luxury again. I worked hard at my job hunt and felt I deserved a break. So do you.

But you don't deserve *too* much of a break. One of the worst things a person can do is start off his or her unemployment with a "well-deserved" vacation. Sometimes the job hunt never gets started. The momentum never builds. Instead, why not look for a job and take two weeks off after you have landed it? If you are unemployed, don't punish yourself, but don't overindulge yourself, either.

Job hunting is a job in itself, hard work that can be discouraging. But since you have to do it, you might as well have fun. You will meet interesting people who may become new friends. And you will learn a lot. That's not so bad.

We can define "purpose" in several ways. For one, when we know our purpose, we have an anchor—a device of the mind to provide some stability, to keep the surprises of a creative universe from tossing us to and fro, from inflicting constant seasickness on us. Or we can think of our purpose as being a master nautical chart marking shoals and rocks, sandbars, and derelicts, something to guide us and keep us on course. Perhaps the most profound thing we can say about being "on purpose" is that when that is our status, our condition, and our comfort, we find our lives have meaning, and when we are "off purpose," we are confused about meanings and motives.

Dudley Lynch and Paul L. Kordis, *Strategy of the Dolphin: Scoring a Win in a Chaotic World*

The world presents enough problems if you believe it to be a world of law and order; do not add to them by believing it to be a world of miracles.

Louis Brandeis

55

The
Five
O'Clock
Club

Conducting a Campaign to Get Interviews in Your Target Markets

The codfish lays ten thousand eggs,
The homely hen lays one.
The codfish never cackles
To tell you what she's done.
And so we scorn the codfish,
While the humble hen we prize,
Which only goes to show you
That it pays to advertise.

Anonymous

An Overview of the Strategy for Your First Campaign

If the only tool you have is a hammer, you tend to
see every problem as a nail.

Abraham Maslow

By now, you have developed preliminary job targets and conducted a Preliminary Target Investigation (through networking, the Internet, and the library) to see which targets are worth pursuing.

Then you selected those you think are worth a full campaign and ranked them in the order in which you want to conduct those campaigns. You are ready to conduct a campaign to contact every organization in your first target. When you are busy meeting with people in Target 1, you will start the campaign preparation for Target 2.

Do not expect to get a job through:

- **Networking**
- **Direct contact**
- **Search firms**
- **Ads (even on the Internet)**

These are techniques for getting
***meetings*, not jobs.**

After you get the meeting, you can think about what to do next to *perhaps* turn it into a job. (See the chapters on Follow-Up in our book *Mastering the Job Interview and Winning the Money Game*.

A Personal Marketing Plan, which you may show to your networking contacts, contains your list of targets, including the organizations in each of those targets. This plan forms the overview of your search.

For Target 1 you will now:

1. **Research to develop a list of all the organizations,** if you have not already done so. Find out—through networking, the Internet, or other research—the names of the people you should contact in the appropriate departments in each of those organizations.

2. **Develop your cover letter.** Paragraph 1 is the opening; Paragraph 2 is a summary about yourself appropriate for this target; Paragraph 3 contains your bulleted accomplishments ("You

may be interested in some of the things I've done"); Paragraph 4 is the close. (Many sample letters appear later in this book.)

3. **Develop your plan for getting a large number of meetings in this target.** There are four basic techniques for meeting people in each of the areas you have targeted for a full campaign. In the following chapters, you will learn more about them. They are:

- networking,
- direct contact (direct mail, targeted mail, walk-in, cold call),
- search firms, and
- ads (both print and online).

Do not think of these as techniques for getting *jobs*, but as techniques for getting *meetings*. After the meeting, think about what to do next to keep the relationship going or perhaps to turn the interview into a job offer.

Organize the names of the people you want to contact, and develop strategies for contacting them:

Only 5 to 10 percent of all job leads are through search firms, and another 5 to 10 percent are through ads. You do not have much control over these leads: you have to *wait* for an ad to appear, and *wait* for a search firm to send you on an interview. Both networking and direct contact are *proactive* techniques you can use to get meetings in your target market. In networking, you contact someone simply by using someone else's name. In direct contact, you contact someone directly—usually after you have done some research and know something about him or her. Networking and direct contact complement each other and gain added effectiveness when used together. You may start your campaign either with direct contact (if you know your target area very well) or with networking (to research an area you don't know well or find a way to contact people), and introduce the other technique as your campaign progresses.

Consider all four techniques for getting meetings, but spend most of your energy and brainpower on networking and direct contact.

Selecting the Techniques

Do not be too timid and squeamish about your actions. All life is an experiment.

Ralph Waldo Emerson

Select the techniques most appropriate for the industry or profession you are targeting, as well as for your own personality. Each technique can work, but the strength of your campaign lies in your ability to use what is best for your particular situation. Contact as many potential employers as possible and then *campaign* to keep your name in front of them.

Use all of the techniques to:

- Learn more about your target area.
- Test what you are offering.
- Let people know you are looking.
- Contact people in a position to hire you.

Opportunities are multiplied as they are seized.

Sun Tzu, *The Art of War*

The Myth of How to Get Interviews: Consider Contacting Organizations Directly

Search firms. Ads. Networking. Ask most people how to get interviews, and they'll mention those ways. But The Five O'Clock Club wanted to find out what really works. Its survey of professionals, managers, and executives clearly shows that *job hunters get more meetings for the time spent through "direct contact" than through any other single technique.*

Articles abound to prove the importance of networking. However, Five O'Clock Club research shows that direct contact is a more efficient way to generate meetings.

Networking means using someone else's name to get a meeting. *Direct contact* means aggressively pursuing people whom you may have known in the past or people you have never met. These might include association members or people identified on the Internet, through newspaper or magazine articles, or from library research. (For entry-level people, direct contact even includes going from one human resources office to another in an office center.) Here are the survey results:

- **Direct contact is the most time-efficient way to get meetings.** Surveyed job hunters spent 45 percent of their time networking, yet networking accounted for only 35 percent of their meetings. On the other hand, surveyed job hunters spent 24 percent of their time on direct contact, resulting in 27 percent of their meetings. Networking is very time-consuming. You have to find people who are willing to let you use their names. With direct contact, there is no middle person.

- **Even executives got almost 1/3 of their meetings through direct contact.** It's a myth that executives must rely on networking to get in to see people more senior than they are. Our surveyed senior executives did in fact get 62 percent of their meetings through networking, but almost 30 percent of their meetings resulted from their contacting executives to whom they had not been referred. Executives should not overlook direct contact.

- **People making a career continuation relied on direct contact even more than networking.** People looking to stay in the same industry or field got about one-third of their meetings through direct contact and a little less by using someone else's name to get a meeting. The job searchers contacted strangers, and got meetings because of their

accomplishments—and their discipline in working follow-up phone calls.

- **Even career changers (42 percent of those surveyed) got 20 percent of their meetings through direct contact.** Career changers often feel they should network to meet people in new fields or industries. However, direct contact can also result in meetings.

- **Search firms accounted for only 8 percent of meetings; newspaper ads accounted for 7 percent; online job boards accounted for 13 percent.** Everyone makes the mistake of placing too much emphasis on published openings. Contact organizations that don't publicize openings now, and stay in touch with them. This increases the chance they'll hire *you*, rather than post the job, when they need help.

We want our job hunters to consider all four techniques for getting meetings in their target markets. See what's working for you.

Using Search Firms

If you are looking for a position that naturally follows your most recent one, you can immediately contact search firms. As I've mentioned, only about 5 to 10 percent of all professional and managerial positions are filled by search firms, so it would seem logical to spend only 5 percent of your effort on them. However, certain professions use search firms more than others do.

Contact reputable search firms that handle positions in your target area. If you don't already have relationships with search firms, find the good ones by asking managers which search firms they use or recommend. Remember, search firms are rarely able to help career changers.

Answering Ads

Five to 10 percent of all jobs are filled through ads—both print and Internet. The odds are against you, so don't spend too much thought or energy on them. And don't sit home hoping for a response. Just answer the ad—as long as it sounds close to what you have to offer—and get on with your search. Maybe you'll hear from them—maybe you won't. (See the chapters in this book on "How to Answer Ads" and "What to Do When You Know There's a Job Opening.")

You must call each thing by its proper name, or that which must get done will not.

A. Harvey Block, President, Bokenon Systems

Networking

Studies show that about 60 to 70 percent of all positions are filled through networking. This is partly because most job hunters mistakenly refer to talking to people as "networking," no matter *how* they wound up talking to them. For example, Pete just found a job. I asked how he got the initial meeting. He said, "Through networking." When I asked him to tell me more, he said, "I'm an accountant, originally from Australia. There is an association here of accountants from Australia. I sent for a list of all the members, and wrote to all of them. That's how I got the job."

Pete got the job lead through a direct-mail campaign, *not* through networking. That's why the survey numbers are off, and that's why you should consider using every technique for getting meetings in your target market. You never know where your leads will come from.

Networking simply means getting to see someone by using another person's name. You are using a contact to get in. You want to see the person *whether or not they have a job for you.* This technique is essential if you want to change careers, because you can get in to see people even if you are not qualified in the traditional sense. To stay in the same field, you can network to get information on which organizations are hiring, which are the best ones to work for, and so on.

Networking can lead you in directions you had not considered and can open up new targets to pursue. You can network to explore even if you are not sure you want to change jobs right now. What's more, it's a technique you can use *after* you land that new job, whenever you get stuck and need advice.

Networking is more popular today than ever before and it is effective when used properly. But, depending on your target, it is not always the most *efficient* way to get meetings. Furthermore, it sometimes gets a bad name because even though people are constantly networking, they often are doing it incorrectly. Learn how to network correctly (see the chapters on networking), but combine targeted mailings (a direct-contact technique) with your networking when you are aiming at small organizations or ones with very few jobs appropriate for you. Networking your way into all of them could take forever. Also, directly contact other people when you would have great trouble getting a networking contact. If the direct contact doesn't work, you can always network in later.

When you combine direct mailing with networking, you can cover the market with a direct-mail campaign and then network certain sections of that market. Or you can network in to see someone, and then perhaps get a list of names you can use for further networking or a direct-mail campaign.

If you do not cover your market, you risk losing out. You may find out later that they "just filled a job a few months ago—too bad we didn't know you were looking." Be thorough. Let *everyone* in your target market know that you are looking.

The beginning of wisdom is to call things by their right names.

Chinese proverb

Direct-Contact Campaigns

Writing directly to executives is a consistently effective technique for generating meetings.

Twenty to 40 percent of all jobs are found this way and more jobs would result from this technique if more job hunters knew about it. You can write to lots of organizations (direct mail) or a few (targeted mail). The techniques are quite different.

Direct contact can save time. You can quickly test your target to see if there are job possibilities for someone like you. If you are familiar with your target area, you can develop your list, compose your letter, send it out, and start on your next target, all within a matter of weeks. Most job hunters contact larger corporations, ignoring smaller firms. Yet new jobs are being created in smaller organizations, so don't overlook them.

Direct contact is also the only technique that allows you to quickly contact *every* employer in the area of interest to you. You are essentially blanketing the market. Networking, on the other hand, is spotty by nature: You get to see only those organizations where your contact knows someone. Direct contact is effective for an out-of-town job search. And this technique works whether you are employed or unemployed. It works for all job levels.

This technique is an effective one for career changers. You can state all the positive things you offer and leave out anything not helpful to your case. Those things can be handled at the meeting.

Direct contact can help you get in to see someone you know you cannot network in to see. Shelli, for example, wanted to see someone very senior in an industry in which she had no experience. But she knew the field would be a good fit for her—she researched the industry and figured out how her background could fit in. She targeted six organizations and was able to network into two of them. She knew she would not be able to network into the other four organizations within a reasonable time frame: It would take her months to find someone who could only *possibly* help her get in to see the people she'd need to see.

Instead of networking, she researched each of the four organizations, wrote to the senior people she was targeting at each one, and followed up

with a phone call. Because of her presentation, three of the executives agreed to see her. This saved her many months in her search. Sometimes a targeted mailing can be *more* effective than networking in getting in to see important people. It takes more brainpower than networking, but you already have that.

Direct contact primarily involves targeted and direct mailing, but a junior person can also go from organization to organization to talk to personnel departments or store managers. As long as job hunters follow up, this technique can work. An executive client of mine used this technique effectively by walking into a small, privately owned, prestigious store, speaking with the store manager to find out the name of the president, and then calling the president. It led to an executive position with that company. This was "direct contact" because he did not use someone's name to get in to see the store manager or the president. Even when I was very young, I used direct contact to get in to see virtually anyone I wanted.

Sometimes I had trouble getting in, but people eventually saw me because I usually had a good reason, did my homework, didn't waste their time, was sincere about why I wanted to see them, and was gently persistent. It suits my personality because I am shy about using someone else's name for the core of my effort, I am comfortable about putting my effort into research and writing, and I don't have the time it takes to see a lot of people who may not be right on target for me. As I go along, I network when appropriate.

Direct contact also includes cold calls, which can work for some personalities in some industries.

We will now focus on targeted mail and direct mail:

Targeted mailings are similar to networking. You target a relatively small number of people (e.g., fewer than 20 or 30) and try to see all of them, *whether or not they have a job for you.* Instead of already having a person to contact, you *establish* your own contact through the research you do. The meeting is handled exactly the same as a networking meeting.

Direct mail is used when you have a large number of organizations to contact (e.g., 200 or more). You mail a brilliant package to all of them and expect seven or eight meetings from the mailing.

If I had eight hours to chop down a tree,
I'd spend six sharpening my ax.

Abraham Lincoln

Using All of the Techniques

A good campaign usually relies on more than one technique to get meetings. Think of how you can divide up your target list. For example, if you have a list of 200 organizations in your target area, you may decide you can network into 20 of them, do a targeted mailing (with follow-up phone calls) to another 20 or 30, and do a direct-mail campaign to the rest. This way you have both blanketed your market and used the most appropriate technique to reach each organization in your target area. In addition, you could also contact search firms and answer ads.

Networking vs. Direct Mail

Let's use the banking industry as an example.

You could easily network your way into a large bank. You could find someone who knew someone at a number of them. Each contact you'd make at a large bank could refer you to other people within the same bank, which would increase your chances of getting a job there. Since one person knows others within that organization, networking is efficient. You can meet many potential hiring managers within one organization.

On the other hand, it may be difficult to network into smaller banks. Fewer of your friends are likely to know someone there, because each small bank has far fewer employees. Each networking meeting would represent fewer jobs and fewer referrals within each bank. Referrals to other small banks would also generally represent fewer jobs than the larger banks have. It could take forever to network to the same number of potential jobs at hundreds of small banks that could easily be covered by networking at large banks. Networking can be inefficient with smaller organizations and you may find that you can't put a dent in the market.

You could contact smaller banks directly. They do not expect you to know someone who works there, so they are more open to intelligent mailings. They tend to get fewer contacts from job hunters. You could categorize the smaller banks in a way that makes sense to you—those strong in international banking, for example, or those strong in lending. Or you could categorize banks by nationality—grouping the Japanese banks, European banks, South American banks, and so on. Then you could *target each segment* with a cover letter customized for that market.

Decide which techniques are best for you. Think about how people tend to get hired within your target industry and profession. Also consider your own circumstances, such as whether you are currently employed, how much freedom you have to go on networking meetings, how much use you can make of the phone, and so on. You can always network your way into a few specific organizations, but networking into a great number is sometimes not possible.

Remember, networking requires a great deal of time and travel. Direct mail is often appealing to those who are working and must ration their meeting and travel time.

A word of caution to very senior executives: Because of your extensive networks, you may be tempted to rely exclusively on them to find your next position. As extensive as they are, your contacts are probably spotty. You may be reluctant to do research because you are used to having others do such things for you. Do your research anyway. Define your targets. List all of the organizations in your target areas that are appropriate for you and the names of the people you need to see in each of these organizations. Most very senior executives skip this step and get their next position serendipitously. That's just fine—if the position is right for you. But many senior executives in their eagerness to land something quickly may land something inappropriate, beneath what they deserve, or nothing at all. If you have listed all of the people you should see in your target areas, you increase your chances of having a thorough campaign and you will not miss out on a good possibility for yourself.

If you can network in to see the people you should see in your target market, fine. But if you can think of no way to network in, contact them directly. You will get plenty of serendipitous leads and meet plenty of people who have business ideas and want to form partnerships with you. These opportunities may be fine, but they are better if you can compare them with those you uncover through an organized search.

Things which matter most must never be at the mercy of things which matter least.

Goethe

In Summary

Make a list of all the people you should meet in *each* of your target areas or, at the very least, make a list of all the organizations in your target areas. Intend to contact all of them. Get meetings with people in your target area through networking, direct contact, search firms, and ads (print and online). Do not think of these as techniques for getting *jobs,* but as techniques for getting *meetings.* Plan how you can contact or meet the *right* people in *every* organization in each of your target areas as quickly as possible.

After the meeting, either keep in touch with networking-type contacts (regardless of how you met them) or think about what you can do next to *perhaps* turn the interview into a job offer.

Getting Polished for a Full Campaign

Although action is typical of the American style, thought and planning are not; it is considered heresy to state that some problems are not immediately or easily solvable.

Daniel Bell, sociologist, *Daedalus*

Before the meeting, be prepared: know exactly what you want and what you have to offer. In the next chapter, you will prepare your pitch to organizations. Have your pitch ready even *before* you contact anyone—just so you are prepared. Read the chapters on interviewing in our book *Mastering the Job Interview and Winning the Money Game,* and *practice.* Be a polished interviewer. Remember the cliché: "You don't get a second chance to make a good first impression."

After you have practiced interviewing, contact the people on your "hit list." Start with those who are less important to you, so you can practice and learn more about your target area. You will want to know, for example, your chances in that market and how you should position yourself.

After you have met with someone, follow up. This method works. Read the chapters on following up. Once you have contacted a target area, contact it again a few months later. Keep following up with the people you meet.

Read magazines and newspapers. Attend organizational meetings. Keep abreast of what is happening in the field. Keep on networking.

Begin at the beginning . . . and go on till you come to the end: then stop.

Lewis Carroll

A Promotional Campaign to Get Meetings

Sometimes I say to a client who is shy, "So far, you and I are the only ones who know you are looking for a job." Get your name out there. Get on the inside track. You must conduct a promotional campaign to contact as many potential employers as possible. *Campaign* to make sure they remember you.

Make a lot of contacts with people in a position to hire or recommend you. If there are sparks between you, and if you help them remember you, you will be the one they call when a job comes up. Or they can give you the names of others to contact. They may even create a job for you if it makes sense.

The goal of your promotional campaign is to let the *right* people know what you are seeking. Some discussions will become job interviews, which will lead to offers. Get a lot of meetings so you will have a number of offers to consider. You want options.

Focus on getting *meetings* in your target area. People who focus on *getting a job* can get uptight when they have a meeting. They do not think of themselves as *looking around* or *finding out what is out there.* They act as if they are in a display case hoping someone will buy them. They may accept the first offer that comes along—even when they know it is inappropriate—because they think they will never get another one.

If you aim to make lots of contacts and get lots of meetings, you are more likely to keep your perspective. If you are an inexperienced job hunter, talk to some people who are not in a position to hire you. Practice your lines and your techniques. Get experience in talking about yourself, and learn more about your target market. Then you will be more relaxed in important meetings and will be able to let your personality come through.

Labor not as one who is wretched, nor yet as one who would be pitied or admired. Direct yourself to one thing only, to put yourself in motion and to check yourself at all times.

Marcus Aurelius Antonius, *Meditations*

You Are the Manager of This Campaign

You are in control of this promotional campaign. After reading this book you will know what to say, how to say it, and to whom. You will select which promotional techniques to use and when and learn how to measure the effectiveness of your campaign.

You will also decide on your image. You can present any picture of yourself you like. You present your image and credentials in your written communications—résumé, cover letters, and follow-up notes. You have *complete* control over what you put in them and how you present yourself.

How you act and dress are also important to your image. Look like you're worth the money you would like. Watch your posture—sit up straight. *Smile!* Decide to feel good and to feel confident. Smile some more. Smile again. Smiling makes you look confident and competent and gives you extra energy. It is difficult to smile and continue being down. Even when you are at home working on your search, smile every once in a while to give yourself energy and the right attitude to help you move ahead. This is true no matter what your level. Even executives are better off doing this as they go through their searches. The ones who cannot do this tend to do less well than those who can.

Whether direct contact or networking, search firms or ads, choose techniques most likely to result in a good response from your target—techniques appropriate to your situation. When you become an expert, change a technique to suit yourself.

Modify your approach or even abandon an effort that is ineffective. You want a good response from your promotional efforts. A *response* is a meeting. A polite rejection letter does not count as a response. Some organizations have a policy of sending letters and some have a policy against them. Rejection letters have nothing to do with you. They do not count. Only meetings count.

This is a campaign to generate meetings. Your competition is likely to have polished presentations. Decide on the message you want to get across in the meeting, and practice it. There are two kinds of meetings: information-gathering (networking) meetings and actual job interviews. Do not try to turn every meeting into a job interview. You will turn people off—and lessen the chances of getting a job. *In the beginning, you are aiming for contact or networking meetings.* (See the chapters on networking meetings, as well as information on handling the job interview, in our book *Mastering the Job Interview and Winning the Money Game.*)

When things do not work, there is a reason. Be aware and correct the situation. There is no point in continuing an unsuccessful campaign. Remember, when things go wrong—as they will—it is not personal. This is strictly business. It is a project. With experience, you will become better at managing your promotional campaigns to get meetings.

Why Stagger Your Campaigns?

Why is it unwise to start all of your campaigns at once? Let's pretend your first target is the telephone industry, and your second target is the environmental industry. If one day you talk to a telephone company and the next day you talk to an environmental organization, you will not sound credible. When you meet with the environmental organization, it does you no good to mention that you met with the telephone company.

If, however, you talk to someone in a telephone company, and then another person in the same or another telephone company, you can say, "I'm talking to four different divisions of your firm right now and I'm also talking to other phone companies." Then it sounds as if you really want to work in their industry.

Similarly, when you want to talk to an environmental organization, you can mention you are talking to a lot of environmental organizations. The information you learn at one organization will make you sound smarter with the next.

As you research and meet with people in a target area, the target becomes richer and less superficial. In the beginning of a search, for example, you may be interested in health care, which is too broad a target. Later, however, you may find that the field is more complex than you thought and learn that people's jobs are not at all what an outsider would expect.

You are an insider when you give back non-proprietary information, such as: "Do you know that Southern Bell has a fulfillment system very similar to yours?"

Or you can say to an environmental organization: "I've been talking to a lot of environmental organizations and it seems that a trend in this industry right now is _____. Do you agree?"

This methodical search is the only smart way to do it because you gain momentum. Most job hunters simply "go on interviews," but that's not enough in this economy. Organizations expect you to know something about them.

On the following page is one Club member's Personal Marketing Plan. There are additional plans in our book *Targeting a Great Career.* You may want to use them as a model for your own.

Sample Personal Marketing Plan

Personal Marketing Plan: Joe Doakes

TARGET FUNCTIONS: VICE PRESIDENT/DIRECTOR/MANAGER

- Management Information Services
- Applications Development
- Information Systems
- Information Systems Technology
- Systems Development
- Business Reengineering

RESPONSIBILITIES:

- Identification of new information systems technologies and how they could affect the profitability of a company.
- Management of projects for the implementation of information systems or new technologies.
- Providing for and managing a business partner relationship between the information systems department and the internal company departments that use their services.
- Implementing and managing a business partner relationship among the company and its primary vendors and its customers using systems technologies, such as EDI (Electronic Data Interchange).

TARGET COMPANIES:

Attributes
- People-oriented
- Growth-minded through increased sales, acquisitions, or new products
- Committed to quality customer service
- Receptive to new ideas on how to do business or using new technologies

Location
- Primary—Northern New Jersey or Westchester/Orange/Rockland Counties in New York
- Secondary—New York City, Central New Jersey, Southern Connecticut, Eastern Pennsylvania
- Other—anywhere along the Eastern Seaboard

TARGET INDUSTRIES:

Consumer Products:	Pharmaceuticals:	Food/Beverage:	Chemicals:	Other:
Unilever	Merck	Pepsico	Castrol	Medco
Kimberly-Clark	Schering-Plough	T.J. Lipton	Witco	Toys-R-Us
Avon	Warner-Lambert	Kraft/General Foods	Allied Chemical	Computer Associates
Carter Wallace	American Home	Nabisco	Olin Corp.	Becton Dickinson
Sony	Products	Hartz Mountain	Union Carbide	Dialogic
Minolta	Bristol-Myers Squibb	Continental Baking	Air Products	Siemens
Boyle Midway	Pfizer	Nestlé	General Chemical	Automatic Data Proc.
Revlon	Jannsen Pharmaceutica	Häagen-Dazs	Englehard Corp.	Vital Signs
L&F Products	Hoffmann-LaRoche	Tuscan Dairies	BASF Corp.	Benjamin Moore
Houbigant	Ciba-Geigy	Dannon Co.	Degussa Corp.	
Mem	Sandoz	BSN Foods	GAF Corp.	
Chanel	A.L. Laboratories	Campbell Soup	Lonza Inc.	
Airwick	Smith Kline Beecham	Cadbury Beverages	Sun Chemical	
Church & Dwight	American Cyanamid	Labatt		
Johnson & Johnson	Boeringer Ingelheim	Arnold Foods		
Reckitt & Colman	Roberts Pharmaceuticals	S. B. Thomas		
Philip Morris	Winthrop	Sunshine Biscuits		
Clairol	Pharmaceuticals			
Estée Lauder	Glaxo			
Cosmair	Block Drug			
	Hoechst Celanese			
	Ethicon			

The
Five
O'Clock
Club

Research: Developing Your List of Organizations to Contact

Wisdom is the principal thing; therefore get wisdom: and with all thy getting get understanding. Exalt her, and she shall promote thee: she shall bring thee to honour, when thou dost embrace her.

Proverbs 4: 7–8

The entire job search process is a *research* process. After all, if you knew exactly the *right* organization and the *right* person and the *right* job for you, you would not be reading this book, and you would not go to The Five O'Clock Club. You would simply go to the organization that had the right job for you—and get hired!

But that's not the way it is. You'll conduct research throughout your *entire* search. Research will help you *home* in on the right place for you: the right industry, the right *organization,* and the right *kinds* of positions—those where you stand a good chance of getting a job right now. Research will also help you pick the right *job*—the one suiting you best for the long term.

If you've been having little luck answering ads and talking with search firms, you may be ready for an organized, methodical search instead. This means you must conduct research. Once you develop your target list, which we also call your Personal Marketing Plan, the rest of your search will be routine. Then you "simply" contact those organizations, arrange to have meetings, and follow up.

Your **Personal Marketing Plan** will guide you in your search, and it will make your search more efficient. You can directly contact people listed in your plan, and use your list in networking

Looking for a place to start your research? Read this chapter and then study the bibliography at the back of this book. Once you have your list of organizations to contact, the rest of your search is clear.

meetings. You'll be able to show people your plan and ask them, "Are you familiar with any of the organizations on this list? What do you think of them? Who do you think I should contact at each organization? May I use your name?"

If you started with our book, *Targeting a Great Career,* during the assessment phase, you accomplished the following:

- You **brainstormed** *all* of the **targets** that you thought might be of interest to you. Later on, when things seem to be drying up, you'll be glad you did this.

- You conducted your ***Preliminary*** **Target Investigation** to check out each one. At this point, you were not trying to get a job; instead, you were conducting a little research to see if it made sense to mount a full campaign aimed at each of those targets. You talked to people to see what they thought, and you conducted research at the library or on the Internet. This helped you eliminate some targets.

- Then you **ranked your targets**, and decided which targets to go after first, second, third, and fourth. If you are desperate for a job, you decided to focus first on the target where you were most likely to get hired. If you have time to explore—maybe you're employed right now—maybe your first target is the dream job you've always wanted to explore.

- Then you ***measured* your targets**. If the total number of positions you're going after is fewer than 200, that's not good. Remember that we are not totaling job openings, but *positions*. And it does not matter if the positions are filled right now. You are trying to avoid having a search that is too small. Those searches are doomed from the start.

  For example, if you want to be a writer in the corporate communications department of a large corporation, you would ask yourself: "How is this large company *organized*? I wonder to whom *corporate communications* reports. I wonder how many *writers* they have in corporate communications." You'd estimate the number of writers you *think* they have. Just take a guess. They certainly have more than one writer in corporate communications! Might they have 5? Or 10? Just take a guess. Of course, a smaller organization would have fewer writers in corporate communications.

  Estimate the number of positions each organization might have and add up all of the positions for the organizations on your target list. If in all of your targets the number does not add up to 200 positions (not *openings* but positions), then brainstorm more targets or more organizations within those targets. If you don't follow this strategy, you're going to have a longer search.

- Next, you ***segmented* your targets**, and segmented *again* if that was reasonable. In the publishing industry, for example, segments could include book publishing, magazine publishing, and publishing online. Magazine publishing is still too big a target, so you would segment it to better manage your campaign. Within magazine publishing, you would list the *kinds* of magazines of most interest to you—for example, sports magazines, health magazines, women's magazines, men's magazines, and so on. You'll find much more on targeting and segmenting in *Targeting a Great Career*.

Successful people often experience more failures than failures do. But they manage to press on. One good failure can teach you more about success than four years at the best university. Failure just might be the best thing that ever happens to you.

Herb True, super-salesman, as quoted by
Robert Allen in *Creating Wealth*

Most people generally target the well-known organizations—the *top* magazines to work for, the *top* museums, the most prestigious hospitals. They target the organizations that *everybody* has heard of and at which everyone wants to work. It's a better idea to research *lesser-known* organizations. These may be even *better* places to work than some of the top-tier organizations. In the second-tier organizations, you may get to do more, have a chance of being a star, and advance more easily. So don't overlook the second-tier organizations.

Your Personal Marketing Plan allows you to *survey all this at a glance*. It lists the industries you're targeting and the organizations within those industries. Your Personal Marketing Plan is so important that it is one of *three key documents* you should share with your small group, in addition to your résumé and cover letter. Show it to your coach and small-group members even when you have just a rudimentary plan, that is, a *tentative* list of industries and subindustries and perhaps a few organizations within each. You will *refine* your Personal Marketing Plan as you move along in your search. Chances are you will change your mind about your most important targets and the most important organizations within each target.

If your small-group members (or your parents or friends) recognize the names of most of the organizations on your list, *you have not yet begun your research!* Dig in more. You'll have to think hard and do your research to uncover organizations that may be *better* places to work.

Job search is just like any other worthwhile project in life. You *make* your plan and then you *execute* it. At the beginning of your search, you'll have a *tentative* Personal Marketing Plan. As you search—and conduct more research—you'll add more organizations to your list. Your Personal Marketing Plan doesn't have to be 100 percent correct before you start contacting prospective employers.

As you move forward, it's best to divide each target into an **A-list, B-list and C-list.** The A-list includes companies where you would love to work. The companies you would consider *okay* go on the B-list, and the C-list companies are of no interest to you.

Contact your C-list companies first to get your feet wet and use them for practice. Because you don't care that much about them, you will probably be more relaxed and confident and will interview well. You are *practicing*. You will also be testing your market to see if you get a good response from these C-list companies.

> **To get a job within a reasonable time . . .
> target 200 positions—not *openings*—
> positions.**

It's important for you to know if the companies on your C-list are *not* interested in you. You need to talk to the people in your small group to find out what you're doing wrong. However, if you are well received by the companies on your C-list, then you can contact the companies on your B-list. You could say something like, "I am already talking to a number of companies in your industry [which is true], but I didn't want to accept a job with any of them [which is also true] until I had a chance to talk with you." This script is just one approach. Be sure to talk to your small group about the right things to say to those on your B-list.

- **Your A-list: You'd love to work there.**
- **Your B-list: They're okay.**
- **Your C-list: They don't interest you.**

Using your Personal Marketing Plan and your A-, B-, and C-Lists together *is* the search: It's a search for organizations to contact and the names of people within each of those organizations. This is a vastly superior approach to what you might have done in the past. Your competitors, on the other hand, are out there contacting search firms, scanning ads, and hitting the "send" button on job-search websites. But *you'll* get in to see hiring managers before they even post their jobs. You'll have less competition and you'll find that a job may be created just for you!

This part of your search *must* be combined with the assessment you did in *Targeting a Great Career*. Review that book again and again during your job-search process. You don't want just a job; you want a career. This means you want a job *that positions you best for the long run;* you can achieve this only if you *know* what your long-run vision is.

Now, let's develop your Personal Marketing Plan. This chapter will give you some ideas and your coach and small group will give you others. In addition, you can use the bibliography at the back of this book or the even more extensive bibliography in the Members Only section of our website (www.fiveoclockclub.com).

The choice of a career, a spouse, a place to live; we make them casually, at times, because we do not know how to articulate the choices . . . I believe that people often persuade themselves that their decisions do not matter, because they feel powerless to make the best decision. Some of us feel that, no matter what we do, our decisions won't matter much . . . But I believe that we know at heart that decisions do matter.

Peter Schwartz, *The Art of the Long View*

Few things are impossible to diligence and skill.

Samuel Johnson, *A Dissertation on the Art of Flying*

Using Search Engines to Develop Your List

Many job hunters use Google or Yahoo for industry information, even if they're going after esoteric industries such as social service agencies, ethics, education policy, and think tanks. Key any industry name into Google or Yahoo and see what comes up. You may have to look through a few pages of information, but there will probably be a site that lists what's going on in that industry, or lists other sites for that industry; one or two of those sites will probably list *organizations* in that industry. Luckily, most organizations have a website and contact information, making it much easier to develop your list right from your own home.

It might be helpful to see how a few people have progressed through this process. Let's start with something that is not as easy as it appears. I'll give you a few examples of *junior-level job searchers* because they can have a more difficult time uncovering the names of people to contact: It's usually easier to find the names of senior people in organizations.

Dan had experience as a computer operator, line assembler (computers), data controller, and mail room clerk. He lived in Magnolia, Texas. Where could Dan find prospective employers without simply responding to ads? To develop a list of companies where Dan could work, I went into Google and simply keyed in "Magnolia, TX businesses." More than 75 *pages* of company listings came up—company name, address, phone number, and distance from Magnolia, TX. Those are a *lot* of companies for Dan to contact. Since Dan's skills are applicable to many industries, he could think about a few industries in which he would enjoy working and focus on those, which would make his job more interesting. How Dan would *contact* those companies is another matter covered in great detail elsewhere in this book.

Jon, a manufacturing engineer/supervisor, had been unemployed quite a while. Manufacturing in Arizona was in a downturn and there were very few jobs. But *some* people were getting hired for jobs that were not advertised. How could Jon find the names of companies to contact so he could become proactive in his search rather than wait for openings? Again, I went into Google. I entered "manufacturers

Arizona." It took me to **Addresses.com**, which returned 548 company names. Then I went to company websites to start my research. The first company I looked up was Allied Tool and Die. It's probably too small for Jon, so he could then go on to the next one. Or he could scan the list to see which companies he recognized or found appealing.

Research is the process of going up alleys to see if they are blind.

Marston Bates, *American Zoologist*

CASE STUDY *Julie*

Targeting Professional Services Firms

Let's take it one step further. The Internet can be a great way to develop your target list and also *contact* hundreds of people within a few hours. This technique works when you want to contact small- to mid-sized professional service firms, such as accounting, architecture, or law firms. It also works if you want to contact small businesses in general. It can work for job hunters at all levels—from college students to executives who want to work for a small business.

Julie had just finished her sophomore year at a small college and was having a problem finding a summer job related to her major, which was architecture. If Julie had gone to a major school such as the University of Michigan, she could have contacted alumni who were in her field, used the job-posting boards on the University of Michigan website, or gone to on-campus job fairs where the employers come to the students. But those options were not open to her. Julie's school was small and not especially geared to helping students get placed.

Here's what it took for Julia to get *four terrific concurrent offers*.

Julie lived in a rural area and there were no architectural firms in her town. So she targeted the major metropolitan area that was closest to her (90 minutes away) because that's where most of the firms were located. She also targeted the suburban areas nearer her home.

Julie would be glad to do administrative work in an architectural firm and also work in CAD, a computer program for architects. She had taken a CAD course and worked on CAD a little at a - previous job. But she didn't want to get stuck as a CAD operator. Instead, she wanted to learn more about the way small architectural firms work. Doing some administrative work would help her get a feel for the firm. So **Julie had defined her targets The Five O'Clock Club way**:

- Industry: architectural firms
- Position: administration or CAD operator
- Geographic area: large metropolitan area and the suburbs near her home.

A basic Five O'Clock Club tenet is that a job hunter must go after 200 job possibilities to get one good offer! This holds true for students as well as for the most senior executives. So it is important to pay attention to the response rate to your e-mailing. Notice how many people ask you to come in for a meeting. If you send 200 E-mails and get only two calls for meetings you must send out 200 *additional* E-mails. Two meetings are not enough!

Architectural firms are generally small, perhaps employing only one student per firm, so Julie would probably need to contact 200 of them. How could Julie come up with the names of 200 architectural firms—and quickly? She was only a week away from the end of the term and had not yet tried to contact many firms.

Julie contacted 200 small firms in less than 10 hours.

Julie used job-posting sites to make a start on her contact list of 200 firms. First, she went into *www.monster.com,* and selected job postings for *architects* in the major metropolitan area near her. Then she selected job postings for architects in the nearby suburban areas. Julie selected only architectural jobs at *firms* as opposed to jobs in the government or major organizations such as hospitals and hotel chains.

Then Julie clicked on the companies she was interested in—*as if* she were responding to the ad. After all, those organizations were hiring! Her approach was to reach out to the person in each small firm who was likely to handle hiring. (This works for students who want to work in a small firm. A more senior person would need to contact the department or division head in a larger firm, which can require making a phone call or looking at the company's website.)

When ads are answered automatically like this—through a job-posting site—the "subject" line contains the ad number so the organization will know which ad a person is responding to. Julie changed the subject line to read (see example on the next page):

Administrator/CAD Drafter— Architecture-related—Employment for top student.

Julie contacted about 50 firms this way, but this was not enough. She needed to find at least 150 additional firms.

Julie responded to ads for senior architects, but asked for a junior-level job instead. Let them know what *you* want.

Next she tried the search engines. Julie went into Google and keyed in the word *architect* and the two geographic areas she was interested in one at a time. The American Institute of Architects was one of the results and is a good source, but she also found lots of individual architectural firms listed. In most cases, Julie had to go to the company website to get an appropriate E-mail address. One by one, she came up with 155 additional organizations to contact, bringing her total to 205 firms (including the 50 from *monster.com*).

**This is the E-mail Julie sent to 205 architectural firms. Her
Five O'Clock Club résumé was an attachment.**

E-mail

To: julieangelo@udallas.edu

Subject: **Administrator/CAD Drafter—Architecture-Related—Employment for Top Student.**

May 11, 200x

Dear Sir or Madam:

I am writing to you because yours is a prestigious firm in the architecture industry and I am an architectural student interested in summer work at a firm such as yours. I'd like to meet with you or someone else in your firm to find out more about your company and to tell you about myself. Even if you have no openings right now, you never know when you may need someone like me.

I have 10 months' experience with a civil engineering firm. You may be interested in some of the specific things I have done:

- Served as an **assistant office manager**, organizing client proposals and setting up manuals. I also answered an 8-line phone.
- Because of my **basic autoCAD experience**, engineers turned to me when they wanted routine things done.

As an architectural studies major, I tend to **be among the best in my class**, winning contests and doing excellent work. I enjoy client contact, helping architects get ready for meetings, putting proposals together, and assisting with autoCAD work. I would appreciate a meeting and look forward to hearing from you.

With thanks,

Julie Angelo

julieangelo@udallas.edu, University of Dallas Box #3124, 76 North Churchill Rd., Irving, TX 99999, 555-666-4693

angelo555@hotmail.com, 863 Erie Avenue, Brewster, TX 99945

Attachment: JAngelo résumé

She sent a mass E-mail. To save time, she stopped e-mailing the firms individually. Instead, she captured the E-mail addresses in a Word document, with one E-mail address per line. After she had gathered 20 or 30 E-mail addresses, Julie sent a "mass E-mail." She didn't put the addresses in the "To" field. She copied all the E-mail addresses into the "bcc" field so the recipients would not be able to tell to which or to how many firms she had mailed. She put the same "subject" as she had for her earlier E-mails, attached her résumé as before, and addressed the E-mail to herself. She did this until she had sent out all 205 E-mails. Then she took her last final exam.

Julie had spent a total of about 10 hours on her research and e-mailing.

> **Using a mass e-mail technique, Julie was able to contact 20 to 30 firms at a time using the "bcc" field.**

Then the calls came in. Within two days, Julie received nine calls for meetings. Interestingly, eight of the calls were from the suburban area and only one call was from the major metropolitan area.

Julie had sent 75 percent of her E-mails to firms in the major metropolitan area—that's where most of the firms were. The major metropolitan area was the *obvious* place to look for architectural jobs. That means, of course, that she had far more competitors and, accordingly, lower response.

Firms in the suburban area were more responsive to her because most job hunters were ignoring the suburbs.

The results of *your* search may surprise you. That's why you have to contact so many places. You never know who will respond.

Julie scheduled seven interviews (she immediately ruled out two firms because the travel would have been more than two hours from home, something she would have found acceptable if she had gotten only a few calls).

Julia was thrilled to have seven meetings lined up because a key Five O'Clock Club maxim is to have 6 to 10 job possibilities in the works. It increases the chances of landing something appropriate for you.

Another Five O'Clock Club maxim is, "Don't chase jobs—chase companies." Contact organizations whether or not they have an opening right now. If your search is solely from postings, you will have competition for the jobs you go after. Everyone is chasing those same job openings. So too, most people target the top-tier firms in major metropolitan areas. If Julie had done that, she would have been discouraged by the results, since she got only *one* call from a firm in the major metropolitan area.

> **Even though 75 percent of her E-mails went to firms in the major metropolitan area, Julie received almost no response from them.**

Some firms may *tell* you they have no openings (regardless of your level) but say they would be glad to meet with you anyway. *Meet with them!* Most jobs are created for people and most companies will hire someone if the right person comes along—even though they have no formal opening and were not looking to hire at the moment. Julie overlooked this and turned down two exploratory meetings because she felt such urgency to get a job.

However, Julie did schedule five interviews over three days' time.

> **The Five O'Clock Club wants you to line up 6 to 10 meetings. Julie lined up 7.**

Julie prepared for the interview; the full scope of that process is covered in our book,

Mastering the Job Interview and Winning the Money Game. At the very least, we can say here: **Go to each company's website** before the interview so you know something about the company. Even managers at small companies will ask applicants, "So, have you seen our website? How much do you know about us?" Because of the web, companies expect you to know something about them.

Her offers poured in. In the end, Julie went on **four interviews and got four offers**. As she got offers, she became pickier about the remaining firms on her list, ruling out those requiring more than an hour and a half of travel. In her last job, Julie earned $10 an hour. Her first offer was at $11, two were at $12.50, and one offer had not yet come in.

Julie seemed very desirable *because* **she had so many possibilities in the works.** Companies were essentially in a bidding war for her. Remember that you need to **see 6 to 10 organizations concurrently to have a good search**.

When Julie interviewed at the last firm, she told them about her other offers, hoping for another offer at $12.50 per hour. They wooed her by promising her she would be able to learn a lot about architecture on the job: She would visit some of the sites where the architects were building, go to client meetings, "shadow" an architect to see what was done all day. They said they would e-mail her an offer later that evening.

Julie would have found it difficult to resist their offer almost regardless of the salary they offered: The experience would have been so extraordinary compared with the others and Julie was trying to keep her long-range future in mind.

However, Julie did not have to choose content over salary. The E-mail came that evening with an offer of $15 per hour!

The last firm knew what it was up against: three other offers. The hiring manager also knew it was difficult to recruit architects in their neck of the woods. But for Julie, the location was perfect: only 45 minutes from her home.

> **Julie increased her pay by 50 percent because she had so many offers and she contacted companies that other job hunters ignored.**

> *Research is to see what everybody has seen and to think what nobody else has thought.*
>
> Albert Szent-Gyorgyi, American biochemist

CASE STUDY *Jack*
A Marketing Executive

You, too, can use search engines to develop your list. Large or even mid-sized organizations are generally easier to research. For example, Jack, a marketing executive, got *all* of the information for his job search online. His targets were pharmaceutical, biotech, and biotech marketing organizations. Jack made lists of companies in all three areas appropriate for him in his geographic area.

You're trying to do the same as Jack. You're trying to make a list of the organizations to contact in each of your targets and find out *whom* to contact at each organization. *Then* Jack started networking and contacting organizations directly. He shortly ended up with four offers—right close to home.

The Internet changes over time. The sites job hunters love and depend on can go out of business or start charging huge fees. So you'll have to find out what's current. Ask your small-group members what they use or check the Members Only area of our website.

However you do it, you'll need a preliminary list of organizations to contact. You'll learn other helpful techniques as you develop your list. Just remember: The list *is* your search. Throughout your search, you refine your target list. That's why they call it a *search*. You have to *search* for the names of people to contact.

73

For what a business needs the most for its decisions—especially its strategic ones—are data about what goes on outside of it. It is only outside the business where there are results, opportunities and threats.

Peter F. Drucker, "Be Data Literate—Know What to Know," *The Wall Street Journal,* December 1, 1992

Associations

Associations are an important source of information. If you don't know anything at all about an industry or field, associations are often the place to start. Attending their meetings will assist you in getting the jargon down so you can use the language of the trade. If you are interested in the rug business, there's a related association.

Maria, a Five O'Clock Club member, was interested in competitive intelligence. Maria went to her local library to consult the massive *Encyclopedia of Associations* (EOA). There would seem to be an association for almost everything, and, believe it or not, she found the Society of Competitive Intelligence Professionals. She called the headquarters, found out about the local chapter, and went to a meeting. She met a lot of people in the field. She also read the association trade journal and learned enough to sound like an "insider." One of these new contacts led her to the job she later accepted.

You can do what Maria did. Go to *your* library, **ask for the *Encyclopedia of Associations***, and spend a few hours with it. Chances are, you'll find one or more associations related to your field of interest. The EOA usually provides information on the national headquarters of associations (many of which are located in or near Washington, DC). Call and ask for information on the **local chapter**. Then call the local chapter and say that you'd like to attend a meeting as a guest. Associations usually *love* to have guests! You'll meet people in the field, hear lectures that will bring you up-to-date, and find copies of their journals, magazines, or newsletters.

Networking is expected at association meetings. When you meet someone you think may help you, ask if you can meet on a more formal basis for about half an hour. If there is no local chapter in your area, the national office may still be willing to send you information.

Associations usually have **membership directories**, which you will have access to when you join. This directory can become the keystone of your search. You can *contact members directly*. You can write, "As a fellow member of the American Rug Association, I thought you could give me some information that would help me in my search." Fellow members are a great source of information.

Associations often publish **trade magazines and newspapers** you can read to stay up-to-date on the business. By reading these, you'll learn about the important issues facing the industry and find out who's been hired and who's moving; you should try to talk to the people you read about. If an association is large enough, it may even have a library or research department, or a public relations person you can talk to. Associations often sell books related to the field.

An association's **annual convention** is a very quick way to become educated about a field. These conventions are not cheap (they run from hundreds to thousands of dollars), but you will hear speakers on the urgent topics in the field, pick up literature, and meet lots of people. You can network at the conference and later.

If you spend a couple of days at a conference, you'll know more about an industry than many people who are *in* the field right now. You can contact people in the industry (many of whom were *not* at the conference) and say, "Were you at the conference? No? Well, I was and maybe I can give you some of the information that I learned there." This is a chance for you to become an insider! A Five O'Clock Club maxim is, "Only insiders get hired." So share the information you pick up.

Since the EOA is the most complete source of association information, we recommend you use it first. A few websites are also helpful. **Associations**

on the Net (www.ipl.org/ref/aon/) lists more than 2000 associations. Simply key in a profession. If you put in "accounting," for instance, you'll find 22 organizations. Also try www.business.com; under each business category, there's a link to "associations." (There are additional sources for associations at the back of this book. Some are in print; some are online.)

On these sites, you'll find links to well-known sites like the one for the National Association of Fund Raising Executives and the Association of Legal Administrators. Or just go to Google, key in the word "association" and an industry or field name (e.g., "accounting"), and you'll come up with leads. But as of this writing, nothing beats the EOA.

Few Americans would lay a large wager that they will be in the same job, working for the same company, ten years hence.

Michael Mandel, *The High-Risk Society*

Alumni Associations

If you went to a prestigious school, you have an advantage over other job hunters because those schools often have great alumni associations. Martin, a graduate of Stanford University, wanted to start a job search. He thought he wanted to target some of the hot technology areas, such as radio frequency identification technology. I told him that his alumni database would be his entire search, and it was. He got a copy of the alumni directory and looked for the names of people who were working in the companies he was interested in. He sent 40 E-mails (which were opened because he put his school's name in the "subject" line) and got responses from 12 alumni who were glad to talk to him about the new technologies and the organizations for which they worked. Martin asked each alumnus about the field, but he also asked for the names of the right person he should contact in each company. Then he used

the alumnus's name when he contacted the appropriate manager. To keep up momentum, Martin sent out 40 more E-mails. Needless to say, all his hard work paid off. Martin accepted a one-year assignment in London with his present employer. He plans to stay in touch with his new Stanford network through E-mail to ensure he will be able to find a job quickly when he returns to the United States.

Network with Five O'Clock Club Alumni

Thousands of successful Five O'Clock Club graduates have volunteered to help current job hunters who are attending the Club. The profile of our alumni is impressive: 40 percent of our attendees earn more than $100,000 per year and a growing number earn in excess of $200,000 (60 percent earn under $100,000 a year).

If you are attending the Club, simply go to our website (www.fiveoclockclub.com), to the "Network with Alumni" area. Just key in the name of the industry or field you're interested in and you will get back up to 20 names at a time. You must have attended four group sessions (so we're sure you know how to network properly, The Five O'Clock Club way) and you must be part of the database yourself. Just fill out the form at this link: www.fiveoclockclub.com/exitsurvey

Be sure you check off that you agree to be contacted yourself (question 26 or 33) and then call us for the code to get in. There is absolutely no risk: After signing up, you will be invited to view, make changes to, or suspend your listing at any time. The only information that will appear will be your name, title, employer, industry, field, and method by which *you select* to be contacted. The information will be available only to graduates and current attendees who have been carefully screened by their career coaches. And of course you have access to the alumni database yourself.

www.linkedin.com

Linkedin.com is a network of professional job seekers. Since members refer each other, it is a network of "trusted professionals." Service is free and peole join by being referred online (via E-mail) by a classmate, coworker, colleague, or other professional. Members fill out a profile, which allows them to search the network for contacts by such things as job title, job function, location, etc.; it also allows others to contact them. Members can access via these searches those who are not in their own network, but in the overall database. There are more than 300,000 job listings from more than 1,000 employers worldwide. Jobs are posted directly on the employers' own sites. This network allows users to get needed introductions to a hiring manager or recruiter. For example, a member can call a hiring manager and say, "Joan Smith of Exco recommended that I call you," even if he or she only knows Joan via a network search.

Linkedin.com has been getting rave reviews at The Five O'Clock Club as of this writing. Says one member, "Linkedin.com is a terrific web-based tool that can help extend a person's network and simplify the process of identifying members of your network in target companies. It's free to join so I've tried to recruit lots of other Five O'Clock Clubbers. As a quick anecdote, I received a cold call this morning from a distant contact in my linkedin network who is looking for help on a number of his projects. I was the perfect fit. A perfect lead! Good luck. And pass it on. If you join, make sure to connect to me; the bigger your network the more effective it will be."

Other Sources

The press. Read newspapers and magazines with *your target in mind,* and you will see all kinds of things you would not otherwise have seen. And don't be afraid to contact the author of an article in a trade magazine. Tell him or her how much you enjoyed the article, what you are trying to do, and ask to get together just to chat. I've made many friends this way. And don't be afraid to contact someone quoted or mentioned in an article.

Mailing lists are not that expensive. You will pay perhaps $100 for several thousand names selected by certain criteria, such as job title, level, industry, size of organization, and so on. You can rent lists from direct-mail houses or magazines. For example, Paul contacted a specialized computer magazine and got the names and addresses by selected zip codes of organizations that owned a specific kind of computer. It was then easy for him to contact all the organizations in his geographic area that could possibly use his skills.

Chambers of Commerce. If you are doing an out-of-town job search, call the local chamber of commerce for a list of organizations in their area. Local business publications can be very helpful as well. In Chicago and New York, for example, *Crain's Business* is a great resource; it publishes annual lists for every industry in the geographic area.

Universities have libraries or research centers on fields of interest. Your research may turn up the name of a professor who is an expert in a field that interests you. Contact him or her.

Networking is a great research tool. At the beginning of your search, network with peers to find out about a field or industry. When you are really ready to get a job, network with people two levels higher than you are.

Don't overlook the obvious! **The Yellow Pages** is a useful source of organizations in your local area. If you're in sales, for example, and you want to know all of the companies within a certain industry with offices in your geographic area, let your fingers do the walking! I can think of no better place than the Yellow Pages. You should look in the hard-copy Yellow Pages, but you could also search in the Yellow Pages online, such as at www.yellowpages.com.

Databases at your library. A CD-ROM database organizes data on a compact disk. This is important because:

1. One disk can hold several volumes' worth of printed material. For example, the *Encyclopedia of Associations* comprises 13 volumes, which would fill a couple of bookshelves. However, all 13 of these volumes are contained on *one* CD!

2. Information can be updated much more frequently on a CD. Publishers can and do release current information on a quarterly basis that is simply "downloaded" onto a disk. Contrast this with print volumes, which can take years to be reprinted and republished. By this time, the new information is often already out of date.

3. You can access and retrieve desired information in a fraction of a second when using CD technology. You simply type the keyword you want to look up. Any information containing the keyword is presented to you almost instantly. When you use printed works, searching for specific pieces of information can be very time consuming.

Libraries. Do not rely only on the Internet for your information. Google cannot replace your local librarian. Libraries have been very enthusiastic adopters of technology. The trend is to continue moving to remote self-service. For example, QuestionPoint is 24-hour live library assistance offered by 1,500 libraries worldwide. Technology inside the libraries themselves is a tremendous source of information for your search, so you may just have to pick yourself up and go there to get the really useful data.

Libraries can often provide you with lists of contacts that will form the basis for your entire search. Many Five O'Clock Clubbers have come into the small-group meetings with disks or computer-printed lists of organizations obtained at the library. See what *your* library has. Many libraries have a system where you can key in the zip codes by which you want to search, the SIC or NAICS codes, and size of the organization. You type, "I'm interested in organizations from $5 million to $10 million in sales," and/or "I want organizations in my geographic area that have between 60 and 200 employees." The system will

download or print out the name of the organization, the address, all of the principals (the president, vice president, and other officers), the type of organization (i.e., the product or service), and other information. This could be your entire job-search list! You can look at that list and do some weeding, "Oh, I'm not interested in this organization. Yes, I'm interested in that one." And you'd refine your target list.

How to access the New York Public Library's directories and guides online. You can now search the New York Public Library's directories and guides via the Internet. Go to: www.nypl.org/research/sibl/guides. The page "Research Guides" will appear. There are a limited number of topics on this page, but if one is of interest to you, click on it; these guides will lead you to a variety of websites, databases, and directories to speed your search.

Also on the "Research Guides" page, click on "Industry Specific Directories," which will open a page **containing links to about 75 industries and professions**. Clicking on one of these will open another page with a list of directories for that topic. Use this list to see if any of these seem helpful and call your local library (or the closest major library in a nearby city or at a nearby college) to see if they have what you want. Join the library online so you can access the databases from your home computer!

These lists are updated regularly. The "Job Targets" section at the back of this book lists the best of these references.

Library-Selected Job Boards—General and Specific

To browse job boards that librarians have researched, go to www.nypl.org/branch. Then access the Mid-Manhattan Library by scrolling down the page and clicking on "Job Information." When the "Job Information Center/Mid-Manhattan Library" page appears, go to "Internet Resources" and click on "Job Search Resources on the Internet." The page titled "Employment" opens. If you click on "Job Searching—General Resources," you will get a listing of job boards with links to all of them. These have been selected by the librarians as the best general job boards. This list is updated every few days.

If you go back to the page marked "Employment," click on "Job Listings—Specific Categories." This will open a page with a list of about 25 categories. Clicking on a specific category will open another page with links for job boards specific to that category. These links are updated regularly by the library staff.

The bibliography in our Members Only area is a great resource containing much more information than is at the back of this book, although in the book it's very handy. Sometimes I meet with a client who says, "I don't know how I can find out the names of organizations in this target area" or "How can I find out about these industries?" I just reach for the *bibliography* at the back of the book and look up the industries in which they're interested. I can point out, "Well, here are five or six sources you might consider— just to find out what's going on in that industry."

Contacting the Company or Organization To Find the Name of the Right Person To Contact

Obviously, it's easier to build lists of *organizations*, but the names of the right people can be more elusive. So, sometimes you just *have* to call the organization and *probe* to find the right person to contact. For example, if you're in customer service, you can call up an organization and say, "May I have the name of the head of customer service?" or "I have to send some correspondence to your head of customer service. Who would that be?" Sometimes you can call and ask for the right person, but sometimes you need to *write* to someone asking for the correct name. (See the chapter, "Handling the Telephone: A Life Skill.")

This can be tough, so brainstorm with your small group to see how you can get the information *you* need for developing your target list. Make sure you get your group to help you. That's why we *have* small groups. You need *other* people's brains to help you in your search. And it's not just enough to get advice from your friends.

Job Postings

Many websites list job postings: Monster.com, AOL, and many field- and industry-specific sites. These sites help you find out who is hiring—even if the postings are not right for you. You don't necessarily need to apply for those jobs, but these sites do give you an idea of what's happening. Consider Businessweek.com, for example. If you click on careers from their home page, you'll find a link entitled, "Who's hiring, looking for an organization?" Clicking there will bring up a huge list of organizations alphabetically with their job postings, a list of the organization job sites, and links to organization websites. See the bibliography of this book for many additional sources.

Classified Ads

Many job hunters place false hopes on the "help wanted" pages. We know most good jobs are never listed in the classified ads and you'll face stiff competitors when you do answer ads. However, studying the ads can be useful. Look at the ads to see *who's hiring*. It doesn't matter whether they list jobs that are appropriate for you. If they're hiring and you're interested in the *organization*, add them to your target list. A Five O'Clock Club maxim is to aim for organizations, not just the jobs. If that industry is not currently on your Personal Marketing Plan, perhaps it's time for you to start a new category.

And no grown-up will ever understand that this is a matter of so much importance!
Antoine de Saint-Exupéry, *The Little Prince*

Additional Resources

Jobvault.com (Vault.com) provides information on more than 1,200 organizations. If you click on "fashion," for example, it will bring up links to articles about the fashion industry and its leading players. You can click on health care, investment banking, and many other major industries. Vault.com doesn't offer information on minor industries; its goal is to provide you with the *inside scoop* on key industries *from a job hunter's point of view*. There are plenty of sites out there where you can find out about an industry from the investor's point of view, but Vault.com offers the *employee* perspective.

Wetfeet.com is a great site for an *introduction* to various industries.

The electric library (elibrary.com) costs about $10 a month and is especially useful for researching small organizations; it often contains full articles on companies that don't catch mainstream attention.

Government websites. Do you want to work for the government? Even at the state level, you will find abundant information. For example, if you wanted a job in Tennessee, try www.tennessee.gov and click on "A to Z Departments and Agencies." It's exciting to see the list of departments. Starting with "A," the listings include the appellate courts, the department of agriculture, the alcoholic beverage commission, the arts commission, and the attorney general. Review the various departments and see if there are a few that are of special interest to you. At the top of the Tennessee.gov home page is a link to "employment." You can search for jobs and submit an application. But you could also target specific agencies that interest you, send your résumé directly to them, call them, and tell them that you are specifically interested in their agency. If you have a specific agency or two in mind, add them to your target list.

Info track, at your library. Info track has full articles and recent stock reports on organizations. On the web, it's **www.Multex.com**. It offers research reports from international brokerage firms and research providers geared to corporate finance specialists, investment bankers, and institutional investors. Stock analysts reports will tell you what's happening in industries as well as in organizations.

PRNewswire.com. When companies and organizations issue press releases, they can also have them listed on prnewswire.com. This is a great way to find out what's going on in any industry you're targeting as well as the major players in that industry.

Nexus, at the library, is a great resource for finding out about a specific *person* to whom you may be talking.

Encyclopedia of Business Information Sources is also a book found at your library. It covers more than *1,000* subjects of interest to business. Select a topic, any topic. If you're interested in "oil," for example, it will tell you the trade journals and books having to do with oil, the associations to join, and helpful websites. If you're interested in rugs, you can find out everything that is happening in the rug industry. The same is true for banking, airlines, or whatever interests you. This is one of my favorite sources.

The "Job Bank" Series of Books

You may live in one of the areas covered by the *Job Bank* series. These are: Atlanta, Austin, Boston, Carolina, Chicago, Colorado, Connecticut, Dallas-Fort Worth, Detroit, Florida, Houston, Indiana, Las Vegas, Los Angeles, Minneapolis, Missouri, New Jersey, Metropolitan New York, Ohio, Philadelphia, Phoenix, Pittsburgh, Portland, San Francisco Bay Area, Seattle, Tennessee, Virginia, Metropolitan Washington, DC. These directories list the industries, as well as the organizations within those industries, and basic contact information. You'll still need to find the names of people to contact in each organization, but these books are great for developing your Personal Marketing Plan.

Not-for-Profits

Business and industry obviously attract a lot of attention and analysis, so it's relatively easy to develop lists of *for-profit* organizations. In the *not-for-profit* arena, you may need to do more digging. It's often helpful to get the annual reports of organizations working with *many* not-for-profits, such as United Way, Catholic Charities, United Jewish Appeal. Look through the annual report and see the agencies they contribute to. If any of them appeal to you, you're on your way to developing your target list.

Also, go to the *Encyclopedia of Associations* to find associations dealing with the not-for-profit areas that interest you. For example, the National Society for Fund Raising Executives is a tremendous organization, as is the Association of Association Executives.

Small and Private Companies

Business Week and *Inc.* magazine both publish lists of small organizations. *The Encyclopedia of Business Information Sources,* mentioned earlier contains more than 1,000 subjects of interest and reference sources. *Dun & Bradstreet's,* (www.dnb.com), at your local public or business school library, has information on some 160,000 U.S. businesses that have indicated net worths of more than $500,000.

Hoovers Handbook of Private Companies has information on more than 900 nonpublic corporations, such as Milliken & Co. and PricewaterhouseCoopers; hospitals and health care organizations such as Blue Cross, charitable and membership organizations including the Ford Foundation; mutual and cooperative organizations such as IGA; joint ventures such as Motiva; government-owned corporations such as the Postal Service; and major university systems, including The University of Texas system.

Another good source is *Ward's Business Directory of U.S. Private and Public Companies,* which lists more than 114,500 companies, 90 percent of which are private. Locate potential clients and create targeted mailing lists in six volumes, arranged A-Z, geographically, by sales, and SIC or NAICS codes.

You can also use the *Small Business Sourcebook*. It is a guide to sources of information furnished by associations, consultants, educational programs, government agencies, franchisers, trade shows, and venture-capital firms for 100 types of small businesses.

The International Market

One terrific online source is the *Directory of Websites for International Jobs: The Click and*

Easy Guide (Click & Easy Series), 2004, Ron and Caryl Krannich, Impact Publications, www.impactpublications.com. Written by two career and international experts, this 45-page report reveals more than 600 websites for anyone seeking an overseas job.

For a serious search, also take a look at *The Directory of Foreign Firms Operating in the United States,* 2004, Uniworld Business Publications, www.uniworldbp.com It has information on foreign firms with branches, subsidiaries, or affiliates in the United States. The foreign companies listed have a substantial investment in American operations—wholly or partially owned subsidiaries, affiliates, or branches.

The Directory of American Firms Operating in Foreign Countries, Uniworld Business Publications, www.uniworldbp.com, contains more than 3,600 U.S. firms with nearly 36,500 branches, subsidiaries, and affiliates in 187 countries. Available in hard cover, soft cover, and on CD-ROM, the directory consists of three volumes that encompass alphabetical lists of U.S. firms with operations abroad. Each entry contains the company's U.S. address, phone/fax, NAICS (North American Industrial Codes System) and description of principal product/service, and lists the foreign countries in which it has a branch, subsidiary, or affiliate.

Finally, there is www.ugamedia.com. You can find European consultants via a Google search. The site has links to more than 35 European portals and search engines.

Don't overlook the importance of worldwide thinking. A company that keeps its eye on every Tom, Dick and Harry is going to miss Pierre, Hans and Yoshio.

Al Ries and Jack Trout,
Positioning: The Battle for Your Mind

Two Kinds of Research

There are two kinds of research. *Primary* research means talking to people who are doing the kind of work you're interested in or people who *know* something about those industries or organizations. You can get in touch with such people through networking or by contacting them directly. *Primary research simply means talking to people*.

Secondary research is reading materials in print, at the library, or online. In a sense, secondary research is *removed* from the source—it is information written by and about people and organizations.

It is vital to conduct *both* primary and secondary research and keep a balance between the two. Some job hunters would rather spend their time talking with people during their job search. Others prefer to spend their time in the library or working at their computers. But whichever one you *prefer,* do more of the other. You need balanced sources of information in your search.

So, if you like to stay at home or in the library, get out more and talk to people. If you're a person who *loves* the Internet, don't kid yourself that you'll get hired online! And don't *waste* time online and claim you've spent *hours* on job search! Be careful how you spend your time online. Or if you're the type who likes to meet people and press the flesh, spend some time at your computer or in the library so you will sound intelligent and well informed when you have meetings.

Primary research—talking to people—doesn't just happen in offices. You're researching when you're talking to people on a bus or a plane or at a coffee shop. They ask, "What do *you* do for a living?" You say, "Well, this is what I do and this is what I am interested in doing next." They may be able to tell you something about the industry you're interested in. That's research—and it does happen!

You're researching when you go to an *association* meeting, talk to people there, and find out more about what is happening in the industry. You can research while you're at a *party*. These are all examples of primary research—talking to people.

Time to Move On

If you've researched smartly and thoroughly, your Personal Marketing Plan should have taken shape nicely—at least a rudimentary version of it. Now it's time to start contacting the companies and organizations on your target lists. Maybe you've been itching to do this all along, but it was better to spend time *planning* first. Now you're on your way!

In this high-risk society, each person's main asset will be his or her willingness and ability to take intelligent risks. Those people best able to cope with uncertainty—whether by temperament, by talent, or by initial endowment of wealth—will fare better in the long run than those who cling to security.

Michael Mandel, *The High-Risk Society*

The greatest obstacle to discovery is not ignorance— it is the illusion of knowledge.

Edward Bond, *Washington Post,* January 29, 1984

Campaign Checklist

Aim for a critical mass of activity that will make things happen, help you determine your true place in this market, and give you a strong bargaining position.

I plan to approach this target using the following techniques:

1. Do research (gather information at the library and through the Internet).
2. Network (gather information through people).
3. Conduct a direct-mail or targeted-mail campaign.
4. Contact selected search firms.
5. Join one or two relevant trade organizations.
6. Regularly read trade magazines and newspapers.
7. Follow up with "influence" notes.
8. Follow up with key contacts on a monthly basis.
9. Answer ads.
10. Aim to give out as much information as I get.

The best techniques for you to use to get meetings depend on your personality and your target market.

For certain targets, search firms may be the most important technique for getting meetings. In other fields, my own for example, people *rarely* get job leads through search firms. When you are networking in your target market, ask people: "Are there certain search firms you tend to use? How do you go about hiring people?"

If I insist that my work be rewarding, that it mustn't be tedious or monotonous, I'm in trouble. . . . Time after time it fails to become so. So I get more agitated about it, I fight with people about it, I make more demands about it. . . . It's ridiculous to demand that work always be pleasurable, because work is not necessarily pleasing; sometimes it is, sometimes it isn't. If we're detached and simply pick up the job we have to do and go ahead and do it, it's usually fairly satisfying. Even jobs that are repugnant or dull or tedious tend to be quite satisfying, once we get right down to doing them. . . . One of the routine jobs I get every once in a while comes from putting out a little magazine. You have to sort the pages. It's a simple, routine, mechanical sort of job. . . . I never realized that this would be one of the most satisfying parts of the whole thing, just standing there sorting pages. This happens when we just do what we have to do.

Thomas Merton, *The Springs of Contemplation*

Information on Research; Additional Personal Marketing Plans

See our book *Targeting a Great Career* for a thorough discussion of how to research your targets (four chapters on research and a 50-page annotated bibliography on the subject, the best on the market). You will also find additional examples of Personal Marketing Plans, including an extensive write-up for targeting the Internet job market.

Getting Interviews and Building Relationships

Four ways to get interviews in your target market

1. Search Firms
2. Ads
3. Networking
4. Direct Contact:
   - *Targeted Mailing*
   - *Direct-Mail Campaign*
   - *Cold Calls*

Plan to contact or meet the *right* people in *every* company in each of your target areas—as quickly as possible.

Get meetings with people in your target areas through:
- Search Firms
- Ads
- Networking
- Direct Contact

Do not think of these as techniques for getting *jobs*, but as techniques for getting *interviews*.

- After a networking meeting, be sure to keep in touch with the person you met.

- After a job interview, think about what you can do next to turn the situation into a job offer.

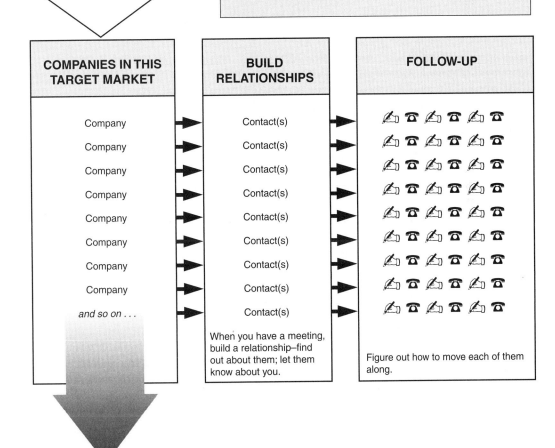

COMPANIES IN THIS TARGET MARKET	BUILD RELATIONSHIPS	FOLLOW-UP
Company	Contact(s)	
Company	Contact(s)	
Company	Contact(s)	
Company	Contact(s)	
Company	Contact(s)	
Company	Contact(s)	
Company	Contact(s)	
Company	Contact(s)	
and so on . . .	Contact(s)	

When you have a meeting, build a relationship—find out about them; let them know about you.

Figure out how to move each of them along.

The
Five
O'Clock
Club

How to Network Your Way In

I use not only all the brains I have, but all I can borrow.

Woodrow Wilson

In the old days, networking was a great technique. We job hunters were appreciative of the help we got and treated those we met with respect and courtesy. We targeted a field and then used networking to meet people, form lifelong relationships with them, and gather information about the area. We called it "information gathering," but it also often led to jobs.

Today, stressed-out, aggressive, demanding job hunters want a job quickly and expect their "contacts" to hire them, refer them to someone important (obviously not the person with whom they are speaking), or tell them where the jobs are. The old way worked; this new attitude does not. This chapter tells you how to network correctly.

Network informally by talking to acquaintances who may know something about your target area. **Network formally** by contacting people at their jobs to get information about their organization or industry. Networking is one way to find out what skills are needed where, what jobs may be opening up, and where you might be able to fit in. Use the networking—or information-gathering—process *to gather information and to build new relationships.*

Gather Information

Networking is one way to find out what skills are needed where, what jobs may be opening up, and where you may be able to fit in. Talking to people because "they might know of something for me" rarely works.

Build Lifelong Relationships

You are also trying to build lifelong relationships. If a target area interests you, get to know the people in it and let them get to know you. It is unreasonable to expect them to have something for you just because you decided to contact them right now. Some of the most important people in your search may provide you with information and no contacts. Be sincerely grateful for the help you get, form a relationship that will last a lifetime, and plan to **recontact regularly the people you meet**.

Remember, you are not talking to people assuming they have heard of job openings. That approach rarely works. For example, if someone asked you if you happen to know of a position in the purchasing department in your old organization, your answer would be no. But if they said, "I'm really interested in your former organization. Do you happen to know *anyone* I could talk to there?" you could certainly give them the name of someone.

This is how people find jobs through networking. As time passes, the people you've met hear of things or develop needs themselves. If you keep in touch, they will tell you what's happening. It is a long-term process, but an effective one.

As you talk to more and more people, you will gather more and more information about business situations and careers in which you think you are interested. And the more people you meet and tell about your career search, the more people are out there to consider you for a job or a referral to a job when they know of one. But, remember, they have to know you first. Networking allows you to meet people without asking them for a job and putting them on the spot. And the fact is, **if they like you and happen to have a job that's appropriate for you, they will *tell* you about it—you will not have to ask**.

People *like* to talk to sincere, bright people and send on those who impress them. People will not send you on if you are not skilled at presenting yourself or asking good questions.

CASE STUDY *Monica*
Networking when You Don't Know Anyone

Monica moved to Manhattan from a rural area because she wanted to work in publishing. She found a temporary job and then thought of ways to network in a city where she knew no one. She told everyone she had always wanted to work in publishing and would like to meet with people who worked in that industry. She told people at bus stops, church, and restaurants. She read *Publishers Weekly*, the publishing trade magazine, to find out who was doing what in the industry and contacted some people directly. She also joined an association of people in the publishing industry. At meetings, she asked for people's business

cards and said she would contact them later. She then wrote to them and met with them at their offices.

Monica found that one of the best contacts she made during her search was a man close to retirement who was on a special assignment with no staff. There was no possibility of her ever working for him, but he gave her great insights into the industry and told her the best people to work for. He saved her from wasting many hours of her time and she felt free to call him to ask about specific people she was meeting.

Over time, lots of people got to know Monica and Monica got to know the publishing industry. She eventually heard of a number of openings and was able to tell which ones were better than others. Monica is off to a good start in her new profession because she made lifelong friends she can contact *after* she is in her new job.

Using the networking technique correctly takes:

- time (because setting up meetings, going on them, and following up takes time),
- a sincere desire for information and building long-term relationships, and
- preparation.

You Are the Interviewer

In an information-gathering meeting, *you* are conducting the meeting. The worst thing you can do is to sit, expecting to be interviewed. The manager, thinking you honestly wanted information, agreed to see you. Have your questions ready. After all, you called the meeting.

Our plans miscarry because they have no aim. When a man does not know what harbor he is making for, no wind is the right wind.

Seneca the Younger, Roman statesman

Questions You May Want to Ask

To repeat: People will be more willing to help you than you think *if* you are sincere about your interest in getting information from them *and* if you are asking them appropriate questions to which you could not get answers through library research or from lower-level people.

If what you really want from them is a job, you will not do as well. At this point, you don't want a job, you want a meeting. You want to **develop a relationship with them**, ask them for information, tell them about yourself, see if they can recommend others for you to talk to, and build a basis for contacting them later.

Before each meeting, write down the questions you sincerely want to ask *this specific person*. (If you find you are asking each person exactly the same thing, you are not using this technique properly.) Some examples:

The Industry

- How large is this industry?
- How is the industry changing now? What are the most important trends or problems? Which parts of the industry will probably grow (or decline) at what rates over the next few years?
- What are the industry's most important characteristics?
- What do you see as the future of this industry 5 or 10 years from now?
- What do you think of the organizations I have listed on this sheet? Which ones are you familiar with? Who are the major players in this industry? Which are the better organizations?

The Company or Organization

- How old is the organization and what are the most important events in its history? How large is the organization? What goods and services does it produce? How does it produce these goods and services?
- Does the organization have any particular clients, customers, regulators, etc.? If so, what are they like and what is their relationship to the organization?

- Who are your major competitors?
- How is the company organized? What are the growing areas? The problem areas? Which areas do you think would be good for me given my background?
- What important technologies does this organization use?
- What is the organizational culture like? Who tends to get ahead here?
- What important challenges is the organization facing right now or in the near future?

The Job or Function

- What are the major tasks involved in this job? What skills are needed to perform these tasks?
- How is this department structured? Who reports to whom? Who interacts with whom?
- What is it like to work here? What is the organization's reputation?
- What kinds of people are normally hired for this kind of position?
- What kind of salary and other rewards would a new hire usually get for this kind of job?
- What are the advancement opportunities?
- What skills are absolutely essential for a person in this field?

The Person with Whom You Are Meeting

- Could you tell me a little about what you do in your job?
- How does your position relate to the bottom line?
- What is the most challenging aspect of your job?
- What is the most frustrating aspect of your job?
- What advice would you give to someone in my position?
- What are some of the intermediate steps necessary for a person to reach your position?
- What do you like or dislike about your job?
- How did you get into this profession or industry?
- What major problems are you facing right now in this department or position?

The Information-Gathering or Networking Process

1. **Determine your purpose.** Decide what information you want or what contacts you want to build. Early on in your job search, networking with people at your own level helps you research the field you have targeted. At this point in your search, you are not trying to get hired. Later, meet with more senior people. *They* are in a position to hire you someday.

2. **Make a list of people you know.** In the research phase, you made a list of the organizations you thought you should contact in each of your target areas. You need lists of important people or organizations you want to contact. Then, when you meet someone who tends to know people, you can ask if he or she knows anyone on your list.

   Now make a list of all the people you already know (relatives, former bosses and coworkers, your dentist, people at your church or synagogue, former classmates, those with whom you play baseball). Don't say you do not know enough appropriate people. If you know one person, that's enough for a start.

   Don't discard the names of potential contacts because they are not in a position to hire you. Remember, you are not going to meet people to ask for a job, but to ask for information. These contacts can be helpful, provide information, and most likely have other friends or contacts who will move you closer and closer to your targets.

People to Contact in Each Target Area

In the chapter "Research: Developing Your List of Organizations to Contact," you made a list of organizations you want to contact in each of your target areas. Then you used the "Sample Personal Marketing Plan" as a model for your own complete list. Now you want to get in to see the people at these and other organizations.

For each target, list on the following page the names of people you know, or know of, or even generic names (such as "lawyers who deal with emerging businesses") who can help you in each target. Whether you contact them through networking or a targeted mailing, the meetings will all be networking meetings.

You will not be idly chatting with these people. Instead, you will have your pitch ready (see the chapter on the Two-Minute Pitch in our book *Mastering the Job Interview and Winning the Money Game*) and will tell them the target you have in mind. The target will include the industry or organization size, the kind of position you would like, and the geographic area. For example:

"I'm interested in entrepreneurially driven, medium-sized private organizations in the Chicago area. I would do well as a chief financial or chief administrative officer in that kind of organization. Can you suggest the names of people who might have contact with those kinds of organizations or do you know anyone who works at such an organization or an organization on my list?"

Tell *everyone* the target you are going after—including people you meet on the train and at the barbershop or beauty salon. You never know who knows somebody.

If you have always done it that way, it is probably wrong.

Charles Kettering

---

3. **Contact the people you want to meet.** Chances are, you will simply call (rather than write to) people you already know—those on your "People to Contact" list. In the beginning of your search, practice on people who know you well. If you say a few things wrong, it won't matter. You can see them again later.

   But as you progress in your search, most of the people you meet should not be people you know well. Extend your network beyond those people with whom you are comfortable. (See the worksheet on the next page.)

People to Contact in Each Target Area

You made a list of organizations to contact in each of your target areas. Now you will show your list to those with whom you network because you want to get in to see those on your list and other organizations as well.

For each target, list below the names of people you know, or know of, or even generic names, such as "lawyers who deal with emerging businesses." You will contact them through networking or a targeted mailing. The meetings you set up will be networking meetings. However, you will not be idly chatting with people. Instead, you will have your "pitch" ready (See Two-Minute Pitch in our book *Mastering the Job Interview and Winning the Money Game*) and will tell them the target you have in mind. The target will contain the industry or organization size, the kind of position you would like, and the geographic area. For example:

"I'm interested in entrepreneurially driven, medium-sized private organizations in the Chicago area. I would do well as a chief financial or chief administrative officer in such an organization. Can you suggest the names of people who might have contact with those kinds of organizations, or do you know anyone who works at such an organization?"

You will tell *everyone* the target you are going after—including people you meet on the train and at the barbershop or beauty salon. You never know who knows somebody.

Target 1	Target 2	Target 3	Target 4	Other Names
				such as: dentist, hairdresser, neighbors

As you build your network of contacts (people you know refer you to people you don't know and they refer you to others), you will get further away from those people with whom you originally began. But as you go further out, you are generally getting closer to where the jobs are. Be willing to go to even further networking levels. Many people report that they got their jobs through someone six or seven levels removed from where they started.

You will probably want to contact people you do not know personally by letter. Force yourself to write that letter and then follow up. People who are busy are more likely to spend time with you if you have put some effort into your attempt to see them. Busy people can read your note when they want rather than having to be dragged away from their jobs to receive your phone call. Often, people who receive your note will schedule an appointment for you through their secretary and you will get in to see them without ever having spoken to them. (On the other hand, some job hunters are in fields where people are used to picking up the phone. "Cold calling" can work for them.)

"I'm sorry, but Mr. Roberts no longer takes meetings, phone calls, cell calls, faxes, snail mail, e-mail, messages, notes or appointments. Is there anything else we can do for you?"

- Identify the link between you and the person you wish to meet; state why you are interested in talking to her or him.
- Give your summary and two short examples of achievements of possible interest to him or her.
- Indicate that you will call in a few days to see when you can meet briefly.

A Sample Note for Information Gathering

Dear Mr. Brown:

Penny Webb suggested I contact you because she thought you could give me the information I need.

I'm interested in heading my career in a different direction. I have been with Acme Corporation for seven years and I could stay here forever, but the growth possibilities in the areas of interest to me are extremely limited. I want to make a move during the next year, but I want it to be the right move. Penny thought you could give me some ideas.

I'm interested in human resources management. My seven years' experience includes the development of an executive compensation system that measures complex human resource variables. For the past two years, I have been the main liaison with our unions and am now the head of the labor relations section. In this position, I managed the negotiation of six union contracts—and accomplished that feat in only 90 days.

I'd like some solid information from you on the job possibilities for someone like me. I'd greatly appreciate a half hour of your time and insight. I'll call you in a few days to see when you can spare the time.

Sincerely,

Levels of Networking Contacts

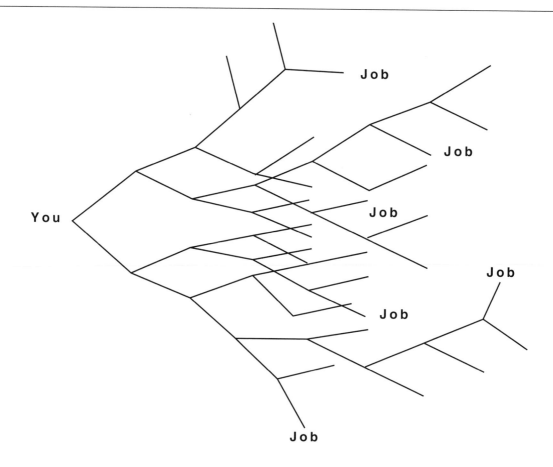

As you build your network of contacts (people you know refer you to people you don't know and they refer you to others), you will get further away from those people you originally knew personally. But as you go further out, you are generally getting closer to where the jobs are.

Be willing to go to further networking levels. Many people report that they got their jobs six or seven levels removed from where they started.

If there are obstacles, the shortest line between two points may be the crooked line.
Bertolt Brecht, *Galileo*

> **Enclose your résumé if it supports your case. Do not enclose it if your letter is enough or if your résumé hurts your case.**

. . . we know that suffering produces perseverance; perseverance character; and character hope.

Romans 5: 3–4

4. **Call to set up the appointment** (first, build up your courage). When you call, you will probably have to start at the beginning. Do not expect the person to remember anything in your letter. Don't even expect him to remember that you wrote at all. Say, for example, "I sent you a letter recently. Did you receive it?"

Remind him of the reason you wrote. Have your letter in front of you—to serve as your script—because you may again have to summarize your background and state some of your accomplishments.

If the person says the organization has no openings at this time, that is okay with you— you were not necessarily looking for a job; you were looking for information or advice about the job possibilities for someone like you or you wanted to know what is happening in the profession, organization, or industry.

If the person says he is busy, say, "I'd like to accommodate your schedule. If you like, I could meet you in the early morning or late evening." If he or she is still too busy, say, "Is it okay if we set something up for a month from now? I would call you to confirm so you could reschedule our meeting if it's still not a good time for you. And I assure you I won't take up more than 20 minutes of your time." Do your best to get on his calendar—even if the date is a month away. (Remember: You are trying to form lifelong relationships. Don't force yourself on people, but do get in to see them.)

Don't let the manager interview you over the phone. You want to meet in person. You need face-to-face contact to build the relationship and be remembered by the manager.

Rather than leave a message, keep calling back to maintain control. If no one returns your call, you will feel rejected. But be friendly with the secretary; apologize for calling so often. An example: "Hello, Joan. This is Louise DiSclafani again. I'm sorry to bother you, but is Mr. Johnson free now?"

"No, Ms. DiSclafani, he hasn't returned yet. May I have him call you?"

"Thanks, Joan, but that will be difficult. I'll be in and out a lot, so I'll have to call him back. When is a good time to call?"

Expect to call 7 or 8 times. Accept it as normal business. It is not personal. (See the section, "How to Use the Telephone.")

5. **Prepare for the meeting.** Plan for a networking meeting as thoroughly as you would for any other business meeting. Follow the agenda listed in step 6. **Remember: It is *your* meeting. You are the one running it.** Beforehand:

- Set goals for yourself (information and contacts).
- Jot down the questions you want answered.
- Find out all you can about the person, and the person's responsibilities, and areas of operations.
- Rehearse your Two-Minute Pitch and accomplishments.

Develop good questions, tailoring them to get the information you need. Make sure what you ask is appropriate for the person with whom you are meeting. You wouldn't, for example, say to a senior vice president of marketing, "So, tell me how marketing works." That question is too general. Instead, do your research—both in the library and by talking with more junior people.

Decide what information you want or what contacts you want to build. Early on in your job search, networking with people at your own level helps you research the field you have targeted. At this point in your search, you are not trying to get hired. Later, meet with more senior people—the ones who are in a position to hire you someday.

Then when you meet the senior vice president, ask questions that are more appropriate for someone of that level. You may want to ask about the rewards of that particular business, the frustrations, the type of people who succeed there, the group values, the long-range plans for the business. Prepare 3 to 5 open-ended questions about the business or organization that the person will be able to answer.

If you find you are asking each person the same questions, think harder about the information you need or do more library research. The quality of your questions should change over time as you become more knowledgeable, more of an insider, and more desirable as a prospective employee. In addition, you should be giving information back. If you are truly an insider, you must have information to give.

If you think education is expensive, try ignorance.
Derek Bok

6. **Conduct the meeting.** If this is important to you, you will continually do better. Sometimes people network forever. They talk to people, but there is no flame inside them. Then one day something happens: They get angry or just fed up with all of this talking to people. They interview better because they have grown more serious. Their time seems more important to them. They stop going through the motions and get the information they need. They interview harder. They feel as though their future is at stake. They don't want to chat with people. They are hungrier. They truly want to work in that industry or that organization. And the manager they are talking to can sense their seriousness and react accordingly.

Nothing great was ever achieved without enthusiasm.
Ralph Waldo Emerson, *Circles*

Business is a game, the greatest game in the world if you know how to play it.
Thomas J. Watson Jr., former CEO of IBM

Format of an Information-Gathering Meeting

Prepare for each meeting. The questions you want to ask and the way you want to pitch, or position, yourself, will vary from one meeting to another. Think it all through. **Review the "Format of a Networking Meeting" before** *every* **networking meeting. If you use it, you will have a good meeting.**

- **Exchange Pleasantries**—to settle down. This is a chance to size up the other person and allow the other person to size you up. It helps the person make a transition from whatever he or she was doing before you came in. One or two sentences of small talk: "Your offices are very handsome" or "Your receptionist was very professional" or "You must be thrilled about your promotion."

- **Why am I here?** The nature of your networking should change over time. In the beginning, you don't know much and are asking basic questions. But you can't keep asking the same questions. Presumably, you have learned something in your earlier meetings. As you move along, you should be asking different, higher-level questions—and you should also be in a position to give some information back to people with whom you are meeting. That's what makes you an insider—someone who knows a lot about the field.

  This is a basic example of *Why I am here*: "Thanks so much for agreeing to meet with me. David Madison thought you could give me the advice I need. I'm meeting with CEOs in the Chicago area because I want to relocate here." If the meeting is *in response to a targeted mailing,* you may say something like: "I'm so

Format of a Networking Meeting

Prepare for each meeting. The questions you want to ask and the way you want to "pitch" or position yourself will vary from one meeting to another. Think it all through.

Be sure to read this chapter in detail for more information on the networking, or information-gathering, process.

The Format of the Meeting

- **Pleasantries**—this is a chance to size up the other person and allow the other person to size you up. It's a chance to settle down. Just two or three sentences of small talk are enough.

- **Why am I here?** For example: "Thanks so much for agreeing to meet with me. Ruth Robbins thought you could give me the advice I need. I'm trying to talk to CEOs in the Chicago area because I want to relocate here." Remind the person of how you got his or her name and why you are there.

- **Establish credibility with your Two-Minute Pitch.** After you tell the person why you are there, they are likely to say something like: "Well, how can I help you?" Then you can respond, for example: "I wanted to ask you a few things, but first let me give you an idea of who I am." There are a number of reasons for doing this:

  1. The person will be in a better position to help you if she knows something about you.

  2. It's impolite to ask a lot of questions without telling the person who you are.

  3. You are trying to form a relationship with this person—to get to know each other a bit.

- **Ask questions** that are appropriate for this person. Really think through what you want to ask. For example, you wouldn't say to the marketing manager: "So what's it like to be in marketing?" You would ask that of a more junior person. Consider having your list of questions in front of you so you will look serious and keep on track.

- As the person is answering your questions, **tell him or her more about yourself if appropriate**. For example, you might say: "That's interesting. When I was at XYZ Company, we handled a similar problem in an unusual way. In fact, I headed up the project . . ."

- **Ask for referrals if appropriate.** For example: "I'm trying to get in to see people at the organizations on this list. Do you happen to know anyone at these organizations ? . . . May I use your name?"

- **Gather more information about the referrals** (such as: "What is Ellis Chase like?").

- **Formal expression of gratitude.** Thank the person for the time he or she spent with you.

- **Offer to stay in touch.** Remember that making a lot of new contacts is not as effective as making fewer contacts and then *recontacting* those people later (see Follow-Up).

- **Write a follow-up note and be sure to follow up again later.**

Remember:

- **You are *not* there simply to get names. You may get excellent information but no names of others to contact. That's fine.**

- **Be grateful for whatever help people give you and assume they are doing their best.**

- **Remember too that this is *your* meeting and you must try to get all you can out of it.**

- **This is not a job interview. In a job interview, you are being interviewed. In a networking meeting, *you* are conducting the meeting.**

93

glad you agreed to meet with me. I've been following your organization's growth in the international area, and thought it would be mutually beneficial for us to meet." Remind the person of how you got his or her name and why you are there. He or she may have forgotten the contents of your letter or who referred you.

Here are additional suggestions on "Why I am here" (Notice how there is a progression going from early on to later in the search process):

- I'm trying to decide what my career path should be. I have these qualifications and I'm trying to decide how to use them. For example, I'm good at ____ and ____. I think they add up to ____. What do you think?

- I want to get into publishing, and I'm meeting people in the field. Dr. Cowitt, my dentist, knew you worked in this industry and thought you would be a good person for me to talk to.

- I've researched the publishing industry and think the operations area would be a good fit for me. I was especially interested in learning more about your organization's operations area and I was thrilled when Charles Conlin at the Publishing Association suggested I contact you.

- I have met with a number of people in the publishing industry and I think some meetings may turn into job offers. I'd like your insight about which organizations might be the best fit for me. I wrote to you because I will be in this industry soon and I know you are one of the most important players in it.

- I've worked in the publishing industry for 10 years and have also learned sophisticated computer programming at night. I am looking for a situation that would combine both areas because the growth opportunities are limited in my present firm. Vivian Belen thought I should speak with you, since your organization is so highly computerized.

- **Establish credibility with your Two-Minute Pitch.** (For more information about this important part of the meeting, see our book.) After you say why you are there, he or she is likely to say something like: "How can I help you?" You respond: "I wanted to ask you a few things, but first let me give you an idea of who I am." There are a number of reasons for doing this:

  1. The person will be in a better position to help you if he or she knows something about you.

  2. It's impolite to ask a lot of questions without telling the person who you are.

  3. You are trying to form a relationship with this person—to get to know each other a bit.

- **Ask questions appropriate for this person.** Really think through what you want to ask. Perhaps have your list of questions in front of you: You will look serious and keep on track.

- **As he or she answers your questions, talk more about yourself** *if appropriate.* "That's interesting. The fact is I've had a lot of public relations experience in the jobs I've held." By the time you leave the meeting, you should know something about each other.

- **Ask for referrals if appropriate.** This is an opportunity to extend your network. "I've made a list of organizations I'm interested in. What do you think of them?" "Are there other organizations you would suggest?" "Whom do you think I should contact at each of the good organizations on this list?" "Could you tell me something about the person you suggested at that organization?" "May I use your name?"

  As you probe, the person may respond that he or she does not know of any job openings. That's okay with you. You simply need to meet with more people in this industry, whether or not they have positions available: "I'm just trying to get as much information as possible."

Some job hunters get annoyed when they go away without contacts. They are thinking short-term and are not trying to build long-term relationships. But you were not *entitled* to a meeting with the manager. He or she was kind to meet with you at all.

If you get no contacts, be very grateful for what you do get. It may be that he or she has no names to give. On the other hand, because many people network incorrectly (aggressively and abrasively), managers are often reluctant to give out names until the job hunter has kept in touch for a number of months and proved his or her sincere interest. Many managers feel used by job hunters who simply want names and are not interested in *them*.

- **Gather more information about the referrals.** (For instance: "What is Harvey Kaplan like?")

- **Formal expression of gratitude.** Thank the person for the time he or she spent with you.

- **Offer to stay in touch.** Constantly making new contacts is not as effective as keeping in touch with old ones. "May I keep in touch with you to let you know how I'm doing?" You might call later for future contacts, information, etc.

- **Write a follow-up note**, and be sure to follow up again later. This is most important and a powerful tool. State how the meeting helped you or how you used the information. Be sincere. If appropriate, offer to keep the manager informed of your progress.

- **Recontact your network every 2 to 3 months.** Even after you get a job, these people will be your contacts to help you in your new job—and maybe you can even help them! After all, you are building lifelong relationships, aren't you? See the chapter "Following Up When There Is No Immediate Job" in this book.

Remember:
- You are *not* there simply to get names. It may

often happen that you will get excellent information but no names of others to contact. That's fine.

- Be grateful for whatever help people give you, and assume they are doing their best.

- Remember, too, that this is *your* meeting and you must try to get all you can out of it.

- This is not a job interview. In a job interview, you are being interviewed. In a networking meeting, you are *conducting* the meeting.

Follow precisely the "Format of a Networking Meeting." If you use it, you will have a good meeting.

Many things are lost for want of asking.
George Herbert, *Jacula Prudentum*

Other Meeting Pointers

- The heart of the meeting is relating your good points in the best way possible. Be concise and to the point. Don't be embarrassed about appearing competent. Be able to recite your Two-Minute Pitch and key accomplishments without hesitation.

- Keep control of the meeting. Don't let the person with whom you're meeting talk too much or too little. If he goes on about something inappropriate, jump in when you can and relate it to something you want to say. Remember, this is *your* meeting.

- Find out which of your achievements he is really impressed with. That's his hot button, so keep referring to those achievements.

- Be self-critical as you go along with this process. Don't become so enamored of the process that you become inflexible. Don't become a professional information gatherer or job hunter.

- Interview hard. *Probe.* Be prepared to answer hard questions in return.

- Take notes when you are getting what you want. This lets the manager know that the meeting is going well and encourages more of the same. The person to whom you are talking is just like everyone else who is being interviewed—everyone wants to do well.

- Show enthusiasm and interest. Lean forward in your chair when appropriate. Ask questions that sincerely interest you and sincerely try to get the answers.

- Don't be soppy and agree with everything. It's better to disagree mildly and then come to some agreement than to agree with everything 100 percent.

- Remember your goals. Don't go away from any meeting empty-handed. Get information or the names of other contacts.

Let your questions focus on the other person. Say, "What do you think?" rather than "Do you agree with me?"

Barry Farber, radio interviewer, *Making People Talk*

- Don't overstay your welcome. Fifteen minutes or half an hour may be all a busy person can give you. Never take more than one-and-a-half to two hours.

- If you are meeting over lunch, go someplace simple so you are not constantly interrupted by waiters.

- If you are looking for a job, don't conceal that fact.

- **If the person you are meeting with suggests passing on your résumé to someone else, that is usually not helpful**—unless you know who the person is and can follow up yourself. Say, "I hate to put you to such trouble. Would you mind if I called her myself and used your name?" If the manager does not agree to this, then you must accept his or her wishes.

- **If the person you are meeting tells you of a job opening**, say, "I'd like to know more about that job possibility, but I also had a few questions I'd like to ask you." Continue to get your questions answered. If you follow up only on the job lead, you will probably wind up with no job and no information.

- It is important to remember that these are only suggestions. You must adopt your own style, your own techniques. You'll find that the more you meet with people, the better you'll get at it. Start out with friends or in low-risk situations. You do not want to meet with your most promising prospects until you are highly skilled at networking meetings. The more you practice, the better you will become.

Who Is a Good Contact?

A contact is any connection between you and the person with whom you are hoping to meet. Most often the contact is someone you've met in another information-gathering meeting, but think a little and you will find other, creative ways to establish links with people. (Also see the chapter "Targeted Mailings: Just Like Networking." Here are a few real-life examples:

Example one: A man's mother used to clean the office of the president of a good-sized corporation. One day the son wrote to the president, "My mother cleaned your office for 12 years." He was granted a meeting with the president and shown a good deal of courtesy. This may seem far-fetched, but it happened.

Example two: Clara wanted to leave an organization where she had worked for nine years. She thought about the person who had taught her data processing years earlier. Her teacher had left the organization to form his own business. She had never kept track of him, but he had impressed her as worldly and she thought he would be a good person to give her advice.

She wrote to him on personal stationery:

Dear Mr. Jones:

You taught me data processing in 1994. I remember it well, since it was the start of my career, and I thought you would be a good person to give me the advice I need.

I'm interested in making a move during the next year or so, but I want it to be the right move.

I now have 10 years of computer experience, specializing in financial and personnel systems. I have used third-generation languages and have designed complicated systems. You may be interested in some of the specific things I've done:

- **Led a three-person team in developing a human resources system that linked salary administration, performance reviews, and employee benefits packages.**
- **Developed a sophisticated accounting system that allowed all of the PCs in the organization to access certain information on the mainframe. All departments in the organization could see the same, updated information.**

I'll call you in a few days to set up a mutually convenient time to get together.

Of course, the man did not know Clara from Adam. She had been one of 28 students in the class he taught at a large organization and was probably the most shy of the group. In fact, after she wrote to him, she became afraid and did not call for two weeks.

When she finally did call, she was told the business had been acquired by another firm and her former teacher had moved from Philadelphia to Chicago. She felt like a fool calling Chicago, but she finally got up the nerve.

When she identified herself to the secretary, she heard, "Clara Horvath! We've been trying to reach you everywhere. Your note didn't contain a phone number!" The secretary said Clara's former teacher was now a senior vice president in Chicago—and had sent the note to the head of the Philadelphia office.

When she called the Philadelphia office, the secretary said, "Clara Horvath! We were hoping you would call. Your note didn't have your phone number."

The secretary arranged for Clara to see the head of the Philadelphia office, who developed a job description for her. According to organizational policy, the job would have to be posted internally and the head of the Philadelphia office would have to interview qualified in-house candidates. After developing a job description to suit Clara, however, the chances were good that he would not find someone internally with her same qualifications.

Clara went to work at the company and it was many months before she finally met the man who was her former teacher. Neither one of them recognized each other, but that was fine!

Life is a series of collisions with the future; it is not a sum of what we have been but what we yearn to be.

José Ortega y Gasset

Other Sources of Contacts

Be sure to read the chapters on research for lots of ideas about associations, alumni groups, and so on. In addition, you can consider:

- Contacting acquaintances—even more than friends. Friends may be reluctant to act as contacts for you. You are more of a reflection on them than you would be for an acquaintance. And if things don't work out, they could lose your friendship—but acquaintances don't have as much to lose.

- Network every chance you get—on the bus, at parties. Don't be like those job hunters who don't tell anyone they are looking for a job. You never know who knows someone who can help you. Everyone you meet knows lots of people.

- Not contacting someone on the strength of *Dun and Bradstreet, Poor's,* or other directories. There is no true link between you and that person. Use your imagination to think of a better link.

Out-of-Town Search

The principles are the same wherever you are. If you have targeted another city, sometimes it is difficult to get face-to-face meetings with some of the people with whom you would like to talk. But plan ahead. If you are making business trips to or attending seminars or taking a vacation in that city, think about who you would like to contact there for your network. Telephone or write to him or her well in advance for an appointment. Keep your ears open about who might be coming through your area and try to get time with him or her if you can.

Summary

Networking is a powerful job-hunting tool—if it is used properly, which most often it is not. It is also a life skill that you can and should use throughout your career. Become expert at it and do not abuse people. Give them something back.

Keep away from people who belittle your ambitions. Small people always do that, but the really great make you feel that you, too, can become great.
Mark Twain

Our dignity is not in what we do but what we understand. The whole world is doing things.
George Santayana, *Winds of Doctrine*

No matter what accomplishments you make, somebody helps you.
Althea Gibson, in *Time,* August 26, 1957

It is better to die on one's feet than to live on one's knees, but some individuals appear actually to believe that it is better to crawl around on one's bare belly.
Nathan Hare, in *The Black Scholar,* November 1969

God does not die on the day when we cease to believe in a personal deity, but we die on the day when our lives cease to be illuminated by the steady radiance, renewed daily, of a wonder, the source of which is beyond all reason.
Dag Hammarskjold

The
Five
O'Clock
Club

Are You Conducting a Good Campaign?

The thing is to never deal yourself out . . . Opt for the best possible hand. Play with verve and sometimes with abandon, but at all times with calculation.

L. Douglas Wilder, in "Virginia's Lieutenant Governor: L. Douglas Wilder Is First Black to Win Office," *Ebony*, April 1986

The Quality of Your Campaign

Getting a job offer is not the way to test the quality of your campaign. A real test is when people say they'd want you—but not right now. When you are networking, do people say, "Boy, I wish I had an opening. I'd sure like to have someone like you here"? Then you know you are interviewing well with the right people. All you need now are luck and timing to help you contact or recontact the right people when they also have a need.

If people are not saying they want you, find out why. Are you inappropriate for this target? Or perhaps you seem like an outsider and outsiders are rarely given a break.

During the beginning of your search, you are gathering information to find out how things work.

Why should someone hire a person who does not already work in the field? Lots of competent people have the experience and can prove they will do a good job.

How You Know You Are in a *Campaign*

You feel as though you know a critical mass of people within that industry. When you go on "interviews," you contribute as much as you take away. You have gained a certain amount of information about the industry that puts you on par with the interviewer—and you are willing to share that information. You are a contributor. An insider.

You know what's going on. You feel some urgency and are more serious about this industry.

You are no longer simply "looking around"— playing it cool. You are more intense. You don't want anything to stand in your way because you know this is what you want. You become more aware of any little thing that can help you get in. Your judgment becomes more finely tuned. Things seem to fall into place.

You are working harder at this than you ever could have imagined. You read everything there is to read. You write proposals almost overnight and hand-deliver them.

Your campaign is taking on a life of its own.

At industry meetings, you seem to know everybody. They know you are one of them and are simply waiting for the right break.

When someone mentions a name, you have already met that person and are keeping in touch with him or her. The basic job-hunting "techniques" no longer apply.

You are in a different realm and you feel it.

This is a real campaign.

There is a test to see if you are perceived as an insider. If you think you are in the right target, talking to people at the right level, and are not early on in your search, you need feedback. Ask people, "If you had an opening, would you consider hiring someone like me?"

Become an insider—a competent person who can prove he or she has somehow already done what the interviewer needs. Prove you can do the job and that the interviewer is not taking a chance by hiring you.

The Quantity of Your Campaign

You need to find a lot of people who would hire you if they could. You know by now that you should **have 6 to 10 things in the works at all times**. This is the only true measure of the effectiveness of your campaign to get meetings in your target area. If you have fewer than this, get more. You will be more attractive to the manager, will interview better, and will lower the chances of losing momentum if your best lead falls apart.

Use the worksheet "Current List of My Active Contacts by Target." At the beginning of your search, these will simply be networking contacts with whom you want to keep in touch. At this stage, your goal is to come up with 6 to 10 contacts you want to recontact later, perhaps every two months. In the middle of your search, the quality of your list will change. The names will be of the right people at the right level in the right organizations. Finally, the 6 to 10 names will represent prospective job possibilities you are trying to move along.

If you have 6 to 10 job possibilities in the works, a good number of them will fall away through no fault of your own (job freezes or hiring managers changing their minds about the kind of person they want). Then you'll need to get more possibilities in the works. With this critical mass of ongoing possible positions, you stand a chance of getting a number of offers and landing the kind of job you want.

There is a tide in the affairs of men, Which, taken at the flood, leads on to fortune; . . . On such a sea we are now afloat; And we must take the current when it serves, Or lose our ventures.

Shakespeare, *Julius Caesar*

Developing Momentum in Your Search

A campaign builds to a pitch. The parts begin to help one another. You focus less on making a particular technique work and more on the situation you happen to be in. This chapter gives you a feel for a real campaign.

In your promotional campaign to get meetings, you see people who are in a position to hire you or recommend you. Keep in touch with them so they will . . .

- think of you when a job opens up,
- invite you to create a job for yourself,
- upgrade an opening to better suit you, and
- give you information to help you in your search.

When you are in the heat of a real campaign, a critical mass of activity builds, so you start:

- hearing the same names,
- seeing the same people,
- contributing as much as you are getting,
- writing proposals,
- getting back to people quickly,
- feeling a sense of urgency about this industry, and
- writing follow-up letters and making follow-up phone calls.

. . . the secret is to have the courage to live. If you have that, everything will sooner or later change.

James Salter, *Light Years*

Eventually, and often after the survival of a long and profound crisis, often after the painful shedding of one skin and the gradual growth of another, comes the realization that the world is essentially neutral. The world doesn't care, and is responsible neither for one's spiritual failures nor for one's successes. This discovery can come as a profound relief, because it is no longer necessary to spend so much energy shoring up the self, and because the world emerges as a broader, more interesting, sweeter place through which to move. The fog lifts, as it were.

Frank Conroy, *The New York Times Book Review,* January 1, 1989

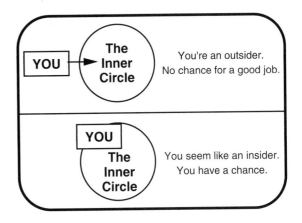

Networking Cover Letters

PHIL GITTINGS
20 Trinity Place
New York, New York 10000
(222) 555-2231
PGittings@earthlink.net

March 10, 200X

Mr. Max McCreery
Executive Vice President
Young & Rubicam
285 Madison Avenue
New York, New York 10017

Dear Mr. McCreery:

I am following up on the suggestion of Nancy Abramson, who refers to herself as a fan of yours, and am writing to ask for your counsel on my current career plans.

I have recently decided to leave my present company, McGraw-Hill Publishing, and continue my career elsewhere. Nancy thought you could give me the advice I need.

I have targeted the advertising industry as part of my search strategy because I believe that my skills in financial planning and problem solving, combined with my international experience, I could make an important contribution to good business management. In addition, I believe I would enjoy working in the dynamic and creative environment of most agencies.

Nancy suggested I ask for your response to my thoughts on how my experience in financial management in the publishing industry can be productively applied in advertising.

Briefly, my experience includes commercial banking (1977–1979) followed by financial analysis at CBS (1979–1981). The largest part of my career was with Time, Inc. (1981–1993), where I served in a variety of financial and administrative assignments, including tours as International Finance Manager, Financial Director of Time's fully independent Mexico subsidiary, and an assignment in the direct marketing group. Following Time, I became a principal in a small publishing company and since 1994 have been Vice President, Administration, at McGraw-Hill Book Clubs.

I look forward to speaking with you and will call in a few days to see when we can meet.

Sincerely,

Phil Gittings

This note was handwritten on informal off-white stationery.

May 19, 200X

Dear Mr. Dittbrenner,

Suzanne Howard suggested I contact you because she thought you could give me the information I need.

I'm interested in heading my career in a different direction. I've been with Rohm and Haas for nine years and I could stay here forever, but the growth possibilities in the areas that interest me are extremely limited. I want to make a move during the next year, but I want it to be the right move. Suzanne thought you could give me some ideas.

I'm interested in human resources. My nine years' experience in data processing included the design and implementation of Rohm and Haas' salary administration system as well as 3 years as Training and Development Director for the MIS Division. For the past two years, I have been in our Advertising Department and am now Advertising and Marketing Services Manager. What I'd like from you is some solid information on the job possibilities for someone like me.

I'd greatly appreciate half an hour of your time and insight. I'll call you in a few days to see when you can spare the time.

Sincerely,

Harvey Kaplan

Jane Hyun

February 2, 200X

Mr. Dwight Clarke
Executive Vice President
Green Card International, Inc.
888 Sixth Avenue
New York, New York 10000

Dear Mr. Clarke:

Rachel Tepfer suggested I get in touch with you.

I am a seasoned financial services marketer at SanguineBank with a strong package goods background and extensive experience in product development and merchandising, branch management, electronic banking, and innovative distribution planning.

- I created the SanguineBank Investment Portfolio, the bank's first complete presentation of its retail savings and investment products, and developed successful ways to sell the SanguineDip account in the retail setting.
- As an Area Director in the New York retail bank, I doubled branch balances in mid-Manhattan in only three years.
- Most recently, I have been developing a set of PC-based fund-transfer products for SanguineBank's Financial Institutions Group.
- Prior to SanguineBank, I rebuilt the baby shampoo division for Johnson & Johnson and managed all bar-soap marketing at Lever Brothers.

A résumé is enclosed for additional background.

I am seeking to move to a new assignment that would take full advantage of my consumer financial services marketing experience, and am extending my search outside of SanguineBank as well as inside. Rachel thought it would be worthwhile for us to meet briefly. I'll call in a few days to set up a mutually convenient time for us to meet.

I'm looking forward to meeting with you.

Sincerely,

Jane Hyun

The
Five
O'Clock
Club

How to Contact Organizations Directly

I don't know anything about luck. I've never banked on it and I'm afraid of people who do. Luck to me is something else: hard work and realizing what is opportunity and what is not.

Lucille Ball

Beth conducted 5 direct-mail campaigns. She selected 5 clear targets and developed lists of names for each, ranging in size from 50 to 200 names. She mailed a cover letter and résumé to her first list. When she started to get calls for meetings, she mailed to her second list. At approximately 2-week intervals, Beth would send out another mailing. She received an excellent response (calls for meetings) from 3 of her 5 mailings.

To develop her interviewing skills and investigate each target area, Beth first had meetings at firms she did not care about. She treated these meetings as networking meetings. Beth probed, for example, to find out what the manager thought of other organizations on her list. If the comments were generally negative, she dropped those organizations. If the comments were positive, she asked if the manager might know someone in the organization whom she could contact. She got a lot of mileage out of her campaign because she combined direct mail with networking and worked the system with great energy.

The entire process took only one-and-a-half months. Beth had clear targets, followed the process, and prepared thoroughly for her meetings. She explored career possibilities in which

she had been somewhat interested and refined her career direction. She turned down a number of job offers before she accepted a high-level position that allowed her to combine her strongest skill area with something that was new to her and satisfied her long-range motivated skills. Beth took a two-week vacation before she started that job. She deserved it.

Jack's campaign strategy was very different. Jack is intelligent, articulate, research oriented—and also very shy. He targeted an industry that would result in a career change for him. He had read a lot about this industry and wanted to find out the job possibilities within it.

Jack meticulously researched organizations and selected 20 in which he was seriously interested. They were huge corporations, which made it relatively easy to get the names of people to contact. If he had simply mailed to that list, however, he might have gotten no response. As you will see later, 20 names is generally not enough for a direct-mail campaign. The effort would have been even more futile in Jack's case because he had, essentially, no hands-on experience in that field.

Jack did a targeted mailing—that is, he wrote to the 20 people and *followed up with phone calls* to all of them. His well-written and convincing letter proved his sincere interest in and knowledge of the field. He sent it without a résumé, because he was making a major career change, and told each of the 20 he would call him or her. He sent all the letters at once and called every person. It was quite an effort. Jack got in to see just about every person on his list and—as usually happens—some of them took a personal interest in his case. They gave him the names of others and told him how to break into the field. Two of his contacts volunteered to sponsor him in their organization's training program.

How It Works

Approximately 20 to 40 percent of all jobs are found through direct-mail campaigns. This technique is even more effective when you combine it with networking—as both Beth and Jack did.

You will do better in your direct-mail campaign when you:

- have clearly identified your target market,
- are familiar with the problems faced by organizations in that market, and
- know what you have to offer to solve its problems.

"I'm sorry, but Mr. Taylor no longer engages in human interaction. He does check his E-mail once a week, though."

Know enough about your target market to compose an appropriate cover letter and to hold your own in a meeting. If you don't know enough, learn more through library research or networking. If you feel you may be caught off-guard in a meeting because of a lack of knowledge of your target market, do not use this technique until you have gained at least some knowledge.

These are not job interviews, but exploratory meetings that may lead to:

- more information,
- names of other people to contact, and/or
- a job interview.

Conduct the meeting using the same format as that of a networking meeting.

Don't let the interviewer know you blanketed the market. If an organization wants to see you, quickly do a little research on it. Tell the manager you wrote to him as a result of your research and name something specific about the organization of interest to you.

It doesn't matter if your meetings come from a direct contact or from networking. What matters is that you get in to see people who are in a position to hire you.

Benefits of This Technique

Direct mail blankets the market. In one fell swoop, you can find out the chances for someone like you in the market. You "market test" what you have to offer and also get your name out quickly to prospective employers. This technique is fast and as complete as you want it to be, as opposed to networking, which is slower and hits your target in a spotty manner.

What Is a Targeted Mailing?

A targeted mailing is direct mail followed by a phone call. Use it when you would like to see every person on your small list. Research so you can write customized letters (you may want to call for annual reports, for example, or talk to people to get information about an organization). Follow the process for networking, paying special attention to the follow-up call, which requires a great deal of persistence. As with networking, you want to meet with people whether or not they have a job to offer.

Passion costs me too much to bestow it on every trifle.

Thomas Adams

An Easy Way to Contact Lots of People

Typically, job hunters do not contact many people. Either the job hunter is unemployed and has the time to contact lots of people but may be suffering from low self-esteem—or is employed and simply does not have the time to contact people during the day. The direct-mail campaign allows a person to contact lots of potential employers despite reluctance or a lack of time.

Sometimes job hunters hit a slump and find networking overly stressful. Direct mail can help you get unstuck. You can hide away for a short while and grind out a mailing. You can sound more self-confident on paper than you actually feel and get your act together before you go out and talk to people. A direct-mail campaign can be a way out of a bind. But eventually you must talk to people. You cannot get a job through the mail. Don't use this technique to avoid people forever. Remember, you are writing so you can get in to see them.

The man without purpose is like a ship without a rudder—a waif, a nothing, a no man. Have a purpose in life, and, having it, throw such strength of mind and muscle into your work as God has given you.

Thomas Carlyle

The Numbers You'll Need

In a small industry, your list will be smaller. In a larger industry, your list may be so large you'll want to hit only a portion of it as a test and then hit another portion later.

The "response rate" is measured by the number of meetings you get divided by the number of pieces you mailed. Meetings count as responses; rejection letters do not. Meetings count because there is the possibility of continuing your job search in that direction. Rejection letters, no matter how flattering, have ended your search in that particular direction.

In direct mailing, a 4 percent response rate is considered very good. The basic rule of thumb is this:

A mailing of 200 good names results in

- seven or eight meetings, which result in
- one job offer.

If your list is smaller, you may still do okay if you are well suited to that target and if there is a need for your services. If, however, your list has only 10 names, you must network in, or use a targeted mailing with a follow-up phone call.

Another factor that affects your response rate is the industry to which you are writing. Certain industries are very people oriented and are more likely to talk to you. Targeting industries that have a great demand for your service should result in a lot of responses.

Assuming that the job you are seeking is reasonable (i.e., you have the appropriate qualifications and there are positions of that type available in the geographic area you are targeting), persistent inquiries will eventually turn up some openings.

What makes men happy is liking what they have to do. This is a principle on which society is not founded.

Claude Adrien Helvetius

Should You Enclose Your Résumé?

If your résumé helps your case, enclose it. Beth enclosed her résumé; Jack did not. Direct-mail experts have proved that the more enclosures, the greater the response rate. You never know what may "grab" the reader and the reader is likely to glance at each enclosure. Your résumé, if it supports your case and is enticing, is another piece to capture the reader's attention. I have been called for meetings because of what was on page three of my résumé.

If, however, your résumé hurts your case, change it or leave it out altogether. A résumé may hurt your case when you are attempting a dramatic career change, as Jack was. (Read the chapter "How to Change Careers" to get more ideas on how you can support your case.)

Cover Letters

The format you follow for your cover letter essentially can be the same whether you enclose your résumé or not. Your cover letter focuses your pitch more precisely than your résumé does and makes the reader see your résumé in that light. You can pitch to a very precise segment of the market by making only minor changes in the letter. The format for your cover letter is:

Paragraph 1—The grabber. Start with the point of greatest interest to your target market. This is the equivalent of a headline in an ad.

If your background is enough of a grabber for the target market to which you are writing, use it. For example, if you want a job in sales and have an excellent track record in that area, then open with a terrific sales accomplishment. Or if your expertise is in turnaround management, your cover letter might start like this:

> As vice president of a $250 million organization, I directed the turnaround of an organization in serious financial difficulty. As a result, this year was more profitable than the previous 10 profitable years combined.

On the other hand, you can open your letter with a statement that shows you understand the problems faced by the industry to which you are selling your services. A successful letter to advertising agencies started like this:

> Many ad agencies are coping with these difficult times by hiring the best creative and sales people available. While this may maintain a competitive edge, many agencies find their bottom line is slipping. The usual response is to send in the accountants. These agencies, and perhaps your own, need more than accounting help. As vice president of operations, I . . .

Here's a variation on the same theme aimed at organizations probably doing well financially:

> I know this is a time of rapid growth and high activity for technology-based firms. I believe this is also a time when technology-based firms must be as effective as possible to maintain their competitive edge. If you are looking for new developers—either on an ad hoc or a permanent basis—consider a person like me.

If you work for a well-known organization in an area that would be of interest to your target market, you could start your letter like this:

> I am at present with X Company in a position where I . . .

Perhaps your background itself would be your key selling point:

> I started out in computers in 1976 and have been involved with them ever since. I am now at . . .

If you are targeting a small number of organizations, mention your specific interest in each one:

> I have been interested in [your organization] for a number of years because of . . .

Paragraph 2—A summary of your background aimed at a target, perhaps taken from the summary statement on your résumé.

Paragraph 3—Your key accomplishments of interest to this target market. These can be written in a bulleted or paragraph format. Make them lively and interesting.

Paragraph 4 (optional)—Additional information. This could include references to your education or personality, or other relevant information, such as:

> I am high in energy and integrity—persuasive, thorough, and self-confident—a highly motivated self-starter accustomed to working independently within the framework of an organization's policies and goals. I thrive on long hours of work, and enjoy an atmosphere where I am measured by my results, where compensation is directly related to my ability to produce, and where the job is what I make it.

Final paragraph—The close. Such as:

> I would prefer working in an environment where my leadership and problem-solving abilities are needed and would be pleased to meet with you to discuss the contribution I could make to your organization.

Or use a statement like this one, which excludes those who may want to hire someone at a lower salary level:

> Hiring me would be an investment in the mid-$70,000 range, but the return will be impressive. I would be pleased to meet with you to discuss the contribution I could make to the performance of your organization.

Or use this statement for a direct-mail campaign where you will not be making follow-up phone calls, especially to a list to which you have some relationship, such as that of an organization of which you are a member:

> I can understand how busy you must be and therefore do not want to bother you with a follow-up phone call. However, I trust that you will give me a call if you come across information that would be helpful to me in my search.

You gain strength, courage and confidence by every experience in which you really stop to look fear in the face. You are able to say to yourself: "I lived through this horror. I can take the next thing that comes along." . . . You must do the thing you think you cannot do.

Eleanor Roosevelt

We African-American women have always worked outside of our homes, in slavery or in freedom—in the fields, in the kitchen, or in the nursery.

Frederica J. Balzano, Ph.D., "And Ar'nt I a Woman?" *The Five O'Clock News*, September 1995

Happiness is not a matter of events; it depends upon the tides of the mind.

Alice Meynell

Pain: an uncomfortable frame of mind that may have a physical basis in something that is being done to the body, or may be purely mental, caused by the good fortune of others.

Ambrose Bierce

The Five O'Clock Club

Targeted Mailings: Just Like Networking

There's nothing to writing. All you do is sit down at a typewriter and open a vein.

Walter ("Red") Smith, in *Reader's Digest,* July 1982

Networking is not the only way to job hunt. Consider targeted mailings when:

- You want to see a particular person but have no formal contact. You must think of how you can create some tie-in to that person and contact him or her directly.
- You have selected 20 to 30 organizations in your target market that you really want to get in to see, and there are only a few jobs that would be appropriate for you in each company. For the 20 or 30 organizations you have chosen, research the appropriate person to contact in each one. Ask each for a meeting—whether or not they have a job for you. You want to get in to see them *all* because your target is very small.

There is no way of writing well and also of writing easily.

Anthony Trollope, *Barchester Towers*

The Letter

- **Paragraph 1:** The opening paragraph for a targeted mailing would follow the format for a

networking letter: State the reason you are writing and **establish the contact** you have with the reader.

> Congratulations on your new position! I know you are extremely busy (I've heard about it from others). After you are settled in, I would be interested in meeting with you. I think it would be mutually beneficial for us to meet, although I have no fixed idea of what could come of it.

After you have found out something about the person or the organization, pretend you are sitting with that person right now. What would you *say* to him or her? Here's what one job hunter wrote to an executive:

> I agree. Your position *is* truly enviable.
>
> With the merger of AT&T and United Telecom completed, AT&T is now positioned to become an even greater force in shaping telecommunications for the future, both domestically and internationally. However, with all the challenges comes the inevitable need for control, resolution of legal and regulatory issues, competitive threats, pricing issues, and reexamination of both the positioning and global packaging of AT&T. Clear, focused strategic and business plans become essential for success. I believe I can help you in these areas.

See the next chapter, "Targeted Mailing Cover Letter: A Case Study," for the rest of this letter. Here's another letter that reflects a great deal of thought:

> As the banks look back on their risky involvement with groups like Campeau, it is clear that a better understanding of the retail business would have saved them from considerable losses. As a result, I'm sure many banks and lending institutions have gone to the opposite extreme. Another solution, however, would be to have an unbiased expert merchant involved in evaluating their retail plans.

Your opening should reflect whatever you know about the organization or the person:

> Whenever people talk about organizations with excellent internal temporary services departments, Schaeffer's name always comes up. In fact, the people who run the Amalgamated Center, where I am now assigned, speak often of the quality of your work. I am interested in becoming a consultant in this field and I hope to meet with you.

- **Paragraph 2:**
  Give a **summary about yourself**.
- **Paragraph 3:**
  Note a few **key accomplishments that would be of interest to this target**.
- **Paragraph 4:**
  Ask for **half an hour** of his time, and say you will **call him in a few days**. For example:

> I am sure a brief meeting will be fruitful for us both. I will call your new secretary in a week or so to see when I can get on your calendar.

or

> I hope you will allow me half an hour of your time and insight to explore this area. I will call you in a few days to set up a mutually agreeable time.

If you plan to follow up with a phone call, say so. (But if you say so, do it—or you may get no response while they wait for your call.)

Life is like playing a violin solo in public and learning the instrument as one goes on.

Samuel Butler

Out-of-Town Search

For an *out-of-town search* (perhaps placed next to the last paragraph):

> As a result of many years' travel to Seattle, I would prefer to live and work in that area. In fact, I am in Seattle frequently on business and can arrange to meet with you at your office.

Who has begun has half done. Have the courage to be wise. Begin!

Horace, Epistles

Scannable Letters

As we have seen, other variations include the use of **underlining key points,** which can increase your response rate. This helps the busy reader scan the letter, be drawn in, and want to read the rest. Underlining makes certain key points pop out at the reader—anywhere in your text. Underline parts of sentences in no more than five places. Read the underlined parts to make sure they sound sensible when read together, have a flow, and make your point.

Even when I look at my own letters, I sometimes don't want to read them before I make them scannable. I rephrase my letters, underlining in a way that will make sense to the reader. People will read the salutation, then the first few words of your letter, and then the parts you have underlined. If they find these things compelling, they'll go back and read the rest of your letter.

Underlining should make sense. Don't underline the word "developed," for instance, which doesn't make sense. Underline *what* you developed, because that's probably the compelling part.

Take calculated risks. That is quite different from being rash.

Gen. George S. Patton, letter to his son, June 6, 1944

Do What Is Appropriate

Strange as it may seem, **sometimes it can be very effective to ignore all of this.** Do what works in your target area. Nat, who was interested in Japanese banks, wrote to 40 banks with a four-line cover letter along these lines: "Enclosed please find my résumé. I have had 20 years of banking experience, am mature, . . ."

Nat knew his market. He thought the Japanese would be put off by the typically aggressive American approach. He got an excellent response rate—and the kind of job he wanted.

Remember, it is sometimes better to follow your instincts rather than listen to the experts. You're smart. You know your market better than we do. Make up your own mind.

The Follow-Up Call (after a Targeted Mailing)

When you call, you will probably have to **start again from the beginning.** Do not expect them to remember anything in your letter. Do not even expect them to remember that you wrote to them. For example, when you phone:

- Say, "I sent you a letter recently. Did you receive it?"
- Remind them of the reason you wrote. You may again have to summarize your background and state some of your accomplishments.

- If they say they have no job openings at this time, that is okay with you—you were not necessarily looking for a job *with them;* you were looking for information or advice about the job possibilities for someone like you, or perhaps you wanted to know what is happening in the profession, organization, or industry.

Leave messages that you called, but do not ask to have them call you back. Chances are, they won't and you will feel rejected. However, be friendly with the secretary and apologize for calling so often. If she would like to have her boss call you back, tell her thanks, but you will be in and out and her boss will be unable to reach you: You will have to call again. After the first call, try not to leave your name again. **Expect to call seven or eight times.** Do not become discouraged. It is not personal.

The way to get good ideas is to get lots of ideas and throw the bad ones away.

Linus Pauling, American chemist

The Meeting

When you go in for your meeting, **handle it as you would a networking meeting** (unless the manager turns it into a job interview):

- Exchange pleasantries.
- State the reason you are there and why you wanted to see this particular person.
- Give your Two-Minute Pitch.
- Tell the manager how he or she can help you. Get the information you want, as well as a few names of other people to whom you should be talking.

As we have said, **be grateful for whatever help people give you.** They are helping you the best they can. If they do not give you the names of others to contact, perhaps they cannot because of a feeling of insecurity in their own jobs. Appreciate whatever they do give you.

For a more detailed description of how to handle the meeting, refer to the chapter "What to Do When Your Networking Isn't Working."

Form a Relationship

Take notes during your meeting. Your follow-up notes will be more appropriate and then you will feel free to contact this person later. Keep in touch with people on a regular basis. Those who know you well will be more likely to help you.

A targeted mailing is a very powerful technique for hitting *every* organization in a small target area. A direct-mail campaign hits every organization in a large target. Both can dramatically move your job hunt along. Try them!

Follow Up

Follow up with a customized note specifically acknowledging the help you received. These notes follow the same concept as follow-ups to networking meetings.

Final Thoughts

You will strike sparks with certain people you meet. They will develop a true interest in you and will surprise you with their help. I have had people invite me to luncheons to introduce me to important people, or call me when they heard news they thought would be of interest to me. I have even made new friends this way.

Of course, I have done my part too by keeping in touch to let them know how my campaign was going. If you are sincere about your search, you will find that the people you meet will also be sincere and will help. It can be a very heartwarming experience.

Without effort we cannot attain any of our goals in life, no matter what the advertisements may claim to the contrary. Anyone who fears effort, anyone who backs off from frustration and possibly even pain will never get anywhere. . . .

Erich Fromm, *For the Love of Life*

CASE STUDY *Ahmed*
Research and Focus

Ahmed had just moved to the United States from Turkey, so he had no contacts here. He had a background in international sales and trading.

He targeted nine major employers and did extensive research on each one. Then he wrote to the head of international sales at each of the nine companies. In his introductory paragraph, he said things like "I notice that your international sales have declined from 6 percent to 3 percent over the last year. I find that very disturbing. I was wondering why that is happening, given the state of the market now . . ."

Paragraph two was his summary. Paragraph three listed his bulleted accomplishments. Paragraph four was the close: "I would really appreciate meeting you . . ."

He called only two of them—because the other seven called him before he had a chance. This targeted mailing resulted in nine meetings and three job offers.

Direct Contact Requires Research and Excellent Writing Skills

Targeted mail works only if you've done your research and if you're a good writer. Furthermore, you must target the right person and have something interesting to say to each person you are contacting. That's why direct contact works best for job hunters who clearly understand their target markets and the important issues in them. And that's also why most people do not attempt direct contact until after they have done their research—through preliminary networking or the library.

Are You Sincere?

It's not enough to write to people and expect to get in to see them. They are probably busy with their own jobs and may be contacted by quite a few people.

Unless you sincerely want to see a person, you won't develop strategies to figure out how to get in to see him or her. You won't do your research. You won't do the follow-up phone calls required to prove your sincerity. You won't prevail when someone doesn't return your phone calls.

If you really want to see this person, you'll persevere. And you won't mind asking for an appointment one month from now if he or she is too busy to see you now. You may even say, "I know you're busy now. How about if we schedule something for a month from now and I'll call you in advance to confirm?"

To Enclose Your Résumé or Not?

A cover story in *Time* magazine was titled "Junk Mail." People said, "Why do junk-mail companies enclose so many things in these envelopes we get? They're wasting paper." In the Letters to the Editor, junk-mail companies said they had no choice because the response rate increased so dramatically with the number of additional enclosures carrying the same message. If they have fewer enclosures, their response rate decreases dramatically.

The same is true for the mailings you are sending. Some people say, "If they see my résumé, they'll know I'm job hunting." But they'll probably know it anyway from your letter. People are very sophisticated today.

My rule of thumb is this: If it supports your case and it has a message that complements your cover letter, then enclose your résumé. You can say, "I've enclosed my résumé to let you know more about me." If you have a brilliant résumé, why not enclose it?

On the other hand, if you want to make a career change, you probably do not want to enclose your résumé because you can probably make a stronger case without it.

Do what is appropriate for you. Try it both ways and see which works better for you and your situation.

Unless you call out, who will open the door?

African proverb

Stating Your Accomplishments in Your Cover Letter

Think of which of your accomplishments are of interest to your target market. You may want to list different accomplishments for the different industries to which you are writing.

Rank your bulleted accomplishments generally in order of importance to the reader, as opposed to chronologically or alphabetically. If some other order would be more appropriate in your case, then do that.

CASE STUDY *Rick*
Out-of-Town Search

A Five O'Clock Club job hunter was looking for a job in Denver. He conducted research by getting a listing of companies from the Denver Chamber of Commerce. He called each company and asked for the name of the department head for the area in which he was interested. He wrote to each one and followed up with a phone call.

He was employed at the time. Yet most of his effort did not take time away from his job. He did his research and wrote his letters evenings and weekends. Networking would have been an impossible way for him to start his search, especially in another part of the country. But after he had made these initial contacts and had traveled to Denver, he could network around.

He wound up with 80 companies to contact—too many for follow-up phone calls. Even 20 is a lot. He followed up with 20 companies and scheduled a three-day trip to Denver. Before he went, he had set up eight meetings for the first two days of his trip. When he met with those first eight, he networked into four additional companies and held those meetings on the third day of his trip.

He didn't have a lot of money, so he couldn't stay long in Denver. But this is also the best way to conduct an out-of-town search—a few days at a time.

When job hunters visit a city for two weeks and hope that something will happen, they usually come home empty-handed. It's better to do your research, contact all of the organizations ahead of time, and go there with meetings already set up. The meetings could be with search firms, in response to ads, or through networking or direct contact.

Go for three days. Tell the people you meet that you are planning to be in town again in a few weeks and would like to meet with other people in their organization or in other organizations. Go back home, do more work, return in another three or four weeks, and stay for another three days. This is how you develop momentum in your out-of-town campaign. A one-time visit rarely works.

Rick went back again six weeks later. It took a few more visits to land the job he wanted, but he did it all with direct and targeted mail as the basis for his campaign, supplemented by networking.

The following pages contain case studies of people who have been successful with targeted mailings. Rather than simply copying their letters, **think of *one* actual individual on your list to whom you are writing and the compelling things you should say to make that person want to meet with you.** Even if you write exactly that same kind of letter to 20 people, it will sound more sincere and have more life if you write that first letter with a particular person in mind.

Targeted Mailing Cover Letter: A Case Study

Faint heart never won fair lady.

Cervantes, *Don Quixote*

Terry was very interested in AT&T. She researched the company and decided to write to the vice chairman of the board. This was an appropriate person for her to write to because he was head of strategic planning, her area of expertise.

She wrote a cover letter using our standard format. The cover letter started out by saying, "I agree with you completely . . ." Then she quoted from an article in which he was mentioned. She was attempting to establish a business relationship with him.

Paragraph two was her summary paragraph. Paragraph three contained her bulleted accomplishments. Paragraph four was her close.

Before sending the letter, she called the company to find out the name of his secretary. It was Kim. Then she called to say that she was writing a letter to Mr. Chase and would Kim please look out for it?

In the last paragraph of her letter, she said, "I would very much appreciate the opportunity to meet with you for half an hour to introduce myself . . . I'll call Kim next week to set up an appointment."

She wound up meeting with the vice chairman, and four other very senior people at AT&T. But the company had a hiring freeze and she ended up working elsewhere.

Was Terry's targeted mailing successful? The answer is yes! Did you forget? Mailings, networking, search firms, and ads are techniques for getting *meetings*. If she got a meeting, the technique was successful. Terry got the meeting she had wanted and more.

By the way, she enclosed her résumé. She was careful not to mention the business she had been in because it was very different from the one at AT&T. But she knew her skills were transferable because she had done so much research on AT&T and could prove it in her letter. She could talk about her background without emphasizing the exact product or service with which she had been involved.

Why Not Network Instead?

When Terry wrote to the vice chairman of the board, she really wanted to see him. If she had decided to network in, it would have taken her a very long time to meet someone who would be willing to introduce her to such an important person. Instead, she did her homework: extensive research and intensive follow-up. Be sure to include targeted mailing in *your* bag of tricks.

Note: Do not necessarily aim for a person at the top of the organization. See people who are appropriate for your level. As a rule of thumb, you want to see people who are two levels higher than you are.

TERRY PILE
Greenwich, CT 02555
212-555-1212 (day)
tpile@trusite.net

August 1, 200X

Mr. Ellis Chase, Vice Chairman
AT&T Corporation
Corporate Planning and Development
One Stamford Forum
Stamford, CT 06904

Dear Mr. Chase:

I agree. Your position *is* truly enviable.

With the merger of AT&T and United Telecom completed, AT&T is now in a position to become an even greater force in shaping telecommunications for the future both domestically and internationally. However, with all the challenges comes the inevitable need for control, resolution of legal and regulatory issues, competitive threats, pricing issues, and reexamination of both positioning and global packaging of AT&T. Clear, focused strategic and business plans become essential for success. I believe I can help you in these areas.

I offer 20 years' experience in management and marketing with more than half that time focused on international markets. In addition, having been primarily involved in start-up and turnaround ventures, I was directly responsible for developing both five- and 10-year strategic plans and one-year operating plans.

Other areas where my experience could assist your corporate planning and development area:

• Established and implemented a global marketing and sales strategy that ensured consistency of message and product delivery to customers.
• Developed an "insider" approach in the local markets for the products and services sold while adhering to corporate values.
• Instituted a global program aimed at ensuring zero defects for multinational clients. Given AT&T's product mix and its strategy for global expansion, superior-quality service is essential for success.
• Developed, installed, and managed a centralized core system for the business noted as the best in the industry.
• Hosted quarterly global sales and marketing conferences and training sessions to cement team spirit and ensure product, corporate and local communications were current and correct.
• Developed a global risk management program to control risk with "common sense" procedures to ensure compliance and support.
• Traveled globally at an 80% level. Focused on visiting/selling/cheerleading clients, prospects, industry leaders, and staff.

(continues)

- Created and implemented a global promotion and advertising campaign to establish an image of a global yet local player.

I would very much appreciate the opportunity to meet with you for half an hour to introduce myself, discuss the AT&T environment, and identify any areas of your organization or the corporation that may need someone with my background and experience. I have the maturity and sophistication to deal with the wide variety of personalities, problems, and opportunities presented by the international markets plus the persistence to see things through to meet your goals.

I'll call Kim next week to set up an appointment. I look forward to meeting you.

Sincerely,

Terry Pile

Targeted Mailing: My Own Case Study

Beginnings are always messy.

John Galsworthy, English novelist

I enjoy research and writing. I sincerely want to meet with the people to whom I write and I therefore don't mind doing a lot of work to get in to see them. I use both targeted- and direct-mail campaigns.

A number of years ago, IBM announced a new president of a company that had to do with employment. I thought I should get to know him because I was in the career-coaching field, although I couldn't find out exactly what the new company would be doing. I knew quite a few people who had tried to network in to see him with no success. The man was inundated with letters from people trying to see him using the name of somebody important at IBM. He turned them all down.

I wrote him a targeted mailing and enclosed a résumé. Before I wrote paragraph one, I tried to think about him as a person. That's what you need to do to make your letters more personal. "Gosh," I thought, "he must be so proud to be president of this company! He's probably never been the president of a company before."

When I am working with my clients, I want them to imagine the person to whom they are writing and write a letter aimed at that specific person—even in a direct-mail campaign, where they may write to 60 or 100 people. It is still better to write that first letter with someone specific in mind (even if you don't really know that person) rather than write to a mailing list.

What you want to say to that specific individual becomes the opening to the letter. In this case, I had to hedge my bets because I didn't know exactly what the company did, so I alluded to that fact. In paragraph two, I gave my summary statement. In paragraph three, I listed bulleted accomplishments.

Before I sent the letter, I called and found he had only a temporary secretary. So, in paragraph four, I referred to this fact.

I said I thought it would be fruitful for both of us if we got together. And I enclosed my résumé.

As usual, I got cold feet after I sent the letter. What happens is that I start thinking, "Why would this person ever want to see me—especially when I know he has rejected so many?" Sometimes I get so scared I wait too long to follow up. Then I write again, usually saying there is some information I left out of my first letter. I send off the second letter and by that time, I can usually get up my nerve to follow up with a phone call.

In this case, the secretary was expecting my call and the company president had asked her to reserve 45 minutes for me.

When I met with him, he told me he had received more than 800 letters, but met with only four people—including me. He said my letter was one of the most intelligent he had received and that I sounded sincere. In case you think the credentials you see in this letter are what got me in, I'd like to point out that I used this same technique even early on in my career when I had virtually no credentials. The four-paragraph approach increases anyone's chances of writing an intelligent letter.

A targeted mailing requires clear thinking, clear writing, and making a case for oneself. Most people realize this. On the other hand, when job hunters have a networking contact, they tend to cut short the hard work required to get in to see someone. And sometimes people resent getting networking letters and feeling as though they are being coerced.

Everyone is networking these days, and it certainly is an important technique, but it's not the only one. At least consider the other approaches to getting interviews in your target market.

I take a simple view of living. It is: keep your eyes open and get on with it.

Laurence Olivier

Targeted Mailing Cover Letters

KATE WENDLETON
444 East Grenopple Street
New York, New York 10000

February 10, 19xx

Mr. Max Lorenz
President, Employment Solutions, Inc.
c/o IBM Corporation
555 Black Horse Pike
Runnemede, NJ 07555

Dear Mr. Lorenz:

Congratulations on your new position! I know you are extremely busy (I've heard about it from others). After you are settled in, I would be interested in meeting with you. I think it would be mutually beneficial for us to meet, although I have no fixed idea of what could come of it.

I have started up, managed, and delivered a number of employment/counseling services. I also have a strong business background:

• I am Founder and Director of The Career Center at the New School for Social Research.
• I am Founder and Director of The Five O'Clock Club®, a career-coaching group that attracts 40 to 60 job hunters a week in Manhattan. We have seven coaches who help the job hunters through their searches.
• When I served as CFO of an outplacement firm with a professional staff of 100, that company was very successful and profitable.
• I counsel senior executives at a major financial institution, a good prototype of an internal service, and the only one with a full-time staff serving clients (others rely on outside consultants).
• One of my books will be published in the fall by the Villard division of Random House under the title, *Through the Brick Wall: How to Job Hunt in a Tight Market.*

I know a *lot* of people in the field and perhaps have knowledge of some important developments in outplacement of which you may not be aware. I am sure our meeting will be fruitful for us both. I will call your new secretary in a week or so to see when I can get on your calendar.

Yours truly,

Kate Wendleton

JAMES J. BORLAND, III
140 West 81st Street
New York, New York 10000
JBorland678@landmine.net

July 17, 200X

Ms. Renée Rosenberg
Merrill Lynch
Liberty Place
165 Broadway
New York, New York 10000

Dear Renée:

I appreciate your offer to review and forward on my résumé. I think you'll see how I've used my skills of persuasion throughout the years. For example, while working on the "Friends of Bill Thomas" Mayoral Campaign, I was on the phone all day long convincing politicians across a broad spectrum to either publicly commit to my candidate or, as was the case at the outset when resistance was strong and reactions negative, to cooperate behind the scenes. The continual give-and-take involved a lot of listening, as people wanted to state their case, vent frustrations with personalities, and so on. I had to cajole and "massage" the local political types in an effort to have them deliver us an audience at events that we staged in their communities. These same techniques—reasoning with people, getting my message across, listening, wanting to please—all these would be assets in a job where rejection is the norm.

On the other hand, I find I enjoy analyzing business. For example, in my current job I monitor revenue and other statistics daily to determine trends and affect policy. While also working on systems problems (we are a computer-driven collections operation), the line management position I hold in day-to-day operations is responsible for a net revenue of $2 million plus per year. I supervise 22 city marshals who participate in the street impoundment program and also deal directly with 3 garage towing operations under contract to us. I've also been negotiating with realtors and prospective subcontractors to expand our operation.

I enjoy working in an atmosphere where there is a lot of activity, where I'm measured by my results, where compensation is directly related to my ability to produce, and where the job is what I make it. I want to be with interesting people, people who matter, people who can have an impact. I feel that the securities business and the opportunity to train and grow the best at Merrill would be a challenge and an education. In this situation, I feel the most severe limitations and constraints would be my own and I like that.

I would be pleased to meet with someone in your organization to further discuss how my qualifications may lead to a career with Merrill.

Sincerely,

Phil sent this letter to 15 pharmaceutical industry executives. He did not include a résumé—it would not have helped his case because his target was dramatically different from his background.

PHILIP GITTINGS
10 West Fortieth Street
West Beach, New Jersey 08000
(222) 555-2231
Gittings 483@aol.com

April 30, 200X

Name
Title
Company
Address
City, State, Zip

Dear _____:

I am writing to you because I am very interested in working for your company.

As biomedical research advances on international fronts, companies with global health-care and pharmaceutical interests are facing intensified multinational competition. Dealing effectively with this kind of environment may require the resources of capable international planning analysts:

- to coordinate diverse, market-driven approaches to worldwide competition,
- to channel regionally developed strategic market plans in the direction of common organizational goals, and
- to establish and communicate that common vision to ensure worldwide leadership.

As an international market planning analyst with Exxon, I have dealt with these issues and would add important expertise to your planning and marketing activities. I have seven years' experience in market planning, operations, and financial analysis, gained through five diverse assignments with Exxon International Company. During this time, I have made some meaningful contributions to the organization's worldwide efficiency, competitiveness, and strength. I have:

- Developed an international market-planning approach for a $4 billion product line. It was acknowledged worldwide for substantially improving overall marketing potential and global communications.
- Analyzed the industry environments of several international product lines.
- Developed corporate outlooks and goals consistent with worldwide perspectives.
- Evaluated the reasonableness of regional market strategies (Europe, Far East, South America, Canada, U.S.A.). Worked with foreign marketing managers to assess competitive strengths and to define appropriate objectives and positioning.

My assignments with Exxon have taught me how to plan, market, and manage effectively the international product lines of a highly decentralized organization. The industry environment is one where widely varying economic conditions, regulatory requirements, and political practices are standard considerations. I would be immediately beneficial to your organization and in your industry because of this tested experience.

In additon to my market-planning responsibilities, I have also performed financial and cost/benefit analyses for efficient use of assets. I have implemented analytical applications on both mainframe and micro computers. I have delivered oral and written presentations to top-level executives. My educational background includes an M.S. in Industrial Administration from Columbia and a B.S. in Mathematics and English.

Due to the restructuring of the oil industry and my assessment of the opportunities there, I am looking to match my skills with organizations that offer potential. Along with my credentials, I bring an intensely personal motivation to meet the challenges of contemporary health-care issues and to participate in the exciting developments promised the pharmaceutical industry by emerging technologies.

I am confident I can contribute importantly and meaningfully to your firm's international marketing and planning efforts. I look forward to an exploratory meeting with you where we can discuss in more detail my qualifications and how they can be of use to you.

I hope you are as interested in meeting as I am. I will call in a few days to see when a personal meeting can be arranged.

Sincerely,

Phil got in to see all of the people he wanted to see—because of his persistence in the follow-up phone calls. He was offered a number of options in the pharmaceutical industry, but he turned them down and accepted a position in a completely different field.

Hélène customized the opening sentence of each letter. She also used a moderate amount of underlining and bolding to make it easier for the reader to scan the letter to see what she had done. This particular letter was aimed at companies involved in electronic commerce.

HÉLÈNE SEILER
2737 Flomenhaft Boulevard
Atlanta, GA 99997
212.555.5228 (Day)

GLOBAL STRATEGY AND MANAGEMENT CONSULTING

Mr. Richard Bayer
KPMG International
Three Chestnut Ridge Road
Montvale, NJ 07645

Most Five O'Clock Club letters use exactly the same format:
Paragraph 1: The opening.
Paragraph 2: A summary about yourself.
Paragraph 3: A few key accomplishments of interest to this target.
Paragraph 4: Ask for a meeting; state who will call whom.

Dear Mr. Bayer:

What an exciting year this is for consulting firms and the explosive growth they enjoy. But clearly what attracts me the most to KPMG is its leadership in strategic marketing. This is why I am writing to you today.

I have been in **global strategic development** and **organizational communications strategies** for the past 20 years, injecting **operational effectiveness** to companies and increasing their revenues massively. During this time, I lived in Paris, London, New York, and Los Angeles (as a base for frequent and lengthy trips to Southeast Asia and Latin America).

By far, the most exciting venture I have been involved with was the strategic consulting and **implementation project** for a $6 billion company. This achievement resulted in moving that company **from #5 to #2** globally. Today that company is a prime target for takeover as its cash flow is one of the most attractive return-on-sale, all industries considered.

I truly help companies build their **global impact** and achieve **long-term profitability**.

You may be interested in some of the specific things I have done:

- I implemented long-range business plans for major entertainment, media, and communications companies: **Time Warner, Sony/USA, and BMG North America**.
- I drove the process forward, made the deals, and brokered trade-offs to ensure company executives saw the added value of **electronic commerce**.

My next goal is to join a top consulting firm and I would appreciate an informational conversation with you or one of your associates to find out more about your needs and to tell you more about myself. As I mentioned earlier, I see electronic commerce consulting as the next tremendous growth area and I have established my expertise in that area.

When I call your office in a few days I would appreciate your telling me who to contact in your Atlanta office to discuss this explosive industry and its challenges.

Sincerely,

Out-of-town search

FRED HOPKINSON

November 10, 200X

Ms. Joy Muench
SVP & Controller
Bankers Trust
433 Market Street
San Francisco, CA 94000

Dear Ms. Muench:

I am writing to you since I am seeking a senior financial and/or operations position in the San Francisco Bay area. Although I enjoy working for Chase Manhattan Bank, I'm afraid my 12 years in San Francisco has spoiled me forever, certainly compared to living in New York.

I am a senior financial manager with a strong background (Bank of America, Wells Fargo, Chase) in financial control and analysis, budgeting, forecasting, and data processing operations. I have strong management and administrative skills, have managed large groups of people, and have successfully turned around problem operations. I have an extensive knowledge of personal computers as well as database and spreadsheet applications.

I would very much appreciate the opportunity to meet with you for half an hour to introduce myself, discuss the current environment at Bankers Trust, and identify any areas of the bank which may, in the future, have a need for someone with my background and experience. I would also appreciate your ideas on other financial institutions in San Francisco that may offer future career opportunities.

I will be in the Bay area in early December (I still maintain my home in San Rafael) and will call you in advance to schedule a mutually convenient time. I appreciate your consideration and look forward to the possibility of meeting you.

Sincerely,

The Five O'Clock Club

Direct-Mail Campaigns

Perfection of means and confusion of goals seem, in my opinion, to characterize our age.

Albert Einstein

Does Direct Mail Work?

A technique "works" if it helps you get meetings in your target market. When you are mounting a full campaign, your goal is to have the organizations in your target market know about you as quickly as possible. You can supplement your networking by using search firms and answering ads, but you will still not have hit most of the organizations in your market. Regardless of how you get in, if you find you are being well received by some organizations in your target market, consider direct mail and/or targeted mail for the rest.

If you use direct mail, consider mounting campaigns to a number of targets. Out of four campaigns, for example, maybe two will be effective and result in meetings and two won't work at all. Part of it is selecting a target likely to be interested in you. Another part is being able to express yourself clearly and compellingly in writing. And a third part is a numbers game. If you get no response when you mail to a very small number, that mailing was not a good test.

Most job hunters expect every letter they write to result in a meeting, which is unreasonable. They don't expect every search-firm contact or every ad to result in a meeting. The same is true for direct contact.

CASE STUDY *Diane*
Getting More Job Possibilities in the Works

Last week, Diane accepted a job offer. She had uncovered two job possibilities through networking, but she wanted to have the requisite "6 to 10 things in the works." So she did a mailing of 250 letters, which resulted in four more job leads. Admittedly, that's a very small response rate from a mailing, but she wound up with four more job interviews than she would have had exclusively through networking.

Act As If This Company Is Important to You

One time I wrote a direct-mail letter to 200 companies. A manager at one company said to me, "How did you hear of us? No one ever writes to us." I said, "Oh, a number of people have mentioned your company." "Really. Who?" I said, "Pierre Charbonneau and Lillian Bisset-Farrell, to name two [making up the first two names that came to my mind]." The manager said, "I don't know them." "Well," I replied, "they've heard of you!"

If they take your letter personally, you cannot tell them you sent that same letter to 200 people.

For direct-mail campaigns using the Internet, see "Using Search Engines to Develop Your List" in the chapter, "Research: Developing Your List of Organizations to Contact."

Helen: Making It Sound Personal

*Out there things can happen to people as
brainy and footsy as you.*

*And when things start to happen don't worry. Don't
stew. Just go right along. You'll start happening too.*

Dr. Seuss, *Oh, the Places You'll Go!*

Helen is an organizational-development person. She wrote a letter to 60 fellow members of the Organization Development Network, saying: "As a fellow member of the OD Network, I thought perhaps you might come across information to help me in my job search. I am interested in making a career move and I sure would appreciate hearing from you." Paragraph two was her summary. In paragraph three, she listed her accomplishments.

Paragraph four was very clever because she had no intention of calling these people, and she didn't want to make it sound like a mass mailing, so she said a variation of "I don't want to bother you with phone calls, but I trust you will give me a call if you come across information that would help me in my search."

She got six calls back about real job openings. She did another mailing to another 60 people in the same organization, got another six meetings, and eventually wound up with a job offer.

Which technique did she use? It was a direct-mail campaign.

If you have an association list, consider using it for a direct-mail campaign, and be sure to mention your membership in that association in your opening paragraph.

---

*Results! Why, man, I have gotten a lot of results. I
know several thousand things that won't work.*

Thomas A. Edison

If you are not going to follow up your letter with a phone call, here's one way to end your letter (if this is appropriate in your situation):

"I don't want to bother you with a follow-up phone call. However, I am very interested in meeting with you. If you feel the same, I hope you will give me a call so we can set up a time to meet."

AURORA BRITO
2421 Maindays Boulevard
Columbus, Ohio 43700
231-555-1212

April 6, 200X

Name
Position
Company
Address
City, State, ZIP

Dear _____:

As a fellow member of the Organization Development Network, I am writing to explore with you potential opportunities in your organization.

Currently with Bell South as an internal corporate human resources consultant, I am seeking an opportunity in organization and management development. Perhaps it would facilitate this process if I share key highlights of my background:

- Management development specialist with more than **6 years of experience** developing and making presentations.
- At **Bell South**, I am responsible for designing and implementing projects to enhance the professionalism of more than 2,000 managers worldwide. This involves:
  — **Executive and high-potential development**—Assessing and identifying top performers to meet specific business talent needs, attend Executive University programs, and facilitate succession planning.
  — **Needs analysis**—Running focus groups throughout the United States and Europe for the purpose of creating and designing training programs.
  — **Organizational research**—Using statistical and research design (SPSSX) to conduct surveys, climate studies, and turnover studies.
- Experience in Asia as a process consultant to an American-based company. **Fluent in Japanese**.
- Hold **2 master's degrees from Columbia University** in organizational and counseling psychology.

What do you think? Are there any possibilities within your purview for someone with my skills and experience base? I realize you are busy and I don't want to be intrusive by phoning; however, if you are interested or would just like to discuss some ideas, please contact me at 231-555-1212. Attached is my résumé. I look forward to your input. Thank you.

Sincerely,

Bruce: Before and after Direct-Mail Letters

Bruce Faulk (his real name) is a young actor who was working as a receptionist while waiting for his big break. Like most actors, he kept in touch with those who might advance his career. But like most job hunters, he left out the substance in his letters.

Because of The Five O'Clock Club approach, he became more methodical about everything he did in his search for his next acting job. Bruce's "after" letter is on the next page.

By the way, after appearing on Broadway as the youngest actor in *Hamlet,* Bruce toured the United States, and is currently touring Europe with *Hair.*

Bruce's letter proves that the approach works for anyone—regardless of their profession. At The Five O'Clock Club, we have worked with everyone from orchestra conductors to fine artists.

This just in from Bruce:

The "before" version of Bruce's direct-mail letter

Dear Martin Reed:

I am sending you my picture and résumé on the advice of Casey Childs, who has directed a number of *A Different World* episodes. I hope you will keep me in mind for any upcoming project for which I might be right. I will keep you apprised of my situation. Thank you.

Sincerely,

Bruce Faulk

Kate—

Europe is all I expected and more—so much so that I've extended my tour here a few more months. So far, most of the tour has been all over—and I do mean *all* over Germany; but there's still a lot of time for Zurich (where I am now), for the rest of Switzerland, for Austria, and a month and a half right outside Amsterdam. Next month, I'm off to Cannes, France, and a week in Sweden.

Not too shabby for a former receptionist?

Hope all is well with you. Please give everyone my love.

Always,
Bruce

The "after" version of Bruce's direct-mail letter

BRUCE J. FAULK
286 North 50th Street—Apt. HL
New York, NY 10099
212-555-9809

March 18, 20XX

Dear Mr. Reed:

Casey Childs, who has directed *A Different World,* suggested I contact you. He thought you and I might be able to work together.

I am a graduate of the High School of Performing Arts and Carnegie-Mellon University. I have performed repeatedly off-Broadway in New York. You may be interested in some of my specific experiences. For example:

- I am particularly proud of my work in *The Island,* a South African one-act by Athol Fugard. Many people said it was the best thing done that year at Carnegie. In fact, we were asked to repeat the show for Black History Month at the Pittsburgh Civic Center. (In addition, I was interviewed on TV as part of the show's promotion.) It was extremely well received and many people came up to me on the streets of Pittsburgh and said how much it meant to them; I have a video of the performance if you are interested in seeing it.
- Another example of my work is *Broadway Cabaret.* I played the part of the emcee, warming up the audience for about 10 minutes before opening the show and then singing and dancing throughout. We played to a packed house and a standing ovation every night of the run; it was the most popular show of the season and was extended. I was glad to develop a serious working relationship with the director/choreographer Billy Wilson.

I am a professional, I know how to put a part together and get a job done and I work very hard on whatever I take on. In addition, I am easy to work with and have a good sense of humor.

I will keep you apprised of my situation so you may have a chance to see me in a piece. Casey thought you and I could work together. I hope we can.

Sincerely,

Bruce J. Faulk

Direct/Targeted Mailing Letters

SYLVAN VON BERG

April 20, 200X

Name
President or CEO
Company
Address
City, State, Zip

Dear _____:

(In many companies) *OR* (In the inorganic chemicals industry), the use of **technology has not kept pace with the expansion of markets** and the need for more sophisticated information to service those sales opportunities. The need for logical, manageable information and its dissemination is paramount in today's world. I can help you with solutions to those issues.

I am a **senior information systems executive** with experience in **managing the information needs for companies ranging from** $250 million to more than $1 billion in annual sales. As a key member of the management team I can direct the implementation of technology to achieve the profit objectives of your organization. My experience has been both domestic and international and I have a unique ability to control major development projects to successful conclusions.

Here are some specific examples of my accomplishments:

- Developed a composite information database. Resulted in **higher market share** and greater penetration into existing market segments.
- Saved $1 million annually on a $5 million data-processing budget.
- Consolidated the technologies and systems of more than $1 billion in acquisitions, avoiding problems frequently associated with multiple acquisitions.

I am a strong hands-on strategic planner and leader and I would welcome the opportunity to discuss how my skills and experience could contribute to your company's objectives. I will call you in a few days to set up a mutually convenient time for us to meet.

Sincerely,

Sylvan Von Berg

Enclosure

Direct-Mail Campaign

TINA DAVIS
2 Bigelow Lane
Nashville, Tennessee 37333
(555) 555-2231 (day)
TimDavis@aol.com

May 10, 200X

Name
President
Bank Name
Address
City, State, Zip

Dear _____:

Many companies' banking relationships are being disrupted because of new controls and regulations and the impact of mergers and acquisitions. In addition, frequent changes in account officers and terms of service are causing a loss of understanding between bank and customer.

Smooth-running banking relationships can make all the difference in the effective conduct of business. How can you, as President of XXX Bank, stay abreast of what is happening and even benefit from current developments?

I can help you with these issues. I offer 20 years' experience in banking, most recently as vice president with Mellon Bank's International Department. Furthermore, few have my connections in and knowledge of the industry.

Here are two specific areas where my experience could benefit you:

Banking Relationships: I know my way around the industry and know what a bank should be able to do for its customers. My experience would enable you to maximize the services available from your bank and enhance the degree of comfort the banks feel toward you, their customer.

Assessment of Credit Risk: Much of my career has been spent in the area of credit assessment and my broad experience could help you avoid many of the pitfalls inherent in doing business.

I have the maturity and sophistication to be able to deal with a wide variety of personalities and problems and the persistence to see things through to a satisfactory conclusion.

I would welcome the opportunity to discuss with you how my skills and background could contribute to your company's goals.

Yours sincerely,

Tina Davis

Direct-Mail Campaign including Out-of-Town Search

Sent to 60 presidents of small/medium-sized advertising agencies or the appropriate people in large agencies. Resulted in 5 exploratory interviews that led to additional interviews and 3 job offers.

M. CATHERINE WENDLETON
410 Main Street Lancaster, PA
(555) 555-2231

May 10, 1983

Dear _____:

Many agencies are coping with these difficult times by hiring the best creative and sales people available. While this may maintain a competitive edge, many agencies find their bottom line is slipping. The usual response is to send in the accountants.

These agencies, and perhaps some of your own subsidiaries, need more than accounting help. As vice president of operations for a $10 million advertising agency, I directed the turnaround of a company that was in serious financial difficulty. As a result, 1982 was the most profitable year in company history and 1983 promises to be better yet.

This experience has taught me what can cause an agency to get into trouble. I know the danger signs and I can teach a company how to run itself with true efficiency and economy—not just with heavy-handed frugality. I have a record of success in making an agency run more smoothly and profitably. My accomplishments include:

- Trouble-shoot in all areas of agency operations (except Creative output).
- Improved employee productivity by 30%. Reduced the number of unprofitable accounts by 83%.
- Set up a management information system that gets to the core of the problems and encourages managers to act. Cleaned up a flawed computer system.
- Dramatically reduced the number of crisis situations in Creative and the number of over-budget situations.
- Instituted a comprehensive salary and performance review system. Developed hiring procedures to reduce turnover.
- As Chairman of the Executive Committee, instituted tight budgetary controls, improved responsibility accounting, and account margin and cost controls.

I have an M.B.A. as well as 12 years of progressive management responsibility in finance and strategic planning, data processing, personnel, and advertising and marketing.

As a result of many years' travel to New York, I would prefer to live and work in the New York area. In fact, I'm in New York frequently.

Hiring me would be an investment in the $xx,xxx range, but the return will be impressive. I would be pleased to meet with you to discuss the contribution I could make to the performance of your organization.

Yours truly,

Kate Wendleton

Direct-Mail Campaign From a Senior Executive

Nick sent this letter to 200 companies, in addition to his targeted mailings. Furthermore, he kept in close contact with search firms and key individuals he had met through the years.

NICHOLAS GARAFALOS
654 Kingston Road, Tampa, FL 99900
(555) 555-4431   nickg@bway.net

May 21, 200X

Mr. James Swann
Teleodymetric Corporation
460 Herndon Parkway
Battlesboro, MD 55170

Dear Mr. Swann:

Building market value is my expertise. Whether challenged to launch a start-up technology venture, orchestrate an aggressive business turnaround, or accelerate growth within a top-performing organization, I have consistently delivered strong and sustainable financial results:

- As Vice President & General Manager with full P&L responsibility for a new IBM business unit, achieved/surpassed all turnaround objectives and restored the organization to profitability with a 55% gain in gross market contribution.
- As General Manager of Paychex Information Consulting Services, orchestrated the start-up of a new strategic business unit and closed new contracts in product, technology, and service sales within an intensely competitive national market.
- As Vice President of Electronic Delivery Systems Development for Chase, led a team of 125 professionals in the development, market launch, and commercialization of advanced electronic and telecommunications technologies.
- Early management achievements include a series of increasingly responsible positions with revenue responsibility for up to $100 million in annual sales from markets throughout Europe, Africa, and the Middle East.

The strength of my performance lies in my ability to define corporate vision and strategy, translate into action, and deliver profitable results. Beginning my career with several major consumer products companies, I was able to transition the marketing, sales, leadership, and general management skills I developed into my more recent positions in emerging information, telecommunications, networking, interactive multimedia, and new media industries.

Currently, I am confidentially pursuing new executive opportunities either in the technology and/or services industries. Aware of the quality of your organization and your commitment to long-term, profitable growth, I would be delighted to have a chance to pursue such opportunities. I look forward to what I anticipate will be the first of many positive communications. Thank you.

Sincerely,

Nick Garafalos

Enclosure

Direct-Mail Campaign

MARJORIE HENDRICKSON

February 2, 20xx

Name
Title
Company
Address
City, State, Zip

Dear _____:

I am a seasoned financial services marketer with **10 years at Asarco Financial** and heavy package-goods experience at Lever Brothers, Johnson & Johnson, and Procter & Gamble.

My experience is in **developing and marketing financial products and services,** including electronic banking products, investment packages, and basic banking services to both consumer and corporate markets. I also have a strong track record in **building effective sales teams and turning around troubled businesses.** I am currently exploring opportunities to build a financial services business or to inject new life into an existing one.

A résumé is enclosed for additional background. If you would like to discuss the possibilities, I would like very much to get together.

I look forward to hearing from you.

Sincerely,

Marjorie Hendrickson

Enclosure

The
Five
O'Clock
Club

How to Answer Ads

Of all sad words
Of tongue and pen
The saddest are these:
"It Might Have Been."

Let's add this thought
unto this verse:
"It Might Have Been
A Good Deal Worse."

Anonymous

Some people get excited when they see an ad in the paper or on the Internet. They *know* this is the job for them and their hopes soar.

But try to keep things in perspective. Don't be surprised if you answer 30, 50, or more ads and *get no meetings*. Your résumé is one of perhaps hundreds or even thousands of responses. What's more, your résumé is not being screened by the hiring manager.

Chances are, your cover letter and résumé will be screened by a computer or by a junior clerk. I once met a 20-year-old woman who reviewed résumés on behalf of blue-chip companies, screening thousands of professionals and managers in the $40,000 to $100,000 range. *She* decided who would get interviewed. This young woman was good at her job and often took a personal interest in the people whose résumés she saw—but she was only 20 years old. Writing a cover letter to intrigue or strike a responsive chord in her wouldn't have worked.

While writing creative cover letters will work for targeted- and direct-mail campaigns, stick to the basics in answering ads. If the ad asks for specific qualifications and experience, highlight those areas from your background. Respond point by point to each item mentioned. Show how you have everything they want. Keep your cover letter crystal clear. Remember, the reader of your letter may be 20 years old. If you don't fit exactly, you will probably be screened out.

Fewer than 10 percent of all jobs are found through ads, including both print and online ads. At The Five O'Clock Club, we say you should consider *all four* techniques for getting interviews in your target market—search firms, ads, networking, and direct contact—and then *notice* which techniques are working for you. "Working for you" means that a technique results in *meetings*. You don't measure the effectiveness of a technique by whether or not you got a *job*. You measure the effectiveness of a technique by whether or not it's resulting in *meetings* for you.

If an average ad in *The Wall Street Journal* or *The New York Times* gets a 1,000 responses, you have 999 competitors. Websites for large corporations can get one million résumés a year. Many people sit at their computers for hours on end, hitting that "send" button and wondering why no one is responding to them. Everyone else is doing the same thing. We frequently hear hiring managers say they don't even consider this accumulating database of résumés. It's a rare job hunter who even includes a cover letter in response to an Internet ad. Yet, the cover letter is the piece that can most significantly increase the chances you'll be called in.

"Actually, we're not hiring. We hold lots of interviews like this one so our competition thinks we're busy."

The Cover Letter for Answering Ads

It's unlikely the hiring manager will be the one who does the screening. Instead, some junior-level person (or a computer) reviews the hundreds or thousands of responses. You can be sure the person wants to get through those résumés as quickly as possible. Their job is to get rid of all but 10 or 20 of them! So make it easy for them to screen you *in*. All you want is to be in the *"include"* pile.

You must *personalize* **the cover letter when answering an ad.** Sometimes when we're looking for people to work in The Five O'Clock Club office, we may post jobs on the Internet and we are deluged with responses. Often we can't tell which job the person is applying for: an accounting job or a public relations job. People just unthinkingly hit the send button without a thoughtful cover letter.

So even when you respond to an Internet ad, be sure to use The Five O'Clock Club's four-paragraph approach. Make your cover letter very clear, very short, very readable. Show a strong

match between you and the position they've posted. Then the résumé screener will at least know which pile to place you in. Here's our formula for the cover letter:

In paragraph one, be sure to mention the *position* for which you are applying, as well as the newspaper or Internet site where you saw the ad, and the date of the ad.

Paragraph two contains your *summary* about you *as it relates to this position*. Such as, "I have 10 years of international marketing experience in the chemical and pharmaceutical industries."

For paragraph three, if you *think* you're qualified for the job, use The Five O'Clock Club's two-column approach when mailing or e-mailing in the response. Your response will definitely stand out compared with all the other responses.

The first column says "You are looking for . . ." or "Your requirements," under which you list everything they've mentioned in the ad. In column two, you say "I have this to offer" or "My experience," and match up what you have to offer to what they're looking for. Of course, make sure what you have to offer seems better than what they're looking for.

List your points in the order in which they're listed in the ad. Most hiring managers will list first in an ad the requirements that are most important to them. So you want to list first those things that are most important to the hiring team. That way, the junior-level person who is screening all of these cover letters (even the ones the computer selected) will have an easier time *including* you rather than *excluding* you.

Use *their* terminology not yours. When answering an ad, make sure you use *their* terminology and not the terminology from your last position. If they say they're looking for a *trainer* and you've been a *teacher*, then just say you've had 12 years of *training* experience. Don't use a word that's inappropriate for their industry or their firm.

Use The Five O'Clock Club's two-column approach if you think you're a good match for the job. On the other hand, if you feel you're *not* a strong match and still want to answer the ad, *don't* use the two-column approach, which would highlight the fact that you're not a strong match. Instead, clearly state what you have to offer and *say* you think you're an ideal candidate and why.

In paragraph four, list any additional information about yourself that you think would be of interest to the hiring company.

Finally, as far as salary in concerned, *say nothing*. Many ads include the words, "Please tell us your salary requirements," yet savvy job hunters decline to mention salary because it increases the chances they'll be *excluded*.

What are the chances you're going to match whatever salary they have in mind? You'll name a number that's too high for them, too low—but rarely just right. The odds are against you. So it's a disadvantage for you to list your salary.

Therefore, job hunters generally say, "I'd be glad to discuss salary requirements upon mutual interest. I look forward to meeting with you to further discuss the position." That way, you're not ignoring their request for salary information.

Sometimes you'll see an ad stating, "You will absolutely not be considered for this job unless you provide your salary history." Those ads are usually placed by academic institutions or by the government. If an ad says you *must* name your salary history, the best approach is to provide *limited information;* don't disclose your *entire* salary history, because you reduce your chance of being called in *and* you reduce your chance of negotiating an appropriate salary. However, you *can* mention a broad range of what you're looking for. Be sure to think strategically. Research the industry you're targeting and its standard procedures and play it accordingly. No matter what the industry, don't disclose too much about yourself before you even get an interview.

By the way, these are the issues and details you should discuss with your small group. That's why we *have* a small group. You may face unusual situations, so be sure to use your group for guidance.

Surround the Hiring Manager

An ad for a job is as good as a flashing neon sign: The company is telling the world it has an opening! Your strategic thinking should go into high gear—if it's a company or a job that *really* interests you. Don't wait to get in by just responding to the ad. Network into the company or contact someone there directly, but not the person mentioned in the ad. "Surrounding the hiring manager" is a very effective technique. Get in to see someone—almost *anyone* other than the hiring manager. An insider can become an advocate for you and refer you in to the hiring manager. You'll have a better chance of standing out from your competitors—because you were referred in and will know more—and you'll do better in the meeting. You're no longer one more grubby job hunter who is simply responding to an ad—you're now someone who is sincerely interested in this company and knows how to go the extra mile. The hiring manager will get to know you in a different way from the other applicants and he or she *may* consider you even though you don't have all of the qualifications they listed. For more information on this technique, see the chapter "What to Do When You Know There's a Job Opening."

Bottom line: **If it's a good ad for you, answer the ad, then forget about the ad and try to get in some other way—without mentioning the ad**.

> **If you meet all the requirements of the job, then make it very clear to the screener that you should *not* be screened out. Be sure to read "What to Do When You Know There's a Job Opening" in this book.**

CIRO DISCLAFANI
38 Cicily Place
West Hamstart, MO 59684
CiroDisc@worldwidenet.com

March 23, 200X

Terry Pile
Employment Manager
National Data Labs
22 Parns Avenue
East Hamstart, MO 59684

Dear Ms. Pile:

I believe I am a good fit for the Assistant Controller position advertised in the *Hamstart Times* on March 20, 20xx.

Having been continually challenged and rapidly promoted at Toronto Dominion Bank, I have a proven track record in controllership functions. I've headed the controllership function in every major area of the company, including credit cards, travelers checks, and private banking. As you may be aware, Toronto Dominion has a rigorous budgeting, financial analysis, and cost-accounting process, similar to National Data Labs, and this has contributed to the success of the organization.

Here is a breakdown of my experience vs. your requirements:

Your Requirements	My Experience
• 12+ years experience in private accounting/management	• 14+ years experience in financial management
• BBA, MBA a plus.	• BBA in finance MBA in financial management
• Financial analysis/cost-accounting skills	• Strong financial analysis skills— controllership functions
	• Strong cost-accounting skills—designed cost-accounting/unit-cost methodologies

I consider myself a sophisticated management professional with a significant number of business accomplishments, coupled with excellent ability to communicate both orally and in writing.

I would welcome an interview with you to review my experience in financial management.

Sincerely,

Ciro Disclafani

Blind Ads

If you are considering a blind ad, be careful. Blind ads don't include the name of the organization seeking to hire someone. It could be placed by a search firm or by the company itself with just a box number. You don't know to whom you're sending your résumé. Be *especially* careful if you're currently employed. That ad could have been placed by your employer or by a search firm who works with your employer. Employed job hunters often respond with just a letter and no résumé. Their letter states why they're a match, but they don't mention their present place of employment. But even this can be risky. If you're employed, you may want to skip those blind ads.

If They Call You

If you do answer an ad, be prepared for a phone call, just in case. Someone may actually respond to your letter! So make sure your message machine doesn't have something silly on it, such as all three of your children saying, "Hi, this is Janet and this is Jim and this is Karen and we all live here." Your message should be professional or you may turn off prospective employers with a silly message or strange music. They may simply hang up and you won't even know they called. Job hunters need to be hypersensitive about *impressions*—and this includes the outgoing message on your answering machine.

If you *do* get a phone call, the first thing you may be asked is your salary range. And that's the *last* thing you want to talk about. So make sure you're ready to handle that. Read our book, *Mastering the Job Interview and Winning the Money Game.* You might say, "I think it's a little early to discuss salary. I'm sure salary is *not* going to be a problem." You want a *meeting*—in person—and you want to be prepared. It's certainly too early to discuss salary.

Remember, however: Most job seekers who respond to ads will never get a call. So don't expect to hear back and get on with your search.

Don't spend too much time trying to figure out how ads work. Figure out how *else* to get in.

Rejection Letters

If you get a rejection letter when you've answered an ad, try not to give it a second thought. That letter is not personal. They don't even *know* you. They're just sending letters out routinely. So ignore the letter, but don't necessarily ignore the *company*! One Five O'Clock Club coach has on his office wall *three* framed rejection letters from the *same company,* which eventually hired him! He put these on public display so his clients could see that rejection letters *don't count.*

If there's a name on the rejection letter, you may want to respond to the letter—especially if you're interested in the company. Remember the person who "rejected" you may be the junior-level person who's going through all those résumés. So you may want to write to the *manager* saying you're disappointed and think you're a great match for the company—if not now, maybe in the future. Be sure to enclose your résumé: Remember that this person may never have even *seen* your résumé! We say at The Five O'Clock Club, "The ball is always in your court"—so a rejection letter may *still* be an opportunity!

Where to Find Ads

Where can you find ads? In your local paper, in the national papers, in association journals having to do with your field or industry. If you have very well-defined targets, association journals, association websites, and other websites having to do with your field or industry can be a terrific place for ads.

> **If the ad gives a fax number, use the fax number to respond. But *also* respond through snail mail—and perhaps E-mail—if possible. You never know which method may get their attention.**

Refining Your Response

Of course, ads point you toward current openings. But remember that ads—whether Internet or print—are great for *research*. Ads tell you who's hiring, what they're looking for, and the jargon they use. You may be able to spot trends by tracking the ads week after week. You can modify the approach to your entire search based on what you find out through this research. And ads give you the names of additional companies to target. Then you can try to get in to see people by contacting them directly or through networking.

Being Effective with Internet Postings

José was a Five O'Clock Clubber who had an e-commerce background. He'd been searching for *four* months before he came to the club, but with slim results—not even one interview. When the small group looked at José's résumé, they couldn't even *see* his e-commerce background. He was positioned incorrectly. So José's small group suggested changes for the top of his résumé. Instead of saying, "international marketing executive," the group suggested that he change it to say, "E-commerce executive with strong marketing background." They suggested he follow *that* headline with bulleted accomplishments related to his e-commerce background, followed by his international background.

José was comfortable with posting his résumé on the web because he was not employed at this time. He got a tremendous number of responses. However, most of them were inappropriate because the person (or machine) saw the words "E-commerce executive" and saw him as a technology person. So his small group suggested he refine his résumé one more time. They suggested he change it to "E-commerce *marketing* executive." *Now* José got called in just for e-commerce *marketing* positions.

José was with The Five O'Clock Club only six weeks. He got four offers. He accepted a job with a terrific firm and his group suggested he *not* close off conversations with the other companies until he had been in the new firm for about two weeks—just to try it out. But it was the *repositioning* that made the Internet work for him.

On the Internet, sometimes *people* are not looking at your résumé. *Computers* are looking at it. So the words you use, and *where* you use them are very important. Because José did not have the word "marketing" in the *first* line of his résumé, but had it in the *second* line, the results he got from the machine were completely different. So you owe it to yourself to think things through: The words on *your* résumé must be carefully chosen.

When you answer Internet ads or post your résumé on an organization's website, don't use esoteric words that were used only in your last firm. Use words that would be *generally* used. If you're *employed, never post* your résumé on the Internet. Respond to ads posted by specific identified organizations. After all, you wouldn't post your résumé on the bulletin board in your local grocery store, would you? You don't want to put your résumé out there for *anybody* to see. Treat your résumé as a confidential document.

For an electronic résumé, put key words at the top. Depending on the software the hiring organization is using, you may need to repeat certain words. For example, certain software packages will rate a résumé higher if it has the word JAVA in it 13 times as opposed to one or two times. Ironically, somebody who may be more qualified but have the word JAVA in the résumé only once may be disqualified. So you might have to be very aware of these things until the software is upgraded. Pay attention to what is working in the market.

Our next chapters cover more about writing an electronic résumé and using the Internet as a job-search tool. And don't forget the bibliography at the back of this book, and a more extensive one in the Members Only section of our website.

SHANA L. KINGSLEY

883 Ledger Lane, Minneapolis, MN 88888
(555) 555-2268
skingsley@msn.com

July 19, 2000X

Mr. Theobold J. Yegerlehner
Vice President, Tax
United Telecom Corporation
United Telecom Building
Minneapolis, MN 88801

Dr. Mr. Yegerlehner,

Could United Telecom benefit from a hands-on tax director and counsel with international expertise and the ability to drive strategic initiatives?

I have designed and implemented tax strategies for businesses in the United States and more than 35 other countries.

I know how to work with operations, finance, and legal people to deliver tailored solutions that get results. I have managed cross-functional teams in North America, Europe, Latin America, and the Asia–Pacific region in complex projects, including

- Executing a **$4 billion U.S. recapitalization**.
- Refinancing global operations to **extract cash from overseas** without crippling operations or paying significant taxes.
- Implementing a global trading company to streamline production, increase sales, and **reduce the global effective tax rate by 50%**.
- Reconfiguring a global sales organization to isolate and manage an estimated **$100 million foreign tax exposure**.

I am very interested in meeting with you. I believe you will find even a brief meeting beneficial. I will call your office in the next few days to see when I can get on your calendar.

Sincerely,

Although hers is a narrow field, when Shana wrote to 20 executives who had no advertised positions; 6 of them contacted *her* immediately for an exploratory meeting.

How to Write an Electronic Résumé

You can have an electronic résumé simply by removing all highlighting so that it can be scanned into a computer. After your résumé is scanned in, it can be searched by companies and search firms through the use of keywords. In this computer age, some predict that scanned résumés will be the driving force in the selection process of the future. As of this writing, however, electronic résumés have had little impact on the job searches of Five O'Clock Clubbers. Let's put electronic résumés in perspective.

In this book, you read that there are four basic ways to get interviews in your target market: through search firms, ads, networking, and direct contact. Five O'Clock Clubbers learn to consider all four techniques for getting interviews and then to assess which approach produces the most *meetings* for them.

You should consider using search firms and ads in your job-search mix. In your particular field, they may be an important source of meetings. However, these approaches are passive: You have little control over the process. The search firm or the company placing the ad must call you in. The use of electronic résumés is also a passive approach to job search. You must wait for someone to call you in.

On the other hand, networking and contacting companies directly are proactive approaches: *You* decide whom to contact and *you* contact *them*. While we encourage job hunters to consider every technique for getting interviews in their target markets, we want them to measure which techniques result in meetings with hiring managers.

Those are the techniques you should use more. If electronic résumés result in meetings for you, then use them.

Companies Using Résumé-Scanning Equipment

Some companies have equipment that scans in thousands of résumés. Theoretically, when someone in that company wants to hire a new employee, the manager would ask for those

"Being a computer champion three years running is impressive. But it's not quite the computer experience we're looking for."

143

résumés that fit the experience for which he or she is looking. In real life, Five O'Clock Clubbers *are* getting jobs with companies using scanning equipment, *but they are not getting many interviews through this technology.* Instead, Five O'Clock Clubbers are getting in to see the hiring managers through networking, direct contact, search firms—or even answering ads. When you contact a company through their résumé-scanning technology, it is usually a dead end. If a company asks for a scannable résumé, give them one, but be proactive: Find some other way in. That's what Five O'Clock Clubbers do. The interview is most likely to come from the "other way," not from the scanned-in résumé.

Posting Your Résumé on the Internet or Other Electronic Medium

Job hunters also use electronic résumés for answering ads on the Internet and for putting their résumés online. To address this issue, I will quote from The Five O'Clock Club's Internet expert, Patricia Raufer. Patricia wrote the following in *The Five O'Clock News* ("The Internet as a Job-Search Tool"):

> Some job hunters have even created their multimedia résumé, with extensive background information; it may include video clips or samples of work—all packaged to be transmitted electronically. This method may be appropriate for creative and technical positions because it demonstrates use and understanding of the technology. Job seekers who respond online to job postings often send an electronic version of their print résumé. However, . . . the electronic résumé has not replaced the standard résumé and cover letter. Using the electronic medium for communication offers the benefit of enabling you to respond quickly, but it is not necessarily the easiest method for the recipient. As with all the communications techniques in job search, choosing the right one is part of the process.

Many of the Internet career websites provide an area in which job hunters post their résumés for access by potential employers. However, access is not always limited to just employers. Therefore by posting your résumé, you're providing personal information, employment history, and credentials to people whom you don't know. Would you tack up your résumé on a public bulletin board or hand it out to strangers simply because they asked for it? And how can you follow up effectively if you don't know who has looked at your credentials?

So, use your judgment about relying too heavily on electronic résumés. We all would like something magical to save us from the grueling work of searching for a job, but many of the ideas you may come across are not effective. Having said that, let's take a look at how you actually do an electronic résumé.

Making Your Résumé Scannable

If you have been using The Five O'Clock Club approach to developing your résumé, you are almost there. First of all, you have gotten rid of company jargon so the outside world can understand what you have done. You have also changed your job titles to reflect what you actually did, rather than using company-dictated titles that may not be as accurate. And you have made your résumé accomplishment oriented—a good approach no matter what kind of résumé you have.

Electronic résumés are scanned into a database. They do not need to look pretty. In fact, you cannot have any underlining, bolding, bullets, or other characters that may confuse the scanner—just use plain, straight text.

Secondly, your résumé must contain keywords the hiring manager is most likely to search for regarding the kind of work you want to do. Therefore, at the top of your résumé, where you may have put Operations Manager, for example, add a string of words that would also be appropriate for you, like this:

Operations Manager, Administrative Manager, Accounting Manager, General Manager,

Strategic Planner, Inventory Control Manager, Materials Manager, Customer Service Manager, Management Consultant.

If you have prepared your résumé The Five O'Clock Club way, the body of your résumé should be fine. Again, choose words they are likely to look for. If you are adept at computers, list the hardware and software you know. Only list generally available software—not the company-specific systems you may have used. For example, you may list Excel, Word, Pagemaker, and Filemaker. But don't list ACS, your company's Accounting Control System. That's a name that would not be recognized in the outside world.

The rest of your résumé would be the same as what you have already prepared, but without any highlighting.

Electronic résumés are just one technique which may or may not be important in your search. At The Five O'Clock Club, we suggest you consider all techniques and do what is appropriate for you.

There are fundamental differences between training and education. If you are trained you become the employee, if you are educated, you become the employer. If you are trained you have a J.O.B. (if you're "lucky"), if you are educated you have a career. If you are trained you have been taught to memorize, if you are educated you have been taught how to think.

Jawanza Kunjufu, *Countering the Conspiracy to Destroy Black Boys*

It isn't possible to win high-level success without meeting opposition, hardship, and setback. But it is possible to use setback to propel you forward.

Dr. David Schwartz, *The Magic of Thinking Big*

The
Five
O'Clock
Club

Using the Internet as a Job-Search Tool

by Patricia L. Raufer

The essence of the high-risk society is choice: the choice between embracing uncertainty and running from it.

Michael Mandel, *The High-Risk Society*

W hen you consider that the Internet is a global network linking individuals, companies, governments, organizations, and academic institutions, it is not surprising it is a valuable job-search tool. Although the Internet can be considered an electronic version of what already happens in a job search, this format offers the benefits of immediacy, connection, and searchability. The Internet, however, does not provide the benefits of personal contact and valuable perspectives that one-on-one information-gathering interviews provide. Consider the Internet as simply another job-search tool to be added to your repertoire of Five O'Clock Club techniques. The following hints will help you make it an effective complement.

Develop an Internet Plan to Coincide with Your Job-Search Marketing Campaign

With the vast amount of information available online, it's easy to spend hours and hours of good job-search time scrolling through databases, accessing career centers, looking at job postings, or chatting in newsgroups. Be very careful not to spend too much time online. The Internet can be interesting but it can also be somewhat addictive. It may seem like productive time because a few hours online can generate a lot of information. However, the time may be better spent elsewhere. Are you as likely to spend hours on end on your networking calls?

The best way to develop your Internet plan is to define specific tasks you will need to accomplish in your allotted Internet time. Include the Internet as part of the research component of your target list and then as a further source when obtaining information about specific companies. Consider online job postings in the same way you would consider ads in periodicals, a great source of open positions but not the only source. Visit the sites sponsored by search firms, but remember: It's your job to find your next position, not theirs.

The Internet has become another means of obtaining interviews to be added to the list: networking, direct mail, search firms, ads, and now the Internet. Also, keep in mind that there may be a lot of hype and media articles about the effectiveness of online campaigns as compared with other job-search methods. Job seekers in certain fields, especially web-related or technical industries, will find that the Internet is an incredible resource, with companies expecting to receive responses to online postings in an electronic format. Job hunters in other fields may get discouraged by the minimal number of postings in their area, especially given the extensive media attention for its effectiveness. Include the Internet among your tools but don't consider it the only source.

Choose the Websites Appropriate for Your Search

Finding the right websites to review online postings should be part of your initial campaign as you develop your target list. In the same way you'll find periodicals the movers and shakers in your industry read, you'll also find industry-specific websites. These websites often contain job postings or have links to affiliate job sites. During the course of your information interviews, ask about industry periodicals and industry websites, too. Check the website of industry organizations and associations as a source for leads through job postings, not to mention activities in your field for networking contacts.

Visit online business periodicals and their affiliated job sites for related business information about your target companies. Current and past editions of these publications contain articles that are often available online for a minimal amount. If the person with whom you're meeting has been quoted or mentioned in the business press, a good way to find out is by searching the newswire and publications website databases.

Portal sites or search engines such as Yahoo (**www. yahoo.com**) and AOL (**www. aol com**) contain career sections and job postings in their business section. Career-specific websites such as Monster.com (**www.monster.com**), and Career Builder (**www.careerbuilder.com**) offer job postings and links to their participating companies. There are even search engines such as Jobhunt (**www. jobhunt. com**) or Dice (**www. dice. com**), which combine a number of career websites, thereby minimizing the number of career sites the job hunter needs to access.

Career sites often contain job postings for a company that are not listed on the firm's own corporate website. If it appears there are no open positions at a company, it may be because their jobs are listed elsewhere, so check through career sites for company-specific listings of your target firm. Keep in mind: Not all open positions are posted to websites and not all positions posted to websites are open.

Search firms often have sites allowing users to complete a profile then included in the candidate database. Complete the profile if you consider the firm reputable but make sure there's a notation about privacy so your résumé is sent out only with your permission.

Responding to Online Job Postings

Before responding to the online posting, verify whether the format you're using to send your cover letter and résumé is correct. Some companies want your résumé included in the body of the E-mail with no attachments. Other firms want two attachments, the cover letter and your résumé. Some companies request responses in text format only, so sending a word-processed document is not appropriate. In that case, convert the word-processed document (.doc) into a text format (.txt) before sending. This may seem trivial but you don't want your response eliminated before it is even reviewed.

When sending your résumé as an attachment, include your last name as part of the document name. For instance, don't call the attachment "My Résumé." If the attachment gets separated from the E-mail or if there is internal E-mail correspondence about a number of candidates, you don't want your documents to be easily confused or misplaced. On the subject line of the E-mail, try to include a notation that will address the topic but will also encourage the reader to open the E-mail. For instance, instead of just "My Résumé" include a notation about your area of expertise (from the first line of your Two-Minute Pitch). Try to keep this line to a minimum as this field is not uniform across all Internet service providers.

Consider online job postings in the same way you would want ads in newspapers and trade periodicals Position your response by matching your background to their requirements. Your response may be scanned by a computer so be sure your résumé contains the appropriate buzzwords for your industry.

Before sending your E-mail response to the company, send it to yourself first. Check the "From" box. If you have a cutesy online name, change it to a more business-appropriate name, even if it means signing on to a new online service or expanding the existing membership with your current Internet service provider. Check your Subject line to see if all the characters you intended are included in this space.

There's often a tendency to be less formal when sending E-mail than when sending written documents. Remember: This is still a job search so spell-check your E-mail before it goes out. If your browser does not have a spell-check feature, cut and paste a word-processed document that you've verified off-line into the body of the E-mail. Always add the E-mail address as the last item so you don't accidentally send an incomplete letter while you're still working on it.

Posting Your Résumé Online

Many of the Internet career websites provide an area in which job hunters post their résumés for access by potential employers. However, access is not limited to just potential employers. Do you want your current boss looking at your résumé online? Who else has access to your personal information, credentials, and employment history? Would you tack up your résumé on a public

bulletin board or hand it out to strangers just because they asked for it? And how can you follow up effectively if you don't know who has viewed your credentials?

However, some job hunters have found posting their credentials helpful in their search and there are ways to minimize some of these concerns. For instance, you can post only a portion of your personal information so interested respondents can call you for further details, allowing you to screen them. Online posting is certainly an option but is not recommended and removing or replacing an online résumé is rarely as easy as posting it.

Remember, the Internet is another tool to supplement your Five O'Clock Club techniques. If you need a quick reminder of this methodology, simply check out our website at **www.fiveoclockclub.com.**

Jobholders do not see the organization as a shifting pattern of needs. The only "opportunities" they recognize are the jobs that are currently posted on bulletin boards down at Personnel. And they grumble about how damned few of those there are, failing to note all the while the expanding range of unmet needs all over the organization.

William Bridges, *JobShift: How to Prosper in a Workplace Without Jobs*

The
Five
O'Clock
Club

How to Work with Search Firms

Once-in-a-lifetime opportunities come along all the time—just about every week or so.

Garrison Keillor, *A Prairie Home Companion*

If you understand how search firms work, your expectations will be more reasonable and you will better understand how to approach them.

Contrary to what some people think, a recruiter in a search firm does not place hundreds of managerial and professional people per year. Their search assignments are very specific and require extensive research, networking, and screening prior to presenting qualified individuals to their client organizations. Therefore, **the average recruiter places *one or two people a month***. This is the most important statistic for you to know about search firms and this information will affect your entire thought process about search firms.

Recruiters who deal with junior-level people need to place 2 people a month. Recruiters who deal with the very highest-level people may place only *6 people a year!* So search firms are not filling as many jobs as you think. It's actually *unlikely* that a search firm and a specific recruiter will be able to place you. Should you talk to search firms? Absolutely. But for goodness' sake don't *count* on them. The numbers are not on your side. Agencies may have lots of openings, but they are usually given the toughest positions to fill: Companies are willing to pay high agency fees to get candidates who walk on water. Agency recruiters would be the first to admit they don't have great hit ratios: Typically only *1* out of every 10 people they send on interviews is hired!.

The work recruiters do is in some respects similar to the work done by realtors. Recruiters "represent" positions that need to be filled (the equivalent of houses for sale), and they recruit qualified people to fill those positions (house hunters). They match qualified candidates with their job opportunities, just as realtors match house hunters with the houses on their lists. The realtor is trying to get buyer and seller to come together on price, and the realtor wants to stay in the middle of the transaction. In both fields, possibilities are sometimes presented as "once-in-a-lifetime" opportunities. And often, the actual matches are just as rare!

Recruiting is basically a sales profession and recruiters are interested in working with individuals who are marketable—just as realtors prefer houses that are marketable. Therefore, the more marketable you are, the more likely a search firm will be interested in handling you. If you are too difficult to categorize, are trying to make a major career change, require an unreasonable compensation, or have other drawbacks, search firms will balk at working with you (although they may not be totally honest about it).

You can increase your odds by *making it easy* for search firms to market you. Here are a few suggestions:

- Summarize your marketable characteristics in your cover letter. Recruiters need to categorize you anyway, so make it easy for them.

- Clearly state your target market (geographic area, industry, and position) and your salary range. For example: "I'm interested in a financial position in the direct-marketing industry in the New York or Chicago areas. I'm looking for a salary in the $65,000 to $70,000 range."

- Next, state your key selling points—your summary and accomplishments. Recruiters present your *accomplishments* to client organizations—not your job description. *Tell them what to say to sell you.* It will make their jobs easier and thus make them more likely to want to handle you.

- Be honest. Assume the search firm will check references and verify whatever information you give to them. Their reputations are based on the caliber of individuals they represent. If you misrepresent information, it could cost you the perfect career opportunity. Even if you get past the search firm, your employer could fire you later if falsehoods are uncovered.

To Redo Your Résumé—or Not

If recruiters want you to redo your résumé, follow their suggestions only if you think you're interested in the job about which they're talking to you. Sometimes customization is appropriate for a specific position, but some recruiters simply want résumés done their own way based on their own habits and biases—and their way may not be *better* at all. They forget that you got in to see *them* with your present résumé. They also forget that their technique "works" not because of their *résumé* approach but because they get on the phone and talk about you to someone. It's okay to change your résumé for them to meet a particular circumstance, but don't change your résumé *for the rest of your search* just because of what a recruiter wanted. Believe it or not, recruiters are *not* résumé experts. Listen instead to your coach and small group.

Sample Search-Firm Cover Letter

Search firms need to know your target: the kind of job you want and where. Your cover letter can

give you a boost here. They also need to know your salary requirements, so you might as well include a range in your cover letter. The letter on the following page uses our formula for cover letters presented earlier.

A Typical Search-Firm Marketing Call

Here's what may happen if you have made it easy for the recruiter by positioning yourself in your cover letter. They place a few phone calls. "Joe," they say, "I've got someone you may be interested in. He's a highly skilled individual who has the exact profile you have hired through me before." And then they may read from your cover letter. "He's got 15 years of financial experience in the direct-marketing industry. [Then they will stress your accomplishments, especially those that saved a past employer time or money.] He's an energetic, ambitious person—a real self-starter. When would it be convenient for us to set up a meeting? He's available next Tuesday or Wednesday morning . . . Oh, I know you don't have any positions currently available. After I met him, I just thought of you. I really think he'd be worth your time to interview."

Should You Keep in Regular Touch with Agencies?

The short answer is no. Recruiters are very aware of the positions they are trying to fill at the moment, and they are very aware of the candidates in their database. All of their energies are going into finding good matches for their client organizations. If they have a position that is appropriate for you and if they are not already too far along with the search, they will call you in. A follow-up phone call from you will do no good and just cuts into their busy day. We advise job hunters to send their résumés to search firms and then *get on with other aspects of their searches*.

It is better to form long-term relationships with reputable search firms. You can do this by helping them when they have an assignment they are trying to fill—even though it is not right for you. Perhaps you could suggest the names of other people they should call. Then when you are ready to make a move, they are already aware of you and your character, and are more likely to consider you when they have an opening that *is* right for you.

Life will give you what you ask of her if only you ask long enough and plainly enough.

E. Nesbitt

Which Organizations Use Search Firms?

Search firms are used by small- to mid-sized organizations with limited personnel departments. The search firm acts as an extension of their human resources staff. In addition, smaller organizations often must use search firms because applicants don't contact them as often as they do larger organizations.

Search firms are also used by major organizations with specific needs. Major organizations expect the search firm to identify the best individual in their industry nationwide—and usually in a very short period of time. Search firms are expected to know—or be able to find out quickly—the important players in a specialty.

Search firms are also used to fill jobs when there is a labor shortage. This could be for a specialty that is much in demand at the moment or for an executive-level position in a field so unusual that the search firm may have to look outside the organization's normal geographic area. Common positions may also be difficult to fill on occasion, leading organizations to turn to agencies.

How to Find Good Agencies and Recruiters

1. One of the best ways to identify good recruiters is by asking hiring managers or other job hunters—that is, through *networking.* When you meet with people during your search, ask them, "Are there any search firms you've used or you think I should talk to?"

2. A primary source of good information is the *Directory of Executive Recruiters.* Despite its title, this book lists firms for most job levels and job categories and also by geographic area. It is found in many libraries, or you can get your own copy from Kennedy Publications, Templeton Road, Fitzwilliam, NH 03447. However, don't contact contingency search firms blindly. (See below for the definition of contingency firms.) Instead, have a targeted list of search firms to contact rather than giving your résumé to everybody.

Search-Firm Cover Letter

Search firms need to know your target: the kind of job you want and where. They also need to know your salary requirements. This letter follows our formula format: Paragraph 2—Summary. Paragraph 3—Bulleted accomplishments.

Dear Ms. Bruno:

In the course of your search assignments, you may have a requirement for a technically knowledgeable IBM AS400—System 38 professional.

I have been both a "planner" and a "doer" of the phases of the System Development Life Cycle at companies such as General Motors and Proctor & Gamble, where I have spent most of my career. My accomplishments span the gamut, including the following:

- Evaluation of application and system software and hardware,
- Installation/setup of a new computer site,
- Conversion of RPG and COBOL programs,
- Requirements for and design of applications,
- Development and programming,
- Quality assurance and testing, and
- Optimization of performance for applications and systems.

At this juncture, after many years of commuting to Manhattan, I'm interested in seeking permanent employment in New Jersey, where I live.

The enclosed résumé briefly outlines my experience over the past 15 years. My base is now in the $70,000 range plus the usual fringes.

If it appears my qualifications meet the needs of one of your clients, I would be happy to further discuss my background in a meeting with you.

Yours truly,

Enclosure

Do not send your résumé to search firms unless you know their reputation. A disreputable agency could "blanket" the market with your résumé and cheapen your value. Make sure the search firm tells you *before* they send your résumé to anyone.

3. Look for search firms in the want ads in newspapers or trade journals. It's easy to identify those that handle the kinds of jobs for which you're looking. You can find out who specializes in your field or industry.

   Just be aware of the game that may be going on here. Not every ad you see in the paper represents a real job. Sometimes, contingency firms need a fresh batch of résumés: The people in their files have already moved on to new jobs. The next time you see an ad in the paper or on the Internet and you think *that job's too good to be true*. It probably *isn't* true. They placed a great, generalized ad to pull in a lot of résumés. Contact those search firms, but not necessarily for the job they have listed in the paper. When you call, they'll say, "That job is filled; let me talk to you about *other* jobs that may be right for you." Working with agencies really is a game.

4. If you're leaving a company because of a downsizing and you plan to stay in the same field, ask your human resources department which search firms *they* use. That will give you

"One of those headhunters called about you today, but it's not what you think. They have offered to pay us to keep you here."

some *clout* because you can say that "Jane Doe in human resources at Databank, Inc. suggested I call you." Since Databank, Inc. pays the search firm for placements, its search firm is likely to try to help you.

Retainer vs. Contingency Search Firms

The "search-firm" field has become more complex in recent years. It now includes new services, such as temporary-service firms.

Whether retainer or contingency, search firms are hired by organizations to fill positions. Organizations pay search firms about one-third of the new person's annual salary. Retainer firms receive an exclusive assignment to fill a position and get paid whether or not they find the person for it. Even if the employer finds a new person through another source, the retainer search firm keeps the fee. Contingency firms are paid only if they fill the position and several contingency firms could be working to fill the *same* position. The one that fills it gets the fee.

Do not send your résumé to contingency search firms unless you know their reputation. A disreputable agency could blanket the market with your résumé, cheapen your value, and even cripple your job search. A careless agency may even send your résumé to your present employer by accident—it's been known to happen!

Aim for a collaborative relationship with the agencies with which you decide to work. Insist on ground rules that will ensure you stay in control. Make sure, for example, that the search firm asks you before it sends your résumé to anyone. A search firm might want to send your résumé to an organization you're trying to get into on your own.

Search firms can help you, but some can actually harm you. For example, a firm—even one that's normally a retainer search firm—could say to you: "Oh, don't worry about your search. I'll take care of it for you." Then they blanket the market with your résumé—or contact employers *you* would have contacted on your own anyway. Now the hiring employer *cannot* consider ever hiring you unless they want to pay a fee. The employer may tell you they already have your résumé from a search firm and "We don't want to pay a fee." Therefore, the search firm becomes your competitor. They got into the organization before you did.

If the employer *is* willing to pay a fee, but two (or more) search firms have sent in your résumé, the organization will not hire you because it does not want to get into an argument about which search firm to pay.

The moral to the story: Yes, use search firms judiciously, but the far better approach is to contact prospective employers on your own wherever possible. If the search firm offers to market you around, this may sound like a gift, **but don't agree to this**. Market *yourself* around. Remember: When an agency represents you, there's a price on your head. You may end up being in competition with a candidate who submitted a résumé directly. Being able to hire without paying a fee may influence the organization's decision.

So tell the search firm, "Don't send out my résumé without calling me first." Keep control of where your résumé is going. Keep control of your search.

For God sake hold your tongue.
John Donne, *The Canonization*

Can I Get the Search Firm to Increase the Salary Being Offered?

The answer is: In most cases, you can't. A search firm is hired by a client organization to fill a certain position at a certain salary. A search firm needs to know your salary requirements. The salary cap can sometimes be negotiated based on the level or experience of the candidate. However, if the search firm does not put you in for the job because your salary requirements are too high,

contact the firm directly. Read the chapter "What to Do When You Know There's a Job Opening."

Let's remember the purpose of search firms: They cannot get you a job. Search firms can help you get *meetings* in your target market. You can also get meetings through ads, networking, and direct contact. When a search firm tells you about a specific job at a specific salary, decide if you want the *meeting*. Once they get you a meeting, you have to do the rest yourself.

Also remember our basic principle regarding salary negotiation: Do not negotiate the salary until you have received an offer. After you have had the interview, turn it into an offer by following up with the organization itself. Once you have the offer, get involved in the negotiating process yourself. There are some search firms that are excellent at negotiating on your behalf if the organization really wants you. In general, however, you will want to do the deal yourself. And you may have to stand up to the search firm if it tries to exclude you from the process.

Who naught suspects is easily deceived.
Petrarch, 1304–1374, Italian poet, *Sonnets*

Develop Long-Term Relationships: Become a Referral Source

Of course, there are always the headhunters who contact you. Establish a rapport with them. Their current job opening may not be appropriate for you, but if they sense that you are cooperative and know what you will accept, they will contact you when the right opportunity crosses their desk. Become a referral source—someone who recommends candidates—and you will receive calls on a regular basis.

In addition, keep the good firms regularly apprised of your situation—over the long term. For your current search, send a letter or E-mail to those with whom you already have a relationship: "It has been a while since we last spoke and I wanted to send you an updated résumé for your files." But be sure to develop a letter that helps the recruiter position you to clients.

When you accept a new position, send each organization with whom you have a relationship the same kind of note and an updated résumé. Good career management is a matter of staying in touch with key people.

Why a Retainer Recruiter May Not Put You in for a Job

Jim, a Five O'Clock Club member and marketer by profession, was one of the best networkers—and researchers—who has ever come to the Club. During the course of his search—through direct contact and networking—he uncovered *52 job openings for marketing management positions*. Jim had first contacted all of the retainer search firms appropriate for him, but he got very few employer meetings. When he networked into or directly contacted prospective hiring organizations themselves, the hiring managers said, "We really like you and we have a job that's out for search right now. Call the recruiter and *use my name*." But Jim had *already* contacted those firms and they had told him nothing about those openings! (Of those 52 openings he uncovered, 48 were being handled by retainer search firms.)

Jim called the recruiters again, restrained himself from being impolite, got the meetings using the names of the hiring manager, and ended up with at least five offers. *Many Five O'Clock Clubbers have had similar experiences landing interviews and jobs after they had been rejected by a search firm.* So a recruiter with a retainer search firm might *not* put you in for a job even though you may be perfect. What's going on here? Several factors are at work. Search firms are hired by the organization to go out and "search" for the right person. Recruiters with retainer firms are supposed to know their markets inside out. So, let's say a retainer search firm has conducted a search and said to the hiring organization, "These are the three best candidates for the job." Then *you* come along. It would be difficult for them to

then say, "Oops, by the way Ms. Hiring Manager, I've found another person for you."

There are other reasons why you may not be put in. In large search firms, there may be one recruiter who is handling that search, but you contacted a different recruiter. Perhaps the one you're talking to doesn't refer you to the recruiter who is handling that search. They're busy working on their own searches or recruiters may be in competition for the most placements that month! They're not going to pass you on to one of their competitors. So they tell you they don't have any appropriate openings right now.

Finally, if a retainer firm fills jobs for your *present* employer, they cannot help you leave your present employer! In fact, some major organizations will actually put a search firm *on* retainer just so the search firm *cannot* recruit from them.

You can see how easy it is for search-firm people not to put you in for a job even if you're the right person: You might make them look bad if they have said their search is complete, they may not be the actual recruiter who is handling the search, or they may have a contract with your present employer.

To take it one step further, a retainer search firm may tell you a hiring manager is not interested in you when they haven't even *told* the manager about you. Because the search firm has already rejected you, *you* contact the organization directly and find the organization has never even heard about you! That's because the search firm was pushing somebody else. They just don't want to tell you they were not going to put you in for the job. Don't be upset by any of this. It's just business and they really can't tell you the truth. They won't say, "I can't put you in for this job because I've already told the client company I've found them the perfect person." So they tell you a white lie. It's business. It's a game. So it's easy to see you shouldn't *depend* on search firms for your search.

But here's the key point: If a search firm refuses to submit your résumé or claims that you were rejected, *pretend you never contacted the search firm at all*. Instead, arrange to have a networking meeting with someone, *anyone* in the firm—not necessarily the hiring manager. After all, you're interested in working there, even if this job is not appropriate for you. **Contact the organization on your own.** However, don't mention you heard about an opening from a search firm. Instead, take the interview as you would with any organization in which you're interested—whether or not they have an opening right now.

The wise man avoids evil by anticipating it.
Publilius Syrus, c. 42 B.C., Roman writer, *Maxims*

Other Points about Salespeople

- Sometimes recruiters may tell you you're a strong candidate for the job when they really see you as *weak* or perhaps as a first or second runner-up. That's because they don't want you to drop out of the picture. They want to have you "in the pipeline." If *you* drop out of the picture, they might have to dig up somebody else. Don't be scandalized by these tactics. It's like any salesman who tells you this is your last chance to buy his product or the price will go up tomorrow. Recruiters are *sales*people.

- Remember: Recruiters are paid *well* if they place you. They get between 25 to 33 percent of your first year's salary when you land. The more money you make, the more money they make. *But* a recruiter may not necessarily be interested in getting you the highest salary possible. It's just like a realtor who wants to make that sale. The realtor gets a percentage, but doesn't mind cutting the price tag $10,000 if it means closing the deal. The recruiter would rather get the placement at a *lower* salary and with a *lower* fee instead of losing the placement. What's more, the recruiter can brag to the employer about the great job he did: "Have I found a bargain for you!" Remember, recruiters work for the *hiring* organization, not for you!

- Be wary of other aspects of the agency business. A contingency recruiter may ask you where else you've interviewed and who you have talked to there. She says, "I really need to know the kind of positions you're looking for. And who have you talked to? I want to know where you're seeing people so I don't send your résumé to the same places." But this may be a fishing expedition. Recruiters need to find *job openings*. As soon as you leave their office, an unethical contingency recruiter could be on the phone to the hiring manager you interviewed with telling him he has the *ideal* candidate for the job—and it *won't be you*! He'll put one of his other clients in for the job to have a shot at getting the fee.

- Be suspicious of recruiters who ask for names of references the first time they meet you. They may be looking for other people to add to their database and recruit for jobs. They shouldn't need references right away anyway. Protect your references.

After the Interview—Back to Five O'Clock Club Basics

When you go on interviews through agencies, be prepared for a tug-of-war concerning follow-up. Chances are, agencies will want you to step out of the way and let them "handle everything." But this is not in your best interests. Remember: The ball should always be in *your* court. Once you have met with the hiring team at the employer's organization, write your follow-up proposals directly to the *hiring* organization, *not to the recruiter.* When we talk about following up after a job interview, we mean **the follow-up you do with the organization itself, not the follow-up with the search firm**.

Most recruiters get nervous when Five O'Clock Clubbers say, "I'm writing a proposal for the employer," because they're afraid you'll ruin the hard work they put in. Most job hunters are not very savvy and might like the idea of letting the agency run the show. But Five O'Clock Clubbers are actually *better* at this process than most search-firm recruiters are. Do your follow-up with the prospective employer. In general, you should *not* copy the recruiter on the follow-up you're doing. Obviously call your recruiter after the interview to find out his impressions—weighing the possibility that what he tells you may not be completely truthful. Then deal with the hiring organization. This is where your small group is invaluable. Ask their advice.

Be courteous to all, but intimate with few; and let those few be well tried before you give them your confidence.

George Washington, 1721–1799, Letter to Bushrod Washington

A Final Word about Search Firms

Some search firms give the industry a bad name. If you are belittled or badgered by a search firm, do not take it personally, but *do move on*. The possible damage to your ego isn't worth it. A recruiter may, for example, hurt your ego so you will accept a position that is rather low in salary.

If you refuse a job offer, a search firm will still present you to their other client organizations. Getting an offer proves you are marketable. If you've received one offer, most will conclude you can get another. They will drop you, however, if they feel you are just shopping the market and are not interested in making a move. After all, they are running a business. So don't be frivolous in refusing offers.

But don't be afraid to turn down an offer if it is not appropriate for you. It is important that you not be talked into accepting an offer you don't want by a recruiter who is trying to satisfy the needs of the client organization. Recruiters are just trying to do their job: selling the benefits of the client organization's position.

Most recruiters are ethical and care about job hunters as well as the employers who pay them. But be smart and be on your guard against those firms that may use tactics that are not in your best interests. When times are good, search firms may be less likely to resort to these tactics. But when times get tough and business is more difficult to come by, firms are more likely to do things you need to guard against. Should you use search firms? Absolutely! Contact a number of search firms in your specialty. Depending on your target market, they may be a very important tool for getting meetings. But should you rely on search firms? Absolutely not! They should represent only a fraction of your job-hunt focus.

Pain: an uncomfortable frame of mind that may have a physical basis in something that is being done to the body, or may be purely mental, caused by the good fortune of others.

Ambrose Bierce

The
Five
O'Clock
Club

What to Do When You Know There's a Job Opening

To paraphrase Peter Drucker, effective people are not problem-minded; they're opportunity-minded. They feed opportunities and starve problems.

Stephen R. Covey, *The Seven Habits of Highly Effective People*

You've heard about a job opening from someone, or you've seen an ad in the paper. Answer that ad. But to increase your chances of getting a meeting, find an additional way in besides the ad (through networking or through directly contacting the organization).

When using networking or direct contact, most job hunters aim for the hiring manager. After all, he or she is the one with the job, so why would you contact anyone else?

But consider contacting someone other than the hiring manager. He or she is being inundated with requests for meetings by people who have heard about the job. To the hiring manager, those who network in may seem just like those who responded to the ad: another job hunter who knows there is a job opening.

But you are different. You're not a grubby job hunter. You're sincerely interested in this organization, aren't you? You want to meet with someone regardless of whether or not he or she has an opening, don't you? In fact, you are so interested in this organization you would be glad to speak with other people there, not just the hiring manager.

If you first meet with others, you will learn a lot about the hiring manager, the organization, its needs, and the kinds of people who work there.

They can refer you in to the hiring manager—with their recommendations. You will be much better prepared than those who got in through the ad. After the formal job interview, you will have advocates in the organization who can coach you and speak to the hiring manager on your behalf.

Some job hunters worry that the job may be filled before they get to the hiring manager. That's possible, but unlikely. Most jobs take a long time to fill. Résumés may sit for weeks before anyone even looks at them. In most cases, you will have time to meet with other people first.

To gather basic information, it's okay to meet with people junior to you or at your level to gather information. But it is sometimes difficult for those lower in the organization to refer you up to the boss. Those at your boss's level, or perhaps higher, are in a better position to refer you up, so make sure you aim to meet with them.

CASE STUDY Madge
I've Followed Your Organization

Jean, a participant at The Five O'Clock Club, met with five people at Conference Associates and received an offer. It was an interesting place, but she decided the job was too low-level and took another job.

When Jean announced at The Five O'Clock Club that she had turned down an offer from Conference Associates, Madge became very interested in the position.

Jean and Madge had dinner so Madge could learn more about the organization, the job, and the people with whom Jean met. Madge also did library research on the organization. Since she knew exactly who all the players were, she could easily have contacted the hiring manager. In fact, she could have networked in through Jean. But that's not what she did.

In this case, we decided Madge should write directly to the president, who was three-up in the chain of command (the person who would be her boss's boss's boss). In her letter, she said she had long been interested in Conference Associates and she referred to issues Jean had told her were important. **She did not refer to the fact that she knew there was a job opening.**

The cover letter Madge wrote (with a résumé enclosed) is on the next page. The president suggested Madge meet with human resources, the hiring manager, and others. By the way, **this is not networking. This is a targeted mailing.**

Through this technique, Madge got the meeting she wanted. Through her follow-up, she got the job. Read about follow-up in our book *Mastering the Job Interview and Winning the Money Game.*

Let your own discretion be your tutor:
Suit the action to the word,
The word to the action.

William Shakespeare, *Hamlet*

This is the cover letter Madge sent. She also enclosed her résumé.

MADGE WRIGLEY
345 East Ball Park Avenue
Scottsdale, AZ 44555
(555) 555-0121

July 3, 200X

Ms. Phyllis Rosen, President
Conference Associates
5637 Columbus Avenue
Phoenix, AZ 44555

Dear Ms. Rosen:

These days, the last thing an executive looking to improve profitability probably wants to hear is, "Go to a conference." But that is precisely what he or she may need to find ideas to solve problems back home. I am writing because Conference Associates' goal of encouraging interaction and furthering the exchange of knowledge is one I would like to promote.

I'm currently a manager at AT&T marketing directly to credit-card customers. I manage about $32 million in revenue annually. I've been successful in building a market for expensive products, some, such as life insurance, with negative connotations to overcome.

The key has been twofold: (1) setting clear-cut goals and guiding both the creative and managerial processes to see them realized and (2) carefully researching and identifying a target market, then developing compelling communications to reach them. Now, though, I would like to put my 10 years of business development and marketing experience to work for Conference Associates, specifically in order to take a broader, and global view, of business.

Several aspects of Conference Associates' activities are particularly aligned with my interests and skills:

- The customer orientation: I would like to make companies my customer, evaluating their needs and delivering the services to meet them.
- The Associates' stated goals for expansion in Europe: I firmly believe my international experience could prove beneficial. I'm fluent in French and Spanish, and have worked in France and Sweden.
- I'm an educator at heart: I enjoy managing and developing staff and making connections among people and ideas.

In sum, I believe I could offer a trained and critical eye to understand the need and persuasive marketing programs to communicate the service.

At your convenience, I would be most interested in having a chance to speak with you. I'll call your office shortly to see if that may be possible.

Sincerely,

Madge Wrigley

MADGE WRIGLEY
345 East Ball Park Avenue
Scottsdale, AZ 44555

August 17, 200X

Mr. Charles Conlon
Director, Personnel
Conference Associates
5637 Columbus Avenue
Phoenix, AZ 44555

Dear Chip:

First of all, it was a pleasure to meet you last Wednesday. I enjoyed hearing your assessment of the potential that exists for C.A., and seeing your commitment and enthusiasm for the organization.

You spoke of the unique position of C.A. as a nonprofit service organization run more and more like any business in a competitive environment. The role of a new marketing director, then, would be to develop a strategy for the business to position C.A. for the next level of growth. It's fortunate that C.A. has a solid base to grow from, including a reputation for quality and service. The challenge would be to enhance that reputation while building new markets and customers.

One of the things we spoke about was the need for the marketing director to work closely and productively with other departments. Ellis Chase and I spoke about that as well. I feel particularly motivated by that type of challenge and have been successful in working with diverse groups. For example, recently at AT&T a major new segmentation strategy and methodology for my product line required tying in systems, finance, and new products, in addition to marketing. It wasn't easy, but the reward is a successful expansion of our business and a precedent set for productive cross-departmental projects.

Getting a business built depends a lot on people who don't report to you and buying them into the goals and the process is the only way of getting the job done well. It requires using a balance of sensitivity and toughness and relating to colleagues with flexibility and creativity. If C.A.'s marketing department is going to become a vital and integral part of the operation, it has to establish itself as responsive, knowledgeable, and resourceful.

I truly believe this position is a solid match with my experience and interests, both for the specific skill base required and the opportunity to build a comprehensive marketing program. I've developed marketing plans for organizations ranging from small nonprofits to AT&T and achieved positive results with the implementation.

The common thread in that success has been what you called "ownership." In both my professional experience and my community volunteer work, I tend to approach the task at hand with energy and commitment. After all, the most effective marketer is the one who can combine strategic development and proven skills with genuine product enthusiasm. I would be most interested in putting that same experience and enthusiasm to work for C.A..

Looking forward to speaking with you again soon.

Best,

Madge Wrigley

MADGE WRIGLEY
345 East Ball Park Avenue
Scottsdale, AZ 44555

August 18, 200X

Mr. Ellis Chase
Senior Vice President, Development
Conference Associates
5637 Columbus Avenue
Phoenix, AZ 44555

Dear Ellis:

It was good meeting with you last Wednesday. I got a clear picture of the requirements of the marketing director position and the kind of challenges to be met.

First and foremost, you expressed a need going forward for someone who can develop a comprehensive, integrated marketing strategy and can communicate that plan effectively and appropriately in all facets of its implementation.

That requires the skills of listener, evaluator and diagnostician, coupled with an ability to generate and harness ideas and turn them into positive results. The goal would be to establish C.A. as a leading source of business intelligence and creativity for corporations and their executives.

I've had a chance to think about some of the ways we discussed to accomplish that goal. It seems that both the stated mission of C.A. and its profitability center on building and enhancing its relationship with members, working to have members' resources and activities become a more familiar and integral part of corporate life. One of the priorities you outlined was devising ways to package existing products and services, maximizing both internal marketing efficiency and external perception of value. That would include targeting different people within the same organization with relevant services, as well as determining the right level of pricing.

You also mentioned C.A.'s global objective, trying to serve both U.S. companies competing internationally and many of their foreign competitors. Although I understand the Paris affiliate handles much of the activity in Europe, one of the components of an integrated marketing plan would be defining the optimum balance between a U.S. and global emphasis.

I firmly believe my experience and personality fit the job at hand and that the skills required play to my strengths. I have demonstrated success in strategic and creative planning, researching, and identifying target markets, then developing compelling and appropriate communications to reach them. At both AT&T and previously at RCA, I have developed new businesses and products, including pricing, positioning, and packaging existing services. Efforts I've directed include advertising that increased response from 58% to 93%, and market expansion of 30% with new targeting programs.

I've found ways to run marketing activities more efficiently, saving on both fixed overhead and variable production costs. Finally, as I mentioned, I'm in charge of all writing for the business unit, working closely with each area to communicate group and corporate monthly results as well as the five-year and annual strategic plans.

From my conversations with you and Deborah, the goals for the position, the products of C.A., and its environment seem to represent a strong match with my background and interests. I look forward to speaking with you again soon and having a chance to discuss the position further.

Sincerely,

Madge Wrigley

MADGE WRIGLEY
345 East Ball Park Avenue
Scottsdale, AZ 44555

October 18, 200X

Ms. Phyllis Rosen
President and CEO
Conference Associates
5637 Columbus Avenue
Phoenix, AZ 44555

Dear Phyllis:

While everything is now official and I'll be starting Thursday, October 24th, I wanted to let you know what a pleasure it was to finally meet with you and how delighted I am to be joining C.A..

When we met, you spoke of approaching the task of marketing C.A. with an eye to challenges and opportunities, building on a strong foundation to find better ways to position ourselves in an increasingly competitive market. That includes keeping the focus on senior-level executives. Your outline of the process you've undertaken to evaluate C.A.'s activities was extremely helpful, as well as your expectations for staff to initiate and persuade, even without direct-line responsibility. I particularly appreciated your straightforward review of the financial position.

You also spoke specifically of the need for someone to bring to the position not only marketing expertise but also an enjoyment of your intellectual, knowledge-based product. I firmly believe in that genuine product combination. I'm looking forward to working with that combination and with colleagues who are clearly committed to the organization.

One of them is certainly Melanie. We had a terrific meeting, reviewing everything from general history to specific programs. Particular attention was paid to the strategic plan and development of C.A. over the past few years and the challenge of communicating that strategy both internally and to our customer base. I'm very much looking forward to working with her on integrating a marketing strategy into the overall planning process and new product development, and incorporating that strategy into marketing the programs. I'll also be able to meet with Aaron before I start.

Over the past few weeks, I've had a chance both to think about my conversations with you and others with whom I've met and to review some of C.A.'s materials (50th anniversary history, last year's annual report, etc.). I believe there is enormous potential to spread the word—and the work—of C.A. to a wider audience and to enhance the value of the organization to its current customers. A major component of the task is communication—defining those characteristics that differentiate us in the marketplace and translating them into language that sells. Your commitment to testing new approaches is welcome, understanding the need for moving thoughtfully and with careful planning.

I look forward to the 24th and to a wonderful association at my new home.

Very best,

Madge Wrigley

Following Up When There Is No Immediate Job

Contrary to the cliché, genuinely nice guys most often finish first, or very near it.

Malcolm Forbes

During each meeting, you have taken up the time of someone who sincerely tried to help you. Writing a note is the only polite thing to do. Since the person has gone to some effort for you, go to some effort in return. A phone call to thank a person can be an intrusion and shows little effort on your part.

In addition to being polite, there are good business reasons for writing notes and otherwise keeping in touch with people who have helped you. For one thing, few people keep in touch so you will stand out. Second, it gives you a chance to sell yourself again and to overcome any misunderstandings that may have occurred. Third, this is a promotional campaign and any good promoter knows that a message reinforced soon after a first message results in added recall.

If you meet someone through a networking meeting, for example, he or she will almost certainly forget about you the minute you leave and just go back to business. Sorry, but you were an interruption.

If you write to people almost immediately after your meeting, this will dramatically increase the chance they will remember you. If you wait two weeks before writing, they may remember meeting someone but not remember you specifically. If you wait longer than two weeks, they probably won't remember meeting anyone—let alone you.

So promptly follow the meeting with a note. It is important to remind those to whom you write who you are and when they talked to you. Give some highlight of the meeting. Contact them again within a month or two. It is just like an advertising campaign. Advertisers will often place their ads at least every four weeks in the same publication. If they advertised less often, few people would remember the ad.

"I'm sorry, but Mr. Konklin is extremely busy today. Can I take a message and have him get back to you?"

What Michael Did

This is a classic—and it worked on me. I wanted to hire one junior accountant for a very important project and had the search narrowed down to two people. I asked my boss for his input. We made up a list of what we were seeking and we each rated the candidates on 20 criteria. The final scores came in very close, but I hired Judy instead of Michael.

In response to my rejection, Michael wrote me a note telling me how much he still wanted to work for our organization and how he hoped I would keep him in mind if something else should come up. He turned the rejection into a positive contact. Notes are so unusual and this one was so personable, that I showed it to my boss.

A few months later, Michael wrote again saying he had taken a position with another firm. He was still very much interested in us and he hoped to work for us someday. He promised to keep in touch, which he did. Each time he wrote, I showed the note to my boss. Each time, we were sorry we couldn't hire him.

After about seven months, I needed another helping hand. Whom do you think I called? Do you think I interviewed other people? Do you think I had to sell Michael to my boss? Michael came to work for us and we never regretted it. Persistence pays off.

We make a living by what we get, but we make a life by what we give.
Winston Churchill

What to Say in Your Follow-Up Note

Depending on the content of your note, you may type or write it. Generally use standard business-size stationery, but sometimes Monarch or other note-size stationery, ivory or white, will do. A *job* interview follow-up should almost always be typed on standard business-size ivory or white stationery.

After an information-gathering meeting, play back some of the advice you received, any you intend to follow, and so on. Simply be sincere. What did you appreciate about the time the person spent with you? Did you get good advice that you intend to follow? Say so. Were you inspired? Encouraged? Awakened? Say so.

If you think there were sparks between you and the person with whom you met, be sure to say you will keep in touch. Then do it. Follow-up letters don't have to be long, but they do have to be personal. Make sure the letters you write could not be sent to someone else on your list.

Sample Follow-Up to a Networking Meeting

PETER SCHAEFER

To: Alexandra Duran

Thanks again for contacting Brendan for me and for providing all those excellent contact names.

There's such a wealth of good ideas in that list that it will take me a while to follow up on all of them, but I'm working hard at it and will let you know what develops.

Again, thanks for your extraordinary effort. (By the way, should you ever want to "review your career options," I would be delighted to share a few names, or more than a few, with you.)

Stay tuned!

Peter

To keep in touch, simply let interviewers/network contacts know how you are doing. Tell them whom you are seeing and what your plans are. Some people, seeing your sincerity, will keep sending you leads or other information.

It's never too late to follow up. For example: "I met you a year ago and am still impressed by . . . Since then I have . . . and would be interested in getting together with you again to discuss these new developments." Make new contacts. Recontact old ones by writing a "status report" every two months telling them how well you are doing in your search. **Keeping up with old networking contacts is as important as making new ones.**

Some job hunters use this as an opportunity to write a proposal. During the meeting, you may have learned something about the organization's problems. Writing a proposal to solve them may create a job for you. Patricia had a networking meeting with a small company where she learned that it wanted to expand the business from $5 million to $50 million. She came up with lots of ideas about how that could be done—with her help, of course—and called to set up a meeting to review her ideas. She went over the proposal with them and they created a position for her.

However, you are not trying to turn every networking meeting into a job possibility. You *are* trying to form lifelong relationships with people. Experts say most successful employees form solid relationships with lots of people and keep in touch regularly throughout their careers. These people will keep you up-to-date in a changing economy, tell you about changes or openings in your field, and generally be your long-term ally. And you will do the same for them.

Has a man gained anything who has received a hundred favors and rendered none? He is great who confers the most benefits.

Ralph Waldo Emerson, "Essay on Compensation"

The Five O'Clock Club

Following Up after a Networking/ Direct-Contact Meeting

The follow-up after a networking meeting—or a meeting resulting from having directly contacted an organization (through a direct-mail campaign or a targeted mailing)—is very different from the way you follow up after a job interview.

Analyze the meeting. In your letter, thank the interviewer. State the *specific* advice and leads you were given. Be personable. Say you will keep in touch. *Do* keep in touch.

Follow up every few months with a "status report" on how your search is going, an article, or news of interest to the manager.

Make sure people are thinking about you. You may contact the manager just as he or she has heard of something of importance to you.

Recontact those you met earlier in your search. Otherwise, you're like a salesman who works to get new leads while ignoring his old relationships. Get new leads but also keep in touch with people you've already met.

It's never too late to follow up. For example: "I met you three years ago and am still impressed by____. Since then I have_____and would be interested in getting together with you again to discuss these new developments." Make new contacts. Recontact old ones. It's never too late.

Trouble getting started? What would you say to the person if he or she were sitting across from you right now? Consider that as the opening of your follow-up letter.

Job hunters make a mistake when they fail to *recontact* people with whom they have formed relationships earlier in their search. Keep in touch on a regular basis so you increase your chances of contacting them just at a time when they have heard of something that may interest you—or may have a new need themselves.

Follow up with a customized note specifically acknowledging the help you received.

JOHN WEITING
163 York Avenue—12B
New York, New York 10000
(212) 555-2231 (day)
(212) 555-1674 (message)
jweiting@attnet.net

June 25, 200X

Ms. Rachel Tepfer
Director of Outplacement
Time-Warner Communications
8 Pine Street
New York, NY 10001

Dear Ms. Tepfer:

Thanks so much for seeing me. Your center is very impressive and seems very well run. But of course, I had heard that before I met you.

As you suggested, I sent for information on ASTD and was pleasantly surprised to see your name in there! It sounds like a great organization and I can't wait until they start to have meetings again in the fall.

I will definitely follow up with both Max McCreery and Marilyn Kaufman, and appreciate your giving me their names. I've called them each a few times, but they and I are very busy people.

After I left your place, I wished I had asked you more about your own career. Only at the very end did you bring up the interesting way you got your job. I had wrongly assumed you came up through the ranks at Time-Warner Communications. Perhaps some other time I can hear the rest of the story. You certainly seem to know your stuff.

I've enclosed The Five O'Clock Club calendar for June, July, and August. In addition, I'll be speaking at The New School in a few weeks and have a lot planned for myself for the fall. I will keep you posted regarding my activities and perhaps I'll even run into you at ASTD meetings.

Thanks again for your time and insight. Till we meet again.

Cordially,

John Weiting

GREGORY BOARDMAN

August 24, 20xx

Dear Mary Ann:

Just a quick note to thank you for taking the time to meet with me yesterday. Even though it seems I've located most of the places that could use my skill set, it's always nice to revalidate that opinion.

I was interested to learn of your new position in national product engineering. Although I understand your current situation, I'm always excited to discover new possibilities for becoming involved in Big Red's national campaign. I've long believed this effort is paramount to Big Red's continued dominance in the industry. In fact I expressed just such an opinion to Julie Ward on Tuesday. Julie is involved in Big Red's advertising program to develop a national brand image and I commented to her how much I liked the concept.

I am very flattered, too, that you would consider involving me in your developing organization. As I mentioned to you, I am quite good at "start-up" positions requiring a great amount of vision to allow for working in an indeterminate environment. Clearly my marketing liaison and consulting activities would be a natural for your charter as well. If I can help you in any way as you define your area, I would be happy to offer you my assistance.

I would like very much to contact you again in a few weeks to learn more about your progress. In the meantime I am going to try to contact Lou Fleming and others involved in the National Marketing effort to keep abreast of this exciting new area.

Thanks again for your time—hope to see you again soon.

Sincerely,

Gregory

Follow-up letters don't have to be long, but they *do* have to be personal. Make sure the letters you write could not be sent to anyone else on your list.

SYLVAN VON BERG

To: Judy Acord

I enjoyed our conversation, which I found most helpful.

I will meet with Betsy Austin when she returns from overseas, and will talk to Jim about seeing Susan Geisenheimer. I'll also contact Bob Potvin and Clive Murray, per your suggestion.

Again, thanks for your help. I'll let you know how things develop.

Sylvan

CARL ARMBRUSTER

To: Nancy Abramson

Thanks again for contacting Brendan for me and for providing all those excellent contact names.

There's such a wealth of good ideas in the list it will take me a while to follow up with all of them, but I'm working hard at it and will let you know what develops.

Again, thanks for your extraordinary effort. (By the way, should you ever want to "review your career options," I would be delighted to share a few names, or more than a few, with you.)

Stay tuned!

Carl

Mr. Miguel Villarin
President
Commerce and Industry Association
Street Address
City, State

Dear Miguel:

Thank you for the time from your busy schedule. I enjoyed our discussion and appreciated your suggestions about marketing myself in the northern part of the state. Your idea on using the Big 8 firms as pivot points in networking is an excellent one. As you requested, I have enclosed copies of my résumé. I plan to call you next week, Miguel, so that I can obtain the names of the firms to which you sent my résumé.

I have been thinking about using Robert Dobbs (Dobbs & Firth) in my networking efforts. Since he is a past president of Commerce and Industry, I would be foolish not to tap such a source. Thanks again, Miguel.

Sincerely,

Janet Vitalis

Enclosures

The Five O'Clock Club

How to Handle Rejection Letters

In nature, there are neither rewards nor punishments—there are consequences.

Robert Green Ingersoll

Organizations generally send the same rejection letter to everyone—complimenting the applicant on his or her credentials and offering regret that there are no appropriate openings at this time. A rejection letter is truly a rejection only when it follows a job interview.

Rejection Letters in Response to a Direct-Mail Campaign

If you received a respectable number of responses (meetings) from your campaign, try another campaign of the remaining organizations in a few months. Direct marketers say you should then expect approximately half the response you got with your first mailing. As an alternative, network into the organizations of interest to you, contact someone else in the same firm, or use a targeted-mailing approach.

If the response rate from your mailing was poor, you picked the wrong market for what you have to offer or the package you sent was lacking. Chances are, you were not as knowledgeable about this market as you thought. Research or network to learn more or network to find out what was wrong with your package.

Rejection Letter in Response to an Ad

This is par for the course. The organization probably received 1,000 résumés. Or perhaps the ad was not for a legitimate opening.

If an organization's name was listed, network in, do a targeted mailing to someone who could be close to the hiring manager, or contact a search firm that handles the type of position mentioned. (See the chapter "What to Do When You Know There's a Job Opening.") Your résumé was probably rejected by someone other than the hiring manager, so it's worth further effort if you're interested in the position. Some organizations have a policy of immediately sending out rejection letters to everyone. Then they call those people they're interested in—even though the applicants have already been "rejected." For organizations that always send rejection letters, this approach saves time.

Rejection Letter in Response to a Networking Contact You Tried to Make

The person did not understand you were seeking information. If many people respond to you this way, reassess your approach to networking.

Rejection Letter Following a Job Interview

This is a true rejection letter. It used to be it took seven job interviews to get one offer, but the figure may now be higher. If you are still interested in the organization, don't give up. (Read what Michael did in the chapter "Following Up When There Is No Immediate Job."

Lessons to Learn

When you get a rejection note in response to a job interview, think about it. How interested are you in that firm? Did you hit it off with the interviewer? If you think there was some mutual interest, see if there might be other jobs with the organization later—perhaps in another department. Or perhaps the person hired instead of you might not work out. Keep in touch. Job hunters rarely do, but employers like to hire people who truly want to work for them and show it by keeping in touch.

CASE STUDY *Stan*
Turning a Rejection into an Offer

Stan was told an offer was being made to another candidate. He was crushed, but he immediately dashed off a letter to the hiring manager and hand-delivered it. The brief letter said in part:

> I was disappointed to hear you have offered the position to someone else. I truly believe I am right for the position and wish you would keep me in mind anyway. You never know— something could happen to the new person, and you may need a replacement. Please consider me no matter when this may occur, because I believe I belong at your institution.

The next day, Stan received a call with an offer. Some people may think the offer to the other candidate fell through. However, I believe Stan's letter influenced the hiring manager. When he saw the letter, he thought to himself, We're offering the position to the wrong person! and he allowed the negotiation with the other candidate to lapse.

The
Five
O'Clock
Club

PART FOUR

Managing Your Campaign
ARE YOU CONDUCTING A GOOD SEARCH?

The
Five
O'Clock
Club

How to Handle the Phone:
A Life Skill

The greatest mistake you can make in life is to be continually fearing you will make one.

Elbert Hubbard

I wrote to Betty, a senior human resources executive whom I have known for years, asking her to be on a panel addressing about 100 other executives. A few days later, I called her office. Her assistant, Jeb, said he could see someone in her doorway talking to her and he would ask her to call me. Betty didn't call: She's a very busy lady and I never expected a return call. When I called again that afternoon, I joked with Jeb, asking him if there was someone still standing in Betty's doorway. I asked him not to interrupt his boss because I understood how busy she was, but he said he would buzz her anyway and I then spoke to her.

This is the way it works in everyday life. When you're making routine work-related phone calls or calling your friends, if they don't return your call, you assume they're busy. And you think nothing of calling them again if you really want to talk to them. But when you're job hunting, you assume they don't call back because they don't *want* to talk to you. You become fearful of rejection. Unfortunately, you cannot get a job unless you actually meet with people—usually lots of people. And it's difficult to get those meetings without using the telephone.

I had no trouble calling Betty. But when I have to recruit speakers I have never met, I dread making those calls even though prospective speakers are usually flattered.

What should you say first? What if they don't answer? What if they do answer? And, yes, in this day of voice mail, things are certainly more complicated.

Making follow-up phone calls is the part of the job-search process people tend to dislike the most. Yet, the calls *must* be made:

- as a follow-up to a letter asking for a meeting—the most common reason for making a call,

- as a follow-up after an interview, and

- as part of your research to find out the name of the right person to contact.

In this chapter, we'll cover how to ask for a meeting.

The Set-Up: Usually by Letter

A letter followed by a phone call is effective because most executives do not like to be caught off guard. They want to know what your phone call is about. If you have been following The Five O'Clock Club process, you have been contacting people with networking letters or targeted mailings. *Networking* means you are using the name of someone else to help you get the meeting: "John Doe suggested I contact you because he thought you could give me the advice I need."

A targeted mailing differs from networking because you are *not* using someone else's name. Instead, *you* create a tie-in to that person. You may write, for example, "I have been following your organization for some time and noticed your international sales have been dropping. I'd like to talk to you about that" or "Congratulations on your new position!"

Whether you are writing a letter using someone else's name or establishing your own connection with that person, the last paragraph of your letter says: "I will call you in a few days."

> **Most people find it difficult to make those follow-up phone calls after having written to someone.**

Learning the Art of Calling

To get the meeting you want, you will have to pick up the phone.

What should you say first? What if they don't answer? What if they *do* answer? And, yes, in this day of voice mail, things can certainly be more complicated.

You'll have to practice to become good at your follow-up phone calls. This means tracking results. Observe what is working and what is not. Modify your script to suit yourself and the situation at hand. You will soon learn to think on your feet and get that meeting or a referral to someone else—without annoying people. But this comes with repetition and practice.

Getting Started

> *I am a great believer, if you have a meeting, in knowing where you want to come out before you start the meeting. Excuse me if that doesn't sound very democratic.*
>
> Nelson Rockefeller

Before you make that call—even before you write that letter—be sure you know the purpose of

your call and what you want to get out of it. If you have unclear goals, you are less likely to accomplish anything worthwhile.

You may be calling to get:

- an in-office meeting with the person, unless the person is in a distant city,
- a phone meeting if that is the only reasonable option, or
- the name of an appropriate person with whom you should talk—if the person you're calling is at too high a level or in a different area.

> **"May I have Mr. Jones call you back?"**
> **"No, thanks, I'll be in and out a lot myself. I'll call him back later. When would be a good time for me to call?"**
>
> **Keep control of this process. If you say to your group, "I've left four messages and they haven't called me back," your group will say, "Stop leaving messages." Instead it's *your* responsibility to put in the effort to make the connection happen eventually.**

Become Friends with the Assistant

A long time ago, I wanted to meet with the person in charge of outplacement coaching at a Fortune 10 company. Even with research, I could not uncover the name of that person. So I wrote to Kevin Altria, the head of human resources, *knowing* he was inappropriate because he was too senior. I didn't need to get in to see Kevin or even speak to him. I just wanted him to refer me on. Then, when I contacted the appropriate person, I would be able to use Kevin's name.

So, before I finished the letter, I called Kevin's assistant to get her name (Jane) so I could include it in the letter and tell her to watch for it.

I followed The Five O'Clock Club format for cover letters. In the opening paragraph to Kevin, I wrote, "I know you're not the right person for me to contact, but I assume you know who's in charge of outplacement coaching at your firm. I'd like to tell that person something about myself and find out more about your company's out-placement department."

Paragraph two was my summary about myself. Paragraph three, the bulleted accomplishments. In the closing paragraph, I said, "I will call *Jane* in a few days to find out who you suggest I contact."

But there's more. On my letter, I put a sticky note saying, "Jane, this is the letter I told you about." When Jane opened her boss's mail, she saw my note with her name on it. She took the letter in to her boss and got the information I needed. Then I called Jane back (by now, we're friends) and I said, "Hi Jane, this is Kate Wendleton again. I'm following up about the letter I sent your boss." And she said, "We sent your letter on to Sylvia Norwood, who is in charge of outplacement here." I never had to bother Jane's boss.

At this point, I could have simply *called* Sylvia. But I didn't want anything to go wrong, so I *wrote* to Sylvia and said, "Kevin Altria suggested I contact you." This was my standard letter. And again, I followed the routine of finding out Sylvia's assistant's name (Jason) and using the sticky note. So, when I called back, I talked directly to Jason again and asked him to help me set up a meeting with Sylvia.

Notice I don't use the assistant as a messenger, asking him simply to tell Sylvia that I called. Instead, I want the assistant to be my ally. I tell Jason a little about my background, why I want to meet with Sylvia, and ask Jason to pass that information on to her. Sometimes, it may take five or six talks with the assistant to set something up. Eventually, Jason said, "Sylvia's very busy and she manages her own calendar, but I'll get her to talk to you."

This is a slow but fairly sure approach for getting in to see appropriate senior-level people. I had a two-hour meeting with Sylvia and was referred on to excellent people in the field.

Very senior people tend to have very smart assistants on whom they rely. So I can "pitch" to

an assistant and ask him to make sure the boss sees my letter. And I don't try to meet with people who are inappropriate for me to see, irritating them and wasting their time.

- **Have goals for your phone calls.**
- **Develop an outline of what you want to say.**
- **Practice to become smooth and natural.**

What Are Your Back-Up Plans?

Sometimes you will not get what you want. Perhaps the person is in the middle of a major project right now or sees herself as an inappropriate person for you to talk to. You can still get something out of the conversation. You can at least try the following tactics.

- Determine when the person may have more time to schedule a meeting with you. The manager may have said to you: "We're in the midst of a crisis" "The next month is murder for me" or "We're reorganizing. I don't even know what's going to happen. The dust isn't going to settle for three months."

  Try to book *something*. "How about if we schedule something for a month from now? I'll call you ahead of time to confirm." Or—in the worst case—"May I call you back in [a month] to see if the situation has changed?"

- Get other names. For example, the manager may have said, "I'm leaving the organization in a few weeks" "This department doesn't concentrate on that" or "We don't use financial people in this department."

  You can say, "Can you direct me to others in your organization you think it would be appropriate for me to talk with?"

For most people, getting in to see a specific, appropriate person is not easy and requires a high degree of motivation. It must be important to you

177

or you will not think of the right things to say and you will give up too quickly. Do you want a meeting with this person or not? If not, go back to *Targeting a Great Career* and rethink what you want to do with your life.

> **Why should a person meet with you *now* just because you wrote to them? You're sitting by the phone, but they're busy.**

It's a Self-Selection Process

You wrote a letter. Why should a person meet with you—and meet with you now—just because you wrote them a letter now? Not only are they busy with their jobs, but personal things come up: There's been a death in the family; he's suffering from the flu; she's on vacation; she is out of the country 90 percent of the time.

You're sitting by the phone, but they're busy.

Part of getting meetings is a self-selection process: You decide how important this meeting is to you and you put in effort *to the extent you want it to happen.* Five O'Clock Club research shows that it takes an average of eight follow-up phone calls to land a meeting. The research also shows the more senior the person, the more calls you will have to make. Senior-level people travel a lot or are in meetings; they are difficult to track down and returning your call is not the most important thing on their "to do" list. If you really want to see them, prove it by your effort. You can show your interest without irritating them, such as when you acknowledge, "I'm sure you must be very busy . . ."

> **It's a self-selection process. If meeting with this person is important to you, put in the effort.**

One Five O'Clock Clubber—a senior-level marketing executive—sent targeted mailings to

20 important, high-profile people. He got in to see people like Craig McCaw of McCaw Cellular and John Kluge, one of the richest men in America. On average, this process required *15* follow-up phone calls—15 conversations with assistants. He met with approximately half the people on his list. He ended up spending four hours with Craig McCaw at Newark Airport—the only mutually convenient place they could arrange. His search was very successful, but he also understood he needed to prove to these in-demand people that it was important that they meet. By the way, he spent four days preparing for his meeting with Craig McCaw.

Busy and important people must have their calls screened or they would never get their work done. On the other hand, part of their job is to look at new talent, make sure they don't miss someone, and keep up with what is happening in the industry.

> **It takes an average of eight follow-up phone calls to get a meeting. The more senior the person, the more calls it takes. But leave a message only once.**

How can an important person decide with whom he should meet? Part of that person's decision is how important the meeting is to *you*. Have you done your homework? Do you know how to talk to his assistant? Do you make a good pitch to the assistant? Do you call back frequently, but without becoming a burden? You have to break through the clutter of all the other people vying for a place on his calendar.

When I was in my early 30s, living in Philadelphia, I had my day job but loved artwork and art museums. I was at the Philadelphia Museum of Art every single Sunday, did a lot of volunteer work there, and knew a lot about that museum. It was announced that Jean Boggs, who was at Harvard, was going to come in as the new head of the museum. *I wanted to see Jean*

Boggs because I had so many ideas for that museum.

Would I be able to network in to see her? Not a chance. *No one* in Philadelphia would have introduced "Kate who?" to Jean Boggs. Instead, I wrote to Jean Boggs at Harvard *six months* before she was scheduled to come to Philadelphia. I said essentially, "You and I should meet. I have a lot of interest in the museum and a lot of ideas."

Then a month before Jean was to arrive at the museum, I wrote to her *again,* saying, "Do you remember me? I know you're coming to Philadelphia in a month and when you get here I think you and I should meet." A little arrogant of me!

When she got to Philadelphia, I wrote to her a *third* time and I said, in so many words, "Hi, it's me again. I know you've arrived and I still want to see you."

When she got to Philadelphia, I was so persistent in making those follow-up phone calls—and not leaving messages for her to call me—that poor Jean Boggs eventually agreed to meet with me. I was passionate about the museum, so these calls were easy despite my shyness.

When I met with Jean, I was enthusiastic and had plenty of ideas. She graciously granted me 15 minutes and then took me down the hall to meet Noble Smith, who actually ran the museum on a day-to-day basis. I had a great meeting with Noble and he came up with a project for me. I worked with about 20 people who were on staff and shared my ideas and we implemented a lot of them. I actually got paid a small amount so I could say I was a paid consultant.

Although I have always been shy, I've managed to meet with anyone I've ever targeted. Who was *I* to get in to see Jean Boggs? I was just a lowly volunteer with no connections. I didn't have great credentials in the art area. I simply wanted to see someone for what I thought was a good reason, I wrote a letter using no one else's name, and I followed up—a *lot.* Being successful in a targeted mailing has to do with being sincerely interested, doing a fair amount of research, contacting the right person, and not

being put off when you make those follow-up phone calls.

> **If I'm afraid of making 20 follow-up phone calls, the good news is that only two people will actually be there!**

The Follow-Up Call

You *must* make those follow-up phone calls. Don't leave a message saying you called and hope they'll call you back. Instead, say to the assistant, "I don't want to leave a message for Ms. Boggs to call me. I'm going to be in and out a lot myself, so I'll call her back."

Do Not Leave Your Phone Number

If you leave two or three messages asking them to call you back and they don't call, you are stuck. Instead, stay in control. Leave one message saying you called, and then keep calling until you reach them.

The first time you call, you can leave a message saying, "Hi, this is Jane Doe. I wrote you a note and I'd like to meet with you." And repeat some of the pitch you made in your note. Have your note in front of you. You can even say, "I'll call you back, but my phone number—just so you have it—is 222-555-3456."

But after that, don't leave messages for them to call you. *You* must call them back. Don't complain to your group, "I've left three messages but they haven't called me back." You shouldn't expect it or complain about it. Hiring managers have their "9 to 5" obligations and plenty of people who want to get in to see them. They don't have time to drop everything and call you back. You screen yourself in by doing your research, by doing those follow-up phone calls, and by becoming friends with the manager's assistant.

CASE STUDY *Philip*

His 28 Follow-Up Phone Calls

Philip, a Five O'Clock Clubber in his 60s, landed three offers from Fortune 500 companies. But this might not have happened. When he had made his 27th call to one of the companies, he said to himself, "My ego can't take this anymore."

But Philip made a "research" call to the purchasing department where he thought there was an opening and asked for the purchasing manager, the job he was hoping to get. The person who answered the phone said, "I'm sorry, we don't have a purchasing manager right now. Maybe I could help you." So he knew the job was still open. He called the hiring manager for the 28th time and the hiring manager said, "Thank you so much for being persistent." That's normally what happens. As long as you don't leave messages for them to call you back, they're usually apologetic when you finally get to talk to them.

If it takes an average of eight follow-up phone calls, some job hunters have to call some people *20* or *30* times to get a meeting. You can call *lots* of times—as long as you don't leave messages or ask to be called back. You know how it is: You get voice mail. Just hang up and call later.

It's a Mental Game

Very few job hunters enjoy doing follow-up phone calls. I've always disliked doing them. But my attitude was this: My anxiety level gets extremely high for even one follow-up call and when I finally make that call, the person isn't there anyway. So I've wasted all that anxiety on one phone call. Making 20 follow-up phone calls takes the same amount of anxiety. And, chances are, *most* of the people I call won't be there anyway! I'll probably reach only 2 people out of 20. So I was able to force myself to make those calls when I was job-hunting because I expected to reach *no one*. If I got someone on the phone, it was almost a surprise.

When I have my list of calls to make, I call a friend first. Or you could call a job-search buddy, and say, "Hi Jim, this is Bob. I've got to make some follow-up phone calls. The minute I hang up this phone, I'm going to dial that first number without even thinking so I can get on that phone and start talking to people." And then your friend Jim may say, "I'm going to talk to you in an hour, Bob, to make sure you *made* those calls." Sometimes you need that kind of help. You might as well call 20 people because you're going to reach almost no one. Make a clump of phone calls at once and don't waste all that anxiety on one call!

It's your responsibility to find some way to get in to see the people on your target list and then keep in touch. I used to get *so* anxious, I would postpone and postpone making those calls. Then I was forced to write to the people again and say, "I wrote to you some time ago, but got off track. I'm contacting you once again because I think it's important we meet." By that time, I was humiliated, but I would *finally* make my follow-up phone calls.

Remember, you are calling people because they really *should* meet with you.

> **Through a targeted mailing—and 15 follow-up phone calls—one client got to spend four hours with Craig McCaw of McCaw Cellular.**

You Do Not Want to Be Interviewed on the Phone

Unless you live far away, there is no substitute for an in-person meeting: You can pick up nonverbal information, there will be fewer distractions (the person is unlikely to be sorting mail while you are in the room), and you will be better able to establish rapport and, hopefully, a relationship.

In addition, the person is more likely to give you more and better information, and may even shuffle through his Rolodex™ to give you names or pick up the phone and make a call on your behalf.

Very senior-level job hunters want to meet others in person even though this may require travel. They may conduct a screening call, but then it may be worth using their frequent-flier miles. "I can be in Chicago early next week so we can meet in person. Which day would be best for you?"

> **Important people must have their calls screened or they would never get any work done. But part of their job is to look at new talent.**

Your Answering Machine

If someone calls you in response to a mailing, be prepared. Have an appropriate, businesslike message on your answering machine—no kids' voices, blaring music, or flip comments ("Hi, this is Jake. You know what to do."). Have your script handy; know your Two-Minute Pitch *cold*. For direct-mail campaigns, you can figure on a *4 percent response rate,* meaning 4 percent of the people to whom you write may call you in for a meeting. So if you mail to 100 people, four are likely to call you for a meeting.

Before Making the Call

- Call into your own phone answering machine, practice your pitch, and listen to your voice. You will probably need to polish your presentation.
- Practice with other people and get feedback. If you don't do this, you may sound canned or unnatural.
- Warm up by calling a friend.
- Don't make just one call at a time. Bunch your calls together so you can get on a roll.
- Sit up straight and smile. The listener will hear the energy in your voice. Some Five O'Clock

Clubbers prefer to *stand up* as they talk so their total presence is focused on the call.

Your Basic Script

If you followed the basic Five O'Clock Club "four-paragraph formula" for your cover letter, use that as the starting point for your script. But people don't talk the way they write, so don't repeat the opening paragraph of your letter verbatim, even though it will be the basis for your introduction on the call.

The quickest way to success is to build a relationship with the person you are calling. Using the key points in your opening paragraph in your greeting, establish potential mutual interests.

"Hi. This is Peter Song. I wrote to you a few days ago because I've researched your organization and I am so impressed with your bold move into the European market. (Pause.) I have 15 years of international marketing experience with companies such as ___ and ___ and I was hoping to meet you at some point to find out more about your organization and tell you something about myself."

The first 15 or 20 seconds establishes the tone of the call. You have to practice so your call will sound *conversational.* An actor doesn't read a script the first time and go on stage; he reads it dozens of times to sound natural.

Prompt the person you are talking with when it's time for a response. In other words, be quiet! If you do all the talking, it's not a conversation. You should also ask open-ended questions: "I'm so impressed with what you are doing . . . I'd love to hear more about that."

> **If you don't practice your pitch, you'll stumble or sound canned or unnatural.**

You want a brief conversation—if only a minute—that covers something of interest to the person you've reached. This helps you form a relationship with the person and increases the odds of your achieving your objectives—in most cases, getting a meeting.

Your cover letter outlined the most important points you want to make in your phone call: the points of mutual interest, why you want to see the person, your background, and your key accomplishments.

Some people find it easier to list their "talking points" and goals on a card. With this kind of miniscript handy when they make the calls, they can cover the bases and become more conversational. Some examples follow.

If the Assistant Answers

The assistant may be a great help. Talk as if you were conducting normal business: You wrote a letter to Mr. Jones and you're following up.

For the first call, leave a message saying you called. After that, do not leave a message. Instead, keep calling back. Keep the ball in your court.

"I'm sorry, Sir, but God is in a meeting at the moment, would you like to leave a message? God's office, please hold . . . God's office, please hold . . ."

You: Hi. Mr. Jones, please.

Assistant: I'm sorry, he's not in right now. May I take a message and have him call you back?

You: This is Kevin Walters. Who am I speaking with, please?

Assistant: My name is Dorothy Black.

You: Hi, Ms. Black. I had written a letter to Mr. Jones asking for a brief meeting. I'll be in and out a lot so I'll have to call him back later. When would be a good time for me to call?

Assistant: I don't know. He'll be in and out of meetings also.

(Become friendly with her. However, it's always preferable to use "Mr." or "Ms." in your first contact. Later it may be appropriate to use first names.)

You: Dorothy, I'll call back later. Maybe I'll be lucky and find him in.

> **Call frequently. If you wait too long, they won't remember who you are and will sense no urgency on your part.**

Later

You: Dorothy, hi, this is Kevin Walters. We spoke earlier. Is Mr. Jones available now by any chance?

Dorothy: He's in a meeting right now. May I have him call you?

You: No, he can't call me back, so I'll have to call him later. You must have your hands full managing his schedule, but I know we will link up soon.

Sometimes you can try early in the morning or in the evening when senior executives may answer their own phones. Voice-mail systems, however, have made this more difficult. Call frequently. If you wait too long, they will not remember your letter. You'll get no momentum going.

If you are calling voice mail—but not leaving messages—you may even call back three times in one day. It's not a bother because the person doesn't know you called. [Note: Remember, your target may have Caller ID, a feature sold by the phone company that identifies your phone number to the person you are calling. Simply call your local phone company and ask them to block your identification.]

Sometimes you may be able to get the assistant to set up a meeting for you or a time to connect:

You: I really wanted a few minutes of his time. (Here's the reason why.) I was wondering if you could facilitate the process. Do you happen to handle his calendar? If not, I'll just keep trying.

Eventually

You: Hi, Dorothy, this is Kevin again. You're probably starting to recognize my voice. I hope I'm not bothering you. Is Mr. Jones in?

Assistant: It's terrible that he is always so busy. You've tried so often. I'll try to get him to talk to you. He's in a meeting right now, but I'll ask him to take your call.

To Get Your Paperwork to the Boss

You: Dorothy, do you know if Mr. Jones read my letter?

Dorothy: No, I don't know. He receives so much mail.

You: Well, I'll fax you a copy. You can put it in his "to read" pile so he'll know why I'm calling.

If They Did Not Receive Your Letter

You: I sent him a note a few days ago. Has he seen it?

Assistant: I don't remember it.

You: Well, let me fax it to you now. What is your fax number?

[Note: Fax your résumé to yourself and see what it looks like. If the type is too small, it may be unreadable by fax. If possible, fax from your computer to lessen degradation. Also, be mindful of the "message" your fax may be automatically printing at the top of transmissions!]

If the Boss Answers

First, establish a connection. For example, "Hello. In my letter to you, I pointed out my interest in your new European campaign." Then, go through your script or checklist.

Handling Objections

In addition to your basic script (which should relate to your cover letter), it is valuable to put together an "objections card." Then you will have a ready response when an objection is thrown at you.

You are most likely to handle objections smoothly if you develop your skills of active and reflective listening. This will help you understand the situation of the person you're calling.

Listed below are a few basic objections from bosses and some possible answers. Believe it or not, objections can be an *opportunity*. You want to uncover the real concerns of the person, even if the objections seem like a closed-end statement. Paul Miller, a Five O'Clock Club member and marketing executive, suggested some of the following responses to objections:

a. There are no jobs here now.

I didn't expect there would be. I'm contacting you because of your knowledge of the industry. I'm very interested in your organization and your industry. I have 20 years' experience in direct marketing and a lot of it has been with an industry directly competing with yours. I thought it would be good for us to meet.

I have read that you are being challenged by Monmouth Company. Is that one of your chief concerns right now?

b. I'm busy.

I can understand with so much going on. May we set up a time a month from now? I will call to confirm to make sure it's still a good time for you.

[Note: If you show consideration of their time, they will sometimes suggest that you "come in tomorrow."]

c. I didn't get your résumé.

I'll fax it to you right now and then I'll give you a call back. What's your fax number?

d. We don't need people with your skills now.

See (a) above. Try to ascertain their one or two greatest issues/problems. You may have experience that is a match.

e. How did you get my name?

You *can't* say you did a mailing to 200 people. You *can* say you found the names of several key players through research or you can say what I have sometimes said:

> "A few people mentioned I should contact you."
> "Really, who?"
> "Sharon Nuskey and Deirdre Cavanagh (two of my friends)."
> "I don't know them."
> "Maybe not, but they know you!"

Prepare an "objections card." Then you will have ready responses for objections they throw at you.

Here are some basic objections from assistants and possible answers:

a. He's very busy.

I'll bet. You must have your hands full with his schedule. What would be a good time to call?

b. I sent your résumé to human resources.

Thank you. However, I really wasn't calling about a human resources matter. I thought Mr. Jones would be interested in discussing a project I've done that relates to what he is doing at United Widget.

c. We have no openings now.

I didn't expect you had openings. See (a) under bosses' objections.

What to Do If You Get Voice Mail

First, you can try the company operator to see if you can get the name and number of Mr. Jones' assistant or the name and number of someone who sits near him. Talk to that person and say you've been trying to reach Mr. Jones, but you only get voice mail. Has he been in? How would they suggest you reach him? Does he have an assistant?

Otherwise, use voice mail as an introduction to begin getting your message across.

Early on: "Hi. This is Kevin Shaw and I'm calling to follow up on my letter." You want them to hear your name and that you sent something. Say that you will call them back.

Here's a danger: If you leave your phone number, you may get a blow-off message on *your* voice mail that would make it very awkward for you to call again. You don't *want* people to call you back *if you have not had a chance to explain yourself.*

Always try to understand the situation of your listener. "I understand how busy you are with so much going on . . ."

How to Handle Rejection

If you aim to talk to 10, 20, or 50 people, you can never expect 100 percent success. There are no perfect scores in this game. But learn to *use* rejection. Hearing *why* you have been rejected is a way to modify your pitch. A "no" requires you to probe.

If you are perceptive, you can pick up on the negatives. One good rule is: Don't ask a question that can be answered "yes" or "no." You want to keep the conversation going and "no" can kill the conversation.

Be polite and direct, but *probe*!

You: I have been trying to break into United Widget (or the Widget category). I'm sure that's a fine place to work. I'd really like your opinion of how I can further my candidacy at United

Widget. . . . Thanks. Is there someone else you suggest I speak with?

Rejection is a way to modify your pitch. A "no" requires you to probe.

They Don't Teach You This in School

Improved telephone techniques are both job-search and *life* skills. With the help of your small group, you can get through this part of the job-search process.

Can we talk?

Joan Rivers

CASE STUDY *My Brother*
Call When You Think They Have Your Letter

My brother, Robert, is a scientist and marketer in a very narrow industry with very few companies in his specialty field. He wrote a very detailed, intelligent letter to the president of one of them, a small company in a remote geographic area. This was a targeted mailing—there were no job openings he knew of.

Because his letter was so intelligent and on target, he thought the president would pick up the phone and call him right away. Well, Robert waited a week and the president didn't call him. So instead of calling him, Robert wrote *another* detailed, very intelligent, analytical letter. Again, no call. Finally, I said to Robert, "Just pick up the phone and call the guy." I come from a *family* of shy people and we're all reluctant to call strangers. So my brother finally found his courage, picked up the phone, called the president, and said, "Listen, this is who I am. I've written to you twice and this is what I said."

The president didn't remember having seen either of the letters. "But," he said, "I'm interested in what you're telling me and I'd be delighted to meet with you." My brother was absolutely dumbstruck that the man had not read his letters! The president dug them up later. In fact, hiring managers will often ask you to send letters again because they can't find them. Those follow-up phone calls are critical.

But don't wait two weeks to call, wasting too much valuable time. Among other things, you need to know if the letter arrived. If you figure it takes four days for your letter to arrive, call on day four. If they haven't received it yet, that doesn't matter. You can say, "Hi, this is so-and-so. I sent you a note recently." In response to, "I don't think I've gotten it yet," you can say, "Well, let me tell you what it said." Have your note in front of you: That's your script. So, you see, there's no *downside* to calling a little bit prematurely—before the letter arrives. If you wait two weeks to call, you may be too late.

Time your call so they get your note and your follow-up call at the same time.

It's now 4-1/2 minutes before 8:00—just in case the time means anything to you.

Heard on a radio show in Jamaica

Someone Offers to Make a Call on Your Behalf

What if Martin, a networking contact, says he'll call a few people on your behalf and ask them to see you? If you don't know who Martin is contacting, you're helpless. Say two weeks pass, and you haven't received any calls from Martin's referrals. Then you call Martin again and ask him if he had a chance to contact any of the people he promised he would. Pretty soon, Martin sees you as a pain. Martin was enthusiastic when he met with you, but now he's back doing his work. He meant to make those phone calls, but life keeps interrupting him. To him, it doesn't feel like so much time had passed, but to you the time is dragging.

What is wrong with this scenario? The ball will never be in your court if you're waiting for *someone else* to make calls for you. If *you* had asked Martin to give you the names of the people he was planning to contact, then you could have immediately written to each person saying, "By now you've probably heard about me from Martin Radice," or, " By now, you may have received my résumé from Martin Radice." And the rest of your cover letter would follow the standard Five O'Clock Club format. You could enclose your résumé and do a follow-up phone call later. You've *got* to ask for the list because if Martin doesn't actually call the people while you're sitting there, chances are good that it won't happen—ever.

So, the next time someone volunteers to make a call or two on your behalf, ask who it is they're planning to call and *help them to help you.*

Keeping Up Your Contacts after Landing That New Job

We tell our job hunters that *after* they land their next job they should make *at least* one networking contact a week, which isn't that much. That's one phone call, or one lunch date, or one getting together for a cup of coffee after work. People who have a solid network in their field have quicker and easier job searches than those who are careless about staying connected. Those with no networking contacts have to start from scratch to build up their contacts, which takes time. So write your long-term career plan and build your networking contacts *now* for the targets you plan to have in the future. That's what successful people do.

Is this the party to whom I am speaking?
Lily Tomlin

When Networking with Fellow Five O'Clock Clubbers

Club members and alumni are important contacts. The Club attracts people who are intelligent, proactive, and helpful. They know how to get along in a group. These are not your average everyday people. Club members expect you to know the process. So be prepared before you contact other members. Wait until your fourth group session before you start networking with other members. Then you'll know your Two-Minute Pitch and you'll know what you want out of meetings with them. You'll also know how to network by then. Five O'Clock Clubbers will bend over backwards to help you, as you will with other members who contact you. So don't abuse or waste these contacts.

Write a letter or E-mail if appropriate. And do your follow-up phone calls. Don't ask for a job—ask for information and guidance! E-mail a thank-you note after a networking meeting. And if a fellow Five O'Clock Clubber opens the door for you to someone else, make sure you go *through* that door, and follow up with the contacts they've set up for you.

The moment you feel foolish, you look foolish. Concentrate, block it out, and relax. Of course, that's not always easy.
Michael Caine, *Acting in Film*

In all human affairs, the odds are always six to five against.
Damon Runyon

Take calculated risks. That is quite different from being rash.
George S. Patton

The
Five
O'Clock
Club

How to Control Your Campaign

Do not fear death so much,
but rather the inadequate life.

Bertolt Brecht

Your overall campaign can be managed with just a few important worksheets:

- Use the **Interview Record** for *every* meeting—both networking and job. (See our book *Mastering the Job Interview and Winning the Money Game*.)

- The most important worksheet for controlling your search is the **Current List of My Active Contacts by Target**. At the beginning of your search, these will simply be networking contacts with whom you want to keep in touch. At that stage, your goal is to come up with 6 to 10 contacts you want to recontact later.

  Later, the quality of your list will change. Then the names will be prospective job possibilities that you are trying to move along.

  If you have 6 to 10 job possibilities "in the works," five of them will fall away through no fault of your own (because of job freezes or the hiring manager changing his or her mind about the kind of person wanted). Then you'll need to get more things in the works. With this critical mass of ongoing possible positions, you stand a chance of landing the kind of job you want.

Other Worksheets

The worksheets mentioned above are critical to the management of your search. Other worksheets guide specific parts of your search.

- In the beginning, the **Seven Stories exercise** and **Your Forty-Year Vision** will help you select job targets appropriate for you (see our book *Targeting a Great Career*).

- **Measuring Your Targets** will assure that you have targets of a size that have a reasonable chance of working.

- The **Summary of What I Have/Want to Offer** will help you "position" yourself appropriately to each of your targets.

- **People to Contact in Each Target Area** is a way to get your search off to a quick start through networking or targeted mailings.

- The **Format of a Networking Meeting** is your guide to properly managing the networking-type meetings you get through networking, targeted or direct mailings, or cold calls.

- The **Summary of Search Progress** and **How to Assess Your Campaign** help you clearly assess how you are doing with regard to each of your targets.

- **The Follow-Up Checklist: Turning Job Interviews into Offers** (in our book *Mastering the Job Interview and Winning the Money Game*) will help you assess the interview and decide what to do next. Your goal, after all, is to move the process along and see if you can create a job for yourself.

- Assessing whether you are at **Stage 1, 2, or 3** of your search will help you see where you really stand, rather than you hoping for a job offer too soon.

Four-Step Salary Negotiation (from our book *Mastering the Job Interview and Winning the Money Game*):

- Are you keeping all four steps in mind?
  — Negotiate the job
  — Outshine and outlast your competition
  — Get the offer
  — Negotiate the compensation package

- Are you **negotiating the job** to make it appropriate for you and for the hiring manager?

- Are you **paying attention to your competition**, what they have to offer, and what you must do to outshine and outlast them? Are you aware that your competitors may not be real people, but may be in the mind of the hiring manager?

- Are you trying to postpone discussion of salary until after you **get the offer**?

Current List of My Active Contacts by Target

Make copies of this page for each target and keep track of your active contacts in each target area. To see how well you are penetrating each target market, compare the total number of appropriate contacts in your market with the number you have actually contacted. Keep adding names to your list. Certain people will become inappropriate. Cross their names off. You should probably have some contact once every month or two with the people who remain on your list.

After your search is up and running, keep track of your contacts by the stage you are in for each one. This will tell you how well you are doing in your search and will give you some idea of how likely it is for you to get an offer.

For Target _____:

Geographic area: _____

Industry or company size: _____

Position/function: _____

Name of Contact	Company	Position	Date of Last Contact	Targeted Date of Next Contact
1.				
2.				
3.				
4.				
5.				
6.				
7.				
8.				
9.				
10.				
11.				
12.				
13.				
14.				
15.				
16.				
17.				
18.				
19.				
20.				

Current List of Active Stage-1 Contacts
Networking Contacts With Whom You Want To Keep in Touch

The Beginning of a Search

Measure the effectiveness of your search by listing the number of people with whom you are currently in contact on an ongoing basis, either by phone or mail, who are in a position to hire you or recommend that you be hired. The rule of thumb: If you are seriously job hunting, **you should have 6 to 10 active contacts going at one time. At the beginning of your search, these will simply be networking contacts with whom you want to keep in touch**. You are unlikely to get an offer at this stage. You are gathering information to find out how things work—getting your feet wet. You look like an outsider and outsiders are rarely given a break. Keep adding names to your list because certain people will become inappropriate. Cross their names off. You should probably have some contact once a month with the people who remain on your list.

Because you have already developed targets for your search, please note below the target area for each contact or note it is serendipitous and does not fit in with any of your organized targets. This will help you see the progress you are making in each target area.

Name of Contact	Company	Position	Date of Last Contact	Targeted Date of Next Contact	Target Area
1.					
2.					
3.					
4.					
5.					
6.					
7.					
8.					
9.					
10.					
11.					
12.					
13.					
14.					
15.					
16.					
17.					
18.					
19.					
20.					

Current List of Active Stage-2 Contacts
The Right People at the Right Levels in the Right Organizations

The Middle of a Search

The nature of your "6 to 10 things in the works" changes over time. Instead of simply finding networking contacts to get your search started, you meet people who are closer to what you want.

Getting a job offer is not the way to test the quality of your campaign. A real test is when people say they'd want you—but not now. Do some people say: **"Boy, I wish I had an opening. I'd sure like to have someone like you here"**? Then you are interviewing well with the right people. All you need now are luck and timing to help you contact (and recontact) the right people when they also have a need.

If people are *not* saying they want you, find out why not. If you think you are in the right targets talking to people at the right level and are not early on in your search, you need feedback. Ask: "If you had an opening, would you consider hiring someone like me?" Find out what is wrong.

Become an insider—a competent person who can prove he or she has somehow already done what the interviewer needs. *Prove* you can do the job and that the interviewer is *not* taking a chance on you.

You still need 6 to 10 contacts at this level whom you will recontact later. Keep adding names to your list because certain people will become inappropriate. Cross their names off. You should probably have some contact once a month with the people who remain on your list.

Name of Contact	Company	Position	Date of Last Contact	Targeted Date of Next Contact	Target Area
1.					
2.					
3.					
4.					
5.					
6.					
7.					
8.					
9.					
10.					
11.					
12.					
13.					
14.					
15.					
16.					
17.					
18.					
19.					
20.					

Current List of Active Stage-3 Contacts
Moving Along Actual Jobs or the Possibility of Creating a Job

The Final Stages of a Search

In this stage, you **uncover 6 to 10 actual jobs (or the possibility of creating a job) to move along**. These job possibilities could come from *any* of your target areas or from serendipitous leads. Find a *lot* of people who would hire you if they could. If you have only one lead that could turn into an offer, you are likely to try to close too soon. Get more leads. You will be more attractive to the manager, will interview better, and will not lose momentum if your best lead falls apart. A good number of your job possibilities will fall away through no fault of your own (such as job freezes or major changes in the job requirements).

To get more leads, notice which targets are working and which are not. Make *additional* contacts in the targets that seem to be working or develop new targets. **Recontact just about everyone you met earlier in your search.** You want to develop more offers.

Aim for three offers: This is the stage of your search when you want them. When an offer comes during Stage 1 or Stage 2, you probably have not had a chance to develop momentum so you can get a number of offers. When choosing among offers, **select the job that positions you best for the long term**.

	Name of Contact	Company	Position	Date of Last Contact	Targeted Date of Next Contact	Target Area
1.						
2.						
3.						
4.						
5.						
6.						
7.						
8.						
9.						
10.						
11.						
12.						
13.						
14.						
15.						
16.						
17.						
18.						
19.						
20.						

How to Assess Your Campaign

Based on Marketing Plan for John Smith
Target Functions: Publishing Sales/Sales Management

Stage 1	Stage 2	Stage 3	Current Offers
Target #1: Consumer Publishing	**Target #1: Consumer Publishing**	**Target #1: Consumer Publishing**	**Target #1: Consumer Publishing**
Time Warner Condé Nast Hearst Hachette Meredith KIII Holdings Gannett Times-Mirror Bertelsmann/G&J Reader's Digest McGraw-Hill Outdoor Services Parade NY Times Corp. Tribune Corp. Contact Perf Arts Network	Time Pathfinder *Inc.* magazine Time Relationship Mktg. *Boston Globe* *Washington Post* Fancy Publications Thirteen-WNET	*USA Today* —Baseball Weekly met w/4 execs Media Vehicles —GE Capital met w/3 execs MAMM and POZ met w/2 execs	Tradewell The Sales Associates —Offered VP, Sales and Head of Internet Sales *Inc.* magazine
Target #2: Trade Publishing	**Target #2: Trade Publishing**	**Target #2: Trade Publishing**	**Target #2: Trade Publishing**
Fairchild Pub. Reed Travel Progressive Grocer James G. Elliot Co.	McFadden M. Shanken Wine and Food BPI Cahners	Supermarket Business Final 2 out of 465 for NE Sales Mgr.	
Target #3: Internet/Computer	**Target #3: Internet/Computer**	**Target #3: Internet/Computer**	**Target #3: Internet/Computer**
CMP Intl Data Mgmt. Ria Group	Preview Travel i33 Communications IDG-Games Mpath-Mplayer	Planet Direct/CMG 2 meetings	Interactive Advertising Net. —1 of 10 selected

The Five O'Clock Club

Stuck in Your Job Search?
What to Do Next

Drive thy business, or it will drive thee.
Benjamin Franklin

How to Measure the Effectiveness of Your Search

Most job hunters say, "I'll know my search was good when I get a job." That's not a very good way to measure your search. You need to be able to tell as you go along whether you are heading in the right direction. There are a number of hints you can pick up along the way.

What Stage Are You In?

As you go along, the basic measurement tool to use in your search is this: Do you have 6 to 10 things in the works? That is, are you talking to 6 to 10 people on an ongoing basis who are in a position to hire you or recommend that you be hired?

The quality of your contacts varies with where you are in your search.

- In the beginning of your search, you will speak to as many people as possible in your target market—regardless of the organization for which they work. At this stage, you simply want market information. If you plan to stay in touch with them on an ongoing basis, they are

Stage-1 contacts. To have any momentum going in the beginning of your search, keep in touch with 6 to 10 people on an ongoing basis (every few months).

Over time, you will talk to more and more people who are Stage-1 contacts—perhaps 60 to 100 people during the course of your search. Some of those contacts will bubble up and become Stage-2 contacts.

- Stage-2 contacts are people who are the right people at the right level in the right jobs in the right organizations in your targeted areas. They are senior to you, perhaps future hiring managers. Your goal is to have contact with 6 to 10 of the right people on an ongoing basis. Then you have a full Stage-2 search going: You are in the middle of your search.

However, you will rarely get a good job offer at Stage 2. You aren't even talking to these people about real jobs at this point. You just want the right people to know you and remember you. And if one later happens to have a job opening, you still need to go after 6 to 10 other job possibilities, because 5 will fall away through no fault of your own. If you do get an offer at Stage 2, you won't have many others with which to compare it. Keep in touch with your current Stage-1 contacts (using *networking* follow-ups), and develop additional Stage-1 contacts so more will bubble up to Stage 2. Some of those will bubble up to Stage 3 (real job possibilities)—and then you're really cooking.

194

- You are in a full Stage-3 search when you are talking to 6 to 10 people on an ongoing basis who actually have a job opening or who have the possibility of creating a job for you. Then you have a number of opportunities that you can move along (using *job* follow-ups), and are in the best possible position to get the right job for you: the one that positions you best for the long term and the one that pays you what you are worth.

If you have 6 to 10 possibilities in Stage 3, you have the chance of getting 3 offers. Remember, these do not have to be ideal jobs—some may even be disgusting. But an offer is an offer and makes you more desirable in the market. You don't have to want to work at each of these places, but at least you will have a fallback position and can honestly say, if appropriate, "I have a number of job offers, but there's no place I'd rather work than yours." With a number of offers in hand, you are less likely to be taken advantage of by a prospective employer who thinks you are desperate.

Life moves on, whether we act as cowards or heroes. Life has no other discipline to impose, if we would but realize it, than to accept life unquestioningly. Everything we shut our eyes to, everything we run away from, everything we deny, denigrate or despise, serves to defeat us in the end. What seems nasty, painful, evil, can become a source of beauty, joy and strength, if faced with an open mind. Every moment is a golden one for him who has the vision to recognize it as such.

Henry Miller

How's Your Search Going?

When I ask you how your search is going, I don't want to hear that a prospective employer really likes you. That's not a good measure of how well your search is going, because one prospect could easily fall away: They may decide to hire no one or they may decide they want an accounting person instead of a marketing person. A lot can happen that is beyond your control.

Instead I expect you to tell me how many things you have in the works. You would say, for example, "My search is going great. I have five Stage-1 contacts in the works. I'm just getting started."

Or you might say, "I have nine Stage-2 contacts and three contacts in Stage 3." If you are expert at this, you may even add: "I want more Stage-3 contacts, so my goal is to get 30 more in Stage 2. Right now, I'm digging up lots of new contacts and keeping the other ones going. With my Stage-2 contacts, I'm generally doing networking follow-ups and with my Stage-3 contacts, I'm generally doing job follow-ups."

That kind of talk is music to my ears.

It usually takes very little effort to get a few more things "in the works." Simply recontact your network, network into someone you haven't met with yet, directly contact someone, talk to a search firm, answer an ad. You will soon have more activity in your search.

I know God will not give me anything I can't handle. I just wish He didn't trust me so much.

Mother Teresa

What Job Hunters Do Wrong

In addition to looking at the *stage* of your overall search, it is also helpful to look at what can go wrong in each *phase* of your campaigns. Some job hunters err in their overall search approach or attitude. Then things can go wrong in the assessment phase or in the other parts of your campaigns (the planning, interviewing, or follow-up phases). We'll examine each of these to determine what you may be doing wrong, if anything.

The Overall Search: What Can Go Wrong?

Here are some problems that are general to the entire search:

- **<u>Not spending enough time</u>** on your search. If you are unemployed, you should be spending 35 hours a week on your search. If you are employed, spend 15 hours a week to get some momentum going. If you spend only two or three hours a week on your job search, you may complain that you have been searching forever, when actually you have not even begun. If you are employed, you can do most of your work in the evenings and on weekends—researching, writing cover letters and follow-up letters. You can even schedule your meetings in the evenings or early mornings.

- **<u>Not having enough fun.</u>** Some job hunters—especially those who are unemployed—say they will start having fun after they get a job. But your search may take many months and you are more likely to come across as desperate if you are not allowing yourself to have some fun. Having fun will make you seem like a more normal person in your meetings and you'll feel better about yourself. The Five O'Clock Club formula is that you *must* have at least three hours of fun a week.

- **<u>Not having 6 to 10 things in the works.</u>** See the beginning of this chapter about Stages 1, 2, and 3 of your search.

- **<u>Talking to people who are at the wrong level.</u>** At the beginning of your search, talk to peers just to gather information to decide whether a prospective target is worth a full campaign. When you have selected a few good targets, talk to those who are at a higher level.

- **<u>Trying to bypass the system.</u>** Some job hunters feel they don't have time for this and simply want to go on job interviews (usually through search firms or answering ads). Others want to skip the assessment process (see our book *Targeting a Great Career*) or don't even do the Seven Stories Exercise. Their campaigns are weaker because they have no foundation.

  At least touch on every step in the process. You will have a quicker and more productive search.

- **<u>Lowering your salary expectations just because you have been unemployed a while.</u>** Even those who have been unemployed a year or two land jobs at market rates. They get what they are worth in the market because they have followed the system.

  At The Five O'Clock Club, half the people who attend are employed; half are unemployed. Many of those who are unemployed have been out of work for a year or two. Usually, they have been doing something wrong in their searches, and the counselor and their group can help them figure out what it is. When they get a job (which they almost certainly will if they stick with the system), they usually wind up getting something appropriate at an appropriate salary level.

  Sometimes, if people really need money, we suggest they take something inappropriate to earn some money and continue to search while they are working.

The world is moving so fast these days that the man who says it can't be done is generally interrupted by someone doing it.

Harry Emerson Fosdick

- **<u>Getting discouraged.</u>** Half the battle is controlling your emotions. Jack had been unemployed one-and-a-half years when he joined us. He seemed very agitated—almost angry—which happens when a person has been working at a job search for so long. I told him I was afraid he might come across that way during meetings. He assured me (with irritation in his voice) that he was completely pleasant during meetings but was simply letting his hair down in the group.

In career coaching, we have nothing to go on but the way the person acts in the group: The way you are in the group probably bears some resemblance to the way you are in the interview. We would recognize you as being the same person. Anyway, it's all we have to go on, so we have to point out to you what we see.

The next week, Jack still seemed angry. I asked the group what they thought and of course they could see it too. It was easier for him to hear it from his peers, and, because he was a mature person, Jack listened to them.

The third week, Jack laughingly announced that he had had a lobotomy and was a completely different person. He said he had changed his attitude and that his meetings reflected this change.

The fourth week he announced that he had had another lobotomy because he felt he still had room for improvement. He was a noticeably different person and did not seem at all like someone who had been out of work a long time. Every day Jack read the books we use at The Five O'Clock Club and provided very good insights to the other job hunters in our small group.

By the fifth week, Jack was almost acting like a cocounselor in the group. He had made great strides in his own search (with three Stage-3 contacts and lots of contacts in Stage 2) and was able to astutely analyze the problems others were having. He was a wonderful contributor.

By the seventh week, Jack was close to a number of offers and in the eighth week, Jack proudly addressed the large group and reported on his successful search. We were sorry to see him go.

By the way, Jack did not have to take a pay cut or a job that was beneath him. His prolonged search did not affect his salary negotiation.

Do what you need to do to keep your spirits up. Don't ask yourself if you feel like searching. Of course you don't. Just do it anyway. And act as if you enjoy it.

- **Not having support.** Looking for a job is a lonely business. You may want to "buddy" with another job hunter. You can call each other every morning to talk about what you are each going to do that day and to review what you each accomplished the day before. You could also join free emotional-support groups at places of worship. You may find you need such help in addition to the job-search strategy you get at The Five O'Clock Club. Or you may find you would like to see a counselor privately to help you with specifics having to do with your search, such as your résumé, a review of your search, salary negotiation, or the follow-up to a very important job interview. Get the help you need.

- **Inflating in your own mind the time you have actually been searching.** You may feel as though you've been searching forever. But if you are searching only three hours a week, you have not yet begun. If at the end of a year, you finally start to put in the required 15 to 35 hours a week, you have just really started to search. Then when people ask how long you have been searching, the correct answer is "a few weeks." It's good to be honest with yourself about how long you have actually been searching.

Procrastination is the fear of success. People procrastinate because they are afraid of the success that they know will result if they move ahead now. Because success is heavy, carries a responsibility with it, it is much easier to procrastinate and live on the "someday I'll" philosophy.

Denis Waitley

During the Assessment Phase: What Can Go Wrong?

In the assessment phase you use our book, *Targeting a Great Career*, to go through the exercises (Seven Stories, Values, Forty-Year Vision, and so on) and select job targets (industries or organizations of a certain size and the position you would like in each target and geographic area).

If you are not sure what you should do with your life, assessment is a time to explore—perhaps with the help of a career coach. What can go wrong in this phase?

- **Selecting 1 or 2 targets too quickly.** Rather than exploring, a job hunter may pick a target, go after it, find out it doesn't work, and then not know what to do next. Instead, brainstorm as many targets as you can at the beginning of your search, rank them, and go after them in a methodical way.

- **Not being specific in selecting a target.** Some job hunters say, "I just want a job. I don't care what it is." You may not care, but the hiring team wants someone who cares about their specific industry and organization. In the beginning of your search, you want to explore and stay calm while you are doing your research to find out what the likely targets are for you. If you don't have targets defined (such as "being a COBOL computer programmer in a medium-sized organization in the Albuquerque area"), then you are still exploring and that's okay. But it is not an organized search. And even when your search is organized and targeted, you will still have plenty of room for serendipitous leads.

- **Not doing the right research.** Read the chapter on research, including the bibliography at the back of this book. Research is critical throughout your search and separates those who follow The Five O'Clock Club method

from other job hunters. Instead of just *doing* research, why not learn to enjoy it and make it part of your life?

The better your research, the richer your targets will become—well defined rather than superficial—and the more knowledgeable you will sound to prospective employers. In addition, you will save a lot of time as you discover where the markets are and which ones are the best fit for you.

- **Not ranking your targets.** Some job hunters go after everything at once. For a more organized search, overlap your targets, but still conduct a condensed search focusing on each target and keeping them separate in your mind.

Take a look at the chart below, which shows a campaign aimed at each target (T1, T2, and T3). Yet the targets overlap to speed up the search.

Next, let's look at what can go wrong in the various phases of the campaign aimed at each target.

Quit now, you'll never make it. If you disregard this advice, you'll be halfway there.

David Zucker

During the Preparation Phase: What Can Go Wrong?

- **Relying on only one technique for getting meetings.** Consider using all four techniques

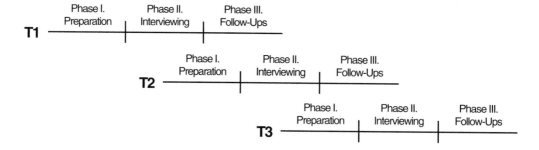

for getting meetings: networking, direct contact, search firms, and ads (in print and on-line). Even in fields where people like to talk to people, such as sales or human resources, though networking is easier, it is not thorough. It is a scattered approach.

Make a list of all the organizations in your target area—say, 120.

— Perhaps network into 20 of them;

— Do a targeted mailing into 20—it's just like networking: use a letter with a follow-up phone call. Remember that you want to see this person whether or not he or she has a job opening;

— Talk to search firms (if appropriate); and

— Answer ads.

— Do a direct-mail campaign (no follow-up phone call) to the remaining 80 organizations—just to be thorough so all the organizations in your target area know that you exist and are looking.

- **Contacting the wrong person.** The human resources person is the wrong one unless you want a job in human resources. The right person is one or two levels higher than you are in the department or division in which you want to work. If you are very senior and want to work for the president, the right person for you to contact is the president or perhaps someone on the board. If you want to be the president, the right person is someone on the board, or whoever may influence the selection of the president.

- **Being positioned improperly.** If you are not positioned properly, you will not be able to get meetings. Write out your Two-Minute Pitch. In your small group, be sure to practice your pitch. Try role-playing. Tell the group who they are pretending to be, and ask them to critique you. You want to make sure you have your pitch down pat. Write it out.

- **Using skimpy cover letters.** We use a four-paragraph approach that is thorough. Most job hunters write paragraphs one and four and skip the meat.

- **Having a weak or inappropriate résumé.** If your résumé doesn't speak for you in your absence and tell them exactly who you are, your level, and what you bring to the party, develop one that helps you. We have a whole book on this topic—along with case studies of real live people.

- **Skipping the research phase to develop a good list of target organizations.** If you have a good list, you will get more out of every one of your networking contacts. Show your list of prospective organizations to your contacts, ask them what they think of the organizations on the list, who they suggest you should contact at the good organizations, and ask, "May I use your name?"

The thing always happens that you believe in; and the belief in a thing makes it happen.

Frank Lloyd Wright

If you want a quality, act as if you already had it. Try the "as if" technique.

William James

During the Interviewing Phase: What Can Go Wrong?

(See our book *Mastering the Job Interview and Winning the Money Game* for a more detailed description of each area listed below.)

- Trying to close too soon.
- Being seen as an outsider.
- Not using the worksheets.
- Not thinking like a consultant.
- Not looking or acting like the level for which you are searching.

- Not seeing the meeting as only the beginning of the process.
- Not getting information/giving information to move it along.
- Not preparing for the meeting by having a 3X5 card or finding out with whom you will be meeting. The 3X5 card contains your summary statement about yourself as well as three to five accomplishments you want to make sure you cover with the hiring team.
- Not being in sync with their timing (trying to close too soon or not moving quickly enough).
- Not listening to what is really going on.

"Mr. Billings realizes you traveled a long way to meet with him. However, he decided to change the meeting until next week."

During the Follow-Up Phase: What Can Go Wrong?

(See our book *Mastering the Job Interview and Winning the Money Game* for a more detailed description of each area listed below.)

In addition to targeting, follow-up is the most important reason Five O'Clock Clubbers land jobs quickly. This is the brainiest part of the process. Notice that the earlier diagram showed the three parts as equal: Preparation, Interviewing, and Follow-Ups. Spend an equal amount of time on each.

Study those parts of this book thoroughly. Some of the obvious things that go wrong include:

- Taking the first offer.
- Not recontacting your contacts.
- Not studying the books.
- Stating your salary requirements too soon.
- Not reassessing where you stand in your search.

Now that we've taken a break from your search to assess how you are doing, it's time to get back to work. Use the work sheets that follow to note the organizations/people you have contacted for each stage of your search.

To laugh often and much; to win the respect and the affection of children; to earn the appreciation of honest critics and endure the betrayal of false friends; to appreciate beauty; to find the best in others; to leave the world a bit better—whether by a healthy child, a garden patch or a redeemed social condition; to know even one life has breathed easier because you have lived. This is to have succeeded.

Ralph Waldo Emerson

If you are distressed by anything external, the pain is not due to the thing itself, but to your estimate of it; and this you have the power to revoke at any moment.

Marcus Aurelius

Sample Summary of Search Progress

For Target 1:

	# of companies in this target	# contacted	# met with	Quality/Status of Contacts
Geog. area: Chicago metro	10	10	3	Stage 3: 1 job lead
Ind. or org. size: Consumer goods companies	Note: Not a great target. Keep in touch with same 5 people.			Stage 2: 2
Pos./function: Director of direct mail				Stage 1: 2

For Target 2:

	# of companies in this target	# contacted	# met with	Quality/Status of Contacts
Geog. area: Chicago metro	200	70	30	Stage 3: 3, 1 close to offer
Ind. or org. size: Direct marketing service cos.	Note: I'll aim to get 80 Stage-1 contacts; 30 Stage-2 contacts.			Stage 2: 9
Pos./function: Director of direct mail				Stage 1: 16

For Target 3:

	# of companies in this target	# contacted	# met with	Quality/Status of Contacts
Geog. area: Chicago metro	120	11	4	Stage 3: 0
Ind. or org. size: Direct marketing— based co.	Note: I need to do a lot more work in this target.			Stage 2: 0
Pos./function: Vice pres., marketing				Stage 1: 4

For Target 4:

	# of companies in this target	# contacted	# met with	Quality/Status of Contacts
Geog. area: Chicago metro	15	15	4	Stage 3: 0
Ind. or org. size: Advertising agencies	Note: This is the field I'm in now, but I want to get out of it.			Stage 2: 0
Pos./function: Director of direct mail				Stage 1: 2

Note: In the far right column, **note those contacts you are keeping in touch with on an ongoing basis:**
Stage 1 contacts: People with whom I want to keep in touch—regardless of level or ability to hire.
Stage 2 contacts: The right people at the right levels in the right organizations. (Potential hiring managers with whom I am keeping in touch. They may be telling me: I wish I had an opening. If I did, I'd like to hire someone like you.)
Stage 3 contacts: Moving along actual jobs or the possibility of creating a job.

Summary of Search Progress

	# of companies in this target	# contacted	# met with	Quality/Status of Contacts
For Target 1: Geog. area: _____ Ind. or org. size: _____ Pos./function: _____				Stage 3: Stage 2: Stage 1:
For Target 2: Geog. area: _____ Ind. or org. size: _____ Pos./function: _____				Stage 3: Stage 2: Stage 1:
For Target 3: Geog. area: _____ Ind. or org. size: _____ Pos./function: _____				Stage 3: Stage 2: Stage 1:
For Target 4: Geog. area: _____ Ind. or org. size: _____ Pos./function: _____				Stage 3: Stage 2: Stage 1:

Note: In the far right column, **note those contacts you are keeping in touch with on an ongoing basis:**

Stage 1 contacts: People with whom I want to keep in touch—regardless of level or ability to hire.

Stage 2 contacts: The right people at the right levels in the right organizations. (Potential hiring managers with whom I am keeping in touch. They may be telling me: I wish I had an opening. If I did, I'd like to hire someone like you.)

Stage 3 contacts: Moving along actual jobs or the possibility of creating a job. (I aim to have a total of 6 to 10 when I am in Stage 3 of my search.)

The
Five
O'Clock
Club

PART FIVE

Career and Job-Search
Bibliography

COMPILED BY RICHARD GREENE

The
Five
O'Clock
Club

Career and Job-Search Bibliography

How to Use this Section (Properly!)

These resources for creating your list of organizations to target were put together in three sections:

Section I: General References of company and industry information, directories, and online compendiums of associations, regional resources, job boards, and more. This is a good way to start making up your list of job targets while finding out more about potential employers and the industries and professions that interest you. A word of caution: Job boards, especially the biggies, are tempting places to hang out. However, only about 6 percent of all jobs get filled via these sites. The Five O'Clock Club approach is not to hang out at your local job board, but rather to develop lists of persons to contact for targeted and direct mailings, as well as for networking. Don't spend more than 6 percent of your time on job boards (6 percent of 35 hours amounts to a little more than 2 hours maximum per week).

Section II: Professions, Industries, Interests . . . , which alphabetically lists some of the most common professions and industries, along with some of the fast-growing segments, such as biotechnology and satellite communications. Also included are listings for minorities, senior citizens, veterans, and more. For each entry, print sources are listed first, followed by online resources. Note that many print sources, particularly directories, are offered with CD-ROMs or as online databases (usually by subscription). Some directories are no longer available in print versions, only as online subscriptions. The trend is away from the printed

page, toward CD-ROMs and online databases. However, many sources are still available in print. Subscription services are geared for businesses and can be costly. Check with your local or main library to see if it subscribes.

Following the print sources is a listing of online resources. Many are or contain job boards, but they usually list resources as well. These include news of the profession or industry, books and other publications, e-newsletters, career advice, user discussion rooms, and much more. If you are trying to enter a new industry or profession, these online sites can provide you with the latest happenings and allow you to chat with better-informed persons, so you can get smarter, faster.

Entries in this section are listed alphabetically, preceded by a short section on Trade Shows, Printed Materials, sources of Free Trade Publications, and Job and Industry Information Sites (Vault.com and Wetfeet.com). Following this is a link to the New York Public Library, which will direct you to sites that contain selected industry and directory information. These sites are kept up-to-date.

The rest of the section's listings are information and job listings on:

Academic and Education

Accounting

Advertising, including Graphic Art and Design

Aging Workers

Apparel, Textiles, Fashion and Beauty

Art and Design

Associations

Automotive

Aviation and Aerospace

Banking, Finance, Investing, Securities, Trading, Credit, and Other

Biotechnology

Business

College/Liberal Arts/Recent Graduates

Communications Equipment and Services, including Telecommunications

Construction and Building

Consulting

Disabled

Diversity and Minorities (except Gay and Lesbian)

Electronics

Energy, Alternative Energy, and Utilities

Engineering

Entertainment, including Media (Broadcasting and Publishing)

Environmental

Ex-Inmates

Film, Video, and Photography

Food and Beverages

Franchising

Freelancing

Furniture

Gay and Lesbian

Government

Health Care and Medicine

Human Resources

Information Technology/High-Tech (Computers, Technology, and e-Commerce)

Insurance

Law

Law Enforcement and Criminal Justice

Library Science

Manufacturing

Nonprofit

Nursing

Public Relations

Publishing (Books, Magazines, Newspapers, Other)

Real Estate

Retailing

Sales and Marketing

Small Business

Summer Jobs and Internships

Transportation (Shipping, Marine, Freight, Express Delivery, Supply Chain)

Travel, Leisure, and Hospitality (including Hotels, Food Service, Travel Agents, Restaurants, and Airlines)

Veterans

Vocational (no four-year college degree)

Volunteering

Wholesaling and Distributing/Importing and Exporting

Section III: International contains print and online resources to tap the worldwide market. Three important things to remember: (1) many of the print and online materials in Sections I and II contain global listings; (2) many of the international listings in this section include the U.S.; and (3) there is loads of additional information on international jobs and careers—too much to include here. So, you can scour the Internet and come up with a long list for your own interests. However, the resources included here are comprehensive and among the best available.

What If I Don't Find Resources That Cover My Job Interests?

If, for example, you want to look for a position as a Whatever Manager and need more specific resources, follow these steps:

1. Consult the Associations section. Almost every kind of job, profession, Whatever has it own association (or associations). Look at the association's website, consider joining, and even be so brazen as to call its office and ask for help.

2. Search the Internet. Type in Whatever and pair it with Job, or Career, or Directory, or Association, or just by itself. The last option will generate millions of hits: Look at the first few for keywords to use with Whatever in another search. You don't have to look through pages and pages of Internet sites. If it isn't on the first or second page, refine your search.

Be careful of directories that are more than a year or so old, since companies and employees change. Does this research method work? It certainly does. That's how this entire listing was put together, albeit with an initial list of resources from the New York Public Library.

Section I: General Reference

Note: For the North American Industry Classification System (NAICS), the official U.S. Census Bureau listing of all NAICS, see www.census.gov/epcd/naics02/.

Help! My Job Interview Is Tomorrow!: How to Use the Library to Research an Employer
Mary Ellen Templeton, Neal-Schuman Publishers, 2nd ed., 1997.
Offers the guidance academic and public librarians themselves would give if they had a few hours to spend with each job seeker. The guide draws on commonly found library sources and includes electronic sources as well. Readers with only a few hours to prepare for their interview will find immediate and specific help from worksheets designed to get answers to frequently asked questions. Special attention is paid to researching small businesses, not-for-profits, and government agencies. Includes an updated, comprehensive bibliography. Although some of the resources are dated, the author offers flowcharts to help job hunters outline the types of information they need.

The Best Places to Live
money.cnn.com
At this site, you can compare the cost of living among cities and create your own "best places" list using the screening tool.

Directories in Print
www.gale.com, annual
Lists about 15,500 active rosters, guides, and other print, nonprint, and address lists published in the U.S. and worldwide. Hundreds of additional directories (defunct, suspended, and unlocatable directories) are cited with status notes in a title/keyword index.

Associations

Directories

Encyclopedia of Associations, Thomson Gale
www.gale.com, annual
This is a comprehensive source of detailed information on more than 135,000 nonprofit membership organizations worldwide. Several versions provide addresses and descriptions of professional societies, trade associations, labor unions, cultural and religious organizations, fan clubs, and other groups of all types. The versions are: *National Organizations of the U.S., International Organizations,* and *Regional, State, and Local Organizations.* An online version is available at some libraries. All versions are indexed by name, keyword, and company, with executives included for the international version.

Associations Yellow Book, Leadership
Directories
www.leadershipdirectories.com
This volume is said to be the nation's leading
directory of major trade and professional associations. Semiannual editions keep you current with
association mergers and executive, staff, and
board member changes. More than 42,000 officers, executives, staff, and board members (with
contact information) at more than 1,000 associations with budgets of more than $2 million. An
industry index organizes associations by their
principal fields. Indexed geographically by budget, political action committees, foundation
(acronyms, association names), and individuals'
names, acronym, and organization name.

Online Resources

Associations on the Net
www.ipl.org
Lists more than 2,000 associations. Simply key in
a profession. If you put in "accounting," for
instance, you'll find 22 organizations. Also try
www.business.com; under each business category, there's a link to "associations."

Associations Unlimited, Gale, Web database,
Thomson Gale
www.gale.com
This web resource, available by subscription, combines data from the entire *Encyclopedia of Associations* series and includes additional Internal
Revenue Service (IRS) information on nonprofit
organizations for a total of more than 456,000
organizations. The database also contains association materials—brochures, logos, and membership applications. An indispensable source for
locating national, international, and local associations; monitoring association trends; identifying
related associations; networking and making
professional contacts; and much more. Five
search methods are available for easy searching:
name or acronym, geographic location, and sub-
ject/SIC/free text; multiple-field searches using
field abbreviations with Boolean operators; and

IRS data on nonprofits. Check with your local
library to see if it subscribes.

Weddle's Association Directory Online
www.weddles.com
Professional associations and societies often
operate websites featuring job boards, résumé
banks, or other employment-related services
(these can include job agents, banner advertising,
and discussion forums for networking). This
Directory is designed to help you find those sites.
It lists several thousand associations from around
the world by their primary professional/occupa-
tional focus and/or industry of interest (e.g.,
Accounting/Finance, Computer Hardware, and
Transportation) and provides a link to the website
they operate. For the most current listing of association sites and a summary of the employment
resources offered at the sites (e.g., job board,
résumé bank), see Weddle's Recruiter's Guide to
Association Web Sites, which was compiled with
the Association for Internet Recruiting and profiles more than 1,500 of the leading associations
and societies in the U.S.

Yahoo
www.yahoo.com
Type in "job" in Yahoo's search window and 148
million results pop up. The first few pages of
entries are job banks. If you need to find a specific
job board, type in "Bond trader job," for example.
Yahoo and **Google**, will lead you to other sites
and publications on a wide variety of job, career,
and company information.

National Directories of Companies

Print and Online

Bizjournals
www.bizjournals.com
Bizjournals is the new media division of American
City Business Journals, the nation's largest publisher of metropolitan business newspapers. It
operates the websites for each of the company's
41 print business journals and recently has

launched its first web-only local business news and information site for Los Angeles. The company plans to launch web-only operations in additional markets. The national Bizjournals site features local business news from around the nation updated throughout the day, top business stories from American City's print editions, industry-specific news from more than 40 industries, advice columns, and a full menu of tools to help business owners and operators manage their businesses more successfully. There's also easy navigation to each of the 42 local business sites. The site's archives contain more than 750,000 business news articles published since 1996. Bizjournals' sites have more than two million unique monthly visitors. E-mail offerings include daily local business updates from any Bizjournals market, as well as weekly updates of industry news from throughout the country. The site also features online local jobs boards, local online business directories, downloadable sales leads and strategic partnership opportunities.

The Corporate Directory of U.S. Public Companies, Walker's Research
www.walkersresearch.com, annual
Essential financial and business data for more than 11,000 U.S. public companies, including foreign companies filing American Depository Receipts (ADRs). Published annually in January; includes eight indexes.

The Corporate Yellow Book, Leadership Directories
www.leadershipdirectories.com
Includes high-growth companies in its listing of more than 1,000 leading U.S. corporations chosen from reports and lists published by numerous nationally recognized business sources. Has names and titles of more than 48,000 executives; direct-dial telephone numbers for executives; more than 10,000 E-mail addresses for officers, management, and administrative services professionals.

Dun & Bradstreet's
www.dnb.com
D&B is now an online subscription service and describes itself as follows: "The leading provider of global business information, tools, and insight has enabled customers to decide with confidence for over 160 years. D&B's proprietary DUNSRight process provides customers with quality information whenever and wherever they need it." Check with your library to see if it subscribes. D&B no longer publishes the Million Dollar Directory and the Reference Book of Corporate Management, America's Corporate Leaders. D&B used to issue annual versions of its directories, but now the information is online. You may find a somewhat recent edition of these and other D&B directories at your library. Be careful, as personnel may change.

Major Market Share Companies: Americas
(See International Directories)

Plunkett Research

Plunkett's Almanac of American Employers, Plunkett Research, Houston
www.plunkettresearch.com, annual.
This volume targets only major corporations. It profiles 500 selected U.S. employers of 2,300+ employees. These firms are located nationwide and represent all industry sectors. The Almanac includes a fully featured CD-ROM. Additional details, including a table of contents, are at www.plunkettresearch.com

Plunkett's Companion to The Almanac of American Employers
This covers selected midsize firms from 150 to 2,300 employees, nationwide, from all industry sectors. Includes a fully featured CD-ROM. Details are at www.plunkettresearch.com. The first section helps you explore various career options; write cover letters and résumés; build job-hunting networks; and master the interview. The second section describes more than 250 career possibilities, providing such data as:

working conditions, employment, job outlook, earnings, related occupations, training, other qualifications, and advancement.

Thomson Gale

Business Organizations, Agencies and Publications Directory 18th Ed., 2005, Thomson Gale
www.gale.com
This Directory is arranged in five broad categories: U.S. and international organizations, government agencies and programs, facilities and services, research and educational facilities, and publications and information services.

Business Rankings Annual, 2005, Thomson Gale
www.gale.com
Contains lists of companies, products, services, and activities compiled from a variety of published sources. Working from a bibliographic file the editors have built up over the years, they have culled thousands of items from periodicals, newspapers, financial services, directories, statistical annuals, and other printed material. The "top 10" from each of these rankings appears in this volume, grouped under standard subject headings for easy browsing. Readers can quickly locate all rankings in which a given company, person, or product appears by consulting the reference's comprehensive index. In addition, a complete listing of sources used to compile this Annual is provided in the bibliography. Each edition includes a separately published cumulative index.

Encyclopedia of Business Information Sources, Thomson Gale
www.gale.com, 19th ed., 2004
Identifies live, print, and electronic sources of information listed under alphabetically arranged subjects—industries and business concepts and practices. Listings are arranged by type of resource (directories, databases, newsletters, indexes, research centers, etc.) within each subject. Many entries also provide E-mail addresses and URLs covering online resources.

Notable Corporate Chronologies, 3rd Ed., 2000
This two-volume set presents concise chronologies for approximately 1,150 of the most significant corporations currently operating in the U.S. and abroad. Coverage focuses on both major established companies and notable newcomers that have had a major impact on the American or world economies, standards of living, and lifestyles.

Small Business Sourcebook, Thomson Gale, 2005
Has listings of live and print sources of information designed to facilitate the start-up, development, and growth of specific small businesses, as well as similar listings for general small-business topics. Entries are provided on a state-by-state basis; also included are relevant U.S. federal government agencies and branch offices.

Ward's Business Directory of U.S. Private and Public Companies, Thomson Gale, 2005
Ward's now lists more than 114,500 companies, 90 percent of which are private. Locate potential clients and create targeted mailing lists. In six volumes, arranged A–Z, geographically, by sales, SIC codes.

Harris InfoSource
www.harrisinfo.com
This directory is on CD-ROM and also in print. Lists manufacturing and all-business industry slices available for every state, region, and the entire U.S. Locate companies by name, geography, product/service category, or SIC. Company profiles include key decision-maker contact information, SICs, product/service categories and descriptions, company size information, sales, employees, contact information, and more.

Hoover's

www.hoovers.com
Hoover's Handbooks
These four volumes provide in-depth information on 2,550 of the world's largest, fastest-growing, and most influential public and private companies.

Hoover's Handbook of American Business 2004

This comprehensive two-volume set contains in-depth profiles of 750 of America's largest and most influential companies, plus a selection of more than 50 of the largest privately owned companies, including Cargill and Mars. Hoover's examines the personalities, events, and strategies that have made these enterprises leaders in their fields.

Hoover's Handbook of Emerging Companies 2004

Covers small, rapidly growing companies in the U.S. and tells the story of 600 such businesses, with in-depth profiles for 200 of these firms. Also includes lists of fast-growing companies from top business publications. This *Handbook* covers selected U.S. public companies with sales of between $10 million and $1 billion, at least three years of reported sales, at least a 20 percent rate of sales growth during that time, and positive net income for their most recent fiscal year. There are, however, a few exceptions to these rules, to cover some interesting companies that don't quite fit the mold.

Hoover's Handbook of Private Companies 2005

This volume covers 900 nonpublic U.S. enterprises, including large industrial and service corporations, such as Milliken & Co. and PricewaterhouseCoopers; hospitals and health-care organizations such as Blue Cross; charitable and membership organizations including the Ford Foundation; mutual and cooperative organizations such as IGA; joint ventures such as Motiva; government-owned corporations such as the Postal Service; and major university systems, including The University of Texas System.

Hoover's Handbook of World Business 2004

Has in-depth profiles of 300 of the most influential firms in Canada, Europe, and Japan, as well as companies from the fast-growing economies of countries like China, India, and Taiwan.

Hoover's Online

www.hoovers.com

Now a part of Dun & Bradstreet, this is a subscription service; however, this site allows free access to an A–Z company directory and an extensive listing of industries, and the latter opens pages of the "most-viewed" companies in each industry sector. Company listings have a paragraph description of the business operation, basic contact information, and a link to the company's website. Subscription services are: The Business Boneyard—a listing that provides a historical view of thousands of companies that have merged, been acquired, or have fallen victim to market trends or weak management. Hoover's Online has more than 2,000 company records with contact information. Also available by subscription is a geographic index and a company listing by stock index. Check to see if your library subscribes.

The National JobBank, Adams Media, Avon, MA

www.adamsmedia.com, annual

Updated annually, this book contains profiles and employment information for 20,000 companies; cross-referenced and indexed. Among data are a list of common positions, phone number for recorded job lines, type of business, locations, and more.

Standard & Poor's

www.books.mcgraw-hill.com

Standard & Poor's 500 Guide, 2004 Edition
Job seekers will find concise and up-to-the-minute overviews of potential employers with critical, often hard-to-find information. Contains market intelligence on all 500 of the companies listed in the S&P 500 Index, including company addresses, phone numbers, websites, names of key corporate directors, earnings and dividends data with three-year price charts, plus extensive stock and other financial information. See also **Standard and Poor's Register of Corporations, Directors and Executives**, which is helpful in locating top personnel.

Industry Profiles and Information

The Occupational Outlook and Salary Information appears as live links at the New York Public Library Job Information Center's website under Job Search Resources on the Internet at **www.nypl.org**. Also see the section Professions/Industries/Interests Industries—look under individual entries for industry information.

Bureau of Labor Statistics

The U.S. Occupational Outlook Employment Projections from the Bureau of Labor Statistics (BLS) www.bls.gov/emp
The Office of Occupational Statistics and Employment Projections develops information about the labor market for the nation as a whole for 10 years into the future. Includes such topics as the occupations with the largest job growth, 2002–12, showing the number of jobs for 2002 and 2012, with changes in the number of positions and the growth rate. Employment projections through 2012 are available for most industries, which are broken down by occupations. For example, "Aerospace Product and Parts Manufacturing" has projections for 50 occupations, including aerospace engineers, aircraft mechanics, arbitrators, lawyers, management analysts—down to writers and authors. Statistics are also given for an occupation across all industries on the same table.

Occupational Outlook Handbook
bls.gov/emp
Also published by the U.S. Dept. of Labor, Bureau of Labor Statistics, this handbook is a nationally recognized source of career information, providing assistance to individuals making decisions about their future work lives. Revised every two years, the Handbook describes what workers do on the job, working conditions, the training and education needed, earnings, and expected job prospects for a wide range of occupations. The

site contains downloadable PDFs of reprints of this handbook. These cover the nature of the work, working conditions, number of jobs in the U.S., job outlook, and median annual earnings. The employment projections mentioned in the reference above are tables of numbers, while the Handbook has no tables but instead discussions on jobs and industries.

Salary Information

Profession-Specific Salary Survey jobsmart.org
Research the salaries of more than 300 professions. This site has links to surveys done by a variety of organizations.

Salary.com
Research salaries, post questions in a forum, and sign up for a weekly newsletter from this site. A free graph of salary ranges is given for different levels of an occupation (from junior to senior) for various cities.

Cutting-Edge Careers and Top Employers Directories

50 Cutting-Edge Jobs, Ferguson, Chicago, 2000
Presents information on 50 newer careers, plus how to break into the field, a glimpse at the future of the field and the specific earnings, responsibilities, and locations of the jobs. This is a potpourri of occupations that have been spawned by changes in technology, business, and the makeup of the population. Some listings are: adventure travel specialist, biotechnology patent lawyer, computer and video game designer, forensic psycho-physiologist, fuel cell technician, Internet quality-assurance specialist, retirement counselor, and wireless service technician. Indexed.

Find Job Vacancies in the Business World or Private Sector, Planning Communications www.planningcommunications.com, new edition available in late 2005 to early 2006 Provides details on the best Internet job and résumé databases, specialty and trade periodicals, job-matching services, job hotline services, directories of employers, directories of professionals for networking purposes, and salary surveys. Covers the business world, high tech, health care, media, science and engineering, and the rest of the private sector. See the table of contents (at the publisher's website) for its full scope.

The Big Book of Jobs 2005–2006 VGM
Career Books Staff, manufactured by McGraw-Hill
Up-to-date data from the U.S. Department of Labor, plus cutting-edge career strategies from VGM. The Big Book lets job seekers save time by offering everything they need in a single volume.

Peterson's Top 2,500 Employers, Thomson Gale Company information provided by Hoover's Online. Be careful—things have changed since the year 2000! Includes indexes. Look for latest edition.

Business Information Websites

Adams Internet Job Search, 6th ed.
www.adamsmedia.com
Completely revised and updated, the sixth edition plugs job hunters directly into millions of opportunities and a comprehensive reference helps to find millions of newly advertised job listings. Get the most up-to-date lowdown on job sites. Find the sites and listings most relevant to your search.

First Research
www.firstresearch.com/
This company offers industry analysis and market research to help "sales and marketing professionals with the targeted understanding needed to engage key prospects and deepen customer rela-

tionships." The 10–12 pages profiles "are designed to deliver the industry knowledge and industry analysis that generate an understanding of the challenges and opportunities facing prospects and customers." More than 150 profiles are offered for $99 each, and are updated quarterly. Each includes an industry overview, financial benchmark data, industry opportunities, business trends, credit and risk issues, and an industry forecast.

Shibui Markets
www.shibuimarkets.com/
SM sells online industry reports and provides free, on-screen information on about 100 industries under "Search by Industry." Each industry has its SIC Code listed. Clicking on one of these industries brings up a screen with basic information on the industry's products, services, and activities, as well as its segments. For example, "Major Group 13: Oil and Gas Extraction" has links to: SIC Code 131: Crude Petroleum and Natural Gas, 132: Natural Gas Liquids, and 138: Oil and Gas Field Services. Clicking on one of these SIC Codes leads to a global list of companies. Free financial information is given for each company, plus users can join online discussions for free. Company reports are available for purchase.

Business.com
www.business.com
Industry-specific and global featured listings of companies and organizations with live links to their websites. A search engine permits browsing The Business Internet to find jobs, products/services, news, etc. Business.com's home page lists about 25 industries, each broken down into three or more subcategories; e.g., financial services is broken down into banking, insurance, and investment. Banking's subcategories include associations, banking institutions, banking law, certificates of deposits, employment, online banking, small business, and software, among others. A section called "Popular Searches" has links to

banking for small business, the banking industry, foreign banking, and sweep accounts, plus more. For each subcategory, clicking on "Jobs" opens a screen showing a limited number of positions. This site is best for putting together a list of potential employers in a specific field. Companies and associations pay to have their listings included.

Regional and Local Directories

Encyclopedia of Associations: Regional, State, and Local Organizations, Thomson Gale
www.gale.com, annual
This is a guide to U.S. nonprofit membership organizations with listings for organizations with interstate, state, intrastate, city, or local scope. Associations include trade and professional associations, social welfare and public affairs organizations, and religious, sports, and hobby groups with voluntary members. Detailed entries furnish association name and complete contact and descriptive text information. This information is not duplicated anywhere in **Encyclopedia of Associations**, also published by Thomson Gale. Name and keyword indexes accompany each volume.

JobBank Series, Adams Media, Avon, MA
www.adamsmedia.com
Currently, there are more than a dozen separate editions that cover the largest metropolitan areas and some states in the U.S. Each book contains profiles of local companies in all industries, with up-to-date information including company descriptions and contact information, hiring managers, common professional positions, projected number of hires, educational backgrounds sought, internship information, and benefits. Also listed are executive search firms and placement agencies, professional associations, websites for job hunters, CD-ROM job-search sources, plus some tips on conducting a search. The guides are

published on: *Atlanta, Austin/San Antonio, Boston, the Carolinas, Chicago, Connecticut, Dallas/Fort Worth, Houston, Los Angeles, New York (including New York City, Long Island, and Rockland and Westchester Counties, and Northern New Jersey), New Jersey, Ohio, Philadelphia, Phoenix, San Francisco Bay Area, Seattle, Virginia, and Washington, DC*

Craig's List
www.craigslist.org
This site is a local bulletin board, with a section on jobs. It has postings for community, housing, personals, and a bit more. The list of cities keeps growing. If your hometown isn't listed here, it may be by the time you read this: *Albany, Albuquerque, Anchorage, Atlanta, Austin, Baltimore, Boise, Boston, Buffalo, Charlotte, Chicago, Cincinnati, Cleveland, Columbus, Dallas, Denver, Detroit, Eugene, Fresno, Hartford, Honolulu, Houston, Indianapolis, Inland Empire, Kansas City, Las Vegas, Los Angeles, Memphis, Miami, Milwaukee, Minneapolis, Monterey, Nashville, New Orleans, New York, Norfolk, Omaha, Orange County, Orlando, Philadelphia, Phoenix, Pittsburgh, Portland, Providence, Raleigh, Reno, Sacramento, Salt Lake City, San Antonio, San Diego, Santa Barbara, Seattle, Spokane, St. Louis, San Francisco Bay, Tampa Bay, Tucson, Tulsa, Washington, DC. Plus Canada: Montreal, Ottawa, Toronto, Vancouver . . . and other countries, too!*

National Job Hotline Directory: The Job Finder's Hot List: 1999–2001 (National Job Hotline Directory), Sue A. Cubbage and Marcia P. Williams
www.jobfindersonline.com
Although published a few years ago, this book contains a state-by-state listing of job hotlines, as well as a list of job-hunting resources and directories of employers by city.

Regional and Local Associations

Thomson Gale

Encyclopedia of Associations: Regional, State and Local Organizations, Thomson Gale
www.gale.com, annual
(See Regional and Local Directories.)

Associations Unlimited

This online database combines data from the entire *Encyclopedia of Associations* series and includes additional Internal Revenue Service information on nonprofit organizations for a total of more than 456,000 organizations. The database also contains association materials— brochures, logos, and membership applications. A key source for locating national, international and local associations; monitoring association trends; identifying related associations; networking and making professional contacts; marketing to associations, their members, and markets; and more. Various types of search methods are available. Check to see if a library in your area subscribes.

Weddle's Association Directory—online
www.weddles.com

Professional associations and societies often operate websites featuring job boards, résumé banks, or other employment-related services. This Directory helps you find these sites. It lists several thousand associations from around the world by their primary professional/occupational focus and/or industry of interest and provides a link to the websites they operate. For the most current listing of association sites and a summary of the employment resources offered at the sites (e.g., job board, résumé bank), see **Weddle's Recruiter's Guide to Association Web Sites**, a print directory compiled in conjunction with the Association for Internet Recruiting with profiles of more than 1,500 of the leading associations and societies in the U.S.

Recruiters

Kennedy Information
www.kennedyinformation.com

The Directory of Executive Recruiters Corporate Edition, 2004

With advice on using executive recruiters and full firm contact information, including phone numbers, fax numbers, and E-mail and web addresses, the Directory is the best source for entering the "hidden" job market with executive recruiters. Five full indexes help the user target information.

The International Directory of Executive Recruiters

Lists full contact information for 2,515 firm locations in 80 countries; indexed by function, industry, firm, and 5,300 search-firm principals; provides tips for job seekers along with recommendations of books and other resources on career management and job changing.

Job Boards and More

Career Fairs

www.careerfairs.com

A locator of job/career fairs searchable by date, job category, and state. Includes high-tech, professional, sales, health care, and college fairs.

www.nationalcareerfairs.com

Provides a listing by date and city for free fairs throughout the U.S.

www.jobstar.org

Lists California job fairs and resources for California job hunters.

How to Participate in a Job Fair
www.jobsearch.about.com

Have a successful job fair experience—in 12 easy steps.

Live Links to Job Boards

This section is taken from the New York Public Library website, Mid-Manhattan Library). This provides links to the most popular job boards, career-information sites, salary information, and more. The library updates this list often, so that all sites are current and active.

This site is accessed by opening **www.nypl.org**, going to the section on the branches, and scrolling down the page and clicking on "Job Information." Then, open the link that says, "Job Search Resources on the Internet." Under "Job Search-ing—General Resources" is a listing of the most popular job boards chosen by the library staff that covers a range of occupations with live links. Here is the listing:

America's Career InfoNet
www.acinet.org/acinet

This is a part of CareerOneStop, an extensive federal and state-sponsored career site. Find wages and employment trends, occupational requirements, state-by-state labor market conditions, millions of employment contacts nationwide, and the most extensive career resource library online.

America's Job Bank
www.ajb.dni.us

U.S. Department of Labor link to 1,800 state employment services. User registration required.

BestJobsUSA
www.bestjobsusa.com
Job seekers may search for jobs, post a résumé, and research the economic prospects of several states, as well as do salary research and get career advice.

Career Builder
www.careerbuilder.com

Search for a job, post a résumé, read articles on working life, and peruse the list of employment agencies.

Career Guides @ Your Library
jobstar.org

Check out these great books available at your local library.

Career Resource Center
www.careers.org/

Extensive links to career-related websites.

FlipDog.com
www.flipdog.com

This site provides job information from big and small companies, public and private organizations.

HOTJOBS
www.hotjobs.com

This site enables job seekers to search by keyword, company, U.S. location, and international location. It also offers useful career tools such as interviewing skills, résumé writing, industry news, and a reloca-tion center.

Internet Career Connection
www.iccweb.com

This site provides job listings, career information, a career guidance service, and a résumé database. You can take a free interest inventory to discover which occupations best match your interests.

Job Bank USA
www.jobbankusa.com

Search employment listings, network, submit an E-résumé, and search the database using specific job requirements.

Job Hunt
www.job-hunt.org

List of online job-search resources and services.

Monster
www.monster.com

Worldwide access for all levels in all fields. Search for jobs, post a résumé, open your own career-management account, and research a featured company.

NationJob
www.nationjob.com

This site provides job information for job seekers and employers, résumé-writing info, a free career test, a salary wizard, career articles, success stories, community programs, and online degree info.

Net Temps
www.net-temps.com

A site targeted to the temporary-employment market. Users may search for jobs and post a résumé.

NYTimes
www.nytimes.com/pages/jobs

Site features an easy-to-navigate design, articles about careers and the workplace, and job listings in the tristate area and nationwide. You can also post résumés on Job Market and sign up for daily E-mail alerts.

The Riley Guide
www.dbm.com/jobguide

A comprehensive site of employment listings and information about job hunting on the Internet.

Vault.com
www.vault.com

Job listings include finance, consulting, law, Internet, health, consumer products and retail, media, marketing, technology, and science. This site offers insider guides, company profiles, message boards, and firm rankings. An excellent source for industry information; however, only a select group of industries are covered.

Wetfeet.com
www.wetfeet.com

Company profiles, industry profiles, career coaching, self-assessment, job listings, internship listings, and international jobs.

www.jobstar.org
Contains career guides, links to salary information for a variety of occupations. Link to **www.careerjournal.com**, the career website from *The Wall Street Journal*. Also, links to the Journal's JobStar Executive (for executives); information on job hunting and career management (from the *Journal* and other sources) and JobStar Job Bank, a searchable database of 30,000+ middle- to senior-level positions is updated daily. A direct way of accessing JobStar is at www.careerjournal.com, which is the *Journal*'s executive career site. This site allows a nationwide search for a particular profession (e.g., physics) or type of job (e.g., IT vice president). The entries include a job description, information on the company, job requirements, and salary. This site also contains articles, discussions, and advice on various aspects of jobs and careers.

www.linkedin.com
This is a network of professional job seekers. The idea behind this site is that, since members refer each other, it is a network of *trusted professionals*. Service is free and persons join by being referred online (via E-mail) by a classmate, coworker,

colleague, or other professional. Members fill out a profile, which allows others to contact them, as well as search the network for contacts by such things as job title, job function, location, etc. Members can access those who are not in their own network but in the overall database via these searches. There are more than 300,000 job listings from more than 1,000 employers worldwide. Jobs are posted directly on the employers' own sites. This network allows users to get needed introductions to a hiring manager or recruiter. For example, a member can call a hiring manager and say, "Joan Smith of Exco recommended that I call you"—even if he or she only knows Joan via a network search.

Guides to Job and Career Websites

Adams Internet Job Search Almanac, Adams Media Corp., 6th ed.
www.adamsmedia.com
Find millions of newly advertised job listings. Get the most up-to-date lowdown on job sites. Find

the sites and listings most relevant to your search. Create electronic résumés readable by computers and intriguing to prospective employers. Post résumés without a hitch. Research the hidden job market to target the right employers. Network with peers in cyberspace.

Best Career and Education Web Sites: A Quick Guide to Online Job Search, Rachel Singer Gordon, and Anne Wolfinger, JIST Works, 4th ed., 2004

www.jist.com

Listings and reviews of the 340 "very best" sites on the Internet for information on careers, college, training, and job searching. This is not a catalog of everything out there; rather it is a carefully considered nomination of the most helpful, crucial, and information-packed sites available on the web. Previously titled **Quick Internet Guide to Career and Education Information**.

CareerXroads, Gerry Crispin and Mark Mehler, MMC Group, Kendall Park, NJ, 2003

www.careerxroads.com

This book has reviews of the top 500 job sites and listings for more than 2,500 in total. The reviews include information on the site's content, the range of jobs posted on the site (10s, 100s, 1,000s, etc.), the range of résumés posted, whether there are any posting fees, the job disciplines and specialties, and a paragraph about the site. An excellent source for finding job boards and much more. Indexes include corporation staffing pages, location, and specialty and industry.

Job Hunter's Sourcebook: Where to Find Employment Leads and Other Job Search Resources, Thomson Gale, Edition 6, 2004

Also lists sources of help-wanted ads, employer directories, employment agencies, placement services, electronic resources, and other information sources for specific careers. Profiles 216 high-interest professional and vocational occupations, from accountant and aircraft mechanic to sports official and stockbroker. A master list of profiled professions lists alternative, popular, synonymous, and related job titles and links them to the jobs

profiled. Entries contain complete contact information and are arranged by type of resource. New profiles on high-growth careers cover such hot jobs as software engineer, database administrator, and environmental engineer. This sourcebook organizes the wide-ranging information available to today's job seeker. Each category features various sources, including reference works, online and database services, software programs, and more. Also included is an alphabetical list of all the publications, organizations, electronic resources, and other sources of job-hunting information.

Plunkett's Employers' Internet Sites with Careers Information, 2004–2005, Plunkett Research, annual

Plunkett's editors have viewed thousands of corporate websites to pick out those with the most useful career information. This book profiles hundreds of those best websites and indexes them by type of business, type of data available, type of jobs available, and more. Each site addresses the following questions: Can you apply for a job online? Is information available for the physically challenged? Are jobs searchable by geographic region? Is the careers section searchable by type of job? Are benefit plan data available? Are international jobs listed? Are specific job openings posted? Are internships listed? Is there a special college recruiting section? In addition, profiles provide a description of the business, size of the firm by annual sales, and human resources contact name, address, and phone number, along with corporate phone and fax numbers. Purchasers of the printed book or PDF version may receive a free CD-ROM database of the corporate profiles, enabling export of corporate data for mail merges and other uses.

Weddle's Directory of Employment-Related Internet Sites 2004

www.weddles.com

This directory lists more than 7,500 websites that specialize in online recruiting. All of the sites are organized and listed by occupational field, industry, and/or geographic focus. The directory covers the global labor market and is said to access sites not easily found by other job hunters. The Directory lists sites in the U.S. and more than 20 countries around the world.

Weddle's Job Seeker's Guide to Employment Web Sites 2004
www.weddles.com

This book is billed as a consumer's guide to online job boards, résumé banks, and career portals. Completely updated for 2004, this reference presents the "best of the 40,000+ employment-related sites currently available on the Internet." It supplies information about each site's services, features, and fees, such as how many and what kinds of jobs are posted, the salary ranges of the posted jobs, and whether the site contains information about employers. Free updates are available at www.weddles.com.

Your 24/7 Online Job Search Guide, Lamont
Wood, Adobe Reader eBooks
Required: Adobe Reader 6.0; Platforms: For Windows, Mac, Palm

Advanced navigation, search, bookmarks, and multiple viewing options. Topics include the search process, electronic résumé, leading job sites, other sites, using usernet and mailing lists, job-related newsgroups, and corporate information sites.

Section II: Professions/Industries/Interests

General

Trade Shows

Events Eye
www.eventseye.com

Trade Shows, Exhibitions, Conferences and Professional Events Worldwide
Features more than 5,200 trade shows, exhibitions, and conferences put on by nearly 1,000 organizers, with a total of more than 8,900 events through July 2006. New trade shows and exhibitions are added every month.

Print

Plunkett's Research, Ltd., Houston, TX
www.plunkettresearch.com

This company offers reports and online subscriptions on industry sector analysis and research, industry trends, and industry statistics. For job seekers, these reports contain industry and company financial and sales information, vertical industry marketing data, product strategy data, trends analysis, statistics, job-search data, company profiles, and executive lists. This enables seekers to develop specific, targeted mailings, as well as be knowledgeable during interviews.

Plunkett's Industry Almanacs
Plunkett's business and industry almanacs contain the latest trends, competitive intelligence, market research, business analysis, data and statistics grouped within specific industry segments. Included are profiles of hundreds of leading companies. Each almanac comes with a CD-ROM that contains its complete core databases. Each almanac contains, among other information, industry information, business statistics, technology trends, and up to 27 executive contacts that are included in profiles of about 500 leading companies in the industry. Individual almanacs are listed below. Check
www.plunkettresearch.com/almanacs.htm for more information on each, as well as a list of upcoming additions to this group. At press time, the industries covered were: *Advertising & Branding, Airlines, Hotels, Travel & Tourism, Apparel & Textiles, Automobiles & Trucks, Banking & Mortgages, e-Commerce & Internet, (Computers, Internet, Software & Hardware), Consulting Industry, Energy Industry (Energy, Alternative Energy & Utilities), Engineering & Research, Entertainment & Media (Entertainment, Media, Film, TV, Radio & Publishing), Financial Services (Finance, Investments, Banking, Insurance & Mortgages), Food & Beverages, Heath Care, Biotech & Genetics, Insurance, Investment & Securities, Real Estate & Construction Industry (Real Estate REITs, Mortgages & Construction), Retail, Telecommunications & Wireless, Transportation, Supply Chain & Logistics.* New titles under

development at press time were: *Banking, Mortgages & Credit Industry, Insurance Industry, Investment & Securities Industry, and Renewable, Alternative & Hydrogen Energy Industry.*

Plunkett's Industry Summary Reports (e-books)

These are downloadable e-books, based on the Industry Almanacs. Each is in PDF form, runs about 30–40 pages, and covers industry information and trends. There is no list of company profiles; thus, there is no executive contact information. Cost is $99.99 for each. The list, at press time, consisted of: *Advertising & Branding Industry, Airline, Hotel & Travel Industry, Apparel & Textiles Industry, Automobile Industry, Banking and Insurance Industry, Biotech Industry, Computer and Software Industry, Consulting Industry, e-Commerce Business, Energy Industry, Engineering Industry, Entertainment & Media Industry, Financial Services Industry Trends, Technologies and Online Access, Food Industry, Health Care Industry, Health Care Technologies Overview, Leading Global Entertainment & Media Companies, Mortgage Industry, Nanotechnology & MEMS Industry, Real Estate & Construction, Renewable, Alternative & Hydrogen Energy, Retail Industry, Telecommunications, Transportation, Supply Chain & Logistics.*

Free Trade Publications

tradepub.com

This site allows professionals to get a free one-year subscription to a wide variety of publications in more than 20 broad categories. These are "controlled subscriptions," which means that readers must fill out a form that includes the company they work for and their title and often what types of equipment and services they use or get involved with during their buying decision.

Job and Industry Information Sites
Industry News and Job Boards

www.vault.com

Vault contains career and industry information, message boards, and lists of "top 20" job boards. This is a good source for industry information. Postings are searchable by keyword, city, and state, except for Consulting, which is categorized by Management & Strategy, Tech, Operations, Human Resources, Change Management, Financial, Health Care, Marketing, and Other. The industries covered are: *Accounting, Advertising and Public Relations, Consulting, Entertainment, Fashion, Government, Health/Biotech/Pharmaceutical, Investment Banking, Investment Management, Law, Media & Marketing, Nonprofit, Real Estate, Technology, Television, Venture Capital.*

www.wetfeet.com

Wet Feet says that it "provides information on companies, careers, and industries that job seekers use throughout their careers to make smarter career decisions. Wet Feet also offers job seekers expert advice, newsletters, salary benchmarking tools, and discussion boards on everything from negotiating a raise to writing better cover letters." This is a good site to find information about various types of careers, what the latest industry news says, and who some of the key players are in each area. Wet Feet sells Insider Guides (under $20 each) on various industries and a limited number of financial institutions, such as Accenture, Deloitte, Citigroup, and Morgan Stanley. Guides, which can be downloaded, are available for *General Career Help, Accounting, Advertising, Biotech & Pharmaceuticals, Brand Management & Marketing, Consulting, Entertainment, Financial Services, Health Care, Human Resources, Law, Manufacturing, Information Technology, Nonprofit & Government, Oil & Gas,* and *Real Estate.* There are also guides for various aspects of job-hunting and career management; e.g., business schools, freelancing, promotions, and more.

New York Public Library Industry-Specific Guides and Directories

www.nypl.org (Science, Industry, and Business Library)

Open the page on research and click on the box "Introductory Research Guides." Guides are provided for a few selected industries. Clicking on "Industry-Specific Directories" will bring up a list of about 75 industries. Clicking on each will open up a page with a listing of appropriate directories. Many of these are included in this listing. There are also materials taken from other sources.

Academic and Education

Print

101 Career Alternatives for Teachers: Exciting Job Opportunities for Teachers Outside the Profession, Margaret Gisler, Prima Pub., 2002
Turnover rates within the teaching industry are skyrocketing, with half of all teachers leaving the profession within their first five years. In addition, an enormous number are scheduled to retire in the near future. This book shows the best fields for teachers to use their skills and experience, and the most attractive and lucrative alternative jobs for teachers.

The World of Learning, Europa Publications, Taylor & Francis Group, U.K., annual
An international directory of educational, cultural, and scientific institutions with contact information on more than 150,000 persons who are the chief personnel in higher education worldwide. Also provides information on more than 400 organizations. An online version is available by subscription.

Online
Academic Employment Network
www.academploy.com
Primary, secondary, and higher learning positions.

Academic Position Network
www.apnjobs.com
Searchable higher education database.

www.academic360.com
Academic360.com is a metacollection of Internet resources that have been gathered for the academic job hunter. It includes links to faculty, staff, and administrative positions.

Chronicle of Higher Education Career Network
chronicle.com
Content and listing of all positions available (for free) from the previous week's edition of the *Chronicle of Higher Education*. Listings from the current week's edition are available online to subscribers only.

Education America Network
educationamerica.net
America's largest online source for education employment opportunities.

Higher Ed Jobs
www.higheredjobs.com
Search for academic jobs by position, location, or keyword.

K-12Jobs
www.k12jobs.com
This site includes information on job fairs, state certifications, education resources, résumés, salaries, and newsgroups.

University Job Bank
UJobBank.com
Job listings for faculty/staff positions, as well as employment opportunities for postdoctoral candidates and a résumé bank.

Accounting

Print

Careers in Accounting, Gloria L. Gaylord and Glenda E. Reid, VGM Professional Careers Series, 3rd ed., 1997
Covers careers in public, corporate, government, and nonprofit accounting, as well as what's required to be a sole practitioner, educator, or

financial planner. Contains career advice and covers recent trends in this field, although some of this book is obviously dated.

Online

Accountemps
www.accountemps.com
Accountemps specializes in providing temporary staffing services by accounting, finance and book-keeping professionals.

Accounting.com
Post a résumé, join a discussion group, view listings of CPAs and accounting firms, and see other resources. Search for jobs by state, city, company name or keywords. This site also has links to other resources for accountants, online discussions, and online professional education courses (this part of the site was under development at press time).

AICPA Online: American Institute for Certified Public Accountants
www.aicpa.org
AICPA Online provides information that includes how to become a CPA, taking the CPA exam, and career opportunities.

Careers in Accounting
www.careers-in-accounting.com
Some of the best info on the Internet on fields such as public accounting, tax, auditing, and managerial accounting. Also links to quite a few other sites and some useful books.

Execu/Search Group
www.execu-search.com
This site is for professional recruitment and temporary staffing in the New York metro area, specializing in accounting/finance, accounting support, financial services, graphics, health care, human resources, information technology, legal, and office support.

Financial Job Network
www.fjn.com
This network lists global job opportunities for financial professionals in the following categories:

Accountant, Auditor, Banking, Investment, CFO, COO, College, Controller, Finance, Insurance, President, CEO.

Vault.com (see previous listing)

Wetfeet Inside Guide, Careers in Accounting, e-book, (see www.wetfeet.com, listed previously)

Advertising, Including Graphic Art and Design

Print

Adweek
Three directories are offered, either online or in print with a CD-ROM. The **Adweek Directory**, **Brandweek Directory**, and **Multicultural Marketing in America Directory**. Electronically, these can be targeted by multiple criteria and viewed in detail. Key contact information for personnel and companies can be downloaded. The data are updated constantly to provide the most current information available. The publication's site, **adweek.com**, also provides industry news that is updated daily.

The Advertising RedBooks, LexisNexis
www.redbooks.com
The RedBooks bills itself as "the most comprehensive, most trusted information source on the advertising industry. Available in print volumes, on CD-ROM and online." The website offers some free searches, but total online access to the more than 30,000 companies listed is by subscription. However, this information is available in the print versions. The website contains an extensive listing of associations related to the ad industry. Individual RedBooks are published for Agencies, Advertisers (Business), Advertisers (Geographic Listing), and International Advertisers and Agencies. The Agency Database contains detailed profiles of nearly 13,500 U.S. and international advertising agencies, including accounts represented by each agency, fields of specialization, breakdown of gross billings by media, contact information on agency personnel, and much

more. The Advertiser Database contains information on more than 15,500 U.S. and international advertisers that each spend more than $200,000 annually on advertising. Each listing includes advertising expenditures by media, current agency, fiscal year-end and annual sales, contact information on key personnel, brand name info, SIC classifications, and other key data.

Breaking into Advertising: How to Market Yourself Like a Professional, Jeannette Smith, Peterson's, Princeton, NJ, 1998
Smith presents an overview of the ad business, how to break into it, and how to get ahead once you're in.

Plunkett's Advertising & Branding Industry Almanac; also **Summary Report** (see **Plunkett's** above)

U.S. Sourcebook of Advertisers, Schonfeld & Associates
www.saibooks.com, annual
A directory of publicly owned corporations that advertise. Corporate name, address, and phone number are provided, along with the names and titles of three senior executives, ad budgets, sales, fiscal year closing, and more. Organized by state and ZIP code.

Online

3 D Site
www.3dsite.com/#jobs
A community-based effort focused on the computer graphics industry (3-D artists, modeling, and special effects).

Adbrands.net
www.adbrands.net
This site contains information about the global advertising industry. Some job postings are here, but this site is best for company profiles and account assignments. Adbrands.net analyzes more than 1,000 leading advertisers, brands, and agencies and provides histories, up-to-date news, financial information, and more than 20,000

external consumer brands, corporate, and worldwide links. The Account Assignments database tracks account management for the world's leading brands and companies, i.e., which advertising agency handles which accounts in which countries. Fully searchable by brand, brand owner, company, or advertising agency, the database now contains more than 10,000 worldwide account assignments for almost 4,000 leading brands. Some information is free to anyone; however, much is by subscription only. A month's subscription is $55.

Advertising Age
www.adage.com
Advertising Age magazine's job bank powered by **Monster.com**.

Adweek
www.adweek.com
Search for a job, post a résumé, read articles, search for job fairs, and read the online version of *Adweek* magazine.

Art Hire
www.arthire.com
For visual/music/sound/voice artists. Lists positions across the U.S., not just in New York and L.A.

Media Bistro
mediabistro.com
Dedicated to anyone who creates or works with content, or who is a noncreative professional working in a content/creative industry. That includes editors, writers, television producers, graphic designers, book publishers, people in production, and circulation departments in industries including magazines, television, radio, newspapers, book publishing, online media, advertising, public relations, and graphic design. Its mission is to provide opportunities (both online and off-line) for you to meet each other, share resources, become informed of job opportunities and interesting projects, improve your career skills, and showcase your work.

Vault.com
www.vault.com
Career and industry information, job postings (see previous listing).

Wetfeet Insider Guide, Careers in Advertising and Public Relations, Wet Feet, San Francisco, 2002
www.wetfeet.com
E-book, also available as PDF. This guide is for those who never took the plunge and wonder what it's like to have a career in advertising or public relations. Topics include how to select the advertising or public relations agency that's right for you, what forces and trends are currently shaping these industries, the take on the top agencies and hirers, what real people working in these fields like and dislike about their jobs, what you're likely to earn, the hours you'll be expected to put in, and typical office culture.

Aging Workers

Print

New Work Opportunities for Older Americans, Robert S. Menchin, iUniverse Pub., 2000
This book speaks to men and women 55 and over. It reviews the new and emerging work opportunities for older Americans, such as job sharing, "bridge" employment, corporate job banks, phased employment, seasonal work, temp jobs, part-time, freelance work, and consulting. Includes job-search tips, how to fight back against age discrimination, how Social Security affects post-retirement income, the pros and cons of working, and advice for housewives returning to work.

Online Resources for Senior Citizens, Charles C. Sharpe, McFarland & Co., 2003
This book facilitates and expands Internet access and usage by seniors, assists them in finding the information they want and need, and contributes to their knowledge of the aging process and the challenges it presents by providing a list of online resources of particular interest to them. Federal government and general resources for seniors are listed first, followed by resources pertaining to such specific topics as abuse, caregivers, computers and the Internet, death and dying, employment, and volunteering.

Online Senior Job Bank
www.seniorjobbank.org
Free to over-50 job seekers. Confidential service matching job seekers over 50 with employers and good jobs. Job seekers: Find full-time, part-time, temporary, and volunteer jobs. Use the Senior Job Alert to be notified of new job postings. Resources have links to many sites for seniors.

Apparel, Textiles, Fashion, and Beauty

Note: *Some of this information is taken from an Industry Guide from the Science, Industry and Business Library of the New York Public Library, "Apparel, Fashion and Textiles" (www.nypl.org). This site contains a large listing of directories for specific segments of these industries.*

Print

Apparel Industry Sourcebook, Fashiondex
www.fashiondex.com
A complete and up-to-date guide listing more than 2,600 nationwide suppliers of all types of fabrics, trims, notions, forecast services, swatch design studios, CAD services, and more for the apparel industry.

Davison's Textile Blue Book, Davison Publishing
www.davisonbluebook.com
Directory of textile mills, dyers, and finishers in the U.S., Canada, Mexico, and Central America allows for simple sourcing of companies. Includes a buyer's guide.

The Directory of Brand Name Apparel Manufacturers, Fashiondex
www.fashiondex.com
The up-to-date directory listing of brand-name labels and manufacturers in the women's, men's, children's, and accessory markets. Developed and

targeted for store and catalog buyers to shop the apparel and accessory markets easily. More than 2,800 brand names listed, broken down by all types of apparel classification. No cross-referencing or legends to consult.

Men's and Boy's Wear—U.S. National Register of Apparel Manufacturing, Davison Publishing, 2003
With more than 2,500 listings, this is a fully indexed directory of American men's and boy's apparel manufacturers. Each profile includes company address, phone, fax, website, officers, year established, annual sales, number of employees, labels, capabilities, fabrics used, lines produced, price range, garments produced, import, export, acceptance of contract work, private-label manufacturing availability, license selling, and retail-outlet information.

Plunkett's Apparel and Textiles Industry Almanac (see previous listing for **Plunkett's**)

Who's Who Guide to Personal Care 2004
Global Cosmetic Industry Magazine's guide includes everything—and everyone—you need to know to get ahead in the personal-care industry. More than 1,300 personal-care companies, as well as 2,000 key personnel, are represented, with products and services ranging from advertising-claims substantiation to zirconium compounds. This special issue is part of a subscription to *GCI Magazine*. Published each year.

Women's and Children's Wear—U.S. National Register of Apparel Manufacturing, Davison Publishing, 2003
www.davisonbluebook.com
With nearly 4,000 companies listed, this register is the most comprehensive directory of the American apparel industry. Fully indexed in easy-to-read format, this directory includes company profile, website, year established, annual sales, number of employees, labels manufactured, fabrics, market, capabilities, and much more.

Online

The Cosmetics Site
www.thecosmeticsite.com
Jobs, networking, news, and other resources.

Fashion Net
www.fashion.net
Global job postings for all types of jobs in fashion, including fashion and graphic design marketing, administration, sales, and more. Site has links to fashion schools, industry news, and articles on what different fashion careers are like, written by professionals.

Fashion Career Center.com
www.fashioncareercenter.com
Job listings, plus links to fashion schools and colleges. Site is said to be a great fit for the New York niche of the rag trade.

Vault.com
www.vault.com
Career and industry information, plus job listings for the fashion industry (see earlier listing for Vault.com)

Professional and Trade Associations

Listed below is a selection of associations, including their websites, that provide industry statistics, news, surveys, and reports:

American Apparel & Footwear Association
www.americanapparel.org
Industry news, consumer information, and statistics.

American Association of Textile Chemists and Colorists
www.aatcc.org

American Textile Manufacturers Institute
www.atmi.org

Associations Directory for the Apparel and Fashion Industry
www.apparelsearch.com
Portal website for links to individual associations in the apparel, fashion, and textile industries; e.g., ATMI, AATCC.

The Fashion Center Business Improvement District, New York City
www.fashioncenter.com

The Institute of Textile Technology in Charlottesville, Virginia
www.itt.edu

National Textile Center University Research Consortium
www.ntcresearch.org

The Textile Institute
texi.org

Trade Shows

Expocentral.com
www.expocentral.com
Information on the textile industry, current trade shows, fairs, exhibitions, conventions, and conferences in the U.S. and other countries.

Selected Databases

Women's Wear Daily Online
www.wwd.com
Women's Wear Daily's entire classified section, including job opportunities. Articles, full text; database. The fashion industry's daily news source, covering business issues, fashion trends, retailing developments, international ready-to-wear, couture presentations, and market overviews. WWD is written for retailers and manufacturers of women's apparel, accessories, fibers, and textiles. Updated daily.

Art and Design

Online

The Art Newspaper
www.theartnewspaper.com
This newspaper provides information on events and trends in worldwide art, including significant sales, theft, and destruction; important new hirings; conservation; and exhibitions. Job openings and courses in art management are listed.

Art Resources
www.artresources.com
A virtual gallery where artists working in any medium can exhibit their works. The site has a large listing of artists, galleries, and museums.

Arts Wire Current
www.artswire.org
Arts Wire is a national computer-based communications network for the arts community. This site includes job listings, opportunities for artists, and opportunities for organizations.

WWAR: World Wide Arts Resources
wwar.com
This site offers information on the visual and performing arts, antiques, film, etc. It includes links to art image collections, artists, education, art history, museums, art agencies, and sources for employment and staffing opportunities.

Associations

Print

The Encyclopedia of Associations,
Thomson Gale
www.gale.com, annual
This is a comprehensive source of detailed information on more than 135,000 nonprofit membership organizations worldwide. Several versions provide addresses and descriptions of professional societies, trade associations, labor unions, cultural and religious organizations, fan clubs, and other groups of all types. The versions are: **National Organizations of the U.S.**, **International Organizations**, and **Regional, State, and Local Organizations**. An online version is available at some libraries. All versions are indexed by name, keyword, company, and for the international version, executives.

Weddle's Recruiter's Guide to Association Web Sites
www.weddles.com, annual
Put together for recruiters, this guide can be an aid to job seekers, as well. Compiled in conjunc-

tion with the Association for Internet Recruiting (Recruiters Network), this guide lists more than 1,500 professional, technical, and trade associations and indicates what kinds of recruiting services they provide (i.e., job board, résumé database, other). Helps you search for job targets by category/profession. For example, for biochemists, this guide will point to such organizations as the American Association of Brewing Chemists, the American Association of Cereal Chemists, the American Chemical Society, the American Institute of Chemical Engineers, and the Canadian Society of Biochemistry and Molecular and Cellular Biologists.

Online

American Society of Association Executives
www.asaenet.org
A job board that is searchable by category (from accounting to sales), job level (entry to experienced), type (full- or part-time, temporary or contract), state, and date posted. The site has links to associations worldwide, as well as career information.

Association Job Boards
associationjobboards.com
This portal provides access to niche job boards operated by professional societies and trade organizations.

Weddle's Association Directory
www.weddles.com/associations/index.cfm
Professional associations and societies often operate websites featuring job boards, résumé banks, or other employment-related services (these can include job agents, banner advertising, and discussion forums for networking). This online Directory is designed to help find those association sites. It lists several thousand associations from around the world by their primary professional/occupational focus and/or industry of interest (e.g., Accounting/Finance, Computer Hardware, and Transportation) and provides a link to the website they operate.

Automotive

Print

Dictionary of Automotive Engineering, 2nd ed., Don Goodsell ed., Society of Automotive Engineers
www.sae.org
The second edition of the *Dictionary* provides complete coverage of more than 3,000 terms and more than 100 detailed drawings currently used in automotive engineering worldwide. This thorough technical reference defines the terminology of the professional engineer and also includes the more informal vocabulary common in industry use. Designed to meet the wide-ranging needs of today's automotive engineers as well as the enthusiast who wants to become familiar with the terminology, the *Dictionary* is a single source to the most up-to-date definitions available. Recommended for automotive engineers and those who want a better understanding of the industry.

Plunkett's Automobiles & Trucks Industry Almanac, Plunkett's Automobile Industry Summary (see previous listing for **Plunkett's**)

Ward's Automotive Yearbook, Southfield, MI, annual
wardsauto.com
Data available on CD-ROM as well as print. Includes hundreds of pages of data, statistics, specifications, and company information; production and sales information; details on Ward's Top 500 dealers; auto company profiles, including key financial data; and a supplement that is a Directory of Suppliers and Product Guide listing more than 1,900 major suppliers under specific product categories, many with detailed company profiles.

Online

Auto Careers
www.autocareers.com
A complete employment resource center for the entire automotive industry. This website matches qualified candidates with auto industry employers in the U.S. and international markets. Site

includes dealerships, independents, manufacturers, distributors, OEMs, vendors, consultants, trade schools, and motor sports.

Auto Dealer Jobs
www.autodealerjobs.com
Jobs for franchise dealers, OEMs, aftermarket, manufacturers, suppliers, repair, rental, collision repair, and independent retailers.

Aviation and Aerospace
Print

International Satellite Directory, Satnews Publishers, 18th ed.
www.satnews.com
Billed as the most complete reference source in the world on communications satellites. Updated annually in two volumes with 16 separate chapters and more than 25,000 entries, this 1,400-plus-page reference source is for all satellite professionals. Comes with a CD-ROM containing over 850 EIRP, G/T, and SFD maps in full color. Also, an online subscription service with information on more than 500 satellites (orbital location, frequencies, EIRP, G/T, SFD, bandwidth, programming, etc.) and 15,000 companies (address, phone, fax, web, products, services, contact names, etc.) in the commercial satellite industry. Containing a fast-search ability plus hundreds of EIRP, G/T, and SFD maps in color not published anywhere else. Other online services are offered for those in the field.

Jane's International ABC Aerospace Directory, Jane's Information Group
www.janes.com
Has details on thousands of organizations and personnel in the aerospace industry. Features government agencies, associations, defense forces, transport carriers, and airports, manufacturers, distributors, sales and service companies, and company divisions and field offices. Entries detail the address, phone, fax, and electronic contact details; previous organization identities, financial and statistical information;

personnel details; parent and subsidiary information; details of products and services, and airfield reference data, all presented in a concise manner. Jane's website contains other resources, news of the aerospace industry, and more.

Job Hunting for Pilots: Networking Your Way to a Flying Job, Gregory N. Brown, Iowa State University Press, 2001

North American Space Directory 2005
www.spacebusiness.com
Expanded to include Canadian companies, the Directory is a reference for industry executives, business development and marketing managers, government officials, and technical and local libraries. This directory features more than 1,200 detailed profiles, each containing one or several paragraphs of information regarding an organization's capabilities, products, and services; business contacts within the organization; and Internet links to speed the gathering of additional information.

World Aviation Directory, *Aviation Week*, publisher, McGraw-Hill
www.aviationweek.com
Source of companies, people, products/services, and fleet information in the aviation/aerospace industry. WAD&AD is the daily business tool for more than 500,000 users worldwide. Lists 19,000 airlines, manufacturers, MRO stations, airports, military/government, distributors/suppliers; 6,000 product/service categories and 150,000 listings; 60,000 aviation/aerospace professionals; and more. Available in print and on CD-ROM.

Online
AV Jobs
www.avjobs.com
Pilots, mechanics, and engineers pay $19.95 for a basic membership. Recruiters can search for detailed pilot background data (types of planes flown, navigation dates). Site has chat rooms and salary data.

Aviation Job Search
www.aviationjobsearch.com
The site has about 4,000 jobs categorized as "in the air" or "on the ground." Many jobs are in Europe. Jobs range from check-in attendants and baggage handlers to flight crew and catering staff.

Nation Job
www.nationjob.com
Contains a comprehensive listing of various aviation jobs in the U.S. The list is searchable by region, salary range, education (from no degree to a postgraduate degree), and whether the job is temporary, full-time or part-time.

Space Business
www.spacebusiness.com
A central point for information on the space industry. Site has a range of products designed to meet the needs of business executives, government officials, and financiers. A bookstore features products such as business directories, technical books, market surveys, training videos and resources, and reference publications.

Space Careers
www.spacelinks.com
Includes links to hundreds of corporation career pages for the worldwide space industry. Civil agencies, satellite manufacturers, ground and launch systems, and more are listed.

Banking, Finance, Investing, Securities, Trading, Credit, and Other

New York Public Library: Science, Industry and Business Library (SIBL)
SIBL's website contains a selected list of Research Guides, each with an extensive catalog of directories, books, websites, and other information. The Guide for Financial Services can be found at: **www.nypl.org**. It contains a large list of reference books, links to annual and 10K reports, bond data, charting services, company financial data, depository receipts, industry data, insurance ratings, IPOs, and much more. The site lists directories and services, with website links. All links are live, except those marked "EIC," which are subscription services available only at SIBL. The entire list is too long to include here, but is an excellent source of information for those seeking jobs in all aspects of financial services. The library staff updates the site frequently. Key resources are included in this section.

Print

30 Days to Success in Real Estate: Fast Track Your Career in Real Estate, Rita D. Santamaria, South-Western Publishers, 2004
Offers financial worksheets and checklists that will get you thinking about your financial goals and networks and help you keep track of your progress on a daily basis. Learn when to send mailings to your clients, schedule and hold open houses, cold call, send notice of listing cards, organize home-inspection tours, and send cards for promotions, among other things. Learn what to say in your calls or correspondence to clients.

ABA Directories (American Banking Assoc.) www.aba.com, published by TFP, **www.tfp.com**

ABA Directory of Trust Banking, pub. June and July
Comprehensive single source of trust banking information. Summary of the contents and explanation of key terminology and financial data. Rankings of the top trust departments in the U.S., based on eight unique criteria. Detailed profiles of more than 3,000 head office and branch locations for trust businesses (banks plus other institutions).

ABA Financial Institutions Directory, pub. June and July
This print directory contains information on U.S.-based financial institutions and provides, in two volumes, all the information needed. Covers

every head office and branch of all banks and thrifts, plus credit unions with more than $25 million in assets in the U.S. Balance sheet data, including net income, leverage ratio, and risk-based capital ratio; names and functional titles of key officers, plus addresses and phone, fax, and routing numbers; alphabetical index with wire transfer address, listing bank's name, head office location, FEDWIRE number.

A.M. Best
www.ambest.com

Best's Key Rating Guide: Overview

Get basic profile information-including Best's Ratings and five years of key performance data-on property/casualty and life/health insurers in the U.S. and Canada. In print with a CD-ROM that can be used to search for and compare insurers, generate custom lists, and more. **Best's Key Rating Guide—Property/Casualty—United States & Canada** and **Best's Key Rating Guide—Life/Health—United States & Canada.**

Graham & Whiteside
www.gale.com
This part of Thomson Gale offers global company and professional information.

Major Financial Institutions of the World, 2003

This directory covers more than 9,000 leading financial institutions worldwide: banks, investment firms, and insurance and leasing companies. Company contact information is included, as well as names of senior management and board members, including more than 7,000 senior executives.

Major Financial Institutions of Europe, 2003

Covers European business and financial institutions, with data like that in the world version.

Leadership Directories
www.leadershipdirectories.com

Financial Yellow Book, semiannual

The nation's "leading directory" of U.S. financial institutions. Published semiannually, it is up-to-date on mergers, acquisitions, and personnel changes for the full range of financial firms. Lists names and titles of more than 30,000 executives, including more than 5,000 board members at more than 800 leading financial institutions and more than 2,800 subsidiaries; provides complete contact information, including address, phone and fax numbers, and E-mail addresses for executives and outside board members, plus administrative contacts in charge of benefits; corporate communications; corporate contributions; foundations; government affairs; information systems; libraries and information centers; meetings, events, and conferences; purchasing; real estate and facilities; recruitment; shareholder relations; and training and development. The Exchanges and Markets section lists leading exchanges and markets in the U.S., such as the New York Stock Exchange. Four indexes: industry, geographic, individual's name, and organization.

Moody's
www.moodys.com
Moody's Investors Service is a widely used source for credit ratings, research, and risk analysis. In addition to its core ratings business, Moody's publishes market-leading credit opinions, deal research, and commentary that reach more than 3,000 institutions and 22,000 subscribers around the globe. The company's ratings and analysis track more than $30 trillion of debt covering approximately 150,000 corporate, government, and structured finance securities; 75,000 public finance obligations; 10,000 corporate relationships; and 100 nations.

Moody's Bank and Finance Manual

Profiles institutions in the U.S. financial industry—banks, savings and loan associations, investment firms, insurance companies, real estate companies and investment trusts, and others. Includes history, contact information, names of officers and directors, and financials.

Nelson Information
www.nelsoninformation.com

Nelson's Directory of Investment Managers, 2003
This Directory is a resource for conducting competitive analysis, determining who should measure your benefit plan, and understanding how the investment-management industry works. Contact, performance, and decision-making information provide a window on the key players, how they do business, and their level of success. Plus, extensive indexes help find the firm or contact person.

Nelson's Directory of Investment Research, 2003
This book now includes information on more than 9,000 analysts who work at more than 700 firms and follows more than 14,000 public companies around the world, including 6,400 U.S.-traded companies and 7,000 non-U.S. companies. This directory covers institutional research firms, U.S. public companies, and international public companies. Plus, cross-referenced indexes help locate exactly the firm, person, service, or industry you're looking for.

Nelson's Directory of Pension Fund Consultants, 2003
Detailed information on pension consulting firms. Organized into five sections: Consultant Profiles—access comprehensive information on the firm's characteristics, including its manager evaluation criteria and requirements to be considered in a search; Geographical—locate firms by region; Services—identify firms offering the specific investment—consulting services of interest to you, Affiliation—a firm's primary affiliations helps determine if it specializes in an area of interest to you; Register of Professionals—access full contact and profile information for key personnel at each firm, including their educational background, past employment, and years of consulting experience.

Nelson's Directory of Institutional Real Estate, annual
Lists 300 real estate investment managers, 1,700 plan sponsor investors in real estate, 1,400 real estate service firms and consultants, 1,000 insurance companies with real estate investments, 2,000 corporations with active real estate operations, and 280 real estate investment trusts. Has three indexes.

Plunkett's Banking, Mortgages & Credit Industry Almanac (see earlier listing for **Plunkett's**)

Plunkett's Banking and Insurance Industry Summary Report (see earlier listing for **Plunkett's**)

Plunkett's Financial Services Industry Almanac (see earlier listing for **Plunkett's**)

Plunkett's Financial Services Industry Summary Report (see earlier listing for **Plunkett's**)

Pratt's Guide to Private Equity Sources, Stanley E. Pratt, Thomson Financial, 28th ed., 2003
Venture capitalists and entrepreneurs use Pratt's comprehensive, accurate profiles and editorial to help raise capital, find the right venture capital firm to do deals with, and keep current on the industry and the competition. More than 4,400 listings offer contact information, capital under management, recent investments, and more. Four indexes by company, personnel, investment stage, and industry preferences enable users to hone their search and target the ideal firm with a minimum of effort. A Web-based version is continually updated. In addition, users can create mailing lists and call sheets from the information provided via the Web version.

Standard & Poor's
www2.standardandpoors.com

Bond Guide
Data on more than 10,000 domestic and Canadian corporate, convertible, and foreign bonds.

Statistical analysis on about 400 convertible bonds and more than 600 of the most active foreign bonds. Corporate bond information includes S&P debt rating, fixed-charge coverage, capitalization, current assets, liabilities, and long-term debt. Each issue includes bond form and eligibility, coupon, interest and maturity dates, yields, amounts outstanding, and underwriter.

Corporation Records

Information on more than 12,000 publicly held U.S., Canadian, and international companies. Full income statements and balance sheets, corporate profiles, equity and fixed-income descriptions, recent news, shareholder reports, SEC reports, newspaper articles, press releases, officers and directors, subsidiaries, and divisions.

Thomson Gale
www.gale.com

Cases in Corporate Acquisitions, Buyouts, Mergers & Takeovers, Thomson Gale, 1999
Presents significant examples and analysis of mergers-and-acquisitions activity, covering both major successes and failures. Approximately 300 entries are arranged alphabetically by the name of the resulting company. The focus is on mergers-and-acquisitions activity where at least one participant is a U.S.-based corporation. Each 2,500-word entry contains three basic parts: brief background information summary of major players, and main essay.

Information, Finance and Services USA,
Thomson Gale, 2003, biennial
Reports, projections, historical data, leading companies, and national and state data from all information, finance, and service industries as defined by the SIC and NAICS classification systems.

Online

Bank Job Search
www.bankjobsearch.com
From the Bank Administration Institute, this site offers forums, information about events, online publications, and free job postings.

Bank Jobs
bankjobs.com
Keeps job hunters up-to-date on industry happenings while providing job services.

BANKERSAlmanac.com, Reed Business
www.bankersalmanac.com
Provides accurate, up-to-date, global banking details on leading financial institutions. This WebLink Directory has links to the websites of banks and other institutions across the world. Detailed information is available by subscription; however, users have free access to links for each bank's website. The Almanac includes a Guide to Suppliers that provides details of IT solutions to the banking sector.

eFinancialCareers
www.efinancialcareers.com
Specializes in securities, investment banking, and asset-management industries. Worldwide job opportunities, but primarily in the U.S. and Europe.

Financial Executive Institute
www.fei.org
For senior finance and accounting professionals. FEI has 15,000 members from about 8,000 companies.

Financial Job Network
www.fjn.com
For companies seeking global finance and accounting professionals. Clients are Fortune 1000 multinational and global executive-recruiting companies.

Financial Planning.com
www.financial-planning.com
Jobs, news, discussion boards, and other resources for the financial community. Much more than a job board.

Financial Times Career Point
www.ftcareerpoint.com
For recruiters who travel in international finance, this is a definite site to post job openings. Site has

news, views, and statistics, plus excellent career articles. Sails on the reputation of the *Financial Times*, which has distribution in cities around the world.

Jobs in the Money
www.jobsinthemoney.com
Designed for mid-level management professionals in finance, banking, accounting, insurance, and investments.

Biotechnology

Print

Biopharma, Biotechnology Information Institute
www.biopharma.com, 2004
The only reference book concerning biopharmaceutical products. Encyclopedic monographs concentrate on products' biotechnology and commercial aspects. Includes all biopharmaceuticals, plus has product and company web databases to locate monographs in the book.

Biotechnology from A to Z, William Bains, Oxford University Press, New York, 1993
www.oup.com
Explanation of 1,000 terms used in the biotechnology field for the nonspecialist.

Biotechnology Guide U.S.A.: Companies, Data, and Analysis, Mark D. Dibner, Institute for Biotechnology Information, Research Triangle Park, NC, 2000
Profiles of more than 1,300 companies involved in biotechnology and analysis of various aspects of the biotechnology industry, including funding, public firms, and resources in commercial biotechnology.

Glossary of Biotechnology Terms, 3rd ed., Kimball Nill, CRC Press, Boca Raton, FL, 2002
www.crcpress.com
Definitions and descriptions of key concepts, acronyms, processes, and materials related to the biotechnology industry for the nonspecialist.

Nature Biotechnology Directory, Nature Press, New York
guide.nature.com
Profiles of biotechnology companies, universities, and research organizations working in various application areas including pharmaceuticals, food, and agriculture.

North American Biotechnology Directory, Atlantic Communications, Houston, TX
www.oilonline.com
On CD-ROM. Directory information for academic and research institutions, companies, financial and legal services, facilities and contractors, suppliers and manufacturers, and government agencies and associations working in the biotechnology field across North America. More than 5,000 companies and 17,000 persons listed.

Plunkett's Biotech & Genetics Industry Almanac (see previous listing for **Plunkett's**)

Plunkett's Biotech Industry Summary (see previous listing for **Plunkett's**)

Online

4Biotech
4biotech.4anything.com
Focus on the business side of biotechnology. Includes links to biotechnology stock and industry information.

Agriculture Network Information Center
www.agnic.org
Guide to quality agricultural information on the Internet as selected by the National Agricultural Library, Land-Grant Universities, and other institutions.

Bio Exchange
www.bioexchange.com
Offers opportunities in molecular biology, biotechnology, and bioinformatics. Lists statistics regarding openings. Job seekers can review company profiles and maintain a list of all openings for which they have applied.

Bio Find
www.biofind.com

Billed as "a one-stop-shop for worldwide biotech industry information." Chat room and "Rumor Mill" are for building community. Site specializes in diagnostics, pharmaceutical, medical devices, and biotech. Jobs listed by category.

Biolink Direct
www.biolinkdirect.com

Database of links to most biotech/pharmaceutical company websites in Europe, U.S., and the rest of the world, grouped by geographical region or name.

BiotechFind
www.biotechfind.com

Searchable directory of international links covering the fields of biotechnology and biofinances.

Bio Space
www.biospace.com

Career center listing links to jobs by company, with hundreds listed in alphabetical order. Also runs career fairs across the U.S.

Bio View
www.bioview.com (Monster)

Openings by job function, including contract work. Covers industry layoffs and conferences and has company profiles.

Nature Biotechnology Directory Website
guide.nature.com

This site is produced in association with Nature Publishing Group, publishers of *Nature Biotechnology Directory*, *The Biotechnology Guide USA*, and *Nature Biotechnology*. This global resource lists more than 8,000 fully searchable organizations. Each entry provides details about an organization, including full name, location, and phone number. Extended entries providing more details about the organization are available for a fee.

U.S. Department of State
usinfo.state.gov/topical/global/biotech

Focuses on the international aspects of biotechnology issues. Links to many international and industry association sites.

U.S. Food and Drug Administration
www.cfsan.fda.gov/~lrd/biotechm.html#reg

FDA announcements, regulations, and recommendations regarding biotechnology.

Vault.com
www.vault.com

Source for information on health/biotech/pharmaceutical.

Wet Feet
www.wetfeet.com

Downloadable guide on biotech and pharmaceuticals.

Business

Print

Great Jobs for Business Majors, Stephen E. Lambert, VGM Career Books, 2003
E-book.

Online

Careers in Business
www.careers-in-business.com

Career opportunities in many areas of business.

MIT Sloan School on Management: Career Center
mitsloan.mit.edu

Links to business home pages and other search resources.

Reeve Associates
www.reevejobs.com

Reeve & Associates is an executive search firm specializing in marketing research disciplines. It conducts searches in all major industries including advertising, automotive, consumer package goods, computer hardware and software, entertainment, financial services, high-tech, health care, internet, gas and oil, pharmaceutical, publishing, and telecommunications.

WSJ.com (Career Journal)
www.careerjournal.com
CareerJournal.com is from *The Wall Street Journal*. It is the premier career site for executives, managers, and professionals.

College/Liberal Arts/Recent Graduates
Print

America's Top Jobs for College Graduates: Detailed Information on 127 Jobs for Those with Four-Year and Higher Degrees, Michael Farr, 5th ed., JIST Works, Indianapolis, IN, 2002
This newest edition has thorough, up-to-date descriptions for 127 major jobs most often held by college graduates. Plus, there are articles on labor-market trends and a section with results-oriented career planning and job-search advice—even some résumé examples for top jobs held by college graduates. Includes The Quick Job Search, a 32-page job section with job-search advice and résumés for some top jobs that don't require a four-year degree.

Broadcast Journalism Internship Directory, The Leadership Institute
Contains information on internships from stations and networks around the country. Visit their website at: www.lead-inst.org or call: (800) 827-LEAD. This directory contains information on how to get an internship, hints to help you succeed, and tips on what to do once you land your internship. Internships are listed under three categories: Prestigious Internships, Hands-On Internships, and Distinguishing Internships.

The College Majors Handbook with Real Career Paths and Payoffs, Neeta P. Fogg, et al., JIST Works, 2004
www.jist.com
Lists job descriptions and reviews career trends relating to 60 college majors. Subtitled, "The Actual Jobs, Earnings, and Trends for Graduates of 60 College Majors."

Current Jobs for Graduates: The National Employment Bulletin for the Liberal Arts Profession
www.graduatejobs.com
Published monthly, these eight newsletters list national jobs appropriate for liberal arts, as well as other, grads:

1. *Jobs for Liberal Arts Graduates*—anthropology, archaeology, classics, college admissions/residence hall, English/writing/literature, government, history, legislative affairs, museum studies, humanities, philosophy, political science, and public administration.
2. *Jobs in Writing, Editing & Communications*—advertising, broadcasting, business communications, editing, journalism, mass communications, public relations, radio/TV/movie production, speechwriting, scriptwriting, technical writing, and telecommuting.
3. *Jobs in Management & Business*—accounting, administration (all fields), advertising, consulting, economics, development, finance/banking, insurance, government, international business marketing, nonprofit management, public interest/policy, public relations, and sales management.
4. *Jobs in Education*—admissions, financial aid, residence life, teaching in private schools, community colleges, four-year colleges; education-related positions in overseas schools; experiential/outdoor schools and language schools.
5. *Jobs International*—American studies, bilingual/bicultural education, classics, diplomacy, English, foreign area studies, foreign languages/literature (all areas), international business, international relations, and translation/interpretation.
6. *Jobs in Art*—applied art, art administration, art education, art history, commercial art, design, graphic art, illustration, printmaking, sculpting and studio art, (positions appropriate for technical, arts, and two-year

college graduates, as well as four-year college graduates).

7. *Jobs in Performing Arts*—arts administration, cinema & film, dance, music, music
education, radio & television, sacred music,
speech & dramatic arts, teaching, theater
arts, and voice, (positions appropriate for
technical, arts, and two-year college graduates, as well as four-year college graduates).

8. *Liberal Arts Career News*—this newsletter
keeps you up-to-date on the latest trends
and information concerning early-career
jobs in the liberal arts disciplines. Each
newsletter also includes reviews of websites
of special interest to liberal arts grads.

Occupational Outlook Handbook
www.bls.gov/oco/home.htm
Provides detailed descriptions for more than 250
career fields, including salary information,
required training, projected growth, and related
professional associations. The *Handbook* is a
nationally recognized source of career information designed to provide valuable assistance to
individuals making decisions about their future
work lives. Revised every two years, the *Handbook*
describes what workers do on the job, working
conditions, the training and education needed,
earnings, and expected job prospects in a wide
range of occupations.

Online

College Grad Job Hunter
www.collegegrad.com
A site for the first-time job hunter and college
graduates. The College Grad Job Hunter takes
you through the steps to successful employment,
from preparation to salary negotiation.

Monster.com's Campus
campus.monster.com
This site is for students and alumni looking for
full- and part-time positions, internships, and on-
campus employment.

Communications Equipment and Services, Including Telecommunications
(See also Information Technology/High Tech)

Print

2003 International Satellite Directory, Satnews Publishers
www.satnews.com
Said to be the most complete reference source
available in the world on communications satellites. Updated annually in two volumes with 16
separate chapters and more than 25,000 entries,
this 1,400-plus-page reference source is for all
satellite professionals. Comes with a CD-ROM
containing more than 850 EIRP, G/T, and SFD
maps in full color.

Plunkett's Telecommunications Industry Almanac (see previous listing for **Plunkett's**)

Plunkett's Telecommunications Summary Report (see previous listing for **Plunkett's**)

Online

Datasheet Locator
www.datasheetlocator.com
A free electronic engineering tool to locate product data sheets from hundreds of electronic component manufacturers worldwide.

MotionNET.com Engineering Directory
www.motionnet.com
Technical web portal designed by experienced
electronic and mechanical design engineers. An
online categorized database for the electronic and
mechanical engineering community. Lists company category (distributor, manufacturer, etc.),
plus contact information, including phone and fax
numbers and E-mail addresses.

Telecom Source Book
www.advanstar.com/marketingservices/
telecomsource
Contains the leading telecom suppliers, including
equipment manufacturers, distributors, and suppliers, and includes contacts at regional Bell hold-

ing companies and Bell operating companies, interconnect organizations, foreign phone companies, long-distance carriers, cellular operators and cellular radio suppliers, and telecommunications associations, regulatory agencies, schools, and colleges.

TelecomCareers
www.telecomcareers.net
Specializing in communications/telecom, this site has links to telecom-related associations. Jobs can be searched by industry, location, or keywords. Includes a telecom directory for those not familiar with industry terminology.

Telecoms.com
www.telecoms.com
Telecoms.com is said to be the definitive source of high-quality information on the mobile telecoms markets and a technology directory of mobile industry research, data sheets, reports, and more. Includes forecasts and tracking data, expert analysis, and comments on international wireless markets all across the globe. Covering the whole cellular market value chain and explaining technologies from 3G rollouts to VoIP (Voice over IP), push to talk (PTT) to mobile content applications, industry experts are the analysts behind the ARC Group, Baskerville, Chorleywood, and EMC.

Construction and Building

Print

The Construction Employer Directory,
Building Industry Exchange
www.building.org
The Building Industry Exchange is said to be the leading online directory for indexing U.S. construction employers. The business directory includes more than 30,000 employer profiles that link to corporate websites and current construction jobs. As a members-only directory, all profiles are monitored and prescreened manually by staff editors for relevance and publishing accuracy. The BIE also has other online directories: *Construction Employer Directory, Architecture Employer Directory,*

Building Products Employer Directory, Real Estate Employer Directory, Engineering Employer Directory, and Related Professions Employer Directory.

National Trade and Professional Associations of the United States 2005, Columbia Books
www.columbiabooks.com
Detailed contact and background information on more than 7,500 trade associations, professional societies, technical organizations, and labor unions in the U.S. All of the listings are updated every year and NTPA remains the definitive, one-volume resource for anyone interested in communicating with, networking within, or carrying out research on associations and the thousands of businesses and industries they represent.

Plunkett's Real Estate & Construction Industry Almanac (see previous listing for Plunkett's)

Plunkett's Real Estate & Construction Summary Report (see previous listing for Plunkett's)

Professional and Trade Associations

Listed below is a selection of associations, including their websites and major publications, where appropriate. This list is taken from the Science, Industry, and Business Library's website (www.nypl.org) "Building and Construction."

American Association of Heating, Refrigerating and Air-Conditioning Engineers (ASHRAE)
www.ashrae.org

American Concrete Institute
www.aci-int.org
Publishes: *Concrete International* (monthly)

American Institute of Architects
www.aia.org

Associated General Contractors of America
www.agc.org
Publishes: *Constructor* (monthly)

Construction Specifications Institute
www.csinet.org
Publishes: *Encyclopedia of Associations and Information Sources for Architects, Designers, and Engineers*

National Association of Home Builders
www.nahb.com
Publishes: *Builder* (monthly)

Online

B4UBUILD.COM
www.b4ubuild.com
Resources for residential construction. Check out the "Building Process" link; includes an organizational directory.

CMD First Source
www.firstsourceexchange.com
Commercial building product information.

Construction Gigs
www.constructiongigs.com
For job seekers in all trades and professions in construction. Recruiters can post links for free. A simple site with great value.

Construction Jobs
www.constructionjobs.com
The job board also participates in trade shows and some job-distribution services. Has alliances with six construction industry associations. Site is easily searchable for job hunters.

Construction WebLinks
www.constructionweblinks.com
Extensive directory of construction-related websites, with annotations, hosted by a law firm. See, for example, link for "New Projects," which includes New York City–specific sites.

Contractor Resource Center
www.contractors.com
This site includes news, information, lists of suppliers, and more.

Engineering News Record
enr.construction.com
News, company rankings for contractors and design firms, directory listings, and materials information.

McGraw-Hill Construction—construction.com
construction.com
From McGraw-Hill's publications, *Engineering News Record, Architectural Record, Design-Build,* and *Dodge.* News, projects, products, and industry-related information. See also links for the *Engineering News Record* and other resources. Free and fee-based information available.

Sweets
sweets.construction.com
Lists 61,300 building products. Find local reps. Sweets Communities are included: Architects, Engineers & Contractors (AEC)—commercial, residential, and facilities building products; Facilities—facilities building products; Residential—residential building products; Canadian—building products distributed in Canada; plus more.

Sweet's Directory Search
sweets.construction.com
Lists 10,700 manufacturers, with 61,300 products.

Ultimate Civil Engineering Directory
www.tenlinks.com
A portal of selected civil engineering Web links chosen by professionals in the field.

Consulting

Print

Consultants & Consulting Organizations Directory, Thomson Gale
www.gale.com, annual
More than 25,000 firms and individuals are arranged in subject sections under 14 general fields of consulting activity ranging from agriculture to marketing. More than 400 specialties are represented, including finance, computers, fund-

raising, and others. Each entry furnishes street addresses or P.O. boxes for headquarters and branches; phone, fax, and toll-free numbers; E-mail addresses and websites; notation of service to international clients; mergers and former names; and more.

Consultants Directory, Dun & Bradstreet
www.dbn.com
Details on more than 30,000 consulting firms representing many areas of specialization. Listings are alphabetical and cross-referenced geographically and by consulting activity. Each listing contains: the D&B D-U-N-S Number, HQ address, phone, year of founding or changed ownership, major business services and consulting areas, recent sales volume, total number of accounts, number of employees, primary customers, geographic territory served, names/titles of principals, other locations with D-U-N-S Numbers. When available: state of incorporation, indication of public ownership, and indication of public family membership.

Plunkett's Consulting Industry Almanac (see previous listing for Plunkett's)

Plunkett's Consulting Industry Summary Report (see previous listing for Plunkett's)

Online

Jobs in the Money
www.jobsinthemoney.com

Pro Savvy
www.prosavvy.com
Has a database of more than 20,000 consultants and matches them with clients. Finance, accounting, and banking consulting and full-time jobs.

Top Consultant
www.top-consultant.com
Domestic and global consulting opportunities. News, free newsletter, and free Top-Consultant Guide to Consulting Firms offers insights into how to differentiate between firms; unique survey data from actual consultants highlighting criteria by which you should assess consulting opportu-

nities; and listings of smaller consulting firms that may be actively recruiting but are not necessarily being targeted by candidates.

Vault.com's Guide to Management Consulting
www.vault.com
This site has a job board for consultants categorized by: management & strategy, tech, operations, human resources, change management, financial, health care, marketing, and other. Offers insider information—what it's like working in the industry, who the players are, and how to get ahead. Reviews top employers in consulting.

Wet Feet
www.wetfeet.com
Downloadable guide on consulting with information on companies, careers, and industries.

Disabled

Print

Job-Hunting for the So-Called Handicapped or People Who Have Disabilities, Richard Nelson Bolles and Dale S. Brown, Ten Speed Press, 2001
Bolles and Brown guide readers through the often frustrating but ultimately rewarding process of securing independence in their lives and personal satisfaction in their careers. The authors begin by demystifying the intricacies of the Americans with Disabilities Act (ADA), describing in clear terms what the Act does and does not guarantee job hunters who have disabilities, and then move on to job-hunting strategies tailored specifically to people with disabilities.

Job Search Handbook for People with Disabilities, Daniel J. Ryan, Jist Pub., Indianapolis, IN, 2000
www.jist.com
Includes preparing for your job search; assessing your skills, abilities, and goals; marketing yourself to potential employers; creating your résumé; writing a great cover letter; applying and interviewing for jobs; and succeeding at work. This

book goes beyond the interview to include negotiating salary and asking for special accommoda-
tions in the work environment.

Job Strategies for People with Disabilities: Enable Yourself for Today's Job Market,
Melanie Astaire Witt, Peterson's Guides.
Princeton, NJ
This guide offers practical, realistic, and sage
advice for the 43 million Americans with disabilities who face the open job market. Witt, a careers
journalist, discusses job-search strategies and the
self-assessment of realistic career and job skills
that can enable and encourage job seekers who
have disabilities to put forth their best selves
without discrimination. In 13 chapters, she also
covers the legal implications of the ADA and
includes occupational surveys, interest surveys,
job-requirement competencies, a job-accommo-
dations study, and adaptive solutions. Three
appendixes list organizations, associations, agencies, and adaptive assistance.

Online

American Foundation for the Blind
www.afb.org
An interactive website for people with visual
impairments to learn about a wide range of
careers with the help of more than 1,500 mentors.

Careers and the Disabled
www.eop.com
Career guidance and recruitment magazines published by Equal Opportunity Publications. Read
articles, peruse help-wanted ads, and post a
résumé.

Disabled Person
www.disabledperson.com
This site includes a résumé database, featured
articles, issues and opinions, disability resources,
and community events.

Job Access
www.jobaccess.org
A combined effort from *Ability* magazine and

Headhunter.net. Job seekers may post résumés
and search the jobs database.

National Business and Disability Council
www.business-disability.com
A corporate resource related to the employment
of people with disabilities. Users may post or
revise their résumés or search for employment.

New York State Education Department; Vocational and Educational Services for Individuals with Disabilities (VESID)
www.vesid.nysed.gov
VESID, an office of the New York State Education
Department, each year offers thousands of New
Yorkers who have disabilities opportunities to
become independent through education, training,
and employment.

U.S. Department of Labor, Office of Disability Policy
www.dol.gov/odep/pubs/ek99/resources.htm
Information and links for those with disabilities.

Diversity and Minorities (Except Gay and Lesbian)

Print

Career Guide and Directory for Immigrant Professionals, 2003, Lesley Kamenshine,
Rowman & Littlefield Publishers, Inc.
www.rowmanlittlefield.com

Finding Diversity: A Directory of Recruiting Resources, 2002, Luby Ismail and Alex
Kronemer, Society for Human Resource
Management
Detailing nearly 300 electronic, print, and on-site
places to recruit diversity candidates with a wide
range of backgrounds, skills, specialties, and abilities, this directory provides a wealth of information on where to advertise positions ranging
from CEO to computer engineer to construction
worker to nurse. Recruiting tools discussed
include **Asiancareers.com**, the Association of
American Indian Physicians website, and
business-disability.com.

Hispanic Network Magazine, Olive Tree Publishing, Yorba Linda, CA, quarterly
www.hnmagazine.com
"Let your skills speak for themselves. Maybe you're fresh out of college and ready to find that perfect career; or you're an experienced professional ready to take the next big step; or maybe it's just time to find that next professional challenge. Whatever the case, our magazine is the place to get where you're going."

Job Choices: Diversity Edition, National Association of Colleges and Employers, Bethlehem, PA
This periodical focuses on job-search and employment issues for minority students. Readers include INROADS interns and students from historically black colleges and universities, Hispanic-serving institutions, and tribal schools. This edition is an ideal way for your organization to demonstrate its objectives for a diverse work force.

The Minority Franchise Guide 2004, Robert Bond and Stephanie Woo, eds., Source Book Publications
Detailed profiles of some 500 North American franchisers that actively solicit minority participation. Listed are companies with recruiting and training programs and financial assistance. Franchises are divided into 45 categories for easy comparison.

National Directory of Minority Owned Business Firms, Thomas D. Johnson, ed., Business Research Services, 2002
The new eighth edition has access to more than 47,000 minority business enterprises. Adding fax numbers and previous government contracting experience, detailed entries furnish up to 17 points of data about each firm, including complete address, contact name, minority type, date founded, certification status, trading area, business description, number of employees, and sales volume. The new edition also has ZIP+4 postal codes. SIC and geographic indexes are included.

2005 National Minority and Women-Owned Business Directory, Diversity Information Resources
www.diversityinforesources.com
Lists more than 9,000 certified minority- and women-owned businesses. Includes company name/contact name & title, address/phone/fax/E-mail/website, products/services, year established, minority type, no. of employees, annual sales, certification(s). Alphabetical, commodity, and keyword indexes facilitate quick searches; extensive keyword index; 84 product/service categories; and NAICS codes.

Pathways to Career Success for Minorities, Ferguson Staff, Facts on File, 2000
Lists hundreds of organizations devoted to the educational and career advancement of minorities. It serves as a directory to help find the tools for starting a business, obtaining a grant, investigating colleges, and tapping into professional networks. In addition to information on scholarships, professional organizations, publications, and websites, the book includes essays on legal rights, affirmative action, and mentoring.

Online

Asia-Net
www.asia-net.com
This site is a clearinghouse for jobs that require bilingual fluency in English and Asian languages, specifically Japanese, Korean, and Chinese.

Black Career Zone
www.blackcareerzone.com
This site introduces the fastest-growing occupations and has links to more than 60 sites for job-search and career planning.

The Black Collegian
www.black-collegian.com
This is the online site of the magazine, which is dedicated to college students and professionals of color. This site includes job-search and employer profiles.

Diversity Employment
www.diversityemployment.com
This site is a multicultural employment resource offering a job and résumé database. Has resources and a list of companies that are diversity leaders.

DiversityLink.com
www.diversitylink.com
View job postings by category or search for specific opportunities. Choose an employer and view its corporate profile and career opportunities. Choose a college/university and view its profile and career opportunities.

Hire Diversity.com
www.hirediversity.com
This site offers channels for African Americans, Asian Americans, people with disabilities, gays and lesbians, Hispanics, mature workers, Native Americans, veterans, and women.

Imdiversity.com
www.IMdiversity.com
IMdiversity.com provides minority professionals with comprehensive job-seeking and career-management tools.

The Online Women's Business Center
www.onlinewbc.gov
OWBO promotes the growth of women-owned business through programs that address business training and technical assistance, federal contracts, and international trade opportunities.

Electronics

(See also Information High Tech Technology, and Communications Equipment and Services, Including Telecommunications)

Online

Electronics Directory
www.sketchpad.net
Directory of electronics, construction, medical, engineering, and other specialist industries. Contact details for suppliers, parts, manufacturers, instruments, and equipment.

Google—Electronics and Electrical
directory.google.com
The Electronics and Electrical section of Google's business directory has about 35 categories, including associations, components, directories, employment, and much more.

Hoover's
www.hoovers.com
Under "Browse Industries," click on "Electronics." This opens up a page with links to the various sectors of this industry. For each sector, individual companies have links.

www.business.com
Under "Browse Our Industries," this site provides links for electrical components, LCDs, and microelectronics. Each category has various subcategories for types of equipment, B2B markets, associations, distributors, and much more.

Energy, Alternative Energy and Utilities
Print

21st Century Complete Guide to Biofuels and Bioenergy: Department of Energy Alternative Fuel Research, Agriculture Department Biofuel Research, Biomass, Biopower, Biodiesel, Ethanol, Methanol, Plant Material Products, Landfill Methane, Crop Residues, U.S. Government (CD-ROM-September 28, 2003)
This CD-ROM provides a thorough guide to information about biofuels and bioenergy. Key topics include biofuels; biomass research and development initiatives; bioenergy; biopower; alternative fuels; United States Department of Energy Alternative Fuels Data Center (AFDC); Biodiesel; Ethanol; Methanol; Biofuels News 1993 through 2002; Alternative Fuel News 1997 through 2003; Alternative Fuel Price Report 2000

through 2002; DOE Pulse Newsletter 1998 through 2003; EPA Landfill Methane Outreach Program (LMOP); USDA Biobased Products and Bioenergy Coordination Council; USDA Agricultural Research Service Bioenergy & Energy Alternatives. In all, this CD-ROM has more than 19,000 PDF pages.

Financial Times Business Global Oil and Gas Directory 2002 (Financial Times Business Global Oil & Gas Directory), Prentice Hall, 102nd edition

Global Mining, Oil and Gas Industry Directory, published by International Business Publications, 2005

International Petroleum Encyclopedia 2004, Rebecca L. Busby, ed., Pennwell Books; Houston, TX
The Encyclopedia contains maps, statistics, and survey charts, country reports, and more by a hand-selected team of industry veterans. Year after year, *IPE* remains the research tool of choice for industry leaders. Available in print and on Windows or Mac format CD-ROM, which contains all the information from the print version in a searchable format.

Major Energy Companies of the World, 8th ed., 2005, Graham & Whiteside
www.gale.com
Covers more than 4,000 companies involved in coal mining and coal products; electricity supply; fuel distribution; natural gas supply; nuclear engineering; oil and gas exploration and production; oil and gas services and equipment; and oil refining worldwide. Entries typically provide company name; address; phone, telex, and fax numbers; E-mail and Web addresses; names of senior management and board members, including more than 20,000 senior executives; description of business activities; brand names and trademarks; financial information for the previous two years; and more.

Plunkett's Energy Industry Almanac (see previous listing for **Plunkett's**)

Plunkett's Energy Industry Summary Report (see previous listing for **Plunkett's**)

Plunkett's Renewable, Alternative & Hydrogen Energy Industry Almanac (see previous listing for **Plunkett's**)

Plunkett's Renewable, Alternative & Hydrogen Energy Summary Report (see previous listing for **Plunkett's**)

Renewable Energy 2005, David Flin, ed., James & James, London, 2005
This publication is sent on a controlled-circulation basis free of charge to senior executives and engineers in major international organizations involved in the renewable energy industry, as well as to relevant senior personnel in government agencies, international trade associations, research establishments, and regulatory bodies. To receive a free copy, log on to the following site and complete the order form: **www.sovereign-publications.com**.

2004 World Directory of Nuclear Utility Management, American Nuclear Society
www.ans.org
Lists personnel at nuclear utility headquarters and nuclear plant sites, including plant managers, maintenance superintendents, radwaste managers, contacts for purchasing and public relations, and more. Worldwide plant listings are arranged alphabetically by country and utility and include operating plants, those under construction, and those being decommissioned. Also included is a listing of international nuclear-related organizations with contact information. Available with or without a CD-ROM that contains all of the names, titles, and addresses of the utility and plant individuals listed in the directory.

Online

Energy Jobs Network
www.energyjobsnetwork.com
This is the job board for 18 different energy associations and media companies. Site includes Canada and Europe.

243

Google—Energy and Environment
directory.google.com
Links to numerous sites that list jobs in the energy, environmental, and gas and oil fields.

Green Energy Jobs
www.greenenergyjobs.com
For professionals in renewable energy. International site has a button that allows searching for positions by country. Site is a gateway to a network of renewable energy jobs, for example, **www.solarpowerjobs.com, www.windpowerjobs.com**, and **www.hydropowerjobs.com**, among others.

Engineering

Print

Peterson's Job Opportunities for Engineering and Computer Science Majors, Peterson's, Princeton, NJ, 1999
This is a good source for engineering company overviews. It lists opportunities in architecture, biotechnology, computer programming, mechanical engineering, civil engineering, electrical engineering, and technology. Listings include a fairly detailed company description, website, human resources manager, phone and fax number, size, location, type, top competitors, and more.

Plunkett's Engineering & Research Industry Almanac (see previous listing for **Plunkett's**)

Plunkett's Nanotechnology & MEMS* Industry Almanac (see previous listing for **Plunkett's**)
* Micro-electro-mechanical systems

Who's Who in Science and Engineering, 8th ed., 2005–2006, Kristin A. Eckes, Marquis Who's Who
www.marquiswhoswho.com
This edition provides key biographical facts on the more than 24,000 men and women leading today's scientific and technological revolution.

Online

EngNet
www.engnetglobal.com
This online directory/search engine/buyers guide service is aimed specifically at the engineering industry to enable engineers, technicians, tradesmen, etc. to find information and communicate effectively with suppliers in the engineering industry. All types of engineering professions are covered.

Tiny Jobs
www.tinytechjobs.com
This is a career website devoted to jobs at the convergence of nanotechnology, biotechnology, and information technology. Both academic and industrial positions in such disciplines as chemistry; physics; materials science; biology; biochemistry; molecular biology; micro- and nano-electromechanical engineering; biomedical engineering and devices; microfluidics; microarrays; information technology; optics; mechanical, electrical, and chemical engineering; and other relevant fields.

NanoGuys
www.nanoguys.com
Nanotechnology jobs, career information, and news.

Vocational Information Center
www.khake.com
This site is a gold mine of links to just about everything in all fields of engineering—engineering basics, national labs, engineering directories, history of science and technology, and dozens of links for civil and structural, electrical and electronic, industrial, materials, mechanical engineers, and job boards. Here are some of the links from this site (*the following sites were compiled by the New York Public Library for all types of engineering jobs*):

ChemIndustry.com
www.neis.com
Lists jobs for chemists, biochemists, pharmaceutical scientists, and chemical engineers worldwide.

Contains a website directory organized by subject—chemical suppliers, services, resources, industrial equipment, industrial equipment, lab and scientific equipment, software, services, and resources (including other job banks).

Engineer Employment
www.engineeremployment.com
List jobs including civil, structural, electrical, chemical, design, and network engineer. Also includes sections on résumés, recruiters, employer profiles, job-search agent, advertising agencies, and salary information.

Engineering Job Source
www.engineerjobs.com
Lists jobs for engineers and technical professionals. You can browse the listings by state or search by keyword.

EngineeringJobs.com
www.engineeringjobs.com
Features links to company employment pages, recruiters, engineering societies and organizations, and résumés of engineers seeking employment.

National Society of Professional Engineers (NSPE)
www.nspe.org
Provides career information on any engineering specialty. Employment section features engineering salary information, career tips, guidelines to professional employment for engineers and scientists, mentoring programs, and other employment links.

Society of Women Engineers
www.swe.org
This site provides tremendous information and career/employment resources for women interested in or currently pursuing engineering careers.

Entertainment, Including Media (Broadcasting and Publishing)
Print

Broadcasting & Cable Yearbook, annual, DecisionMaker Media Management (DM2), Oak Brook, IL
www.dm2lists.com
Offers access to general managers, programming directors, vice presidents, promotion managers, music directors, and others at 14,000 facilities.

Gale Directory of Publications & Broadcast Media, Thomson Gale
www.gale.com, annual
Contains thousands of listings for radio and television stations and cable companies. Print media entries provide address, phone, fax numbers, and E-mail addresses; key personnel, including feature editors; and much more. Broadcast media entries provide address, phone, fax, and E-mail addresses; key personnel; owner information; hours of operation; networks carried; and more.

Bacon's
www.bacons.com
Bacon's has online services, plus annual print versions of the following directories: Newspaper/Magazine Directory, Radio/TV/Cable Directory, Media Calendar Directory, Internet Media Directory, New York Publicity Outlets Directory, Metro California Media Directory. These contain listings that have editors, producers, and journalists, with their specialties; contact information; how they like to be contacted (phone, E-mail, etc.); plus detailed information on each publication or broadcast medium.

Industry Yellow Pages
www.theindustryyellowpages.com

AV Market Place 2004: The Complete Business Directory of Audio, Audio Visual, Computer Systems, Film, Video, and Programming with Industry Yellow Pages. Industry Yellow Pages: The Official Radio, Retail and Distribution Music Directory Listing, 2004

Has more than 2,000 radio stations, 660+ record stores, and 360+ music distributors.

Leadership Directories
www.leadershipdirectories.com
News Media Yellow Book is the "nation's leading personnel directory of national news media organizations." Fully updated quarterly editions give complete contact information for journalists, including assignments, direct phone numbers, and E-mail addresses. More than 33,000 journalists at more than 2,200 leading national news media organizations. Also contains contacts for administrative services, such as circulation, information systems, libraries and information centers, public relations, and recruitment. With a biographical appendix with photographs and contact and career information for leading journalists.

Plunkett's Entertainment & Media Industry Almanac (see previous listing for **Plunkett's**)

Plunkett's Entertainment & Media Industry Summary Report (see previous listing for **Plunkett's**)

Television & Cable Factbook, Warren Communications News
www.warren-news.com
More than 740,000 detailed records in four sections. Covers cable systems, television stations, media ownership, and media services, with data on companies and individuals.
Sources for more specific entertainment directories and books are listed under **www.nypl.org**.

Online

EntertainmentCareers.Net
www.entertainmentcareers.net
This site lists jobs and internships in the entrainment industry.

Film Staff
www.filmstaff.com
Film and television production listings are updated daily, as well as jobs for commercials, music videos, theater, and interactive projects.

MediaRecruiter
www.mediarecruiter.com
Internet's largest listing of media positions nationwide, serving the advertising and communications industries. MediaRecruiter specializes in the following employment areas associated with media: management, marketing, research, promotion, co-op, traffic, engineering, production, technical, and sales support.

Playbill
www.playbill.com
This site provides listings of acting and theatrical support positions on and off Broadway and throughout the U.S., London, Canada, and Brazil.

ShowBizjobs.com
www.showbizjobs.com
This site provides job information on the film, television, recording, and attractions industry job markets.

Vault
www.vault.com
Entertainment jobs are searchable by function, keyword, state (or non-U.S.); plus industry information.

Variety
www.variety.com
Almost 4,000 media and publishing jobs are listed.

Wet Feet
www.wetfeet.com
Information on entertainment companies, careers, and industries.

Environmental

Print

The Environment Encyclopedia and Directory
2004, Europa Publications (UK); 4th ed., 2005
www.europapublications.co.uk
Examines environmental issues throughout the world, with thorough definitions and explanations of terms related to the environment. The

volume includes detailed maps, an extensive bibliography, and a Who's Who section (leading personalities actively involved with environmental affairs), making this a one-stop reference for anyone interested in environmental issues. A comprehensive directory section is organized alphabetically by country, listing main governmental and nongovernmental organizations, both national and international. Contains an extensive bibliography of relevant periodicals.

Environmental Guide to the Internet, 4th ed., Toni Murphy and Carol Briggs-Erickson, Government Institutes
govinst.scarecrowpress.com
Contains the top 1,200 environmental Internet resources, including environmental discussion groups and mailing lists, newsgroups, newsletters and journals, and websites. New features include 45 new newsgroups, including 30 from the newly created government hierarchy; 75 new electronic journals and newsletters; 200 new websites, and other resources.

U. S. Environmental Directories
www.geocities.com
Provides a sample of the more than 2,000 websites listed in its parent publication, **The Directory of Environmental Web Sites**. In print and on CD-ROM.

Who's Who in Environmental Engineering, 2004, American Academy of Environmental Engineering
www.aaee.net
Lists all of the board-certified diplomates of environmental engineering. Cross-referenced geographically and by specialty.

Who's Who in Science and Engineering, 8th ed., 2005–2006, Kristin A. Eckes, Marquis Who's Who
www.marquiswhoswho.com
This edition provides key biographical facts on the more than 24,000 men and women leading today's scientific and technological revolution.

Indexes

Environmental Policy Index (EBSCO)
Abstract & index. Contains nearly 750,000 indexed citations of articles from scientific, technical, and popular journals spanning the whole range of environmental topics from 1973 to the present. Updated monthly.

General Science Abstracts
Articles. Abstract and index database. Locate articles in periodicals covering astronomy, biology, the environment, conservation, health, microbiology, oceanography, and other subjects from 1984 to the present. Updated monthly.

Online

Environmental Career
www.environmentalcareer.com
The website for the Environmental Career Center in Hampton, VA. Users may search for jobs in a variety of fields, including biology, forestry, environmental science, and environmental engineering. The site also includes a calendar and training links.

Environmental Opportunities
www.enviropps.com
Environmental Opportunities, Inc. is a strategic environmental management and project services firm dedicated to helping industrial and commercial clients achieve their business and financial objectives through advanced environmental policies, programs, and practices.

Green Dream Jobs
www.sustainablebusiness.com
Employment listings for the environmentally conscious job seeker. Links to more websites about environmental careers.

Ex-Inmates

Online

Binding Together, Inc.
www.bindingtogether.org
Binding Together provides job training and placement, financial incentives, and counseling to people recovering from substance abuse with multiple barriers to employment.

The Fortune Society
www.fortunesociety.org
The Society offers counseling, referrals to vocational training, job placement, tutoring in preparation for the GED, Basic Adult Literacy and English as a Second Language classes, and substance abuse treatment.

The Osborne Association
www.osborneny.org
The Osborne Association assists defendants, former offenders, people on probation and parole, and prisoners and their families. It offers a wide range of educational, vocational, support, and health services.

Film, Video, and Photography

(See also Entertainment, Including Media)

Print

VNU Business Media
www.hcdonline.com
This company provides directories and books for the entertainment industry.

The Hollywood Creative Directory, 52nd ed.
Lists up-to-date information on production companies, television shows, and studio and network executives.

Hollywood Music Industry Directory, Premier Edition
Complete contact information, including company name, job title, address, phone, fax, E-mail, assistants' names, and website URL. Sections cross-referenced by person.

2004 Blu-Book Production Directory, Staff of **The Hollywood Creative Directory, eds.**
The Hollywood Creative Directory has joined forces with **The Hollywood Reporter** to make the *Blu-Book* even better. For professionals and new filmmakers alike, the 2004 edition has comprehensive contact information on everything you need to produce a film, TV show, commercial, or music video. More than 250 product and service categories and more than 6,000 listings.

Online

Film Land
www.filmland.com
Links for industry news, crew calls, and services, and a bulletin board.

Mandy's Film and TV Production Directory
www. mandy.com
Search the U.S. or the world for production jobs, agents, producers, support services, and equipment.

Show Biz Jobs
www.showbizjobs.com
Browsing can be done by region, company, salary, or keyword.

Variety
www.variety.com
In addition to the print version, Variety.com has industry news and a job board.

Food and Beverages

Print

Beverage Marketing Directory, 2005, Beverage Marketing Corp.
www.beveragemarketing.com
Contact information, brand affiliation, production capacity, sales volume, and fleet data for virtually every U.S. and Canadian beverage producer and distributor, plus the industry's largest personnel database, featuring nearly 30,000 beverage executives.

Major Food and Drink Companies of the World 2004, manufactured by Graham & Whiteside
www.gale.com
Covers more than 9,800 of the leading food, alcoholic, and nonalcoholic drink companies worldwide. Entries typically provide company name; address; phone, telex, and fax numbers; names of senior management, including more than 45,000 senior executives; description of business activities; brand names and trademarks; subsidiaries and associates; financial information for the previous two years; and more.

Plunkett's Food Industry Almanac (see previous listing for **Plunkett's**)

Plunkett's Food Industry Summary Report (see previous listing for **Plunkett's**)

Thomas Food and Beverage Market Place, manufactured by Grey House Publishing
Three-volume directory combining Thomas Food Industry Register and Grey House Publishing's Food and Market Place and Food and Beverage Market Place, Supplier's Edition, databases. Contains 45,000-plus profiles with contact details, company descriptions, and executive names for companies in categories including food and beverage manufacturers, transportation firms, warehouse and broker companies, wholesalers and distributors, importers and exporters, and equipment, supplies, and services.

Wine & Spirits Industry Marketing Handbook 2004, Adams Beverage Group
beveragehandbooks.com
This "who's who and what's what" handbook has been revised to include listings and brand information on leading distillers, vintners, importers, and marketers. Virtually all of the leading brands and major executives are included, as is an extensive brand index showing product type, country of origin, and supplier.

World Drinks Marketing Directory, Euromonitor Staff
www.euromonitor.com, 2003
Profiles of the leading drink companies worldwide, together with authoritative market analysis on the industry from acknowledged experts and sources to consult for further information. Companies are selected for inclusion based on their national market share. Full contact details plus company key events, financial information, annual growth, market shares, major subsidiaries, and leading brands.

Online

Food Info Net
www.foodinfonet.com
Search for jobs. This is an online food job center to help both job seekers and hiring companies maximize their effectiveness. Food companies and recruitment firms can post food-related jobs.

Food Industry Jobs
www.foodindustryjobs.com
Includes restaurant, hospitality, food, supermarket, chef, retail, distributor/wholesaler, beverage, food broker, tourism, seafood, agricultural, hospital, hotel/resort, casino, catering, educational, transportation/logistics, and more.

Franchising

Print

Bond's Franchise Guide, 2004 Source Book Publications, Oakland, CA
www.franchising.com
Annual guide to more than 1,000 franchise opportunities. Franchiser profiles are listed by industry. Contains two indexes—one alphabetically by franchiser and the other alphabetically by attorneys, consultants, and service providers. Individual profiles contain contact information, background data (when established, number of units, qualifications, etc.), financial/terms, types of support and training offered, and specific expansion plans.

Online

International Franchise Association
www.franchise.org
Site has a job bank for searching a comprehensive franchise database with Web and E-mail links to more than 800 companies. Also, information on the world of franchising and how it works, a preview of the Association's Annual Convention, plus Franchise Buyer, an online service in which clients fill out a form and a team of experts helps them find the franchise opportunities best suited to their personal goals.

Freelancing

Online

Craig's List
www.craigslist.com
Individual sites for a large number of metro areas, plus some foreign cities. Listings for part-time jobs, personals, discussion forums, housing: it's an electronic bulletin board with lots of job categories.

Freelance Exchange
www.freelanceworkexchange.com
Positions include writing and editing jobs, web design and development projects, medical and legal transcription jobs, research and E-mail support work, data-entry and administration jobs, programming and technical projects, and graphic design and illustration jobs. Includes freelance job report, forums, testimonials, and more.

Furniture (See also Retailing)

Print

Directory of Home Furnishings Retailers, Shelley Alsaker, Lebhar-Friedman Books **www.lfbooks.com, 2000**

Furniture Industry in the United States and Canada, report by CSIL, Centro Studi Industria Leggera Staff, Stefan Wille (ed.) AKTRIN Furniture Information Center, May 2001

www.furniture-info.com
This report describes trends in household furniture production and consumption, international trade, prices, marketing policies, and distribution. Furniture imports and exports are broken down by country and product (kitchen furniture, bedroom furniture, upholstered furniture, and furniture parts). Profiles of the most representative furniture producers and distributors, with analysis of sales performance and product mix, are provided. The report was written by CSIL, the Italian Furniture Research Center, an affiliate of AKTRIN.

Gay and Lesbian

Print

Lavender Road to Success: The Career Guide for the Gay Community, Kirk Snyder, Ten Speed Press, 2003
Based on a two-year study of more than 300 gay, lesbian, bisexual, and transgendered alumni from the University of Southern California, this is the first career guide written specifically for the gay community. Identifying how the right career decisions can level the workplace playing field, author Kirk Snyder presents a personal and comprehensive look into the career paths of gay professionals, giving voice to those who have experienced both success and failure as a direct result of their career decisions.

Straight Jobs, Gay Lives: Gay and Lesbian Professionals, the Harvard Business School, and the American Workplace, Annette Friskopp, Sharon Silverstone, Simon & Schuster, 1996
Based on a Harvard Business School study, this book on gays and lesbians offers surprisingly upbeat news for all those hoping to climb the corporate ladder. The men and women who discuss their experiences talk frankly about such issues as coming out versus being closeted in the workplace, harassment, discrimination, and

health and insurance benefits. Contact listings for gay employee and professional groups nationwide and an overwhelming list of resource materials and guides.

Online

Gay Work
www.gaywork.com
A job-search listing service designed to connect employees with gay-friendly employers. Allows the user to post a résumé, perform a job search, view employer websites, and research a company. Guide: Employment Issues for People Living with HIV/AIDS and much more.

Gay/Lesbian Careers
www.glpcareers.com
This is a job-search engine providing employment opportunities and resources to gay, lesbian, bisexual and transgendered job seekers in the U.S., helping them find the right job at the right company. Posting jobs on this site enables any company to position itself as a forward-thinking entity committed to diversity employment. Employer profiles describe a company's diversity programs and policies.

Government

Print

The Book of U.S. Government Jobs, 8th Edition: Where They Are, What's Available and How to Get One, Dennis V. Damp and Salvatore Concialdi, Bookhaven Press, June 2002
Thorough reference for anyone considering a career in governmental public service. Individual chapters address basics of governmental employment and processes of being interviewed and taking civil service exams, as well as jobs specifically for military veterans, overseas employment, U.S. Postal Service, law-enforcement jobs, and much more. Exhaustive reference with appendixes of contact lists for federal agencies, straightforward checklist for job hunters, and much more.

Encyclopedia of Governmental Advisory Organizations, Ed. 20, Thomson Gale, next edition is June 2005
www.gale.com
Contains entries describing activities and personnel of groups and committees that function to advise the president and various departments and bureaus of the federal government, as well as detailed information about historically significant committees. Complete contact information is provided, including fax numbers and E-mail and URL addresses when available. Features five indexes: alphabetical and keyword; personnel; publications and reports; organizations by federal department or agency; and organizations by presidential administration.

Government Job Finder: Where the Jobs Are in Local, State, and Federal Government, Daniel Lauber and Jennifer Atkin, Planning/Communications, November 2004
www.planningcommunications.com
Details some 1,400 sources of vacancies for professionals, labor, trade, technical, and office support positions in local, state, and federal government in the U.S. and overseas. Also includes federal agency personnel office phone numbers and salary surveys.

Online

Browse Government Resources, The Library of Congress
www.loc.gov/rr/news/extgovd.html
Links to many sites that yield federal government information. Maintained by the Serial and Government Publications Division, Library of Congress. Has links to all U.S. government agencies, alphabetically and by hierarchy. Excellent site to find out all kinds of information about the federal government.

Federal Job Search
www.federaljobsearch.com
Captures your job-search profile online and matches it daily against a database of 26,580 U.S. federal government job openings all across the

U.S. and around the world. Free job-search alerts; your E-mails will contain matching job titles, job location, a brief description, deadline for the posting, and federal grade and salary information for each position. Some services are by subscription.

Federal Jobs Digest
www.jobsfed.com
From Breakthrough Publications; not an official U.S. government website. Provides listings for federal job openings, job descriptions, résumé advice, and a job-matching service.

FedWorld
www.fedworld.gov/jobs/jobsearch.html
FedWorld is maintained by the National Technical Information Service. Job hunters may search for and read descriptions of U.S. government jobs and print copies of required forms.

Jobs @ Census
www.census.gov/hrd/www/index.html
Search for jobs with the U.S. Census Bureau.

U.S. Department of Justice
www.usdoj.gov/06employment/index.html
Search for jobs in the many bureaus of the U.S. Department of Justice.

U.S. Geological Survey: Employment
info.er.usgs.gov/ohr
Job opportunities and application information for the U.S. Geological Survey.

USA Jobs
www.usajobs.opm.gov
U.S. government's official site for jobs and employment information from the U.S. Office of Personnel Management.

Health Care and Medicine

Much of this information is from the Mid-Manhattan's Job Information Center link, "Careers in Health Care" (www.nypl.org).

Print

Encyclopedia of Medical Organizations and Agencies, 15th ed., 2005, Thomson Gale
www.gale.com
This resource provides access to public and private agencies concerned with medical information, funding, research, education, planning, advocacy, advice, and service. Its 69 subject chapters represent an entire range of contemporary medical fields: allergy and immunology, alternative medicine, biomedicine, chiropractic, gastroenterology, hypnosis, neurology, osteopathic medicine, reproduction and family planning, substance abuse, and more. Entries provide contact and descriptive information for the organizations listed. A name and keyword index, as well as a subject cross-index, make finding information easy.

Health Professions Career and Education Directory, 30th ed., 2004–5, American Medical Association
www.ama-assn.org
Lists 6,500 educational programs and 2,800 educational institutions in 64 different health professions, from radiographer and medical assistant to art therapist, physician assistant, and rehabilitation counselor. Includes occupational descriptions, employment characteristics, and information on educational programs, such as length, curriculum, and prerequisites. Program listings include contact information as well as class capacity, month classes begin, program length, yearly tuition, awards granted, and availability of evening/weekend classes.

Health Resources Online
www.healthresourcesonline.com
Offers a variety of health care directories and resources, including Payor-Provider Directories by

State, Three-on-One CD-ROM; The National Directory of Adult Day Care Centers, Third Edition; The National Directory of Medical Directors, Database on CD-ROM, 2004.

Major Pharmaceutical & Biotechnology Companies of the World, 7th ed., 2005, Graham & Whiteside
www.gale.com
Covers the world's largest pharmaceutical companies, providing essential business profiles of the international leaders in the industry. Entries typically provide company name; address; phone, telex, and fax numbers; E-mail and website addresses; names of senior management and board members, including senior executives; description of business activities; brand names and trademarks; subsidiaries and associates; financial information for the previous two years; and more.

Medical and Health Information Directory, 18th ed., 2005, Thomson Gale
www.gale.com
Comprehensive guide to organizations, agencies, institutions, services, and information sources on medicine and health-related fields. Three volumes: Volume 1—Organizations, Agencies, and Institutions; Volume 2—Publications, Libraries, and Other Information Resources; and Volume 3—Health Services.

Plunkett's Health Care Industry Almanac (see previous listing for **Plunkett's**)

Plunkett's Health Care Industry Summary Report (see previous listing for **Plunkett's**)

Massage: A Career at Your Fingertips, VGM Career Horizons, Mahopac Falls, NY, Enterprise Pub., 2003

Opportunities in Eye Care Careers, Lincolnwood, IL., VGM Career Horizons, 2004

Opportunities in Pharmacy Careers, Lincolnwood, IL., VGM Career Horizons, 2004

Online
American Medical Association: Job Center
www.ama-assn.org
Use their website to find a job with the American Medical Association.

America's HealthCare Source
www.healthcaresource.com

Biotech Information Directory
www.cato.com
Contains more than 3,000 links to companies, research institutes, universities, sources of information, and other directories specific to biotechnology, pharmaceutical development, and related fields. Emphasizes product development and delivery of products and services.

Biotechnology Industry Organization
www.bio.org
Contains industry information and resources, as well as their Guide to Biotechnology, a guidepost for both industry and mainstream journalists to key information about the biotech industry and how it influences and improves many lives each day, and their BIO Member Directory, which contains lists of BIO members and profiles, BIO state and international affiliates, and a link to BIO Online Member Directory.

Business.com
www.business.com/directory/healthcare
News, events, jobs, associations, online references.

Careers In Health
www.careers-in-health.com
Start a career in the health field.

CompHealth
www.comphealth.com

Corey Nahman .com
www.coreynahman.com
Pharmaceutical news and information. More than 4,500 pharmaceutical jobs at more than 500 companies worldwide; drug lists; news; female health; pharmaceutical sales jobs. Also contains informa-

tion on and links to medical portals, books, journals and databases for doctors, and others.

DocJob
www.docjob.com

Health Care Job Store
www.healthcarejobstore.com

Health Care Careers
www.health-care-careers.org
Get career information and find degrees offered by many health care schools

Health Care mart.com
www.healthcaremart.com

Healthcare Recruitment On Line
www.healthcarerecruitment.com

Healthlinks.net
www.healthlinks.net
A site for health-care consumers and professionals that provides links to services and products, alternative health, education, dental and medical resources, hospitals, employment, health-care publications, mental health, and much more.

Hirehealth.com
www.hirehealth.com

JAMA Classifieds
www.ama-assn.org
Search for jobs in various medical specialties by state.

MedHunters.com
www.medhunters.com

NP Central
www.nurse.net

Vault
www.vault.com
Covers health/biotech/pharmaceutical jobs and industries.

Wet Feet
www.wetfeet.com
Information on companies, careers, and industries in health care.

Human Resources

Print

Directory of Executive Recruiters, Kennedy Publications, 2005
www.kennedyinfo.com
Lists 13,250 recruiters at 5,600 search firms with all the contact information needed to start networking immediately with executive recruiters: address, phone, fax, E-mail, and web addresses. Now available online, with updates for up to one full year.

Online

American Society for Training and Development
www.astd.org
More than 70,000 members in 100 countries representing 15,000 corporations. Posted jobs are easy to view via a search engine or by scrolling through the listings.

Career Development and Training
www.tasl.com
Training and Seminar Locators (TASL) is an award-winning free education and training resource center/database for career/business. Includes offerings of more than 1,000 of the best universities, industry associations, media, and training companies. Online database of training and seminar providers, searchable by event or service, product or provider.

HR.com
www.hr.com
About 1,800 jobs are posted. When a job hunter's qualifications match those of a recruiter, the site automatically e-mails the person's résumé to that organization. Newsletter. Free basic membership, but other features are by subscription.

HR Connections
www.hrjobs.com
HR connections is a service-driven professional recruiting firm specializing in placement of human resources professionals nationwide.

HR Junction
www.hrjunction

A well-designed site from JobMark, a site-hosting firm. More than 100 positions are free to see and post.

Jobs4HR
www.jobs4hr.com

A career and recruiting site for human resources professionals by human resources professionals. Offers an online jobs database and Personal Career Agent.

Society for Human Resource Management
www.shrm.org

Award-winning site has jobs searchable by location, keyword, or date of postings. Viewing job openings is free to nonmembers. Society has more than 170,000 members, making this site "the first place to post a human resources opening" (CareerXRoads comment). Only paid members can access the entire site; however, there is a still lot of information for free. Latest news on trends, training, compensation, tools and resources, articles, and more.

The Training Registry
www.tregistry.com

A directory of trainers, workshops, and training seminars. Lists hundreds of trainers, consultants, and consulting services, and thousands of training topics, workshops, and seminars covering all delivery media, including instructor-led, web-based, or online courses; computer-based training; videos; and more.

Information Technology/High Tech (Computers, Technology and E-Commerce)

(See also Communications Equipment and Services, Including Telecommunications)

Print

The Best Computer Jobs in America: Twenty Minutes from Home, Carol L. Covin, Twenty Minute Press, Bristol, VA, 2002

Designed to give techies an edge. Whether a virtual interview with the top hiring managers, or a focused view of technology and job opportunities, the Guide provides the research for which techies don't have time. College degree or certification? Entry-level or experienced? Legacy or new economy? This Guide provides the insight candidates need to tune their résumé and stand out from the crowd when applying for jobs in today's market. Companies profiled are drawn from the ranks of top-rated employers leading the way in technical and business innovations, as listed in publications ranging from *Computerworld* to *Fortune* to *Industry Week.*

Career Guide for the High-Tech Professional: Where the Jobs Are Now and How to Land Them, David Perry and Jay Conrad Levinson, 2004

No shortcuts, tricks, or anything unethical. Solid advice along with the rich details of landing the job of a lifetime. Job-finding wisdom and actual things you must say in your cover letter, on your résumé, and during your interviews.

Career Opportunities in Computers and Cyberspace, 2nd ed., 2004, Career Opportunities Set, 25 Volumes, Harry Henderson, Ferguson Publishers
www.fergpubco.com

Straightforward guide to jobs in the computer industry. Covers more than 80 jobs, profiling everything from programming and manufacturing to software instruction and sales. For 2004 edition, all entries have been reviewed and updated with latest information and many new profiles have been added to cover emerging jobs, including data miner, bioinformatics specialist, system administrator, technical recruiter or agent, and online writer/editor. The Industry Outlook section reflects recent changes in the field, such as areas that have fallen off (dot-com business) and areas likely to grow (bioinformatics).

The E-Business Book: A Step-by-Step Guide to E-Commerce and Beyond, Dayle M. Smith, Bloomberg Press, 2001

Informed by loads of real-world examples of Internet initiatives that have worked. Lays out a dozen essential steps for entrepreneurs building a solid plan for long-term success.

Major Information Technology Companies of the World, 7th ed., 2005, Graham & Whiteside
www.gale.com
Covers more than 3,100 of the leading information technology companies worldwide. Entries typically provide company name; address; phone, telex, and fax numbers; E-mail and website addresses; names of senior management and board members, including more than 12,000 directors and senior executives; description of business activities; brand names and trademarks; subsidiaries and associates; financial information for the previous two years; and more. Includes a comprehensive index and an index listing company names alphabetically by country.

Major Telecommunications Companies of the World, 8th ed., April 2005, Graham & Whiteside
www.gale.com
Profiles more than 3,500 of the leading telecommunications companies worldwide, including many of the top Internet companies. Each listing typically includes company name; address; phone and fax numbers; E-mail and Web addresses; names of senior management and board members; description of business activities; brand names and trademarks; subsidiaries and associations; number of employees; financial information for the previous two years; principal shareholders; and public/private status.

Plunkett's E-Commerce and Internet Business Almanac 2003–2004: The Only Comprehensive Guide to the E-Commerce & Internet Industry, Jack W. Plunkett
www.plunketts.com
A ready-reference guide to the e-commerce and Internet business. Complete profiles of the 400 largest, most successful corporations in all facets of the business. Industry analysis covers B2C,

B2B, online financial services, and Internet access and usage trends.

Plunkett's InfoTech Industry Almanac, Plunkett Research, Houston, TX
www.plunkettresearch.com
Contains industry and company information on leaders in the "movement and management of voice, data and video." Includes statistics and trends in wireless technologies, hardware, software, networking, the Internet, and semiconductors. Lists more than 500 firms chosen for their dominance. Company profiles include contact information, key personnel, financials, salaries/benefits, number of women and minority officers, types of products and services, plus a paragraph on growth plans/special features. Has index of subsidiaries, brand names, and affiliations.

Telecommunications Directory, 15th ed., September 2005, Thomson Gale
www.gale.com
Lists detailed information on telecommunications companies providing a range of products and services from cellular communications and local exchange carriers to satellite services and Internet service providers.

Top 500 Computer VARs & Systems Integrators, CSG (Chain Store Guide) Information Services
www.csgis.com
Profiles 500 of the leading VARs, software VARs, computer dealers, and systems integrators that sell value-added products, solutions, and services to corporations, government agencies, educational institutions, and various other trade classifications. Lists key personnel, markets served (government, general business, health care, etc.), and more.

Vault.com's Guide to High Tech
www.vault.com
All about the industry, what working in it is like, the key players, and more.

Online

From the Mid-Manhattan Library, Job Information Center:

CompInfo.ws
www.compinfo-center.com

Bills itself as "the top one-stop reference resource for corporate IT, computer software, computers and communications. Millions of IT users worldwide rely on our Web-based support resources." Site contains events, books, downloads, news, conferences, Web seminars, plus everything from applications and systems to website development. A real wealth of information.

ComputerJobs.com
www.computerjobs.com

Provides quality computer-related job opportunities and career-related content for 19+ major metropolitan markets.

ComputerGraphicsWorld
cgw.pennnet.com

A site from Pennwell's magazine of the same name, this site has news, conference/event listings, and a free e-newsletter, but not a job board.

Dice
www.dice.com

Leading online technology job board, with permanent, contract, and consulting jobs. Home to a world of career-development resources and expertise.

JobCircle.com
www.jobcircle.com

Provides careers, content, and community to IT professionals in Pennsylvania, New York, New Jersey, and Delaware.

New York State High-Tech
www.hightechNY.com

Lists some of the most exciting and rewarding high-technology jobs available.

Yahoo
dir.yahoo.com

Journals, conferences and links to job boards.

Yankee Group
www.yankeegroup.com

The Yankee Group is a global player in communications and networking research and consulting. Spanning numerous industries, the company provides strategic planning assistance, technology and market forecasting, and cross-industry analysis to support a wide range of clients on a worldwide basis with the development of their business, market, technology, and enterprise initiatives. Provides research of key technology issues and the industry's only personalized one-to-one approach for client interaction. The Yankee Group's results-driven research helps clients understand their target customer, technology demand, and shifting market dynamics, thereby enabling them to shape successful business strategies. Registering as a guest gives you access to both summaries of Yankee Group research and a customized My Yankee site and E-mail updates on new research.

Insurance

(See also the section Banking, Finance, Investing, Securities, Trading, Credit, and Other)

Print

Plunkett's Insurance & Mortgages Industry Almanac (see previous listing for **Plunkett's**)

Weiss Ratings
www.weissratings.com

Offers a complete line of products designed to direct consumers and business professionals alike toward safe investment and insurance options while avoiding unnecessary risks that could lead to financial losses. Every quarter, the company evaluates the financial strength of more than 15,000 institutions, including life, health, and annuity insurers; property and casualty insurers; HMOs; Blue Cross/Blue Shield plans, banks, and savings and loans. In addition, Weiss tracks the risk-adjusted performance of more than 12,000 mutual funds and more than 9,000 stocks.

Weiss Ratings' Guide to Life, Health, and Annuity Insurers provides extensive coverage of the life insurance industry. Each quarterly edition delivers independent Weiss Safety Ratings and supporting analysis on more than 1,700 U.S. insurers, including all Blue Cross/Blue Shield plans. The Guide also includes a list of Weiss Recommended Companies, with information on how to contact them and the reasoning behind any rating upgrades or downgrades.

Online

A.M. Best Company
www.ambest.com
This company claims to be the leading provider of information on the insurance industry and its Best's Ratings are viewed as the global benchmark of insurer financial strength. Best offers an online service to rate insurers globally. The site contains links to the most recent coverage of the captive market, including **Best Ratings, Best's Review and BestWeek Special Reports, Statistical Studies**, and news. For complete news coverage, visit the NewsRoom or BestDay, a roundup of the insurance news from **A.M. Best's Daily Newsletter**.

Insurance National Search
www.insurancerecruiters.com
INS is a nonprofit professional association of a highly select group of more than 40 insurance recruiting firms operating on a regional, national, and international basis. Member firms work with each other on a cooperative basis to assist in a job search. Positions can be searched by lines of business (annuities, employee benefits, etc.) or by departments (accounting, legal, marketing communications, etc.).

Insurance File
www.insfile.com
A wide variety of insurance organizations from all geographic regions do their own recruiting on this site. Usually several means to respond to a

posting, including phone, fax, mail, and E-mail. Insurance Careers database provides efficient job finding for insurance professionals and recruiting of insurance personnel for insurance and health-care companies, insurance agencies, brokerage firms, corporate risk-management departments, financial institutions, law firms, public accounting firms, and information systems companies.

Law

Print

Guerrilla Tactics for Getting the Legal Job of Your Dreams, Kimm Alayne Walton, J.D., Harcourt, 1995
Step-by-step guide to the legal job-search process.

Law and Legal Information Directory, Thomson Gale, May 2005
www.gale.com
Provides descriptions and contact information for institutions, services, and facilities in the law and legal-information industry.

National Association for Law Placement
www.nalp.org

Behind the Bench: The Guide to Judicial Clerkships, NALP, Debra Strauss, 2002
Includes information about courts, range of judicial clerkships, and all aspects of application process (including new clerkship hiring plan).

Changing Jobs: A Handbook for Lawyers in the New Millennium, Heidi McNeil Staudenmaier, ed. ABA, NALP, 3rd ed., 1999
Many NALP members contributed their expertise to *Changing Jobs*, which helps law students and attorneys achieve a better understanding of career paths and job-search strategies.

Choosing Small, Choosing Smart—Job Search Strategies for Lawyers in the Small-Firm Market, Donna Gerson, NALP, 2001
Comprehensive guide to the small-firm market.

2005-06 NALP Directory of Legal Employers
(No longer available in print; visit **www. nalpdirectory.com**
Most widely used legal-recruitment directory available includes information on more than 1,600 employers nationwide. Indexed by location, practice-area keyword, and office size.

Vault Guide to the Top 100 Law Firms, Brook Moshan Gesser and Chris Prior
www.vault.com, 2004
Bigger and better than ever before. More than 14,000 associates ranked the most prestigious law firms in the nation and revealed their opinions about hours, diversity, training, offices, relationships with partners, compensation, and other essential details.

Online
The Federal Judiciary
www.uscourts.gov
Includes information on federal courts, including employment opportunities. Covers all areas supporting U.S. courts, their services, and areas of responsibilities.

FindLaw Career Center
www.careers.findlaw.com
Offers information on careers and resources for the legal industry. Features legal news, U.S. federal law, U.S. state law, and government, international, and community resources.

Law.com: Career Center
www.lawjobs.com
Research legal jobs, law firms, and practice centers, recruiters, and trends.

Lawyer's Listings
www.lawyerslistings.com
Find law firms and individuals by state, city, discipline, or name. Contains legal forms, letters, documents, and guides. Users can find attorneys at **www.lawchek.com**, a free service.

The National Federation of Paralegal Associations
www.paralegals.org
Offers information on how to get started, where to study, legal resources, professional development, and links to international associations and information. Career Center offers information on positions, directory of recruiters, and referral service.

Law Enforcement and Criminal Justice Majors
Print
Great Jobs for Criminal Justice Majors, VGM Career Books, Chicago, 2001
Helps students explore career options within their field of study. Every aspect of the job-search process is covered, including assessing talents and skills, exploring options, making a smooth transition from college to career, conducting an effective job search, and landing the job. Filled with a variety of career choices. Available as an e-book.

Seeking Employment in Criminal Justice and Related Fields, J. Scott Harr and Karen M. Hess, Thomson/Wadsworth, Belmont, CA, 2003
Provides specific information on many criminal justice professions, helpful tips on résumés and cover letters, and practical advice on interview techniques. Among other resources, this book contains latest information on using Internet to research careers and find job openings. Includes CD-ROM. Careers in Criminal Justice Interactive.

Online
Corrections Connection
www.corrections.com
Weekly news source committed to improving the lives of corrections professionals and their families. Open forum where practitioners exchange ideas and use best practices, resources, case studies, and new technologies. More than 500,000

users every month. Host to industry's leading sites: ACA, AJA, NCCHC, ACHSA, and ACFSA. Lists job openings and has links to other job sites.

Jobs 4 Police
www.jobs4police
Posted by city and state. Site has practice exams, home-study CD-ROMs, and online and classroom courses for every entry-level and promotional police exam in the country.

Law Enforcement Jobs
www.lawenforcementjobs.com
Jobs and resources for police officers, field agents, security officers, sheriffs, international justice specialists, and more.

Library Science

Print

Jump Start Your Career in Library and Information Science, Priscilla K. Shontz, Scarecrow Press, Lanham, MD, 2002
Designed to help new librarians manage a successful and satisfying career in the library and education science profession. Although the first years are often overwhelming, they can be key to creating a successful career as a librarian or information professional. New librarians can drift into unsatisfying careers without good mentors and/or strong support groups. Emphasizes value of defining one's own idea of success and positioning one's self to be prepared to take advantage of opportunities that arise. Although aimed at students and new information professionals, much of the book's advice may apply to a librarian at any stage of his or her career.

The Librarian's Career Guidebook, Priscilla K. Shontz, ed. Scarecrow Press, Lanham, MD, 2004
63 information professionals from diverse positions, workplaces, and regions discuss a variety of career issues and offer advice to prospective librarians, MLS students, and librarians in various stages of their careers, from entry-level to highly

experienced. Covers career options, education, job search, on-the-job experience, professional development, essential skills, and strategies for enjoying your career.

Online

American Association of Law Libraries
www.aallnet.org
Information on the profession, professional development workshops offered by AALL and other organizations, jobs, and other good resources.

American Library Association: Education and Employment
www.ala.org
Job listings from *American Libraries* magazine, College and Research Libraries NewsNet, and LITA (Information Technology). Site also connects to ALA's Office of Human Resources and Development and other websites for job seekers.

ARLIS/NA JobNet
www.arlisna.org
Art Libraries Society of North America lists vacancy announcements for art librarians, visual resources professionals, and related positions.

Association of Research Libraries Career Resources Online Service
db.arl.org
Provides job hunters with easy-to-use resource for finding positions in ARL libraries.

BUBL Information Service
bubl.ac.uk
Information service for U.K. higher education community. Extensive international information resources for librarians, including job announcements for U.K., Europe, U.S., and worldwide.

C. Berger and Company: Library Consultants
www.cberger.com
Provides employment services, including temporary positions for professional, paraprofessional, and clerical personnel, as well as permanent professional library and information-management

positions in libraries and information centers. Based in but not limited to the Midwest.

Job Resources from the University of Illinois at Urbana-Champaign
www.lis.uiuc.edu
Developed by Graduate School of Library and Information Science at UIUC. Offers long list of links to resources for library and information professionals.

Librarian Job Site
www.librarianjobsite.com
Dedicated to finding jobs for librarians; users may post their résumé or search for a job.

Library Job Postings on the Internet
www.libraryjobpostings.org
Search for jobs in all types of libraries all over the world. Compiled by Sarah Nesbeitt, Reference/Systems Librarian.

The Library & Information Science Professional's Career Development Center
www.liscareer.com
LISCareer offers career-development resources for new librarians and information professionals, MLS students, and those considering a library-related career. Features practical articles contributed by information professionals, along with links to online and print resources.

Music Library Association (MLA)
www.musiclibraryassoc.org
Job list includes current positions as well as a review of positions posted in previous years. Placement Service assists music librarians who seek initial or new employment in positions requiring both music and library expertise.

The Networked Librarian: Job Search Guides
pw2.netcom.com
Virtual clearinghouse of all concerns related to library employment.

University Library at California State University, Long Beach
www.csulb.edu
Provides information for students. Whether you call yourself a librarian, information scientist or specialist, knowledge liaison, or information technologist, it is the same field that has been invigorated by the computer and the Internet.

Manufacturing

Print

American Manufacturers Directory, 2002,
published by American Business Directories, 2002

Encyclopedia of American Industries: Vol. 1, Manufacturing, Thomson Gale, 2004
www.gale.com
This two-volume edition provides detailed, comprehensive information on a wide range of industries in every realm of American business. Also available as an e-book.

National Association of Manufacturers
www.nam.org
NAM is the nation's largest industrial trade association, representing small and large manufacturers in every industrial sector and in all 50 states. Headquartered in Washington, DC, NAM has 10 additional offices across the country.

Plunkett's Transportation, Supply Chain & Logistics Almanac (see previous listing for Plunkett's)

Thomas Register
www.thomasregister.com
Comprehensive online and print resource for finding companies and products manufactured in North America where you can find links to thousands of online company catalogs and websites. *Thomas Register* in print gives you current information on more than 165,000 U.S. and Canadian manufacturers including phone, fax, and toll-free numbers, as well as addresses, subsidiaries, sales offices, and corporate affiliations. With a wide

array of details, the comprehensive print version makes it easy to trace a brand name back to the manufacturer for 72,000 separate product and service headings. All listings are alphabetical by state and city.

Online

American Business Directory, Thomson Dialog, produced by InfoUSA
library.dialog.com
Contains company address, current address, phone number, employment data, key contact and title, primary SIC code, Yellow Pages and brand/trade name information, actual and estimated financial data, and corporate linkages on more than 12 million U.S. business establishments. Data are compiled through a continuous updating cycle of compilation from print sources (including more than 5,000 Yellow Pages books) and phone interviews, capturing additional information, such as primary line of business, key contacts, and actual number of employees. Annual reports are used for public company data.

Jobs in Manufacturing
www.jobsinmanufacturing.com
Find careers in manufacturing, engineering, purchasing, logistics, and transportation. Search manufacturing jobs by category and city; register and post your résumé. Has a weekly job alert and a career center and discussion boards.

Manufacturing Jobs.com
www.manufacturingjobs.com
Premier industry-specific employment resource for manufacturing. Employers and recruiters will find a targeted approach connects them with only the most qualified applicants with relevant experience. Job seekers use a Confidential Career Profile feature. We showcase your skills and work experience to prospective employers while keeping your identity and contact information secure. From the front office to the plant floor.

NationJob
www.nationjob.com
Searchable by location, salary, education, and duration (temporary, full-time, etc.)

U.S. Manufacturers Directories and Databases, Manufacturer's News
www.mnistore.com
Directories by state, industry, and nationally, by SIC code. Metro, international directories, plus databases by state.

Nonprofit

Print

See also Gale's **Encyclopedia of Associations**
www.gale.com

100 Best Nonprofits to Work For, 2nd ed., 2000, Leslie Hamilton & Robert Tragert, Planning/ Communications
www.planningcommunications.com
Profiles 100 of today's best-paying, most secure, and most gratifying nonprofit organizations for which to work, including public television and radio stations, state-of-the-art wildlife parks, environmental groups, and more. Each nonprofit is rated by stability, career prospects, pay and benefits, and work environment, plus the pros and cons of working for each organization.

Associations USA 2004: A Directory of Contact Information for NonProfit Associations and Organizations in the United States, Omnigraphics, Inc.
www.omnigraphics.com
Lists 14,200 active associations and other nonprofit organizations in the U.S. Include organization's name, address, and phone number, and most have website addresses, fax numbers, and toll-free numbers.

Foundation Directory 2000, Foundation Center
fdncenter.org
Data on the nation's most influential foundations, those holding assets of at least $2 million or distribute $200,000 or more in grants each year. Part

2 is designed specifically for nonprofit organizations that want to broaden their funding base to include midsized foundations.

National Directory of Nonprofit Organizations: A Comprehensive Guide Providing Profiles & Procedures for Nonprofit Organizations, 18th ed., 2005, Taft Group
www.gale.com
Includes Taft's National Directory bibliographical references and index. Foundations, endowment funds, scholarships, research centers, trusts, religious organizations, associations, chambers of commerce, hospitals, and universities are just a few of the kinds of influential organizations listed.

Non-Profits Job Finder: Where the Jobs are in Charities & Nonprofits, 5th ed., 2005, Daniel Lauber, Kraig Rice, and Jennifer Atkin, SCB Distributors
www.scbdistributors.com
Job leads at nonprofits and charities and all the tools job seekers need to conduct a savvy, balanced job search; 2,000+ places to find job vacancies; how to use the job databases, résumé banks, E-mail job-notification systems, directories, and salary surveys on the Internet sites; free online updates; salary surveys; details on specialty and trade periodicals; job-matching services; print and CD-ROM directories of employers.

World Guide to Foundations, 3rd ed., Vol. 1, 2004, K.G. Saur
www.gale.com
As a crucial source of grants, studies, research, and other not-for-profit services, the world's growing roster of foundations each year dispenses literally billions of dollars to causes ranging from eradicating AIDS to monitoring human rights abuses to promoting free speech on the Internet. Whether you're looking for the phone number of the Ford Foundation or a list of scientific foundations in Switzerland, you'll find everything you need to know in this guide. It

brings together more than 21,750 foundations on six continents and some 112 countries, from Albania to Zimbabwe.

Online
Council on Foundations
www.cof.org
Membership organization of more than 2,000 grant-making foundations and giving programs worldwide. Provides leadership expertise, legal services, and networking opportunities, among other services, to members and the general public.

Foundation Center
www.fdncenter.org
Philanthropy News Digest of The Foundation Center offers the Job Corner. You can search jobs by category, organization types, job functions, and states.

GuideStar and Philanthropic Research, Inc.
www.guidestar.org
A free interactive "marketplace of information" that connects nonprofit organizations, donors, foundations, and businesses. 400,000 users per month. Programmatic and financial information about more than one million American charitable nonprofit organizations.

Idealist
www.idealist.org
A global network of individuals and organizations. Provides information about nonprofit organizations, including services, events, volunteer opportunities, and job listings.

The NonProfit Times Online
www.nptimes.com
The classifieds section lists different levels of nonprofit jobs.

Opportunity NOCs: Nonprofit Organization Classifieds
www.opportunitynocs.org
Job listings and career resources.

Nursing

Print

Careers in Nursing, 2003, Terence J. Sacks and Thomas A. Schweich, McGraw-Hill
www.mcgraw-hill.com
With increased demand for home care, community health nursing, and hospital care, the Bureau of Labor Statistics has listed nursing as one of the top 40 growth jobs for the next 10 years. A wide variety of rewarding and lucrative opportunities abound for those with nursing skills and training. This book offers a concise, comprehensive overview of the positions available and their respective requirements. Topics covered include the history, current status, and future of the profession; getting into nursing school and financing your education; choosing a specialty e.g., (ER, intensive care, pediatrics); current salaries and benefits; and where jobs are and what it takes to succeed.

Nursing Now: Today's Issues, Tomorrow's Trends, 3rd ed., Joseph T. Catalano, F. A. Davis
www.fadavis.com, 2002
Topics such as rights of nurses and patients, burnout, ethical decision making, and NCLEX licensure. Explores the evolution and history of nursing and examines the impact of reform, the legal system, and politics of the nursing system. Numerous examples, true-life situations, case studies, and practical applications.

Nursing Today: Transitions and Trends, 4th ed., JoAnn Zerwekh and Jo Carol Claborn, eds., Elsevier Science
www.elsevier.com, 2002
Focuses on information students need to make a successful transition from the classroom to practice. Provides solid understanding of the problems and opportunities professional nurses face and details the practical skills essential for success. New and expanded coverage on nursing management, delegation of nursing care, community-based care, and alternative/complementary health care. Specific career-management tools include workplace communication, time management, résumé writing and interviewing tips, budgeting basics, and NCLEX-RN exam.

Online

National NurseSearch
www.nursesearch.net
Recruiting site working to fill nursing openings in many specialties and at all experience levels.

NurseRecruiter.com
www.nurse-recruiter.com
Nursing Jobs Directory is exclusively for nurses by nurses. U.S. and international employment opportunities for nursing professionals. Jobs are in hospitals, travel, agencies, offices, clinics, long-term care, camps, home health care, management, education, and more.

Nursing Jobs Online
www.nursingjobs.org
A nursing-owned company that provides "features you won't find available from any other job board. . . .We are the busiest job board exclusively for Nursing Jobs." Not a free service. Nursing Jobs's goal is to provide all health-care professionals and providers with the most complete and comprehensive source of career-related information. Site also has resources.

Nursing Spectrum
www.nursingspectrum.com
Offers career information and jobs database of current RN employment listings.

Nursing World
www.nursingworld.org
American Nurses Association website offering a wide variety of resources—books, career information, nursing issues, information on the nursing shortage. Only full-service professional organization representing nation's 2.7 million registered nurses (RNs) through 54 constituent member associations. Advances nursing profession by fostering high standards of nursing practice, promoting the economic and general welfare of

nurses in the workplace, projecting a positive and realistic view of nursing, and by lobbying the Congress and regulatory agencies on health-care issues affecting nurses and the public.

Public Relations

Print

O'Dwyer's
www.odwyerspr.com
O'Dwyer's publishes several public relations (PR) directories, allows free searching of its directories online (however, not all entries are accessible online), allows job hunters to post résumés, and contains news and advice about PR industry. Access to 400 PR firms and 1,500 PR service companies is free. Total database, available to subscribers and in print versions, contains 2,900 PR firms worldwide, 6,000 companies, and 2,100 associations. Monthly online subscription costs $14.95 and lets the user access full database. Directories are:

Directory of Public Relations Firms, 2004
Lists 2,900+ firms in the U.S. and abroad. 19,000+ clients are cross-indexed; the only place you can look up a company and determine its outside PR counsel.

Directory of Corporate Communications, 2004
Lists over 7,800 companies and associations. All 2,800 companies listed on New York Stock Exchange, with PR contacts, CEOs. Includes about 2,000 associations and 189 foreign embassies, 350+ federal governmental departments, bureaus, agencies, and commissions. More than 18,000 PR/IR professionals are listed, plus thousands of CEOs.

O'Dwyer's PR Buyer's Guide, 2004
Lists 1,500 products and services for the PR industry in 56 categories, including annual report design, photo distribution, media lists, and website development.

Online

Media Bistro
www.mediabistro.com
Job boards and resources for a variety of media professionals, including PR.

PR Week.Jobs
www.prweekjobs.com, or **www.prweek.com**
PR Week Magazine's site for jobs and industry information, in U.S. and globally.

Public Relations Society of America Career Resources
www.prsa.org
Career Resources Center offers a new, fully searchable Job Center. Posting a résumé is free to members and costs $40 for three months for non-members.

Publishing (Books, Magazines, Newspapers, Others)

Print

Bacon's, www.bacons.com
Publishes annual Bacon's Media Directories, which are available in print and as online, subscription database:

Bacon's Newspaper/Magazine Directories
Two separate volumes; all U.S., Canadian, Mexican, and Caribbean daily newspapers, with nearly 15,000 magazines and newsletters; lists syndicated columnists by specialty, editors with their beats and pitching profiles, plus details on each publication with contact information.

Information Today
www.infotoday.com

American Book Trade Directory 2003–2004, 49th ed.
Profiles nearly 30,000 retail and antiquarian book dealers, plus 1,000 book and magazine wholesalers, distributors, and jobbers in all 50 states and territories, too.

International Literary Market Place, 2004,
Information Today
www.infotoday.com
Covers more than 180 countries worldwide—
from Afghanistan to Zimbabwe. Contains up-to-
date profiles for more than 16,500 book-related
concerns around the globe, including 10,500 publishers and literary agents, 1,100 major
booksellers and book clubs, and 1,520 major
libraries and library associations

Literary Market Place 2004
This 64th edition carries some 13,000 entries,
3,300 being publishers (166 listed for the first
time) in two volumes that have 54 sections organizing everyone and everything in the business-
from publishers, agents, and ad agencies to
associations, distributors, and events. More than
14,000 listings in all, featuring names, addresses,
and numbers; key personnel, activities, specialties, and other relevant data; e-mail addresses
and websites; and more. Some 24,000 decision
makers throughout the industry listed in a separate Personnel Yellow Pages section in each volume; plus more information.

Oxbridge Communications
www.oxbridge.com
Over the past 40 years, Oxbridge Communications
has built one of the largest databases of U.S. and
Canadian periodicals and catalogs in existence—
more than 72,000 titles. All information is also on
CD-ROM and online at **www.mediafinder.com**.
Oxbridge publishes four print directories:
The Standard Periodical Directory (magazines, newsletters, newspapers, journals, and
directories)—62,000 listings with contact information. **The National Directory of Magazines**—
more than 16,000 listings. **The Oxbridge
Directory of Newsletters**—more than 14,000
listings. **National Directory of Catalogs**—more
than 9,000 listings.

Publishers Directory, 28th ed., March 2005,
Thomson Gale
www.gale.com

According to the publisher, it is the most comprehensive source of detailed information on U.S.
and Canadian publishers, distributors, and
wholesalers. Also covers small independent
presses and virtual publishers.

Online
Authorlink
authorlink.monster.com
Search thousands of jobs and instantly submit
your résumé online. Job Search Agent lets site do
the searching. Create your job profile and you'll
get a message when a match is made.

CompInfo-The Computer Information Center
www.compinfo-center.com

Links to many desktop publishing databases,
magazines, user groups, manufacturers, where to
get help, and much more.

desktoppublishing.com
Site for jobs, career information, and resources for
graphic and Web designers, editors, and more,
with links to other job sites. Powered by Google,
this site is for desktop publishing only.

**Journal of Electronic Publishing, University
of Michigan Press**
www.press.umich.edu
Contributions from expert and experienced practitioners on a particular theme, as well as longer
pieces from publishers, scholars, and others interested in electronic publishing.

Media Bistro
www.mediabistro.com
Dedicated to anyone who creates or works with
content or is a noncreative professional working
in a content/creative industry. Includes editors,
writers, television producers, graphic designers,
book publishers, people in production, and circulation departments in industries including magazines, television, radio, newspapers, book
publishing, online media, advertising, PR, and
graphic design. Its mission is to provide opportu-

nities (both online and off-line) for you to meet each other, share resources, become informed of job opportunities and interesting projects, improve your career skills, and showcase your work.

MediaProfessional.info
www.mediaprofessional.info
Free. Brief profiles of more than 200 job sites, recruiters, career resources, and salary guides for job seekers in media, marketing, advertising, sales, PR, publishing, and journalism. Updated quarterly. Also, media and marketing news and resources.

The Write Jobs
www.writejobs.com
Jobs in books, journalism, freelancing, technical writing and editing, and medical writing.

Real Estate
Print

Careers in Real Estate
www.wetfeet.com
Insider Guide to learn how the real estate industry breaks down; latest trends in real estate industry; looks at top-ranked companies and how they got there; typical jobs, salaries, and career paths for real estate professionals, from loan officer and site acquisition specialist to REIT manager and commercial broker; typical day in the life of a real estate broker, real estate agent, or director of asset management; plus more.

Careers in Real Estate Management, 2000, Inst. of Real Estate Management
www.irem.org
Explores opportunities and rewards of real estate management, including how to get started, earning potential, and the challenges real estate managers may encounter.

Directory of 2,500 Active Real Estate Lenders, 2004, Tyler G. Hicks, International Wealth Success
www.iwsmoney.com

Lists 2,500 names and addresses of direct lenders or sources of information on possible lenders for real estate.

Directory of Institutional Real Estate, Nelson Information
www.nelsoninformation.com, annual
Lists 300 real estate investment managers, 1,700 plan sponsor investors in real estate, 1,400 real estate service firms and consultants, 1,000 insurance companies with real estate investments, 2,000 corporations with active real estate operations, and 280 real estate investment trusts. Plus, three indexes to help find the needed contact. Complete addresses and phone numbers for decision makers and prospects.

Internet Resources and Services for International Real Estate Information: A Global Guide, Sheau-yueh J. Chao, Greenwood Publishing Group, 2001
www.greenwood.com
Guide to nearly 2000 real estate websites, including data for more than 220 regions, states, and countries.

Plunkett's Real Estate & Construction Industry Almanac (see previous listing for **Plunkett's**)

Plunkett's Real Estate & Construction Summary Report (see previous listing for **Plunkett's**)

U.S. Real Estate Register and Property Digest, 36th ed.
www.usrealestateregister.com
Print directory and free online searchable version. Real estate industry professionals can locate the properties and services they need—real estate brokers, mortgage bankers, investors, appraisers, architects, engineers, builders, developers. Includes priority website listings. Locates airparks, business, industrial, land, office, shopping centers, warehouses, and research technology parks. Contacts and listings.

Online

iHireRealEstate
www.ihirerealestate.com

Highly rated by "CareerXRoads" book, 2003
Finalist out of 6,000 sites reviewed for real estate.
Jobs are fresh, unique, and individual—no mass
job loads; continuous monitoring of job postings
by our staff; upload your résumé; no need for
time-consuming typing; live phone customer
support; site spends tens of thousands of dollars
each month attracting new employers.

Institute of Real Estate Management, Online Member Directory
www.irem.org

Quick and advanced searches are free to non-members.

National Association of Realtors
www.realtor.org

All kinds of resources, links, and information for
realtors, including news, meetings, career advice,
publications, and more.

Real Jobs-Real Estate
www.real-jobs.com

Contains more than 700 résumés with contact
information. Recruiters post jobs, ranging from
sales agents to land barons. Jobs can be searched
by company name, location, job category, and
education.

Real Estate Careers
www.restatecareer.com

State-by-state listing of information on getting a
license and advice on real estate careers.

Real Estate Best Jobs
www.realestatebestjobs.com

Dedicated to real estate and all real estate—
related industries in all 50 states. Listings for all
mortgage positions, corporate real estate, residential and commercial real estate, property management, all title positions, real estate attorneys and
paralegals, home inspectors, appraisers, and other
positions related to real estate.

Real Estate Job Store (about.com)
jobsearch.about.com

Sales, marketing, finance, and construction job
listings and career resources. Links to the following sites:

Jobsite.com

Real estate, real estate finance, and construction
jobs.

Real-Jobs

Commercial real estate job listings.

Real Estate Best Jobs

Searchable database of real estate jobs.

Real Estate Career Guide

Information on real estate careers from Century
21.

Property managerjobs.com

Nationwide searchable database of property
manager jobs.

Vault.com
www.vault.com

Career and salary information, message boards,
and job listings.

Retailing

Print

Career Opportunities in the Retail and Wholesale Industry, 2001, Shelly Field Groveman, Facts on File
www.factsonfile.com

Profiles more than 70 careers available in retail and
sales settings. Broken down into four key sections-
Malls and Shopping Centers; Stores, Shops, and
Boutiques; Department Stores; and Automobile
Sales. Each entry provides a job overview and
description of a likely career path. Jobs profiled
include property manager, mall marketing director,
event coordinator, leasing director, district man-

ager, buyer, merchandiser, billing manager, wholesale sales representative, manufacturer's representative, sales trainer, sales supervisor, purchasing agent, personal shopper, department store manager, loss-prevention manager, payroll specialist, and automobile sales manager.

World Retail Directory and SourceBook 2003, published by Euromoney Publications Ltd., Thomson Gale
www.gale.com
Contact details for leading retailers in 52 countries, company rankings, overview of global trends in retailing, key information sources, and latest statistical data. Retailers featured include buying groups, cash and carries, convenience stores, cooperatives, department stores, discount stores, franchises, hypermarkets, mail-order companies, specialized multiples, supermarkets, variety stores, and voluntary chains. Company profiles have full contact details, year established, activities, parent company, major subsidiaries, key personnel, outlets/operations, number of employees, financial information, and notes on company.

Plunkett's Retail Industry Almanac (see previous listing for **Plunkett's**)

Plunkett's Retail Industry Summary Report (see previous listing for **Plunkett's**)

Online

AllRetailJobs.com
www.allretailjobs.com
Lists more than 34,000 jobs, plus other resources.

hCareers.com
www.hcareers.com
Said to have the most restaurant jobs, retail jobs, hotel jobs, hospitality jobs, and job seekers anywhere. Lists nearly 40,000 retail positions.

Retailology.com
www.retailology.com
Site for Federated Department Stores—Macy's, Bloomingdale's, Goldsmith's, Burdine's, and more.

Sales and Marketing
(See also Advertising, Including Graphic Art and Design and Public Relations)

Print

Dictionary of Marketing Communications, 2003, Norman A. P. Govoni, SAGE Publications
Contains more than 4,000 entries, including key terms and concepts on the promotion aspect of marketing, with coverage of advertising, sales promotion, public relations, direct marketing, personal selling, and e-marketing.

Directory of International and E-Marketing: A Country-by-Country Sourcebook of Providers, Legislation and Data, 7th ed., 2003, Roderick Millar (consultant ed.), Kogan Page (with Federation of European Direct Marketing and American Direct Marketing Association)
Includes more than 4,000 direct- and e-marketing company analyses, strategies, and trends and lists providers of direct-marketing services in more than 50 countries. First part examines new opportunities in the field and includes statistics, new techniques, regulatory regimes, regional developments, and internationalization of sales. Second part is country-by-country directory of providers profiles.

Green Book
www.greenbook.org
Who's who for finding suppliers of more than 400 types of marketing-research services, including advertising, brand, media and product research, analytical services, computer services and programs, interviewing, surveys, and technical services.

Internet Resources and Services for International Marketing and Advertising: A Global Guide, 2002, James R. Coyle, Greenwood Publishing Group
www.greenwood.com
More than 150 countries and regions covered, including more than 2,000 websites with

information on international marketing and advertising. Resources and services provide information on country's advertising and marketing industries, as well as related marketing subspecialties, including direct marketing, customer relationship management, graphic design, retailing, distribution, and packaging.

Resumes for Sales and Marketing Careers, 3rd ed., 2005, (VGM's Professional Resumes Series) McGraw-Hill
Nearly 100 sample résumés and 20 cover letters, tips on highlighting your strengths and using active vocabulary, worksheets for gathering personal information, and more.

Vault Career Guide to Marketing & Brand Management, Jennifer Goodman, John Phillips, and Andy Kantor, 2002
www.vault.com
Learn about marketing careers and jobs, path to brand-management success, how to ace brand-management case interviews, and more.

Vault Career Guide to Sales and Trading, Gabriel Kim
www.vault.com, 2004
Everything from the basics, the traders, and financial markets to career paths and getting hired.

Online

6FigureJobs.com
www.6figurejobs.com
Online resource for connecting senior managers with employers and recruiters.

CareerSite
www.careersite.com
Job seekers can search for openings locally, regionally, or nationally. They can access detailed company information, get advice about managing a career or conducting a job search, and develop an online résumé.

MarketingJobs.com
www.marketingjobs.com
Provides job information on sales, marketing, advertising/PR, sales management, marketing management, and advertising/PR management.

Marketing Jobs/Sales Jobs
www.marketingjobs.com
Jobs in sales, marketing, PR, sales management, and marketing management; salary survey; and bookstore.

MarketingManager.com
www.marketingmanager.com
Employment Center with opportunities in sales and account management. Many of the industry's best-known employers regularly advertise their job openings here. Provides resources for both job seekers and employers. Now hosted and powered by Top Echelon.

SalesJobs.com
www.salesjobs.com
Affiliated with Recruit USA and IQ Post. Allows job seeker to search by base salary, total compensation, position, title, name of company, industry, location, or area code. More than 13,000 jobs listed, plus links to sites for meetings, trade shows, sales training, and portals.

Small Businesses
Print

The Complete Book of Small Business Management Forms, Dan Sitarz, Nova Pub. Co., Carbondale, IL, 2001
www.novapublishing.com
Quick reference containing more than 140 useful forms for managing small-business sales, accounting, inventory, administration, and much more. Each form is displayed on a whole page, fully explained by the comprehensive and easy-to-understand text, and also included on a CD, enabling anyone to personalize or predesign forms on their own computer. "Superb tool" for anyone starting up or operating small business of his/her own.

Small Business Sourcebook, 2005, Thomson Gale
www.gale.com
Guide to sources of information furnished by associations, consultants, educational programs, government agencies, franchisers, trade shows and venture-capital firms for 100 types of small businesses. Volume 1 profiles 224 specific small businesses (from accounting/tax preparation services to word-processing services), with each profile containing listings for up to 19 key sources of assistance (essentially a complete directory of sources for each business). This edition adds profiles of 30 new small businesses. Volume 2 provides additional information on general small-business resources for 39 topics, such as franchising, marketing, and management, and contains various sources of information and assistance available from state and federal agencies. SIC codes provided for all businesses profiled. Glossary of small-business terms explains buzzwords and phrases of contemporary business.

Sole Proprietorship: Small Business Start-up Kit, 2004, Nova Publications
www.novapublishing.com
Provides clear and easy-to-follow blueprint for setting up any type of business entity in any state. Authoritative, accurate, and up-to-date, each guide includes state-by-state appendices of relevant state law. Written in concise, straightforward, and understandable language. Includes legal, accounting, tax, and marketing forms; business plans; questionnaires; and clear instructions.

The Ultimate Small Business Marketing Directory: 1500 Great Marketing Tricks That Will Drive Your Business through the Roof, 2003, Entrepreneur Press, McGraw-Hill
www.mcgrawhill.com
Marketing tricks and secrets that top business and sales professionals use daily to devour competition, close more sales, win new customers, and keep them coming back. Developed for small-business owners looking for cost-effective, innovative, and time-tested ways to market their

businesses, products, and services. Chapters on research, planning, competition, customer service, advertising, direct marketing, networking, websites, and many other topics. Also provides hundreds of handy online resources, checklists, and sample forms.

Online
Starting Your Business from the Small Business Administration (SBA)
www.sba.gov/starting
Offers information on starting your own business, success series, FAQs, business plans, counseling help, special assistance, assets for sale, training, patents, and trademarks.

Summer Jobs and Internships
Print
Getting Your Ideal Internship: The WetFeet Insider Guide, 2004, Saleem Assaf and Rosanne Lurie
www.wetfeet.com
Learn how to find or create an ideal internship; structure an internship at a company that doesn't have a formal intern program; make cold calls to prospective summer employers; maximize chances of getting an offer for permanent work while working as an intern; and make yourself more attractive to future employers.

Summer Jobs and Opportunities for Teenagers, 2003, Lifeworks
Useful tools and tips, from figuring out what kind of job or opportunity you want to targeting and applying for a position and managing a paycheck.

Summer Jobs in Britain 2005, David Woodworth eds., Vacation Work Publications, UK
Lists more than 30,000 vacancies in England, Scotland, Wales, and Northern Ireland for Summer 2005, including paid jobs, voluntary work, and vacation traineeships providing on-the-job work experience relevant to a possible future career. Explains when and to whom to apply;

gives information on wages (up to $400 per week); when the work is available; covers what previous experience, if any, is required; if there are age limits; and whether accommodations are provided and at what cost.

Summer Jobs in the USA 2004–2005: More Than 55,000 Exciting and Fun Jobs for High School and College Students, Thomson's/ Peterson's staff
www.gale.com
Includes details on more than 55,000 summer jobs for high school and college students with nearly 800 employers in the U.S., Canada, and overseas. Facts and figures on salaries, type and number of open positions, benefits, preemployment training, and contact information.

Online

The Corporation for National Service
www.nationalservice.org
Provides opportunities for Americans of all ages and backgrounds to serve their communities and country through Senior Corps, AmeriCorps, and Learn and Serve America.

CoolWorks
www.coolworks.com
Find a seasonal job or career in some of the greatest places on earth. Get a summer job in Yellowstone, Yosemite, or another national park. Find a summer job as a camp counselor. Ski resorts, ranches, theme parks, tour companies and more are waiting for you.

Peace Corps
www.peacecorps.gov
Employment Center provides information on domestic and overseas vacancy announcements; headquarters, regional recruitment, and overseas opportunities; working at Peace Corps; how to apply; and vacancy status listing.

SnagAJob
www.snagajob.com
Click "Summer Job." Applicants enter their zip code to search and can browse a partial list of employers plus create profile on themselves.

Studentjobs.gov
www.studentjobs.gov
Sponsored by the U.S. Office of Personnel Management and U.S. Department of Education's Student Financial Assistance Office. Provides information on federal job opportunities, co-ops, internships, summer employment, Outstanding Scholars Program, volunteer opportunities, and plenty of temporary and permanent part- and full-time jobs.

Transportation (Shipping, Marine, Freight, Express Delivery, Supply Chain)
Print

Lloyd's, Informa UK Ltd.
www.lloydslist.com

Lloyd's Maritime Directory, 2000
Two-volume reference work covering shipping industry. Completely revised for Year 2000, it contains updated company and vessel details and more than 130 previously unclassified firms.

Lloyd's Shipping and Nautical Yearbook 2000
Offers updated directory of nautical schools, colleges, and maritime lawyers, as well as detailed country and general information sections providing wealth of useful facts and figures.

Moody's Transportation Manual
Covers financial and operating data on all major public and private air, rail, bus, trucking, vehicle leasing and rental, and shipping companies.

Plunkett's Transportation, Supply Chain & Logistics Industry Almanac (see previous listing for **Plunkett's**)

Plunkett's Transportation, Supply Chain & Logistics Industry Summary Report (see previous listing for **Plunkett's**)

Online

Consultant Directory
www.consultant-directory.com
Online directory has listings for transportation,

Wet Feet
www.wetfeet.com
Online summary of the transportation industry.

Jobs4Transportation
www.Jobs4Transportation.com
Jobs in customer service, logistics, warehousing, management, sales/marketing, and driving. Site has salary information, list of schools, and more. Free links to employment agencies, employers that post jobs online, career resources, and job banks serving the U.S.

Travel, Leisure and Hospitality (Including Hotels, Food Service, Travel Agents, Restaurants, Airlines)

Print

Careers in Focus: Travel and Hospitality, 2nd ed., 2002, Ferguson Publishing
www.fergpubco.com
Describes education, training, earnings, and outlook associated with 22 careers in the fields of travel and hospitality, including bellhop, bartender, flight attendant, hotel manager, pilot, resort worker, and tour guide.

Career Opportunities in Casinos and Casino Hotels, 2000, Shelly Field, Facts on File
www.factsonfile.com
Gives readers everything they need to know to start a career in the growing casino and gaming industry. Covers 100 specific jobs and provides an overview of the industry and extensive appendixes of professional organizations, schools, associations, unions, and casinos.

Opportunities in Culinary Careers, 2003, Mary Deirdre Donovan, VGM Career Horizons/ McGraw-Hill
books.mcgraw-hill.com

Inside scoop on culinary arts, and all essential aspects of a potential career, no matter how specialized. Comprehensive, up-to-date information, from latest training requirements to current salary statistics to the lowdown on life on the job. Apprenticeships, cooking schools, and certification programs. Detailed descriptions of job duties and responsibilities for a wide variety of positions, from pantry cook to dining room manager to executive chef.

Plunkett's Airline, Hotel & Travel Industry Almanac (see previous listing for **Plunkett's**)

Plunkett's Airline, Hotel & Travel Industry Summary Report (see previous listing for **Plunkett's**)

Working in Tourism: The UK, Europe & Beyond, Verite Reily Collins, Vacation Work Publications, 2004
Covers range of types of work available, including jobs to be found in ski and beach resorts, hotels and airlines, campsites, and sailing flotillas. Country-by-country guide covers more than 30 countries and describes the prospects for finding work there for both career tourism staff and seasonal workers. Also included is information on work permits, other regulations, and addresses of employment agencies and other specialist companies that can help you find work. Also features a directory of more than 300 placement agencies and travel companies.

Online

Hospitality Careers Online
www.hcareers.com
Search jobs by industry, position, management level, domestic and international locations, and keywords. Post résumés and create Job Detective, which sends E-mail whenever a new job is posted that matches the type of job for which you are looking.

Hospitality Net Virtual Job Exchange
www.hospitalitynet.org
Provides job information for hotels, restaurants, and food and beverage industry.

Hotel Online
www.hotel-online.com
Provides job information and online directory for the hospitality industry.

Resort Jobs
www.resortjobs.com
Features worldwide resort jobs with ski resorts, camps, national parks, cruise ships, restaurants, and hotels.

Veterans

Print

Military Advantage: Your Path to an Education and a Great Civilian Career, 2001, Lynn Vincent, Delmar Learning
www.delmarlearning.com
For those deciding to enter or preparing to leave the military, this shows how to capitalize on your service. The U.S. Armed Forces offer a unique opportunity to develop skills for success in today's job market.

Military-to-Civilian Career Transition Guide, 2004, Janet I. Farley, JIST Works
www.jist.com
worksheets and advice in this book help you compare job offers and point you in the right direction. After you land that job, you can use this book to help your adjustment to the civilian world of work.

Online

VeteranEmployment.com
www.veteranemployment.com
Largest online military website, run by Military.com, offering free resources to serve, connect, and inform 30 million Americans with military affinity, including active duty, reservists, guard members, retirees, veterans, family mem-

bers, defense workers, and those considering military careers.

VetJobs.com
www.vetjobs.com
Endorsed by Veterans of Foreign Wars and Veteran Service Organizations. Long list of resources, in addition to a job board.

Veterans Resource Advisor
www.dol.gov/vets
Helps veterans prepare to enter the job market. Includes information on broad range of topics, such as job-search tools and tips, employment openings, career assessment, education and training, and benefits and special services available to veterans.

Vocational/No Four-Year College Degree

Print

America's Top Jobs for People without a Four-Year Degree: Detailed Information on 190 Good Jobs in All Major Fields and Industries, 7th ed., 2004, Michael Farr
www.jist.com
Offers practical information for students who do not plan to attend college and/or who are looking for good-paying jobs that don't require a four-year degree. Includes The Quick Job Search, with job advice for some top jobs that don't require a four-year degree.

Vocational Careers Sourcebook, 5th ed., 2002, Thomson Gale
www.gale.com
Wide array of sources, including profiles of 139 vocational occupations, ranging from agricultural worker and assembler to welder and woodworker. Job descriptions, contact information, fully updated contact/order information, E-mail and URL addresses, electronic career resources, state occupational and professional licensing agencies, and employment-growth rankings and statistics.

Online
Vocational Information Center
www.khake.com

Vocational and technical careers; check out skills employers really want; find a trade school; research technical topics; and take a look at the current job market.

Volunteering

Online
CharityFocus
my.charityfocus.org

Volunteer-run 501(c)(3) nonprofit organization that empowers nonprofits with web-based technological solutions, building websites, providing technical assistance, and engaging in wide variety of projects designed to benefit nonprofit organizations dedicated to public service. CharityFocus volunteers help nonprofits to better serve their beneficiaries. By working together and sharing a common vision of service, volunteers of Charity-Focus create a mechanism through which they and others can act in the service of others.

Project America Home Page
project.org

Nonprofit organization to promote community involvement. Volunteers experience challenging and fun projects in 21 countries. Conversations, care work, teaching, building, and more, open to all ages.

Teach for America
www.teachforamerica.org

National corps of college graduates from all academic majors and backgrounds who commit two years to teach in urban and rural public schools in need.

Volunteer Jobs
www.careers.org

Links to volunteer job sites.

VolunteerMatch
www.volunteermatch.org

Nonprofit online service that helps interested volunteers get involved with community service organizations throughout U.S.

Wholesaling and Distributing/Importing and Exporting

Print

American Wholesalers and Distributors Directory, 14th ed., Sept. 2005, Thomson Gale
www.gale.com

Discover more than 27,000 large and small wholesalers and distributors throughout the U.S and Puerto Rico. Name and address of the organization, fax number, SIC code, principal product lines, total number of employees, estimated annual sales volume, and principal officers. Access information four easy ways: by broad subject terms derived from each company's principal product line; by SIC index; by state and city (geographic index); and by company name (alphabetic index).

Career Opportunities in the Retail and Wholesale Industry, Shelly Field Groveman, Facts on File, 2001
www.factsonfile.com

Profiles more than 70 careers available in retail and sales settings. Broken down into four key sections: Malls and Shopping Centers; Stores, Shops, and Boutiques; Department Stores; and Automobile Sales. Each entry provides a job overview and description of a likely career path. Jobs profiled include property manager, mall marketing director, event coordinator, leasing director, district manager, buyer, merchandiser, billing manager, wholesale sales representative, manufacturer's representative, sales trainer, sales supervisor, purchasing agent, personal shopper, department store manager, loss-prevention manager, payroll specialist, and automobile sales manager.

Directory of United States Exporters, and Directory of United States Importers (set), 2004, Commonwealth Business Media
www.cbizmedia.com
Two annual publications that provide logistics professionals with active confirmed leads for more than 60,000 U.S. companies involved in world trade. Each volume is a cross-referencing index of company listings by geographical location, alphabetical name, and products. Every listing provides a detailed picture of company's trade activity, including U.S. ports of entry, countries of origin, SIC codes, number of shipments, product descriptions, executive personnel, and extensive contact information. Available separately or as a two-volume set. Also available as CD-ROMs that contain all of the information from print publications plus downloadable E-mail addresses and more.

U. S. Export-Import and Business Directory: Ultimate Directory for Conducting Export-Import Operations in the Country. Largest Exporters and Importers, Strategic Government and Business Contacts, Selected Export-Import Regulations and More, International Business Publications, 2000

World Business Directory, 11th ed., 2002, **Thomson Gale**
www.gale.com
Information on nearly 136,000 companies active in international trade. Profiles global marketplace with comprehensive data on market leaders, small- and medium-sized firms, and local niche companies in more than 180 countries. Includes 25,000+ Latin American companies, 10,000+ top U.S. companies, 50,000+ European and U.K. companies, and nearly 17,000 Asian companies.

Online

Directory of U.S. Importers & Exporters, Dialog OnDisc, Dialog
www.dialog.com
Combines data from two print directories, Directory of United States Importers and Directory of United States Exporters, plus summary data from the PIERS (Port Import Export Reporting Service). Databases and primary research all on one CD. This combination of data is not found in any other single source and is not available online. Identifies top U. S. companies involved in importing or exporting goods from more than 55,000 U.S. exporters and importers. All 50 states and Puerto Rico are included. Target export and import managers for direct-mail or telemarketing campaigns. Internet access via one of Dialog's @Site servers. Standalone/laptop—delivered on CD/DVD (uses DOS/MAC/WIN software).

Federation of International Trade Associations
www.fita.org
International Trade/Import-Export Portal is source for trade leads, news, events, and links to 7,000 international trade-related websites. Also has Job Bank.

Retail/Wholesale Jobs
www.salary.com
Lists a wide range of various positions.

Section III: International Directories

Note: For North American Industry Classification System (NAICS), official U.S. Census Bureau listing of all NAICS, see **www.census.gov/epcd/naics02/**. In the section, Professions Industries/Interests many of the resources contain information on international companies and job sources. See this listing for additional information. The Science, Industry, and Business Library of the New York Public Library contains an extensive listing of international directories. The list is too specific and too long to include here. For details, see **www.nypl.org**

Print Directories

Asia's 7500 Largest Companies, 2004, ELC International
www.bernan.com
Available with or without a CD-ROM.

Craighead's International Business, Travel and Relocation Guide to 84 Countries, 12th ed., 2004, Craighead Publications
Covers 84 countries; designed specifically to meet the needs of individuals who require in-depth information about doing business, living, and working in countries most important to international business. Provides data necessary to understand and evaluate political, economic, and business environment and everyday living conditions of foreign destinations.

Directory of American Firms Operating in Foreign Countries, 17th ed., 2003, Uniworld Business Publications
www.uniworldbp.com
Contains more than 3,600 U.S. firms with nearly 36,500 branches, subsidiaries, and affiliates in 187 countries. Available in hard cover, soft cover, and on CD-ROM. Three volumes encompassing alphabetical lists of U.S. firms with operations abroad. Each entry contains the company's U.S. address, phone/fax, NAICS and description of principal product/service, and lists the foreign countries in which it has a branch, subsidiary, or affiliate. Some key personnel are noted, when provided. Also contains listings by country of U.S. firms' foreign operations. Each country listing includes, alphabetically, name of U.S. parent firm, address, phone, fax, website address, and name and address of its branch, subsidiary, or affiliates in that country.

Directory of Foreign Firms Operating in the United States, 2004, Uniworld Business Publications
www.uniworldbp.com
Information on foreign firms with branches, subsidiaries, or affiliates in the U.S. The foreign companies listed have a substantial investment in American operations, being a wholly or partially owned subsidiary or affiliate, or having a branch in the U.S. Three parts: Part I: Country of American Affiliates; Part II: Foreign Firms; and Part III: American Subsidiaries.

Directory of Websites for International Jobs: The Click and Easy Guide (Click & Easy Series), 2004, Ron and Caryl Krannich, Impact Publications
www.impactpublications.com
Lists 600+ websites for anyone seeking an overseas job. Packed with practical information on the how, who, and where of finding the perfect overseas job. Includes contact information on key steps in conducting an effective job search: search engines; virtual networking communities; major employment websites; international executive-search firms; country employment websites; publishers; nonprofit organizations; educational groups; federal government agencies; international organizations; contracting and consulting firms; and teaching abroad.

Encyclopedia of Associations: International Organizations, 2004, Thomson Gale
www.galegroup.com
This three-volume reference covers multinational and national membership organizations, including U.S.-based organizations with a binational or multinational membership. Provides names of directors, executive officers, or other personal contacts; phone, fax, telex, E-mail, websites, and bulletin boards; group's history, governance, staff, membership, budget, and affiliations; goals and activities of international organization, including research, awards, certification, education, lobbying, and other important activities; and publication and convention information. Entries are arranged in general subject chapters. Geographic, executive, and keyword indexes help research.

Encyclopedia of Global Industries, 3rd ed., 2002, Thomson Gale
www.gale.com
Chronicles the history, development, and current status of 115 of the world's most lucrative and high-profile industries. Provides comprehensive, international coverage organized by industry. Additional features include an alphabetical table of contents; contents organized by industry; gen-

eral and geographic indexes; harmonized system/SIC conversion index; and industry index.

Europe's 15,000 Largest Companies, 2004, ELC International, Oxford, UK (publisher), Dun & Bradstreet, Parsippany, NJ (U.S. distributor). Contains a guide to SIC activity codes by industry. Ranks companies by sales for each SIC category and provides country, headquarters, financial data, and year established. Trade index shows country in which company pays land. Alphabetical index has address, phone, fax, website, and name of company's most senior executive. Also offered with a CD-ROM.

European Marketing Data and Statistics, 2004, Euromonitor
www.euromonitor
Compendium of statistical information on the countries of Western and Eastern Europe. Provides detailed and up-to-date statistical information relevant to international marketing planning. Data are presented in spreadsheet format and a number of extrapolated tables have been included, together with graphs, marketing maps, and diagrams. There is also information on smaller European nations and principalities.

F&S Index-Europe, 2005 edition, Thomson Gale
www.gale.com

F&S Index-International, 2005 edition, Thomson Gale
www.gale.com
Compilation of company, product, and industry information from financial publications, business-oriented newspapers, trade magazines, and special reports. Contains valuable information on corporate acquisitions and mergers, new products, technological developments, and social and political factors affecting business. Good for competitive product analysis, market and demographic research, and sales strategies.

Hoover's Handbook of World Business, 2004, Hoover's Business Press
www.hooversbooks.com
In-depth profiles of 300 of most influential public, private, and state-owned firms from Canada, Europe, and Japan, as well as companies from such countries with fast-growing economies as China, India, and Taiwan. Hoover's also publishes **Brazil Company Handbook** and **Japan Company Handbook**.

International Directory of Business Biographies, 2004, St. James Press, Thomson Gale
www.gale.com
Provides current information for business leaders worldwide. Biographical essays on more than 600 individuals, nearly half of whom are outside the U.S.

International Directory of Company Histories, St. James Press, Thomson Gale
www.gale.com, annual
Detailed information on the development of the world's 4,550 largest and most influential companies. Entries provide information on founders; expansions and losses; labor/management actions; NAIC codes; key dates; ticker symbol; principal subsidiaries, divisions, operating units, and competitors; and other significant milestones, all with statistics, dates, and names of key players. Volumes 1-6 are organized alphabetically by major industries; volume 7 and subsequent volumes are arranged alphabetically by company name within each volume. Each volume includes a cumulative index to companies and personal names.

International Job Finder: Where the Jobs Are Worldwide, 2002, Daniel Lauber, SCB Distributors
www.scbdistributors.com
For students, recent graduates, and others attracted by work opportunities in foreign countries. Claims that Internet is more effective for obtaining international jobs than domestic ones. Advantages discussed include searching data-

bases of jobs to fit your employment and location criteria, placing your name in job banks, signing on for E-mail notification, speeding résumé transmission, using news groups for networking opportunities, and obtaining current country information. Readers are also warned to beware of potential pitfalls and gives advice on how to recognize and avoid scams. Some 1,200 online and print resources are organized into worldwide gateways and eight geographic regions.

International Jobs: Where They Are and How to Get Them, 6th ed., 2003, Nina Segal and Eric Kocher, Basic Books
www.basicbooks.com
Covers federal government, business, communications, banking, nonprofit organizations and foundations, and multinational organizations such as the United Nations.

Marketing Information Sourcebooks

Euromonitor International
www.euromonitor.com

Asia-Pacific, 2003

European, 2003

Latin America, 2003
Provides full contact details for a wide variety of business information providers, including trade associations, national statistics offices, government departments, business information libraries, trade and business journals, and business websites. Offers an at-a-glance guide to information publishers across nearly 100 market sectors.

Major Companies series, Graham & Whiteside
www.gale.com
Up-to-date volumes containing thousands of companies, institutions, etc., along with contact information.

Major Companies of Africa South of the Sahara, 2005, Graham & Whiteside
www.gale.com
More than 1,700 major companies in South Africa are covered, plus 4,500 businesses in non-Arab countries south of the Sahara.

Major Companies of the Arab World, 2004
Provides information on more than 7,800 of the largest companies in Abu Dhabi, Ajman, Algeria, Bahrain, Dubai, Egypt, Fujairah, Gaza/West Bank, Iraq, Jordan, Kuwait, Lebanon, Libya, Mauritania, Morocco, Oman, Qatar, Ras Al Kaimah, Saudi Arabia, Sharjah, Somalia, Sudan, Syria, Tunisia, Um Al Quwain, and Yemen. Also includes names of more than 38,000 senior executives.

Major Companies of Central & Eastern Europe and the CIS 2004, C. Tapster, ed.
Covering 27 countries from Albania to Yugoslavia, this directory details leading trade organizations, privatized companies, manufacturers, financial institutions, and government-related business organizations, including new EC member states for 2004. Combining the research expertise of both Graham & Whiteside and Dun & Bradstreet, this joint publication has been completely revised to include more than 9,500 of the most important business organizations in Central and Eastern Europe and former Soviet Republics. The number of named contacts in the directory has been increased by more than 10,000 to 38,000 since the last edition. Directory has essential facts and contacts, including address, phone, and fax numbers; E-mail and web addresses, plus listings of company's activities, parents, subsidiaries, and agents; brands and trademarks; and financial information for previous two years.

Major Companies of Europe, 24th ed.
Provides current and comprehensive information on more than 24,000 of Europe's largest companies, including names of 194,000 senior executives. Entries typically include company name; address; phone and fax numbers; E-mail and web addresses; names of senior management and board members; description of business activities; brand names and trademarks; subsidiaries and affiliates; number of employees; financial information for last two years; principal shareholders; and private/public status.

Other titles in this series:
Major Companies of the Far East and Australasia

Major Companies of Latin America and the Caribbean

Major Companies of South West Asia

Major Employers of Europe, 6th ed., 2005, Graham & Whiteside, annual
www.gale.com
Useful reference for job seekers, recruitment agencies, and all those seeking to do business with Europe's largest employers. Provides valuable summary information, identifying top 10,000 companies in Europe by number of employees. Among information provided for each company is company name and address; phone, fax, and E-mail; website URL; names of managing director and personnel/human resources director; description of business activities; brand names and trademarks; subsidiaries and associates; number of employees; financial information for last two years; principal shareholders; and date of establishment. Two indexes to company data: by country and by business activity.

Major Market Share Companies
www.euromonitor.com
Published by Euromonitor International, several volumes are kept current:
Major Market Share Companies: Americas, 2004
Major Market Share Companies: Asia-Pacific, 2004
Major Market Share Companies: Eastern Europe, Middle East and Africa, 2004
Major Market Share Companies: Western Europe, 2004
Each volume profiles leading consumer-brand-owning companies operating in its area. Provides full details for every company and allows you to identify brands they own, their market-share performance, and their ultimate holding company. Product areas covered are drinks, food, and household and personal-care products. Fully indexed by country, sector, and company name, with information needed to contact top players.

Principal International Business, Dun and Bradstreet's
www.dnb.com
This D&B WorldBase File uncovers business opportunities abroad with key information on up to 500,000 companies outside of the U.S. Multi-element search capabilities enable quick and easy access to businesses, allowing targeted lead generation. Users can locate employment opportunities abroad and identify key executives in the international business world. Available in print and on CD-ROMs.

Trade Associations and Professional Bodies of the Continental European Union, 3rd ed., 2004, Graham & Whiteside
www.gale.com
Provides information on more than 3,600 trade associations and professional bodies in continental Europe. Typical entries include name; address; phone and fax numbers; E-mail and website addresses; number of members; year founded; number of staff; contact name; fee; library type; details of meetings and conventions; and description of activities.

Trade Shows Worldwide, 22nd ed., 2005, Thomson Gale
www.gale.com
Contains information needed by every segment of the trade show industry. With its global perspective and clearly organized format, it gives industry professionals, city planners, information professionals, and business executives quick access to information vital for success and timely decision making.

Who's Who in International Organizations: A Biographical Encyclopedia of More Than 13,000 Leading Personalities, 4th ed., 2002, K.G. Saur
This three-volume reference provides concise biographical and contact data for approximately 14,000 individuals from more than 7,000 organi-

zations worldwide. Renowned people in science and technology, social sciences, medicine, politics, religion, communications, industry, finance, trade unions, education-every field of human endeavor.

World Directory of Trade and Business Associations, 2002, Euromonitor International
www.euromonitor.com
Profiles trade and business associations in many countries and market sectors. Dozens of categories of business and trade organizations are covered. Provides full contact details for trade and business associations worldwide, as well as publication, membership, and activity details. Fully indexed.

Work Abroad: The Complete Guide to Finding a Job Overseas, Transitions Abroad Publishing, 2002
www.transitionsabroad.com
Said to be the first comprehensive guide to all aspects of international work, including work permits, planning out an international career, short-term jobs, teaching English, volunteer opportunities, international internships, K-12 and university teaching, starting your own business, and much more. For anyone who wants to find a job overseas.

Online Directories

Business International & Company ProFiles, Thomson Gale
www.gale.com
Business International & Company ProFiles integrates information from *Business ASAP* and full text of *PR Newswire* releases with 200,000 combined directory listings, including Graham & Whiteside international company directories. By subscription.

The Global Yellow Pages
www.globalyp.com
Links to phone directories from Argentina, Australia, Austria, Belgium, Bermuda, Canada, Chile, China, Colombia, Denmark, Europe, Finland, France, Germany, Holland, Indonesia, Ireland,

Israel, Italy, Japan, Latvia, Luxembourg, Malaysia, Mexico, New Zealand, Norway, Pakistan, Poland, Romania, Russia, Singapore, Slovenia, South Africa, South America, Spain, Sweden, Switzerland, Turkey, the United Kingdom, and the United States.

LexisNexis Corporate Affiliations, compiled by the LexisNexis Group
www.corporateaffiliations.com
Provides current accurate corporate linkage information on nearly 200,000 of the most prominent global public and private parent companies and their affiliates, subsidiaries, and divisions, down to seventh level of corporate linkage.

World Trade and Industrial Enterprise
www.worlddirectory.com
Digital information network permits searches of world online for different types of businesses. Listings are limited; e.g., for Europe, fewer than 1,000 companies are included.

Worldclass Supersite
web.idirect.com
Offers free access and step-by-step commentary for 1,025 top business sites from 95 countries, chosen based on usefulness to world commerce, timeliness, ease of use, and presentation. Seven sections, including Reference (Market Guides, Regional Institutions, U.S. Government Megasites), Money (World & U.S. Stocks, Stocks by Country, Foreign Investment), and Networking (Gathering Places, Bilateral Organizations, Leads and Tenders). This section links to a database of 30,000 world business exhibitions and has a Forums page, with 35 of the most active web-based forum, chat, trade-lead bulletin board, Q&A, and discussion screens with diverse areas of focus.

Yearbook of International Organizations, 2002/3, K. G. Saur
www.saur.de
UIA has selected the most important 31,086 organizations from its database of current and previous organizations. Provides profiles of 5,546

intergovernmental and 25,540 international non-governmental organizations active in nearly 300 countries and territories. Organization descriptions listed in Volume 1 are numbered sequentially to facilitate quick and easy cross-referencing from other volumes. Users can refer to Volumes 2 and 3 to locate organizations by region or subject, respectively; comprehensive indexes are included.

International Job Boards

JobPilot AG
www.jobpilot.net
Includes Austria, Belgium, the Czech Republic, France, Germany, Hungary, Italy, the Netherlands, Poland, Switzerland, and the United Kingdom.

JobsAbroad.com
www.jobsabroad.com
Appeals to college students and recent graduates who want to work and study abroad. Includes information on internships, language schools, volunteering and teaching abroad, and travel.

Monster International
international.monster.com
Includes Australia, Belgium, Canada, Denmark, Spain, France, Hong Kong, Ireland, India, Italy, the Netherlands, New Zealand, Singapore, and United Kingdom.

Overseasjobs.com
www.overseasjobs.com
Provides international job listings and links to other career resources.

The
Five
O'Clock
Club

PART SIX

What Is
The Five O'Clock Club?

AMERICA'S PREMIER CAREER-COACHING NETWORK

The
Five
O'Clock
Club

How to Join the Club

The Five O'Clock Club: America's Premier Career-Coaching and Outplacement Service

One organization with a long record of success in helping people find jobs is The Five O'Clock Club.

Fortune

- Job-Search Strategy Groups
- Private Coaching
- Books and Audio CDs
- Membership Information
- When Your Employer Pays

THERE *IS* A FIVE O'CLOCK CLUB NEAR YOU!

For more information on becoming a member, please fill out the Membership Application Form in this book, sign up on the web at: www.fiveoclockclub.com, or call: **1-800-575-3587** (or **212-286-4500** in New York)

The Five O'Clock Club Search Process

The Five O'Clock Club process, as outlined in *The Five O'Clock Club* books, is a targeted, strategic approach to career development and job search. Five O'Clock Club members become proficient at skills that prove invaluable during their *entire working lives.*

Career Management

We train our members to *manage their careers* and always look ahead to their next job search. Research shows that an average worker spends only four years in a job—and will have 12 jobs in as many as 5 career fields—during his or her working life.

Getting Jobs . . . Faster

Five O'Clock Club members find *better jobs, faster.* The average professional, manager, or executive Five O'Clock Club member who regularly attends weekly sessions finds a job by his or her 10th session. Even the discouraged, long-term job searcher can find immediate help.

The keystone to The Five O'Clock Club process is teaching our members an understanding of the entire hiring process. A first interview is primarily a time for exchanging critical information. The real work starts *after* the interview. We teach our members *how to turn job interviews into offers* and to negotiate the best possible employment package.

Setting Targets

The Five O'Clock Club is action oriented. *We'll help you decide what you should do this very next week to move your search along.* By their third session, our members have set definite job targets by industry or company size, position, and geographic area and are out in the field gathering information and making contacts that will lead to interviews with hiring managers.

Our approach evolves with the changing job market. We're able to synthesize information from hundreds of Five O'Clock Club members and come up with new approaches for our members. For example, we now discuss temporary placement for executives, how to use voice mail and the Internet, and how to network when doors are slamming shut all over town.

The Five O'Clock Club Strategy Program

The Five O'Clock Club meeting is a carefully planned *job-search strategy program.* We provide members with the tools and tricks necessary to get a good job fast—even in a tight market. Networking and emotional support are also included in the meeting.

Participate in 10 *consecutive* small-group strategy sessions to enable your group and career coach to get to know you and to develop momentum in your search.

Weekly Presentations via Audio CDs

Prior to each week's teleconference, listen to the assigned audio presentation covering part of The Five O'Clock Club methodology. These are scheduled on a rotating basis so you may join the Club at any time. (In selected cities, presentations are given in person rather than via audio CDs.)

Small-Group Strategy Sessions

During the first few minutes of the teleconference, your small group discusses the topic of the week and hears from people who have landed jobs. Then you have the chance to get feedback and advice on your own search strategy, listen to and learn from others, and build your network. All groups are led by trained career coaches with years of experience. The small group is generally no more than six to eight people, so everyone gets the chance to speak up.

Let us consider how we may spur one another on toward love and good deeds. Let us not give up meeting together, as some are in the habit of doing, but let us encourage one another.

Hebrews 10:24–25

Private Coaching

You may meet with your small-group coach—or another coach—for private coaching by phone or in person. A coach helps you develop a career path, solve current job problems, prepare your résumé, or guide your search.

Many members develop long-term relationships with their coaches to get advice throughout their careers. If you are paying for the coaching yourself (as opposed to having your employer pay), please pay the coach directly (charges vary from $100 to $175 per hour). **Private coaching is *not* included in The Five O'Clock Club seminar or membership fee.** For coach matching, see our website or call **1-800-575-3587** (or **212-286-4500** in New York).

From the Club History, Written in the 1890s

At The Five O'Clock Club, [people] of all shades of political belief—as might be said of all trades and creeds—have met together. . . . The variety continues almost to a monotony. . . . [The Club's] good fellowship and geniality—not to say hospitality—has reached them all.

It has been remarked of clubs that they serve to level rank. If that were possible in this country, it would probably be true, if leveling rank means the appreciation of people of equal abilities as equals; but in The Five O'Clock Club it has been a most gratifying and noteworthy fact that no lines have ever been drawn save those which are essential to the honor and good name of any association. Strangers are invited by the club or by any members, [as gentlepeople], irrespective of aristocracy, plutocracy or occupation, and are so treated always. Nor does the thought of a [person's] social position ever enter into the meetings. People of wealth and people of moderate means sit side by side, finding in each other much to praise and admire and little to justify snarlishness or adverse criticism. People meet as people—not as the representatives of a set—and having so met, dwell not in worlds of envy or distrust, but in union and collegiality, forming kindly thoughts of each other in their heart of hearts.

In its methods, The Five O'Clock Club is plain, easy-going and unconventional. It has its "isms" and some peculiarities of procedure, but simplicity characterizes them all. The sense of propriety, rather than rules of order, governs its meetings, and that informality which carries with it sincerity of motive and spontaneity of effort, prevails within it. Its very name indicates informality, and, indeed, one of the reasons said to have induced its adoption was the fact that members or guests need not don their dress suits to attend the meetings, if they so desired. This informality, however, must be distinguished from the informality of Bohemianism. For The Five O'Clock Club, informality, above convenience, means sobriety, refinement of thought and speech, good breeding and good order. To this sort of informality much of its success is due.

Fortune, The New York Times, Black Enterprise, Business Week, NPR, CNBC, and ABC-TV are some of the places you've seen, heard, or read about us.

The Schedule

See our website for the specific dates for each topic. All groups use a similar schedule in each time zone.

Fee: $49 annual membership (includes Beginners Kit, subscription to *The Five O'Clock News,* and access to the Members Only section of our website), **plus** session fees based on member's income (price for the Insider Program includes audio-CD lectures, which retails for $150).

Reservations required for first session. Unused sessions are transferable to anyone you choose or can be donated to members attending more than 16 sessions who are having financial difficulty.

The Five O'Clock Club's programs are geared to recent graduates, professionals, managers, and executives from a wide variety of industries and professions. Most earn from $30,000 to $400,000 per year. Half the members are employed; half are unemployed. *You will be in a group of your peers.*

To register, please fill out form on the web (at www.fiveoclockclub.com) or call 1-800-575-3587 (or 212-286-4500 in New York).

Lecture Presentation Schedule

- History of The 5OCC
- The 5OCC Approach to Job Search
- Developing New Targets for Your Search
- Two-Minute Pitch: Keystone of Your Search
- Using Research and Internet for Your Search

- The Keys to Effective Networking
- Getting the Most Out of Your Contacts
- Getting Interviews: Direct/Targeted Mail
- Beat the Odds When Using Search Firms and Ads
- Developing New Momentum in Your Search
- The 5OCC Approach to Interviewing
- Advanced Interviewing Techniques
- How to Handle Difficult Interview Questions
- How to Turn Job Interviews into Offers
- Four-Step Salary-Negotiation Method
- Successful Job Hunter's Report

All groups run continuously. Dates are posted on our website. The textbooks used by all members of The Five O'Clock Club may be ordered on our website or purchased at major bookstores.

The original Five O'Clock Club was formed in Philadelphia in 1883. It was made up of the leaders of the day who shared their experiences "in a spirit of fellowship and good humor."

The
Five
O'Clock
Club

Questions You May Have about the Weekly Job-Search Strategy Group

Job hunters are not always the best judges of what they need during a search. For example, most are interested in lectures on answering ads on the Internet or working with search firms. We cover those topics, but strategically they are relatively unimportant in an effective job search.

At The Five O'Clock Club, you get the information you really need in your search—*such as how to target more effectively, how to get more interviews, and how to turn job interviews into offers.*

What's more, you will work in a small group with the best coaches in the business. In these strategy sessions, your group will help you decide what to do, this week and every week, to move your search along. You will learn by being coached and by coaching others in your group.

We find ourselves not independently of other people and institutions but through them. We never get to the bottom of our selves on our own. We discover who we are face to face and side by side with others in work, love, and learning.

Robert N. Bellah, et al., *Habits of the Heart*

Here are a few other points:

- For best results, attend on a regular basis. Your group gets to know you and will coach you to eliminate whatever you may be doing wrong— or refine what you are doing right.
- The Five O'Clock Club is a members-only organization. To get started in the small-group teleconference sessions, you must purchase a minimum of 10 sessions.

- The teleconference sessions include the set of 16 audio-CD presentations on Five O'Clock Club methodology. In-person groups do not include CDs.
- After that, you may purchase blocks of 5 or 10 sessions.
- We sell multiple sessions to make administration easier.
- If you miss a session, you may make it up any time. You may even transfer unused time to a friend.
- Although many people find jobs quickly (even people who have been unemployed a long time), others have more difficult searches. Plan to be in it for the long haul and you'll do better.

Carefully read all of the material in this section. It will help you decide whether or not to attend.

- The first week, pay attention to the strategies used by the others in your group. Soak up all the information you can.
- Read the books before you come in the second week. They will help you move your search along.

To register:

1. Read this section and fill out the application.
2. After you become a member and get your Beginners Kit, call to reserve a space for the first time you attend.

To assign you to a career coach, we need to know:

- your current (or last) field or industry,
- the kind of job you would like next (if you know), and
- your desired salary range in general terms.

For private coaching, we suggest you attend the small group and ask to see your group leader—to give you continuity.

The Five O'Clock Club is plain, easy-going and unconventional. . . . Members or guests need not don their dress suits to attend the meetings.

From the Club History, written in the 1890s

What Happens at the Meetings?

Each week, job searchers from various industries and professions meet in small groups. The groups specialize in professionals, managers, executives, or recent college graduates. Usually, half are employed and half are unemployed.

The weekly program is in two parts. First, there is a lecture on some aspect of The Five O'Clock Club methodology. Then, job hunters meet in small groups headed by senior full-time professional career coaches.

The first week, get the textbooks, listen to the lecture, and get assigned to your small group. During your first session, *listen* to the others in your group. You learn a lot by listening to how your peers are strategizing *their* searches.

By the second week, you will have read the materials. Now we can start to work on *your* search strategy and help *you* decide what to do next to move your search along. For example, we'll help you figure out how to get more interviews in your target area or how to turn interviews into job offers.

In the third week, you will see major progress made by other members of your group and you may notice major progress in your own search as well.

By the third or fourth week, most members are conducting full and effective searches. Over the remaining weeks, you will tend to keep up a full search rather than go after only one or two leads. You will regularly aim to have 6 to 10 things *in the works* at all times. These will generally be in specific target areas you have identified, will keep your search on target, and will increase your chances of getting multiple job offers from which to choose.

Those who stick with the process find it works.

Some people prefer to just listen for a few weeks before they start their job search and that's okay, too.

How Much Does It Cost?

It is against the policy of The Five O'Clock Club to charge individuals heavy up-front fees. Our competitors charge $4,000 to $6,000 or more, up front. Our average fee is $360 for 10 sessions (which includes audio CDs of 16 presentations for those in the teleconference program). Those in the $100,000+ range pay an average of $540 for 10 sessions. For administrative reasons, we charge for 5 or 10 additional sessions at a time.

You must have the books so you can begin studying them before the second session. (You can purchase them on our website or at major bookstores.) If you don't do the homework, you will tend to waste the time of others in the group by asking questions covered in the texts.

Is the Small Group Right for Me?

The Five O'Clock Club process is for you if:

- You are truly interested in job hunting.
- You have *some* idea of the kind of job you want.
- You are a professional, manager, or executive—or want to be.
- You want to participate in a group process on a regular basis.

- You realize that finding or changing jobs and careers is hard work, but you are absolutely willing and able to do it.

If you have no idea about the kind of job you want next, you may attend one or two group sessions to start. *Then* see a *coach privately* for one or two sessions, develop tentative job targets, and return to the group. You may work with your small-group coach or contact us through our website or by calling **1-800-575-3587** (or **212-286-4500** in New York) for referral to another coach.

How Long Will It Take Me to Get a Job?

Although our members tend to be from fields or industries where they expect to have difficult searches, *the average person who attends regularly finds a new position within 10 sessions.* Some take less time and others take more.

One thing we know for sure: **Research shows that those who get *regular* coaching during their searches get jobs faster and at higher rates of pay than those who search on their own or simply take a course.** This makes sense. If a person comes only when they think they have a problem, they are usually wrong. They probably had a problem a few weeks ago but didn't realize it. Or the problem may be different from the one they thought they had. Those who come regularly benefit from the observations others make about their searches. Problems are solved before they become severe or are prevented altogether.

Those who attend regularly also learn a lot by paying attention and helping others in the group. This *secondhand* learning can shorten your search by weeks. When you hear the problems of others who are ahead of you in the search, you can avoid them completely. People in your group will come to know you and will point out subtleties you may not have noticed that interviewers will never tell you.

Will I Be with Others from My Field/Industry?

Probably, but it's not that important. If you are a salesperson, for example, would you want to be with seven other salespeople? Probably not. You will learn a lot and have a much more creative search if you are in a group of people who are in your general salary range but not exactly like you. Our clients are from virtually every field and industry. The *process* is what will help you.

We've been doing this since 1978 and understand your needs. That's why the mix we provide is the best you can get.

Career Coaching Firms Charge $4,000–$6,000 Up Front. How Can You Charge Such a Small Fee?

1. We have no advertising costs, because 90 percent of those who attend have been referred by other members.

   A hefty up-front fee would bind you to us, but we have been more successful by treating people ethically and having them pretty much *pay as they go.*

   We need a certain number of people to cover expenses. When lots of people get jobs quickly and leave us, we could go into the red. But as long as members refer others, we will continue to provide this service at a fair price.

2. We focus strictly on *job-search strategy,* and encourage our clients to attend free support groups if they need emotional support. We focus on getting *jobs,* which reduces the time clients spend with us and the amount they pay.

3. We attract the best coaches, and our clients make more progress per session than they would elsewhere, which also reduces their costs.

4. We have expert administrators and a sophisticated computer system that reduces our overhead and increases our ability to track your progress.

May I Change Coaches?

Yes. Great care is taken in assigning you to your initial coach. However, if you want to change once for any reason, you may do it. We don't encourage group hopping: It is better for you to stick with a group so that everyone gets to know you. On the other hand, we want you to feel comfortable. So if you tell us you prefer a different group, you will be transferred immediately.

What If I Have a Quick Question Outside of the Group Session?

Some people prefer to see their group coach privately. Others prefer to meet with a different coach to get another point of view. Whatever you decide, remember that the group fee does *not* cover coaching time outside the group session. Therefore, if you wanted to speak with a coach between sessions—even for *quick questions*—you would normally meet with the coach first for a private session so he or she can get to know you better. *Easy, quick questions* are usually more complicated than they appear. After your first private session, some coaches will allow you to pay in advance for one hour of coaching time, which you can then use for quick questions by phone (usually a 15-minute minimum is charged). Since each coach has an individual way of operating, find out how the coach arranges these things.

What If I Want to Start My Own Business?

The process of becoming a consultant is essentially the same as job hunting and lots of consultants attend Five O'Clock Club meetings. However, if you want to buy a franchise or existing business or start a growth business, you should see a private coach.

How Can I Be Sure That The Five O'Clock Club Small-Group Sessions Will Be Right for Me?

Before you actually participate in any of the small-group sessions, you can get an idea of the quality of our service by listening to all 16 audio CDs that you purchased. If you are dissatisfied with the CDs for any reason, return the package within 30 days for a full refund.

Whatever you decide, just remember: *It has been proven that those who receive regular help during their searches get jobs faster and at higher rates of pay than those who search on their own or simply attend a course.* If you get a job just one or two weeks faster because of this program, it will have more than paid for itself. And you may *transfer unused sessions to anyone you choose.* However, the person you choose must be or become a member.

The
Five
O'Clock
Club

When Your Employer Pays

*D*oes your employer care about you and others whom they ask to leave the organization? If so, ask them to consider The Five O'Clock Club for your outplacement help. The Five O'Clock Club puts you and your job search first, offering a career-coaching program of the highest quality at the lowest possible price to your employer.

Over 25 Years of Research

The Five O'Clock Club was started in 1978 as a research-based organization. Job hunters tried various techniques and reported their results back to the group. We developed a variety of guidelines so job hunters could choose the techniques best for them.

The methodology was tested and refined on professionals, managers, and executives (and those aspiring to be) from all occupations. Annual salaries ranged from $30,000 to $400,000; 50 percent were employed and 50 percent were unemployed.

Since its beginning, The Five O'Clock Club has tracked trends. Over time, our advice has changed as the job market has changed. What worked in the past is insufficient for today's job market. Today's Five O'Clock Club promotes all our relevant original strategies—and so much more.

As an employee-advocacy organization, The Five O'Clock Club focuses on providing the services and information that the job hunter needs most.

Get the Help You Need Most: 100 Percent Coaching

There's a myth in outplacement circles that a terminated employee just needs a desk, a phone, and minimal career coaching. **Our experience clearly shows that downsized workers need qualified, reliable coaching more than anything else.**

Most traditional outplacement packages last only 3 months. The average executive gets office space and only 5 hours of career coaching during this time. Yet the service job hunters need most is the career coaching itself—not a desk and a phone.

Most professionals, managers, and executives are right in the thick of negotiations with prospective employers at the 3-month mark. Yet that is precisely when traditional outplacement ends, leaving job hunters stranded and sometimes ruining deals.

It is astonishing how often job hunters and employers alike are impressed by the databases of *job postings* claimed by outplacement firms. Yet only 10 percent of all jobs are filled through ads and another 10 percent are filled through search firms. Instead, direct contact and networking— done The Five O'Clock Club way—are more effective for most searches.

You Get a Safety Net

Imagine getting a package that protects you for a full year. Imagine knowing you can come back if your new job doesn't work out—even months later. Imagine trying consulting work if you like. If you later decide it's not for you, you can come back to The Five O'Clock Club.

We can offer you a safety net of one full year's career coaching because our method is so effective that few people actually need more than 10 weeks in our proven program. But you're protected for a year.

You'll Job Search with Those Who Are Employed—How Novel!

Let's face it. It can be depressing to spend your days at an outplacement firm where everyone is unemployed. At The Five O'Clock Club, half the attendees are working, and this makes the atmosphere cheerier and helps to move your search along.

What's more, you'll be in a small group of your peers, all of whom are using The Five O'Clock Club method. Our research proves that those who attend the small group regularly and use The Five O'Clock Club methods get jobs faster and at higher rates of pay than those who only work privately with a career coach throughout their searches.

So Many Poor Attempts

Nothing is sadder than meeting someone who has already been getting job-search *help*, but the wrong kind. They've learned the traditional techniques that are no longer effective. Most have poor résumés and inappropriate targets and don't know how to turn job interviews into offers.

You'll Get Quite a Package

You'll get up to 14 hours of private coaching—well in excess of what you would get at a traditional outplacement firm. You may even want to use a few hours after you start your new job.

And you get up to one full year of small-group career coaching. In addition, you get books, audio CDs, and other helpful materials.

To Get Started

The day your human resources manager calls us authorizing Five O'Clock Club outplacement, we will immediately ship you the books, CDs, and other materials and assign you to a private coach and a small group.

Then we'll monitor your search. Frankly, we care about you more than we care about your employer. And since your employer cares about you, they're glad we feel this way—because they know we'll take care of you.

What They Say about Us

The Five O'Clock Club product is much better, far more useful than my outplacement package.

Senior executive and Five O'Clock Club member

The Club kept the juices flowing. You're told what to do, what not to do. There were fresh ideas. I went through an outplacement service that, frankly, did not help. If they had done as much as the Five O'Clock Club did, I would have landed sooner.

Another member

When Your *Employer* Pays for The Five O'Clock Club, *You* Get:

- **Up to 14 hours of guaranteed private career coaching** to determine a career direction, develop a résumé, plan salary negotiations, etc. In fact, if you need a second opinion during your search, we can arrange that too.

- Up to **ONE YEAR of small-group teleconference coaching** (average about 5 or 6 participants in a group) headed by a senior Five O'Clock Club career consultant. That way, if you lose your next job, you can come back. Or if you want to try consulting work and then decide you **don't like it, you can come back**.

- **Two-year membership** in The Five O'Clock Club: Beginners Kit and two-year subscription to *The Five O'Clock News*.

- **The complete set of our four books** for professionals, managers, and executives who are in job search.

- **A boxed set of 16 audio CDs** of Five O'Clock Club presentations.

COMPARISON OF EMPLOYER-PAID PACKAGES

Typical Package	Traditional Outplacement	The Five O'Clock Club
Who is the client?	The organization	Job hunters. We are employee advocates. We always do what is in the best interest of job hunters.
The clientele	All are unemployed	Half of our attendees are unemployed; half are employed. There is an upbeat atmosphere; networking is enhanced.
Length/type of service	3 months, primarily office space	1 year, exclusively career coaching
Service ends	After 3 months—or *before* if the client lands a job or consulting assignment	After 1 full year, no matter what. You can return if you lose your next job, if your assignment ends, or if you need advice after starting your new job.
Small-group coaching	Sporadic for 3 months Coach varies	Every week for up to 1 year; same coach
Private coaching	5 hours on average	Up to 14 hours guaranteed (depending on level of service purchased)
Support materials	Generic manual	• 4 textbooks based on over 25 years of job-search research • 16 40-minute lectures on audio CDs • Beginners Kit of search information • 2-year subscription to the Five O'Clock Club magazine, devoted to career-management articles
Facilities	Cubicle, phone, computer access	None; use home phone and computer

The
Five
O'Clock
Club

The Way We Are

The Five O'Clock Club means sobriety, refinement of thought and speech, good breeding and good order. To this, much of its success is due. The Five O'Clock Club is easy-going and unconventional. A sense of propriety, rather than rules of order, governs its meetings.

J. Hampton Moore, *History of The Five O'Clock Club*
(written in the 1890s)

Just like the members of the original Five O'Clock Club, today's members want an ongoing relationship. George Vaillant, in his seminal work on successful people, found that "what makes or breaks our luck seems to be . . . our sustained relationships with other people." (George E. Vaillant, *Adaptation to Life,* Harvard University Press, 1995)

Five O'Clock Club members know that much of the program's benefit comes from simply showing up. Showing up will encourage you to do what you need to do when you are not here. And over the course of several weeks, certain things will become evident that are not evident now.

Five O'Clock Club members learn from each other: The group leader is not the only one with answers. The leader brings factual information to the meetings and keeps the discussion in line. But the answers to some problems may lie within you or with others in the group.

Five O'Clock Club members encourage each other. They listen, see similarities with their own situations, and learn from that. And they listen to see how they may help others. You may come across information or a contact that could help

someone else in the group. Passing on that information is what we're all about.

If you are a new member here, listen to others to learn the process. And read the books so you will know the basics that others already know. When everyone understands the basics, this keeps the meetings on a high level, interesting, and helpful to everyone.

Five O'Clock Club members are in this together, but they know that ultimately they are each responsible for solving their own problems with God's help. Take the time to learn the process, and you will become better at analyzing your own situation, as well as the situations of others. You will be learning a method that will serve you the rest of your life, and in areas of your life apart from your career.

Five O'Clock Club members are kind to each other. They control their frustrations—because venting helps no one. Because many may be stressed, be kind and go the extra length to keep this place calm and happy. It is your respite from the world outside and a place for you to find comfort and FUN. Relax and enjoy yourself, learn what you can, and help where you can. And have a ball doing it.

There arises from the hearts of busy [people] a love of variety, a yearning for relaxation of thought as well as of body, and a craving for a generous and spontaneous fraternity.

J. Hampton Moore, *History of The Five O'Clock Club*

The
Five
O'Clock
Club

Lexicon Used at The Five O'Clock Club

Use The Five O'Clock Club lexicon as a shorthand to express where you are in your job search. It will focus you and those in your group.

I. Overview and Assessment

How many hours a week are you spending on your search?
Spend 35 hours on a full-time search, 15 hours on a part-time search.

What are your job targets?
Tell the group. A target includes industry or company size, position, and geographic area.

The group can help assess how good your targets are. Take a look at *Measuring Your Targets.*

How does your résumé position you?
The summary and body should make you look appropriate to your target.

What are your backup targets?
Decide at the beginning of the search before the first campaign. Then you won't get stuck.

Have you done the Assessment?
If your targets are wrong, everything is wrong. (Do the Assessment in *Targeting a Great Career.*) Or a counselor can help you privately to determine possible job targets.

II. Getting Interviews

How large is your target (e.g., 30 companies)? How many of them have you contacted?
Contact them all.

How can you get (more) leads?
You will not get a job through search firms, ads, networking, or direct contact. Those are techniques for getting interviews—job leads. Use the right terminology, especially after a person gets a job. Do not say, "How did you get the job?" if you really want to know "Where did you get the lead for that job?"

Do you have 6 to 10 things in the works?
You may want the group to help you land one job. After they help you with your strategy, they should ask, "How many other things do you have in the works?" If *none*, the group can brainstorm how you can get more things going: through search firms, ads, networking, or direct contact. Then you are more likely to turn the job you want into an offer because you will seem more valuable. What's more, 5 will fall away through no fault of your own. Don't go after only 1 job.

How's your Two-Minute Pitch?
Practice a *tailored* Two-Minute Pitch. Tell the group the job title and industry of the hiring manager they should pretend they are for a role-playing exercise. You will be surprised how good

the group is at critiquing pitches. (Practice a few weeks in a row.) Use your pitch to separate you from your competition.

You seem to be in Stage One (or Stage Two or Stage Three) of your search.

Know where you are. This is the key measure of your search.

Are you seen as an insider or an outsider?

See *How to Change Careers* for becoming an insider. If people are saying, "I wish I had an opening for someone like you," you are doing well in meetings. If the industry is strong, then it's only a matter of time before you get a job.

III. Turning Interviews into Offers

Do you want this job?

If you do not want the job, perhaps you want an offer, if only for practice. If you are not willing to go for it, the group's suggestions will not work.

Who are your likely competitors and how can you outshine and outlast them?

You will not get a job simply because "they liked me." The issues are deeper. Ask the interviewer: "Where are you in the hiring process? What kind of person would be your ideal candidate? How do I stack up?"

What are your next steps?

What are *you* planning to do if the hiring manager doesn't call by a certain date or what are you planning to do to assure that the hiring manager *does* call you?

Can you prove you can do the job?

Don't just take the *trust me* approach. Consider your competition.

Which job positions you best for the long run? Which job is the best fit?

Don't decide only on the basis of salary. You will most likely have another job after this. See which

job looks best on your résumé and will make you stronger for the next time. In addition, find a fit for your personality. If you don't *fit,* it is unlikely you will do well there. The group can help you turn interviews into offers and give you feedback on which job is best for you.

> *"Believe me, with self-examination and a ot of hard work with our coaches, you can find the job . . . you can have the career . . . you can live the life you've always wanted!"*
>
> Sincerely,
> Kate Wendleton

Membership

As a member of The Five O'Clock Club, you get:

- A year's subscription to *The Five O'Clock News*—10 issues filled with information on career development and job-search techniques, focusing on the experiences of real people.

- Access to *reasonably priced* weekly seminars featuring individualized attention to your specific needs in small groups supervised by our senior coaches.

- Access to one-on-one coaching to help you answer specific questions, solve current job problems, prepare your résumé, or take an in-depth look at your career path. You choose the coach and pay the coach directly.

- An attractive Beginners Kit containing information based on over 25 years of research on who gets jobs . . . and why . . . that will enable you to improve your job-search techniques—immediately!

- The opportunity to exchange ideas and experiences with other job searchers and career changers.

All that access, all that information, all that expertise for the annual membership fee of only $49—plus seminar fees.

How to become a member—by mail or E-mail:

Send your name, address, phone number, how you heard about us, and your check for $49 (made payable to "The Five O'Clock Club") to The Five O'Clock Club, 300 East 40th Street - Suite 6L, New York, NY 10016, or sign up at www.fiveoclockclub.com.

We will immediately mail you a Five O'Clock Club Membership Card, the Beginners Kit, and information on our seminars followed by our magazine. Then, call **1-800-575-3587** (or **212-286-4500** in New York) or e-mail us (at info@fiveoclockclub.com) to:

- reserve a space for the first time you plan to attend, or
- be matched with a Five O'Clock Club coach.

Membership Application

The Five O'Clock Club

□ **Yes! I want to become a member!**

I want access to the most effective methods for finding jobs, as well as for developing and managing my career.

I enclose my check for $49 for 1 year; $75 for 2 years, payable to *The Five O'Clock Club*. I will receive a Beginners Kit, a subscription to *The Five O'Clock News*, access to the Members Only area on our website, and a network of career coaches. Reasonably priced seminars are held across the country.

Name: _____

Street Address: _____

City: _____ State: _____ Zip Code: _____

Work phone: (_____) _____

Home phone: (_____) _____

E-mail: _____

Date: _____

How I heard about the Club: _____

Shortcut Your Job Search: The Best Ways to Get Meetings

The following *optional* information is for statistical purposes. Thanks for your help.

Salary range:

□ under $30,000   □ $30,000–$49,999   □ $50,000–$74,999

□ $75,000–$99,999   □ $100,000–$125,000   □ over $125,000

Age: □ 20–29   □ 30–39   □ 40–49   □ 50+

Gender: □ Male   □ Female

Current or most recent position/title: _____

Please send to:
Membership Director, The Five O'Clock Club,
300 East 40th St.-Suite 6L, New York, NY 10016

The original Five O'Clock Club® was formed in Philadelphia in 1893. It was made up of the leaders of the day who shared their experiences "in a setting of fellowship and good humor."

Index

About the Author

Kate Wendleton is a nationally syndicated columnist and a respected authority and speaker on career development, having appeared on the *Today Show,* CNN, CNBC, *The Larry King Show,* National Public Radio, and CBS, and in *The Economist, The New York Times, The Chicago Tribune, The Wall Street Journal, Fortune* magazine, *Business Week,* and other national media.

She has been a career coach since 1978, when she founded The Five O'Clock Club and developed its methodology to help job hunters and career changers of all levels in job-search strategy groups. This methodology is now used by branches of The Five O'Clock Club that meet weekly in the United States and Canada.

Kate also founded Workforce America, a not-for-profit affiliate of The Five O'Clock Club that ran for 10 years. It served adults in Harlem who were not yet in the professional or managerial ranks. Workforce America helped adults in Harlem move into better-paying, higher-level positions as they improved their educational level and work experience.

Kate founded, and directed for seven years, The Career Center at The New School for Social Research in New York. She also advises major corporations about employee career-development programs and coaches senior executives.

A former CFO of two small companies, she has 20 years of business-management experience in both manufacturing and service businesses.

Kate attended Chestnut Hill College in Philadelphia and received her MBA from Drexel University. She is a popular speaker for associations, corporations, and colleges.

When she lived in Philadelphia, Kate did long-term volunteer work for the Philadelphia Museum of Art, the Walnut Street Theatre Art Gallery, United Way, and the YMCA. Kate currently lives in Manhattan with her husband.

Kate Wendleton is the author of The Five O'Clock Club's four-part career-development and job-hunting series, among other books.

About The Five O'Clock Club and the "Fruytagie" Canvas

Five O'Clock Club members are special. We attract upbeat, ambitious, dynamic, intelligent people—and that makes it fun for all of us. Most of our members are professionals, managers, executives, consultants, and freelancers. We also include recent college graduates and those aiming to get into the professional ranks, as well as people in their 40s, 50s, and even 60s. Most members' salaries range from $30,000 to $400,000 (one-third of our members earn in excess of $100,000 a year). For those who cannot attend a Club, *The Five O'Clock Club Book Series* contains all of our methodologies—and our spirit.

The Philosophy of The Five O'Clock Club

The "Fruytagie" Canvas by Patricia Kelly, depicted here, symbolizes our philosophy. The original, which is actually 52.5" by 69" inches, hangs in the offices of The Five O'Clock Club in Manhattan. It is reminiscent of popular 16th century Dutch "fruytagie," or fruit tapestries, which depicted abundance and prosperity.

I was attracted to this piece because it seemed to fit the spirit of our people at The Five O'Clock Club. This was confirmed when the artist, who was not aware of what I did for a living, added these words to the canvas: "The garden is abundant, prosperous and magical." Later, it took me only 10 minutes to write the blank verse "The Garden of Life," because it came from my heart. The verse reflects our philosophy and describes the kind of people who are members of the Club.

I'm always inspired by Five O'Clock Clubbers. They show others the way through their quiet behavior . . . their kindness . . . their generosity . . . their hard work . . . under God's care.

We share what we have with others. We are in this lush, exciting place together—with our brothers and sisters—and reach out for harmony. The garden is abundant. The job market is exciting. And Five O'Clock Clubbers believe that there is enough for everyone.

About the Artist's Method

To create her tapestry-like art, Kelly developed a unique style of stenciling. She hand-draws and hand-cuts each stencil, both in the negative and positive for each image. Her elaborate technique also includes a lengthy multilayering process incorporating Dutch metal leaves and gilding, numerous transparent glazes, paints, and wax pencils.

Kelly also paints the back side of the canvas using multiple washes of reds, violets, and golds. She uses this technique to create a heavy vibration of color, which in turn reflects the color onto the surface of the wall against which the canvas hangs.

The canvas is suspended by a heavy braided silk cord threaded into large brass grommets inserted along the top. Like a tapestry, the hemmed canvas is attached to a gold-gilded dowel with finials. The entire work is hung from a sculpted wall ornament.

Our staff is inspired every day by the tapestry and by the members of The Five O'Clock Club. We all work hard—and have FUN! The garden *is* abundant—with enough for everyone.

We wish you lots of success in your career. We—and your fellow members of The Five O'Clock Club—will work with you on it.

—Kate Wendleton, President

The original Five O'Clock Club was formed in Philadelphia in 1883.
It was made up of the leaders of the day, who shared their experiences
"in a spirit of fellowship and good humor."

 **THE GARDEN OF LIFE IS** abundant, prosperous and magical. 🍇 In this garden, there is enough for everyone. 🍇 Share the fruit and the knowledge 🍇 Our brothers and we are in this lush, exciting place together. 🍇 Let's show others the way. 🍇 Kindness. Generosity. 🍇 Hard work. 🍇 God's care.

The Five O'Clock Club Job-Search Series
for Professionals, Managers and Executives

THOMSON
DELMAR LEARNING

We'll take you through your entire career. 1. Start by understanding yourself and what you want in **Targeting a Great Career**. 2. *Package Yourself with a Targeted Résumé* done The Five O'Clock Club Way. 3. Then *Shortcut Your Job Search* by following our techniques for getting meetings. 4. Turn those interviews into offers with *Mastering the Job Interview* and *Winning the Money Game*. 5. Finally, do well in your new job with *Navigating Your Career*.

- Figure out what to do with your life and your career
- Develop a résumé that separates you from your competitors
- Shortcut your search by using the Internet and other techniques properly
- Learn how to turn those job interviews into job offers
- Use our Four-Step Salary Negotiation Method to get what you deserve

Launching the Right Career
Now, students, recent grads, and those who want a career instead of a job can use the same techniques used by thousands of professionals, managers and executives. Get that internship, develop a resume that gets you interviews, and learn how to interview well.

Targeting a Great Career
ISBN: 1-4180-1504-0

Packaging Yourself: The Targeted Résumé
ISBN: 1-4180-1503-2

Shortcut Your Job Search: The Best Way to Get Meetings
ISBN: 1-4180-1502-4

Mastering the Job Interview and Winning the Money Game
ISBN: 1-4180-1500-8

Navigating Your Career: Develop Your Plan, Manage Your Boss, Get Another Job Inside
ISBN: 1-4180-1501-6

Launching the Right Career
ISBN: 1-4180-1505-9

258 pp., 7 3/8" x 9 1/4", softcover

The Five O'Clock Club's Book Series has enabled thousands of professionals, managers, and executives to correct their job-search mistakes. Most who attend regularly and read our books–even those unemployed up to two years—have a new job within only ten weekly sessions.

Most people conduct a passive job search. Their approach is ordinary, non-directed, fragmented, and ineffective.

The Five O'Clock Club was started in 1978 as a research-based organization. The methodology was tested and refined on professionals, managers, and executives (and those aspiring to be)–from all occupations and economic levels.

Ever since the beginning, The Five O'Clock Club has tracked trends at every meeting at every at every location. Over time, our advice has changed as the job market has changed. What worked in the past is not always sufficient for today's job market. Today's Five O'Clock Club Book Series contains all the relevant old strategies–and so much more. The Five O'Clock Clubbers who do best read and re-read the books, marking them up and taking notes. Do the same and you will do better in your search.

About the Author:
Kate Wendleton is a nationally syndicated careers columnist and recognized authority on career development, having appeared on *The Today Show*, CNN, CNBC, *Larry King Live*, National Public Radio, CBS, and in the *New York Times, Chicago Tribune, Wall Street Journal, Fortune, Business Week*, and other national media. She has been a career coach since 1978 when she founded The Five O' Clock Club and developed its methodology to help job hunters and career changers at all levels. A former CFO of two small companies, Kate has twenty years of business experience, as well as an MBA.

www.delmarlearning.com

To place an order please call: (800) 347-7707 or fax: (859) 647-5963
Mailing Address: Thomson Distribution Center, Attn: Order Fulfillment, 10650 Toebben Dr., Independence, KY 41051